LANDSCAPE DESIGN

A Practical Approach

LANDSCAPE DESIGN

A Practical Approach

Fourth Edition

Leroy G. Hannebaum

 Prentice Hall, Upper Saddle River, New Jersey 07458

Library of Congress Cataloging-in-Publication Data

Hannebaum, Leroy G.
    Landscape design: a practical approach/Leroy G. Hannebaum.—
    4th ed.
        p.   cm.
    Includes bibliographical references and index.
    ISBN 0-13-163230-2
    1. Landscape design.   2. Landscape architecture.   I. Title.
SB472.45.H36   1998   97-6511
712—dc21   CIP

Acquisition editor: Charles Stewart
Editorial/production supervision and interior design: Janet M. McGillicuddy
Director of production and manufacturing: Bruce Johnson
Managing editor: Mary Carnis
Electronic page composition: Janet M. McGillicuddy
Electronic art: Mark LaSalle
Cover design: Maria Lange
Cover photo: Leroy Hannebaum
Manufacturing buyer: Marc Bove
Marketing manager: Melissa Brunner
Assistant editor: Kate Linsner
Editorial assistant: Kimberly Yehle

 © 1998 Prentice-Hall, Inc.
A Division of Simon and Schuster
Upper Saddle River, New Jersey 07458

Printed in the United States of America

10   9   8   7   6   5   4

ISBN 0-13-163230-2

Prentice-Hall International (UK) Limited, *London*
Prentice-Hall of Australia Pty. Limited, *Sydney*
Prentice-Hall Canada Inc., *Toronto*
Prentice-Hall Hispanoamericana, S.A., *Mexico*
Prentice-Hall of India Private Limited, *New Delhi*
Prentice-Hall of Japan, Inc., *Tokyo*
Simon & Schuster Asia Pte. Ltd., *Singapore*
Editora Prentice-Hall do Brasil, Ltda., *Rio de Janeiro*

*For Glenn and Opal Hannebaum, my parents,
who opened the doors for learning*

Contents

Chapter 9
MATCHING PLANT MATERIALS TO DESIGN CRITERIA   191

Chapter 10
COVERING THE GROUND   207

Chapter 11
EMBELLISHMENTS   228

Chapter 12
SPECIAL LANDSCAPE PROBLEMS: BUSINESS AND RENTAL PROPERTIES   246

Chapter 13
SPECIFICATIONS, ESTIMATIONS, AND BIDS   267

Chapter 14
THE ROLE OF THE DESIGNER/SALESPERSON   288

PREFACE

The motivating factor during the initial writing of this book resulted from my frustration while attempting to identify a suitable text for a landscape design class I instructed for the Department of Horticulture at Kansas State University. None of the books I evaluated gave information on all of the subjects I felt the students needed. *Landscape Design: A Practical Approach* was, and remains, principally a text for horticultural students and a reference book for those practicing landscape design for a vocation. I have also been pleased to receive much positive response from landscape architects, both those who teach and those who practice. Because of the positive responses, and virtually no negative feedback, I have not made changes simply for the sake of change.

It is my hope that the material presented here will make students curious enough to pursue reading those books that are listed in the appendices. The goal of this book is to provide a good, basic understanding of the landscape design process, including design analysis, study of land forms and planning of land form manipulation, area creation and circulation, environmental adjustments, the aesthetics of good design, appropriate materials selection, and the proper use of enriching materials in the landscape. In addition, materials are presented that are of great importance to would-be designers/salespeople in the areas of specification reading and writing, bidding and estimating, and sales.

Contemporary landscape-oriented businesses commonly combine the design and sales functions under one umbrella heading of "salesman." I have altered that title to read "salesperson" in this book out of a desire for fair play, since I found my classes to be fairly equally divided between young men and women from the standpoints of both numbers and abilities. These young people are excited about careers in landscape design and sales, as well they should be. It is a wonderfully creative and ever-changing field, full of challenges and rewards. The products of a landscape salesperson's efforts are good for people, both physically and psychologically, and financial rewards are plentiful for those who are well trained and diligent.

This book should also serve as a good guidebook for those already in the design/sales field, as it offers tables of useful information for estimating and plant selection and a good review of principles. It is my hope that at least portions of the book will also serve the landscape architectural student and the practicing landscape architect, if only by offering some different perspectives on familiar subject materials. Some original materials concerning the landscaping of business and rental properties should prove interesting for all readers, while providing many landscape selling points.

Because this book is oriented toward presenting the maximum coverage of the landscape design process in a short amount of space, it may appear, in places, to take a formulaic approach. That is not my intention; but because horticulture students have such brief exposure to the subject, an approach of this type is often necessary to ensure that factors will be considered without fail. As experiences are broadened, much of the design sequence becomes committed to the designer's memory, so simultaneous and in-depth design considerations come more naturally.

I would like to acknowledge the help and support of a number of individuals and companies during the writing of this text. Dr. Gustaaf A. van der Hoeven, Extension Specialist in Landscape and Environmental Horticulture at Kansas State University, gave generously of his time and expertise to review the manuscript and make valuable suggestions.

My appreciation also goes to Mr. William K. Doerler, the National Landscape Association, and *American Nurseryman* magazine for allowing me to reprint the excerpt that appears on page 2 in this text, and to the National Association of Homebuilders for their permission to reprint an excerpt from *Cost Effective Site Planning*. The Westinghouse Electric Corporation supplied several of the night-lighting photographs.

New Image Industries, Inc., generously supplied information and photographs, as did LaSICO, and LANDCADD, Inc. Design Specialties, Inc., supplied some of their rubber plant stamps as well as illustrations of others.

Finally, I must recognize the support and encouragement of my wife, Linda, and my children, Ty, Tanya, Tara, and Todd.

Leroy G. Hannebaum

LANDSCAPE DESIGN

A Practical Approach

Chapter **1**

INTRODUCTION TO TODAY'S LANDSCAPING

In this chapter, you will learn who the landscape planners are and what differences exist between their professions. You will also learn about the makeup of the landscape plan, and you will study each component of the total plan.

Landscaping is a very complex subject. It is practical yet aesthetically demanding. An art, it requires the many and varied skills of craftspeople for implementation.

Good landscaping should be beautiful, of course, but on the practical side of the ledger, landscaping should also serve many functions. In fact, every part of a well-conceived landscape should be functional; there are no "frills." From such practical achievements as cooling in the summer, allowing the sun's warmth to heat in the winter, blocking winds, and sheltering from rain or snow while controlling the drainage of surface water, to merely providing colors and fragrances to be sensed with enjoyment, well-designed landscaping handles many problems.

Landscaping should not be considered an expense but, rather, a capital improvement that will increase property values significantly. It is an investment that should always provide an excellent return if properly designed, implemented, and maintained. From an environmental standpoint, it results in savings on utility bills, but investment possibilities notwithstanding, perhaps the most important contribution of landscaping has to do with the feelings people have for it and not the money. Spaces made useful, comfortable, relaxing, and stimulating contribute much to enjoyable living.

This book is primarily concerned with the landscape designing process. The many skills of specialized craftspeople may be required to implement a good landscape, but these skills are wasted without a good initial design.

The Landscape Planners

Many people perform this complex design process, but those who are successful at it are the ones who are well prepared. Several different groups of people, all with their own unique relationships to landscape design, are represented. These groups are usually landscape architects, landscape designers, extension-service specialists, and property owners.

There exists some confusion between the definitions of "landscape architect" and "landscape designer." However, in the June 1, 1980, issue of *American Nurseryman* magazine, in which William K. Doerler reported the results of a survey conducted by the National Landscape Association, the following definitions were given:

> *Landscape architect.* A landscape architect is literally an architect of the landscape, bringing together the natural balance between the needs of people and ecology. Architects also consider wise land use and aesthetics in their work.
>
> This individual has the ability to create designs for everything from small intimate gardens to new cities and parks of varying sizes.
>
> The landscape architect's skill in drafting and art helps him or her to prepare line drawings that can be used by contractors. The landscape architect's drawings enable him or her to transform creative ideas into clearly understood presentations. The ability to write and understand detailed

specifications is another skill the landscape architect must possess so his or her plans can be correctly followed. His or her understanding of the inter-relationship of people and their surroundings enables him or her to solve the problems of land planning.

Landscape architects may become specialized in certain fields, such as golf courses, municipal parks, community or regional planning, and residential or commercial properties.

The landscape architect usually has a formal education from an accredited school or has acquired the knowledge through years of experience in the design field.

Landscape designer.   This individual is employed by a landscape nursery to design the work that the firm builds. The landscape designer is familiar with basic design principles, plant cultural requirements, and landscape construction methods.

The landscape designer's services are provided by the landscape nursery as a service to his or her customers. Sometimes there is a separate charge for these designs, but usually they are provided as part of a job package. Projects are usually residential or small commercial jobs and consist primarily of planting designs.

The landscape designer is a person with a flair for design who has an ornamental horticultural background. This design knowledge is obtained through practical experience or formal education. The landscape designer enters the scene after a project is built. The landscape designer sells as well as designs.

These definitions indicate how the members of the National Landscape Association view landscape architects and landscape designers as groups. As is usually the case, group definitions leave room for overlaps to occur—some landscape architects do work for landscape operators, and some landscape designers operate independently. Individual training, experience, and capabilities vary widely within each group.

If major differences exist between landscape architects and landscape designers, they most likely occur in their training. Formally trained landscape architects are better trained in the graphic arts and in engineering and architectural technology. Landscape designers, as a group, are better trained in the horticultural sciences. These gaps are narrowing as each group seeks to strengthen its weakest training areas.

Because landscape architects are relatively few in number, and because they are in constant demand for large, lucrative planning projects, the small property owner often finds them relatively unavailable. The landscape designer, who is usually employed by a firm that sells to the small property owner, is more easily engaged to design for small homes or business properties. The fact that these designers work for commercial firms should not negate the value of their work, providing they are honestly interested in providing clients the best service available. Reputations are at stake, and the landscape designer who puts customer needs first enjoys high esteem in the community.

Among themselves, the landscape designers are a diverse group. They may be employed by landscape nurseries, landscape contracting firms, or garden-store operations. Many are college-trained horticulturists. Specific courses in landscape design, along with plant identification and plant culture courses, are included in such college programs. Graphic arts courses are encouraged, as curriculum limits permit, to strengthen design capabilities, and a wide range of art and science courses helps round out these programs.

Vocational–technical schools and junior colleges are also responsible for training many of today's landscape designers. These schools offer intensive training in a shorter period of time than is required in a four-year college curriculum. Since they tend to be more vocationally oriented than colleges, the courses taken are more concentrated and more tightly focused.

There is also a substantial group of landscape designers who have had no formal training. This group consists of nursery-owners, landscape contractors, garden-store operators, and others who have learned their skills through experience, reading, or other independent means.

Extension-Service Specialists

Land-grant colleges and universities across the nation employ landscaping specialists who disseminate current information to the public. They write extension publications, talk to groups, and even do some individual consulting. They present seminars designed to teach the principles of landscape design to homeowners and nursery groups. Aiding these specialists at the local level is the county extension agent, who supplies information and consults within county boundaries. All of these specialists are trained to help others help themselves, but they are largely overworked and understaffed. It is not their job to plan individual landscapes, but they can, and will, help with landscape designs.

Property Owners

Given the right information and proper preparation, some property owners can design satisfactory landscapes for themselves. Unfortunately, many homeowners either do not seek or do not make use of good information. Inferior landscapes that will not function are the result. Any homeowner who wishes to design his or her own landscape well should solicit guidance from extension personnel or local nurseryowners or should study reliable literature; he or she should then prepare to spend long hours in the planning process.

THE LANDSCAPE PLAN

Images of graphically impressive blueprints, depicting circular plant symbols and elaborate planting beds, come to mind at the mention of landscape plans. It is true that landscape plans are recorded on paper so the ideas will not be forgotten, but those concepts must originate in the designer's mind. They are merely recorded on paper.

This should not be construed to mean that graphic representation is unimportant. But designers can get so involved in the way a design looks on paper that they forget they are planning for real, three-dimensional items. Inexperienced designers tend to be overwhelmed by the need to arrive at the final product—a magnificently represented blueprint of a landscape that is, by itself, a work of art. But it is the actual landscape that is represented on the paper that is important. That three-dimensional concept, complete with color and texture, must exist in the designer's mind before it can be transferred onto paper. Even a poor landscape design often can be graphically represented to look good on a blueprint. By contrast, an excellent design can be drawn on the back of an envelope in crude loops and circles. It is the ideas that count most.

The importance of the landscape plan on paper is, first, as a means of evaluating, then of communicating, ideas. Those ideas that have been conceived in the designer's mind during the design process are recorded on paper in such a way that others can read and understand them. The plan must communicate those ideas to the property owner as well as to any potential installer. Perhaps most importantly, the landscape designer uses the plan to communicate ideas to himself or herself throughout the design process. Recording the various design concepts on paper during the design process allows the designer to relate one area to another, comparing concepts for compatibility. Unlike the ideas floating around in a person's head, those recorded on paper do not get lost.

Scale

Landscape plans are drawn to an absolute scale, so that a unit of measurement on the plan represents an exact, longer distance on the property. Different scales may be used, but a scale of 1/8" to 1' is commonly used for small properties. This scale is pleasant to view on a drawing and comfortable to read, and it can be measured with an ordinary ruler or tape measure. The larger the property being landscaped, the larger the scale must be in order to fit the drawing on manageable pieces of paper. Larger commercial or institutional landscape plans are often drawn at scales of 1" to 50' or even 100'. Although they are necessary, these scales are more difficult to read and to draw, and they cannot show great detail. Whatever scale is used, it must always be clearly stated on the plan.

Plan View

The most prominent portion of a landscape plan is the plan view of the property (see Figure 1-1). This is a bird's-eye view of the entire property, as if the viewer were suspended in the air directly over the property. Property lines form the borders of the plan view. All permanent features on the property are represented at accurate scale—the walls of buildings, driveways, sidewalks, patios, and so forth. Easements and building setback lines are represented by dotted

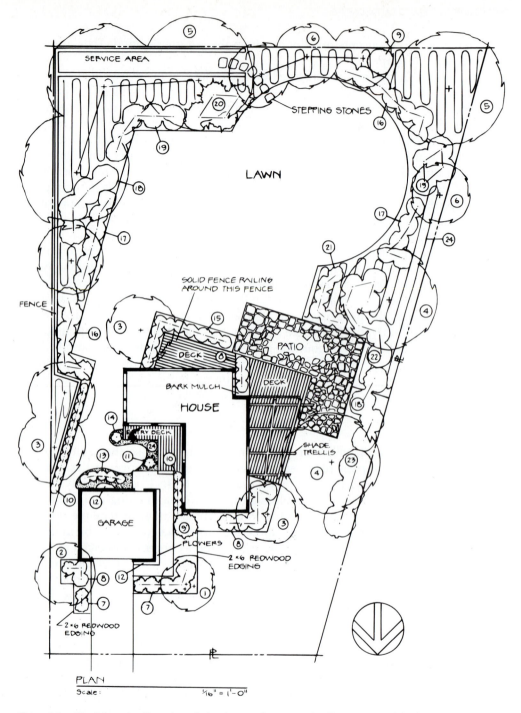

Figure 1-1. The "plan-view" portion of a landscape plan gives a bird's-eye view of the landscape as designed.

lines. Windows and doors are indicated by open spaces in the solid lines that depict the walls of buildings. Fluctuations in the levels of the ground surface are represented by broken lines, called *existing contour lines*. (See Chapter 4, "Studying the Land Forms", for more details.) Proposed alterations in ground levels are represented by solid lines, which indicate proposed contours.

Symbols

The various symbols on landscape plans represent distinct features of the design. Plants are normally symbolized by circles of various designs. The diameter of such a circle approximates the plant's spread at maturity. A dot or cross is usually placed in the center of the circle to indicate the exact location for planting. Some optional styles of these symbols are shown in Figure 1-2.

The choice of symbols for the plants on a plan depends on the designer's individual preference as well as on the density of the plan. Some of the symbols represent only the outer edge of a tree, allowing the viewer also to see clearly any shrubs, groundcovers, or planting-bed edges that might be below the tree's canopy. The more elaborate tree symbols that depict the tree's branches or leaves do not afford such opportunity; attempting to show any features below such symbols would only clutter the design, creating confusion. In order to communicate ideas properly, the symbols chosen should allow a crisp, clean, uncluttered view of all features on the plan view.

Why use different symbols at all? Because they communicate feelings to property owners. The more elaborate symbols are quite attractive when they are well drawn, and it is, of course, necessary to convince the property owner that the landscape will be attractive. Symbols also allow the designer to communicate texture or foliage type. Differentiating between deciduous trees and evergreen trees by choice of symbols makes it easier to understand the plan's contents.

Every other feature of the landscape plan view is represented by lines. Groundcovers, gravels, bark, and other types of surfacing materials can easily be distinguished from grass and from each other by textural representation (see Figure 1-3). There is no reason why anyone seeing a plan view for the first time should not be able to differentiate between a brick patio and one to be made of flagstone merely by looking at the symbolic representation. These changing representations make the plan view easier to read and understand, while providing pleasant contrasts.

The measurements needed to prepare cost estimations are taken from plan views. For that reason, also, the scale must always be accurate. If the individual bricks are drawn in on a patio, they should be at absolute scale with the actual bricks to be used in construction. If only an approximation of size is shown, someone might mistakenly count the bricks for estimation purposes. The resulting miscommunications would be both costly and irritating.

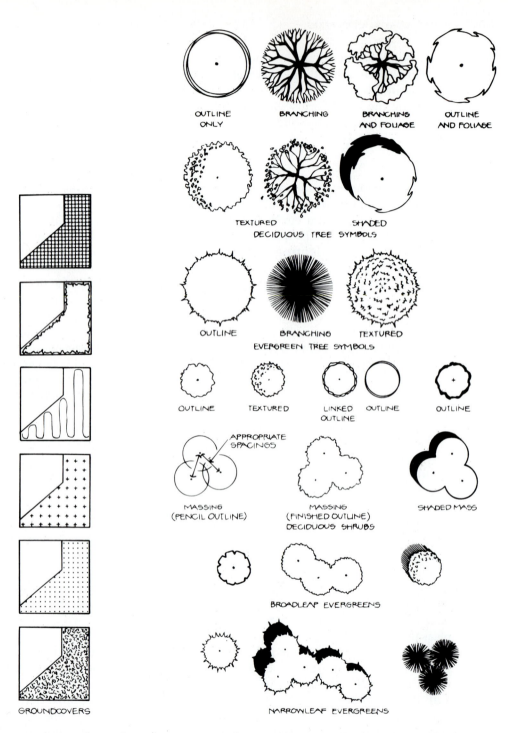

OUTLINE ONLY   BRANCHING   BRANCHING AND FOLIAGE   OUTLINE AND FOLIAGE

TEXTURED   SHADED

DECIDUOUS TREE SYMBOLS

OUTLINE   BRANCHING   TEXTURED

EVERGREEN TREE SYMBOLS

OUTLINE   TEXTURED   LINKED OUTLINE   OUTLINE   OUTLINE

APPROPRIATE SPACINGS

MASSING (PENCIL OUTLINE)   MASSING (FINISHED OUTLINE)   SHADED MASS

DECIDUOUS SHRUBS

BROADLEAF EVERGREENS

GROUNDCOVERS   NARROWLEAF EVERGREENS

Figure 1-2. The symbols chosen to represent plant materials on a landscape plan are largely a matter of designer's choice. Some represent only the outline, some represent textures, and still others represent branching patterns. Regardless of the choices made, the symbols must blend together well on each plan and communicate the ideas clearly.

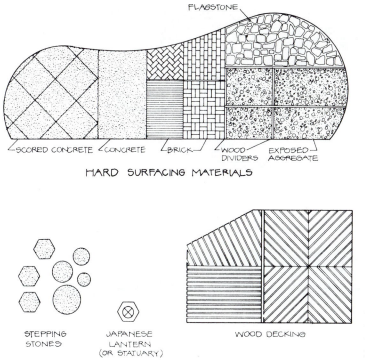

FLAGSTONE

SCORED CONCRETE CONCRETE BRICK WOOD DIVIDERS EXPOSED AGGREGATE

HARD SURFACING MATERIALS

STEPPING STONES

JAPANESE LANTERN (OR STATUARY)

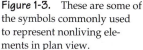

WOOD DECKING

Figure 1-3. These are some of the symbols commonly used to represent nonliving elements in plan view.

If plantings are not drawn as individual units, as groundcovers often are not, it is the square area and the indicated spacing that provide the figures for estimation purposes.

Rubber ink stamps can save the designer much time, particularly when intricate symbols are desired. Since these symbols are applied in ink, some practice is necessary to learn how to make the symbols appear of the same darkness, and care is advised to avoid smudging the ink. Properly applied, these symbols can add interest to a plan view, elevational drawing, or a perspective sketch. Figure 1-4 shows a landscape plan and elevational view done primarily with rubber stamp symbols. In Figure 1-5, both hand-drawn and rubber stamp symbols are used.

Another source of ready-made plant symbols is the dry transfer symbols. These symbols are printed on a clear mylar sheet with adhesive—when they are needed, they are removed from the mylar backing and the adhesive holds them to the paper. In addition to symbols for plants, many types of shading and texturing can be represented by dry transfer materials, as can many styles and sizes of lettering. As with rubber stamps, practice is also required to set transfer symbols straight and on the appropriate line.

Lettering

No matter how descriptive the symbols used in the plan view are, labeling is an absolute necessity for clarification. Plan effectiveness as a communication

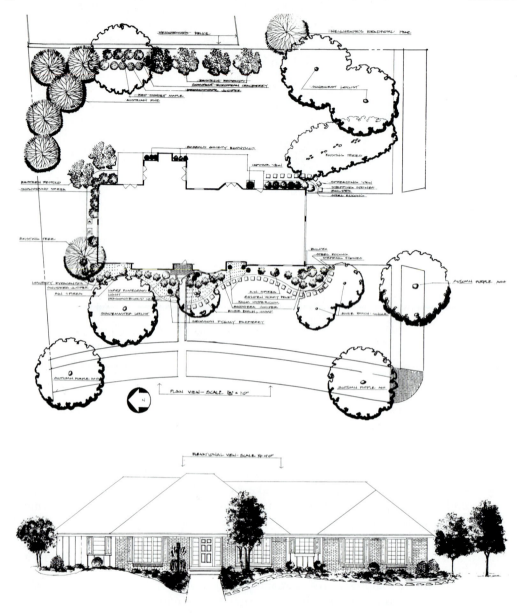

Figure 1-4. This landscape plan and elevation were done primarily with rubber stamps. Only the largest trees were hand-drawn. The symbols were then lightly shaded to make them stand out better. (Leroy G. Hannebaum, designer, Blackburn Nursery & Lawn Service, Topeka, KS.)

Figure 1-5. A plan view, using hand-drawn as well as stamped symbols, lightly shaded. (Leroy G. Hannebaum, designer, Blackburn Nursery & Lawn Service, Topeka, KS.)

device is very much dependent on the placement and style of lettering chosen. Labeling does little good if the lettering cannot be read, or it is difficult to find because it is poorly located.

Generally, the lettering style chosen for a landscape plan should be simple, clean, and consistent for easy reading. Elaborate script has no place on a landscape plan. Remember, the primary purpose of the lettering is to communicate ideas—a purpose that will not be accomplished if the reader has to struggle to decipher each word (see Figure 1-6).

The lettering used for each purpose should be uniform in size. All labels on the plan view, for example, should be of equal size, so they do not distract from one another. Letters should not be equally spaced, however, since some letters are wider than others. The spacing should balance within each word. Letter size can change, however, from one segment of the plan to another; for example, the letters used on the plant list might be larger than those on the plan view. Changing size from one use to another can contribute favorably to the balance and appearance of the entire landscape plan.

Labels should always be placed in close proximity to where the information is needed. It is always frustrating to have to search for information. All labels can be located for easy reference and the lettering still can be balanced over the entire plan if the designer is careful.

Plants may be labeled either directly on the plan view or on a separate *plant list* (see Figure 1-7). Instant recognition of a plant's name is an advantage of direct plan-view labeling. If the plan view is already filled with lettering and symbols, a separate plant list contributes to a less cluttered appearance. The use of a separate plant list also allows more information to be given. Botanical names of plants, quantities, sizes, and conditions of plants at planting time can all be included on a separate plant list but would clutter the plan view. When a separate plant list is used, key numbers or letters are used to identify each plant, both on the plan view and on the plant list.

ALWAYS USE GUIDELINES FOR CONSISTENT LETTER HEIGHT

USE CONSISTENT SPACING BETWEEN LINES FOR ATTRACTIVE LETTERING

STRIVE FOR EQUAL AREAS BETWEEN LETTERS
INSTEAD OF EQUAL SPACING BETWEEN LETTERS

WRONG   RIGHT
A J I L O P   A I J L O P
|| |||| || ||
↑ ↑ ↑ ↑ ↑   ↑   ↑
EQUAL SPACING   EQUAL AREAS

Adjust Letter SIZE and *STYLE*
AS NEEDED TO COMMUNICATE IDEAS EFFECTIVELY

Figure 1-6. The lettering size, style, and quality are all important contributors to plan quality and effective communication.

PLANT LIST

KEY	COMMON NAME	BOTANICAL NAME	QTY
1	EUROPEAN WHITE BIRCH	BETULA PENDULA	1
2	GOLDEN RAINTREE	KOELREUTERIA PANICULATA	1
3	EASTERN REDBUD	CERCIS CANADENSIS	5
4	SUGAR MAPLE	ACER SACCHARUM	2
5	SKYLINE HONEYLOCUST	GLEDITSIA TRIACANTHOS 'SKYLINE'	4
6	RADIANT CRABAPPLE	MALUS 'RADIANT'	3
7	BLUE RUG JUNIPER	JUNIPERUS HORIZONTALIS 'WILTONI'	7
8	COMPACT OREGON HOLLYGRAPE	MAHONIA AQUAFOLIUM 'COMPACTA'	12
9	MANHATTAN EUONYMUS	EUONYMUS KIAUTSCHOVICAS 'MANHATTAN'	2
10	JEWEL EUONYMUS	EUONYMUS KIAUTSCHOVICAS 'JEWEL'	18
11	MUGHO PINE	PINUS MUGO 'COMPACTA'	1
12	SARCOXIE EUONYMUS	EUONYMUS FORTUNEI 'SARCOXIE'	1
13	GOLD DROP POTENTILLA	POTENTILLA FRUTICOSA	5
14	VICARY PRIVET	LIGUSTRUM X VICARI	1
15	KOBOLD BARBERRY	BERBERIS THUMBERGI 'KOBOLD'	11
16	COMMON FLOWERING QUINCE	CHAENOMELES SPECIOSA	13
17	KALM ST JOHNSWORT	HYPERICUM KALMIANUM	11
18	'SPRING GLORY' FORSYTHIA	FORSYTHIA INTERMEDIA 'SPRING GLORY'	8
19	HIGHBUSH CRANBERRY	VIBURNUM OPULUS	9
20	PFITZER JUNIPER	JUNIPERUS CHINENSIS PFITZERANA	4
21	CRANBERRY COTONEASTER	COTONEASTER APICULATA	6
22	GLACIER MOCKORANGE	PHILADELPHUS X VIRGINALIS 'GLACIER'	7
23	PERIWINKLE	VINCA MINOR 'BOWLESII'	
24	CARPET BUGLE	AJUGA REPTANS	

Figure 1-7. When plants are not labeled individually on the plan view, a separate plant list is included on the landscape plan.

The *title block* (see Figure 1-8) is used on a landscape plan to provide general information about the drawing itself. The name of the client, address of the property being landscaped, date the drawings were completed, and name or initials of the designer or draftsperson are included. If the drawing is a revision, the fact should be noted along with the date. Ordinarily, a title, such as "A Landscape Plan," or "Residential Landscape Design," precedes the remaining information. Title blocks provide the information needed for indeterminate storage with easy retrieval. Although it is usually concentrated in the lower right-hand corner of the plan, the title block may be incorporated elsewhere, if desired, to help balance the plan's appearance.

Many times, landscape designers prefer to place title-block information at other places, helping balance the total drawing and adding some "pizazz." They believe that by doing so, they contribute positively to the plan's appearance. Since landscape plans promote beauty by their design, that feeling should also be promoted by the appearance of the plan itself.

A LANDSCAPE PLAN

THE HANNEBAUM RESIDENCE

MANHATTAN, KANSAS
LEROY HANNEBAUM, DESIGNER   SEPTEMBER, 1980

Figure 1-8. The title block gives all the data pertinent to identification of the landscape plan and of the landscape designer.

A *directional indicator* pointing north should be displayed prominently and close to the plan view, along with the *written scale* of the drawing.

An *elevational drawing*, or even a *perspective view* of a portion of the proposed landscape, is sometimes included on a landscape plan (see Figure 1-9). An elevational drawing shows the height, width, and form of suggested plantings, with no depth perspective. Every feature of the elevational drawing shows the height, width, and form of suggested plantings, with no depth perspective. Every feature originates from the same horizontal base. Perspectives do show all three dimensions of the landscape but they are more difficult to draw correctly. Textures can be represented well on either elevational drawings or perspectives. These drawings more clearly communicate to property owners the desired landscaping intent for an area.

Construction-detail drawings are incorporated into the landscape plan when only inadequate detail can be communicated on the plan view. These drawings enlarge the scale of a given area so that area can be more meticulously labeled or symbolically represented. These details, when used, should be separated from the plan view, with their own separate scale clearly marked.

Figure 1-9.   An elevational drawing shows the two-dimensional size and forms of various elements in the landscape. Perspective drawings are more realistic because depth is added. (perspective drawing by Marguerite Koepke)

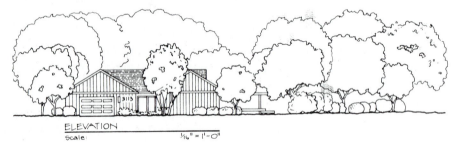

The condition of a finished landscape plan reflects the attitude of its designer. A neat, concise, well-labeled plan impresses readers and communicates ideas well (see Figures 1-10 and 1-11). On the other hand, a sloppy, poorly represented, and ill-labeled plan conveys an attitude of disinterest on the designer's part, so property owners and installers are less likely to hold the finished product in high esteem.

To commit landscape ideas to paper requires drafting. Drafting can be accomplished by hand (manually) or by machine (computer). For each process, equipment is required. We will look at each, beginning with manual drafting equipment in this chapter, and computer drafting equipment in Chapter 15, "Computers in Landscape Design."

Drafting Tools

Many specialized drafting tools are used in the preparation of a formal landscape plan, beginning with the drafting table. A drafting table is a special-

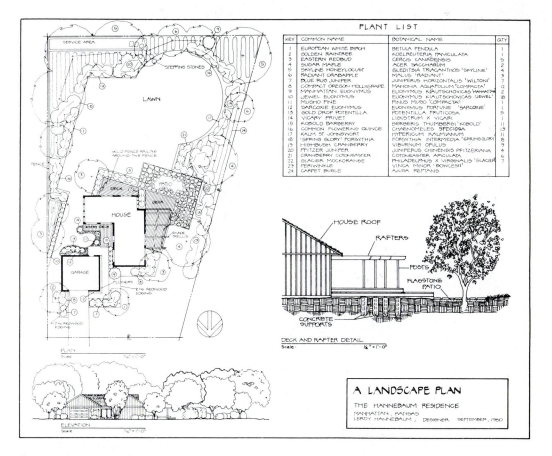

Figure 1-10. A representative landscape plan, complete with plant list and elevations.

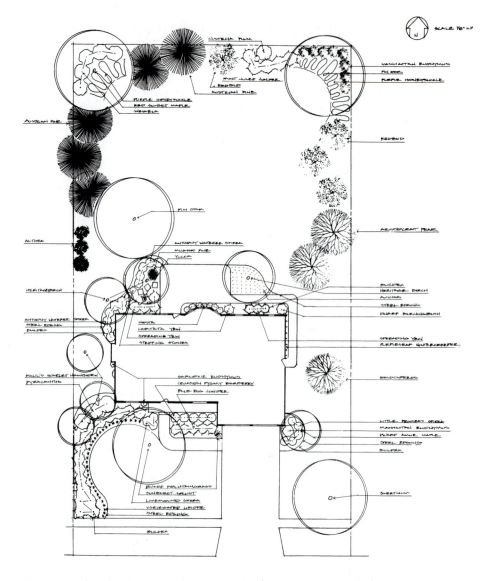

Figure 1-11. A typical landscape plan for a small residence. (Leroy G. Hannebaum, designer, Blackburn Nursery & Lawn Service, Topeka, KS.)

ized desk with a smooth, rectangular surface and square corners. Many sizes and styles are available, usually having a wood or plastic surface. Most have adjustable tops, meaning that the surface can be angled as the designer finds most comfortable. Wood-surfaced tables are often covered by a plastic, adhesive-backed material that protects the wood and provides a smoother drafting surface (see Figure 1-12).

Figure 1-12. A typical drafting table. Courtesy Alvin & Co. Inc.

A T-square is used to draw horizontal lines across a drafting board, or as a horizontal base for instruments used to draw vertical lines. The "T" is hooked onto the left side of the drafting table for a right-handed draftsperson, the right side for a left-handed drafter (see Figure 1-13).

Alternatively, the drafting table might be equipped with a parallel bar, which is fixed onto the table, providing a level horizontal base as the bar slides from bottom to top of the surface (see Figure 1-14).

Stationary triangles are used with the T-square or parallel bar to draw vertical or angular lines. These are plastic triangles that are composed of one right angle (90 degrees) and two other angles. These angles might be one sixty-degree

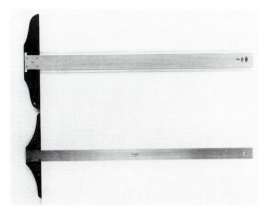

Figure 1-13. Two T-squares. Courtesy Alvin & Co. Inc.

Figure 1-14. A parallel bar attached to a drafting table. Courtesy Alvin & Co. Inc.

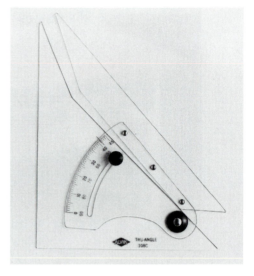

Figure 1-15a. Two stationery triangles. Courtesy Alvin & Co. Inc.

Figure 1-15b. An adjustable triangle. Courtesy Alvin & Co. Inc.

angle and one thirty-degree angle, or two forty-five-degree angles. Adjustable triangles are also available. These are used to represent angles that are not covered by the stationary triangles (see Figure 1-15).

The drafting machine might be the ultimate piece of manual drafting equipment. It consists of an articulated arm with an L-shaped clear acrylic piece on its end (see Figure 1-16). Wherever this right-angled piece of plastic is positioned over the board's surface, a ready horizontal guide and a ready vertical guide are always present for use. The right-angled arm can be swiveled by degrees, enabling lines with angles other than horizontal or vertical to be drawn.

Figure 1-16. A drafting machine, attached to a drafting table. Courtesy Alvin & Co. Inc.

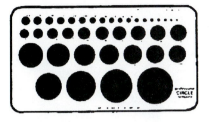

TD1200

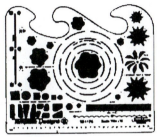

TD1178

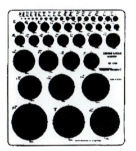

TD1204

Figure 1-17.   Three of many available drafting templates. Courtesy Alvin & Co. Inc.

Templates

Plastic templates are useful for drawing shapes quickly and consistently. A template is a flat, thin piece of plastic into which shapes have been cut. Those most often used are circle templates, into which variable sizes of circles are cut, allowing the draftsperson to draw circles by tracing the outer edge of the cutout. Other templates offer square, hexagonal, or rectangular shapes. Specialized templates even offer tree, fence, hedging, and other symbols (see Figure 1-17).

SPECIALIZED TEMPLATES.   One specialized template is called a French curve, which consists of many curved lines, none of which are based on a true radius, as are circles. This is used to create lines in a free-curving style (see Figure 1-18). A flexible lead-filled bar can also be used to draw smooth, curved lines.

Drawing Instruments

PENCILS.   Many types of writing instruments are available for drafting. The simplest and least expensive is the wood pencil. The numbers and letters on a wood pencil, such as 2B or 4H, identify the relative hardness or softness of the

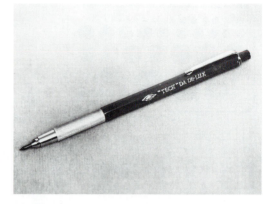

Figure 1-18. French curves are specialized templates used to draw free curves. Courtesy Alvin & Co. Inc.

Figure 1-19. A typical lead-holder. Courtesy Alvin & Co. Inc.

lead. Pencils marked with the letter "H" contain harder leads, while those marked with the letter "B" contain softer leads. The higher the number before each letter, the harder the lead. For example, a 4H pencil contains a harder lead than a 2H pencil, and a 4B lead is softer than a 3B lead. It should be noted that modern pencil leads are made of graphite or plastic, and contain no actual lead.

A special type of wood pencil is called a nonphoto lead pencil. The marks made by a nonphoto pencil are a specific blue shade that will not reproduce on a blueprint.

Pencils of other colors are often used to render colored plan views, elevational views, or perspectives.

Pencils can be sharpened with a knife, a manual pencil sharpener, an electric pencil sharpener, or a sandpaper block. The type of line desired dictates the method of sharpening and the type of lead used. A very fine line requires a pencil with a hard lead, sharpened to a pin-point. Broad, heavy lines result from soft lead sharpened to a wedge-shape on a sandpaper block, which is a piece of wood onto which are stapled many layers of small sandpaper rectangles. While softer leads smudge more easily, the harder leads are more difficult to erase.

LEAD-HOLDERS. A lead-holder is a hollow metal or plastic sleeve that holds long individual leads of the same hardness range as the lead pencils above (see Figure 1-19). At the top of the lead holder is a button which, when depressed, opens a gripping device at the opposite end of the holder, freeing the lead to slide lower, to be gripped again when the button is released. These leads are sharpened in a lead pointer, as pictured in Figure 1-20, then further shaped with a sandpaper block when a broader point is desired. A lead pointer produces an extremely fine, long-tapered point. Most mechanical lead pointers set on a flat surface, but some are hand-held and one type clamps onto the drafting board.

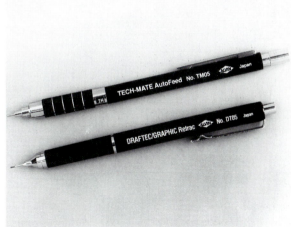

Figure 1-20. Lead pointers are used to sharpen the lead in a lead holder. Courtesy Alvin & Co. Inc.

Figure 1-21. Two types of mechanical drafting pencils. Courtesy Alvin & Co. Inc.

There is also a lead pointer that attaches to the top of most electric erasers, allowing the electric motor to power it.

MECHANICAL PENCILS. Mechanical pencils are very popular. Mechanical pencils are easy to use, hold several leads, and do not require sharpening. The leads are sized by millimeters, generally from .3mm to .9mm, the latter making the broadest line. One drawback to the mechanical pencil is that the leads are quite thin, requiring a delicate touch to avoid constant breakage. The thicker leads used in a lead holder are stronger.

An efficient draftsperson often possesses a number of mechanical pencils, each one equipped with a specific size of lead. Furthermore, this draftsperson might own mechanical pencils of the same size, each equipped with lead of a particular letter-number. This allows the draftsperson simply to change pencils to draw various line values within a given lead size, rather than using just one mechanical pencil and having to keep changing the lead (see Figure 1-21).

PENS. While many landscape plans are drawn in pencil, ink is also used. Ink is particularly useful for finished drawings where consistent line quality is desired. The highest quality ink utensils are called technical pens. These have points rendering lines of variable widths. The widths of inked lines are referred to as line weights. Line weights are 00, 0, 1, 2 1/2, and 4, with 00 being the narrowest line, 4 the broadest. Replaceable ink cartridges make these technical pens reusable indefinitely (see Figure 1-22).

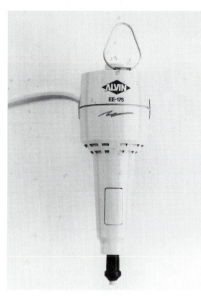

Figure 1-22. A set of technical pens for inking drawings. Courtesy Alvin & Co. Inc.

Figure 1-23. An electric eraser. Courtesy Alvin & Co. Inc.

Rolling ball-point pens can also be used for drafting, albeit with less flexibility of line weight and less consistency of line quality. Micro-point pens make the narrowest lines, fine-point are broader.

ERASERS. Erasers of various strengths and forms are available to correct the inevitable mistakes. An electric eraser is particularly necessary when drafting in ink. Eraser strips of varying strengths can be purchased to fit an electric eraser (see Figure 1-23).

To avoid erasing more of the drawing than is necessary, an eraser shield is used (see Figure 1-24). An eraser shield blocks nearby lines that the draftsperson wants to retain.

DRAFTING MEDIUM. Most landscape plans are drafted onto layers of differing types of paper. Tracing paper, a thin and inexpensive product, is used first, for formulating ideas on a throw-away medium. When all design criteria have been formulated, the tracing paper is overlaid with a high-quality vellum, upon which the final draft is prepared. Vellum is thin paper, made entirely of cloth rags. Vellum is more opaque than tracing paper, but porous enough that the lines on tracing paper beneath can be seen and traced. Vellum paper is also available containing grid lines of a specific scale. These grid lines, printed in nonphoto blue, do not reproduce on a blueprint. Several commonly used scales are avail-

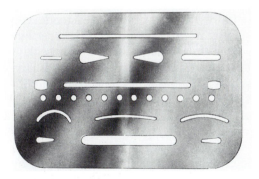

Figure 1-24. An eraser shield prevents erasing lines to be kept. Courtesy Alvin & Co. Inc.

Figure 1-25. Scalesticks are used to measure distances on plans at various scales. Courtesy Alvin & Co. Inc.

able. Because the grid lines eliminate much measuring with a scale stick, using this type of vellum paper can speed up the drafting process.

Tracing paper and vellum paper are fastened to the drafting board with pieces of drafting tape or drafting dots. Drafting tape is thin tape, with adhesive strong enough to hold drafting papers secure to the drafting board, but not so strong as to tear the paper when is is carefully removed. Typically, strips of tape are placed over each of the four corners of the paper, holding it securely. Drafting dots are circular pieces of the same tape, which are dispensed one-at-a-time from a box and placed at each corner of the paper.

MEASURING DEVICES. Landscape plans are drawn in absolute scale, which means that a length of measurement is used on the plan to represent a larger measure of feet, meters, etc., on the property for which plans are being developed. Typical scales used on landscape plans are: 1/8" equals 1', 1/16" equals 1', or 3/32" equals 1'. These scales are called architectural scales. They are represented on a foot-long measuring device, similar to a ruler, that is usually triangular in shape and called an architect's scalestick. An architect's scalestick allows for eleven different scales to be represented in all. Similarly, an engineer's scalestick is a triangular stick representing scales such as 1" equals 10', up to 1" equals 60'. A metric scalestick includes scales that are in increments of a meter, such as 1:1000, or 1:500 (see Figure 1-25).

LETTERING GUIDES. Lettering guides are, in fact, specialized templates. There are several types of lettering guides. Some allow horizontal guidelines to be drawn across paper to serve as guidelines for the height of letters. Others work like stencils, allowing the draftsperson to trace the letter-forms cut into the template, using a pencil or pen.

BLUEPRINTS.   Original drawings are valuable because of the time invested in creating them. Also, vellum is fragile in the field, so prudent designers keep original drawings safe in the office, hopefully in fireproof cabinets. Inexpensive blueprints, imminently replaceable, are given to clients or taken to the field. A blueprint is a print made by passing a special reproduction paper, which is covered with a light-sensitive chemical, through a blueprint machine, coupled with the sheet of drafting vellum upon which the plan is drawn

High-intensity light shines through the vellum, burning off the chemical coating in all places not masked by pencil lead or ink. Therefore, where lines and symbols occur on the vellum, the chemical coating remains on the blueprint paper below the vellum. This remaining chemical coating is then developed by being exposed to an ammonia solution as the blueprint paper continues through the blueprint machine. When exposed, all lines and symbols turn blue, while other portions of the paper that were unprotected from the light, turn an opaque white. Blackline print paper can be purchased, which results in black lines rather than blue.

Original drawings can be blueprinted many, many times, as long as they are kept dry and protected from light, which causes the paper to deteriorate. Storage in plan files or tubes safely protects them from light.

Large photocopy machines are now available that can be used to reproduce landscape plans, instead of blueprinting. These provide a copy that looks more like the original, with generally a whiter background.

Computer-Aided-Drafting (CAD)

The other type of drafting that is gaining rapidly in popularity is accomplished with computers. To perform this type of drafting, one substitutes computer hardware and software for pencils, triangles, templates, and the like. These tools will be discussed in Chapter 15, "Computers in Landscape Design."

THE SEQUENCE OF BUILDING A LANDSCAPE

The process of building a good landscape involves three distinct steps: design, installation, and maintenance. Failure to consider any one facet can affect the success of a landscaping project. An extremely well-conceived landscape cannot succeed if it is poorly installed, nor can a poorly designed landscape be redeemed by good installation procedures. Development of the landscape throughout its history requires high maintenance standards.

It is not enough to design a potentially beautiful and functional landscape. A good landscape designer follows up a design by making sure the plan is properly implemented and maintained. Cost estimations to ensure project feasibility, specifications to guide installation for quality, and attention to ease of maintenance during the design process are all ways in which the designer can contribute to landscaping success. Supplying sound information to clients for their subsequent maintenance of the landscape is also a designer's duty.

The Design Process

Many of the stages in the landscape designing process are interrelated so closely that it is necessary to consider them simultaneously. A logical order exists for the completion of a landscape design, ensuring that all factors are considered. But, because of the interrelationships, experienced designers find their minds flashing from one area of concern back to another until all problems are solved.

The design process begins with a thorough *design analysis*, consisting of a *site analysis* and an *analysis of people's needs*. Until the needs of the property and the people using it are known, they cannot be met. As part of the site analysis, the land itself must be studied to determine if alterations are necessary to provide drainage, usable areas, and a more comfortable environment. A general study of these beneficial land features, as well as those requiring alteration, is best; they are refined later as plans are completed.

After all factors surrounding the land and its occupants have been studied, the designer can start to formulate specific design concepts. The property is divided into usable portions for the functions indicated in the design analysis, and necessary terrain alterations are planned. Shade, wind protection, screening, and enclosure can then be provided. At this stage of the design process, it is best to make general choices, not choosing specific materials until all design criteria have been evaluated.

All circulation routes are also considered during this design stage. Again, it is best to determine the general size and shape of sidewalks, drives, patios, and so forth, without specifically determining the surfacing to be used. Aesthetic decisions can come later.

After all general determinations have been made about area sizes and shapes, environmental requirements, and circulation routes, the aesthetic design factors can be considered. The design becomes more specific at this point. Choices are made: a trellis or a tree for shade; a wall, fence, hedge, or mass planting for a screen; and so forth. Ground-surface patterns take form as surfacing materials are chosen and lines of demarcation are determined. All elements in the landscape can be tied together effectively in a unified design that is aesthetically pleasing. Textures, colors, and forms are blended together to form a functioning landscape that is pleasant to view. Materials selection climaxes the design process.

Each of these separate parts of the design process must necessarily be discussed here individually, but the experienced designer will mull them over simultaneously as he or she proceeds. The designer continually shifts attention from one factor to another, ensuring that the final design will be unified in all phases. The resulting landscape plan might look something like those illustrated in Figures 1-26 and 1-27.

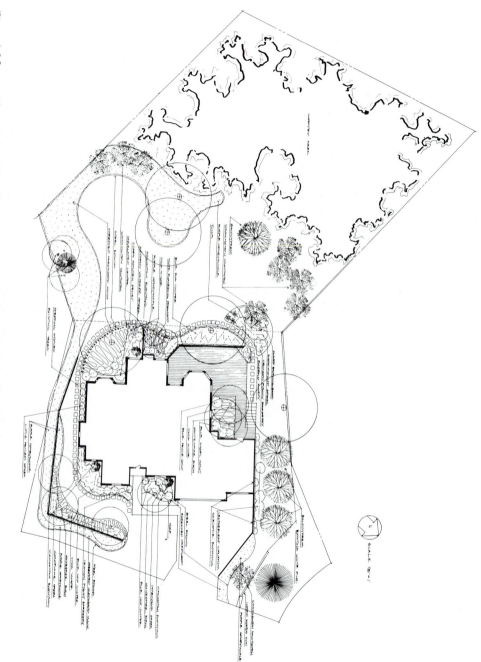

Figure 1-26. Another residential landscape plan. (Leroy G. Hannebaum, designer, Blackburn Nursery & Lawn Service, Topeka, KS.)

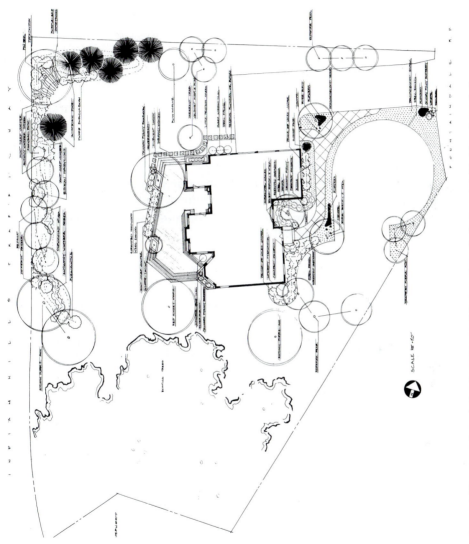

Figure 1-27. A residential plan featuring earth berms along the back and right side, a large deck, and a designed entry-walk treatment. (Leroy G. Hannebaum, designer, Blackburn Nursery & Lawn Service, Topeka, KS.)

Although the primary intent here is to study the design process, this book will also address those questions of installation and maintenance that are encountered as part of the designer's duties. The writing of specifications—which, when mastered, means also a mastery of the reading of others' specifications—is covered later in the book. Estimating and bidding are covered, since a landscape designer's duties commonly include this financial responsibility. Sales, which are also a part of the designer's job in most cases, are also discussed. It is further recommended that anyone who wishes to become a good landscape designer should supplement the material in this book by reading books about landscape implementation, maintenance, and so forth.

POINTS TO REMEMBER

- Landscape design is a complex process that combines the practical with the artful in a unified, functional composition.
- Landscape designers differ from landscape architects, primarily because of a variation in training and differing vocational tendencies.
- A landscape plan is a printed means of communicating design intent to property owners and installers.
- The concepts formed in the landscape designer's mind are more important than the symbols chosen to represent them.
- The landscape plan consists of some or all of the following: the plan view, elevational or perspective drawings, the plant list, construction details, title block, directional indicator, and scale indicator.
- Labeling on the landscape plan must be uniform, simple, neat, and easy to read. All labels must be placed close to where information is needed.
- The manner in which a landscape plan is finished indicates the designer's attitude toward the project, further influencing the property owner and installers.
- Drafting is the process of drawing a formal landscape plan on paper and the person who actually draws the final plan is a draftsperson.
- Many specialized drafting tools are used in the preparation of a formal landscape plan, including the drafting table, T-square, plastic triangles, templates, and the drafting machine.
- A variety of drawing instruments are used in landscape design, including wooden pencils, mechanical pencils, and technical pens.
- The letters and numbers on a wood pencil identify the relative hardness or softness of the lead.
- Tracing paper and vellum paper are both used in the landscape design process.
- Landscape plans are drawn in absolute scale.

- Since original landscape drawings are both fragile and valuable, blueprints are made from these plans for routine use.
- To be successful, a landscape must be well designed, well installed, and well maintained. Skimping on any one facet destroys the landscape's potential.
- Though landscape design can be broken into a sequence of procedures, careful designers evaluate all parts of the sequence simultaneously, drawing the best from each for a given landscape.

REVIEW QUESTIONS

1. What differences exist between landscape designers and landscape architects?
2. How does an elevational view differ from a perspective view?
3. What does the use of absolute scale mean, as it applies to a landscape plan?
4. Why is it sometimes advantageous to use a separate plant list, instead of directly labeling plants on the plan view?
5. Why does a scale of 1/8″ = 1′ work well for many landscape plans?
6. Why is it important to make a landscape plan look good?
7. What does the title block of a landscape plan contain?
8. What does the use of absolute scale mean as it applies to a landscape plan?
9. Is a drafting machine part of the computer hardware used in computer-aided-drafting?
10. Does a pencil marked 4H contain harder lead than one marked 2B?

PRACTICAL TIP FROM A PRACTICING DESIGNER

While many designers complete preliminary designs on tracing paper, then trace the final draft onto vellum, I've found that it saves time to work directly on vellum with nonphoto blue lead, which does not reproduce on a blueprint. Then, I ink the final drawing directly over the blue lines.

When drafting in ink, it is virtually necessary to own an electric eraser.

Nonphoto blue graph-vellum is available in different scales. This can speed the drafting process by eliminating the need to measure lines with a scalestick. The blue graph-lines do not reproduce on blueprints.

A large, plan-sized photocopy offers another advantage to the designer, because one can use it to copy a plan onto vellum, as well as copy paper. If several sheets are required with the same base-map, photocopies save much drafting time. Photocopied lines on vellum erase easily as changes are made.

Chapter 2

DESIGN ANALYSIS

In this chapter, you will study the ways a good landscape designer prepares to design a landscape—by evaluating the needs of the property itself as well as the needs of those using the property.

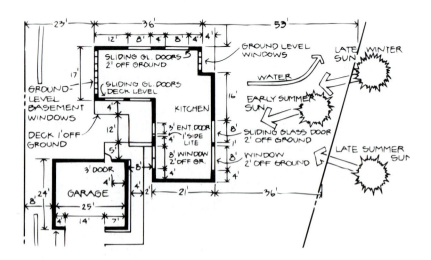

Landscape design is largely a problem-solving activity. The problems encountered can originate with the land itself, with buildings on the land, or with the people who occupy or use the land. In the end, a good landscape design must solve these problems, regardless of their origin, in a functional and harmonious manner. The initial step in this problem-solving activity is called design analysis; it consists of a site analysis and an analysis of people's needs.

SITE ANALYSIS

The analysis of a building site includes an assessment of its better features as well as of the problems it presents. Site analysis is most fruitful when it is completed prior to building construction. The buildings then can be designed and placed to take advantage of the best features of the site, while many site-related problems can be prevented. For example, proper building orientation permits passive solar heating in the winter while minimizing exposure to the sun's rays in the summer. Planning for a minimum of northern glass exposure allows the designer to concentrate plantings for further insulation value, rather than for mere protection. Valuable plants and other site features that might otherwise be lost can be retained. Structural materials can be blended with site characteristics to a larger extent when site analysis precedes building design and construction.

Unfortunately, the landscape designer is usually first involved in a design project after buildings have been constructed. The site problems then become building problems as well, and all are considered during the site analysis (see Figure 2-1).

A site analysis is recorded on paper while the designer is on the site. This rough diagram is made in a notebook or on other conveniently carried paper. Later, the information may be transferred to tracing paper overlaying a scaled drawing of the site and buildings for a more proportionate view. Of course, the measurements for the scaled drawing are also made during the site analysis. Accurate measurements of the placement of permanent features on the site, notes about all site problems, and the site's assets are all recorded on this diagram (see Figure 2-2).

Residential site analysis includes the following steps:

- Obtain a plot plan for the building site from city or county offices before visiting the site. Study easements, building setbacks, parking strips, and other legal requirements.
- Measure lot dimensions. Locate property stakes to determine boundaries.
- Locate the house on the lot. Measure from one corner of the building to two property lines to position the building. Repeat the process at another corner of the house to situate the angle of the house.
- Measure and record building features. Locate all windows, doors, and so forth.

Figure 2-1. Even when great care is taken during the building process, some landscape development is necessary to erase construction scars.

- Locate water outlets, electric meters, and other utility structures on the site and buildings.
- Make notations about changes in house siding, trim, shutters, and so forth.
- Measure to locate and assess the value and condition of existing plants on the site.
- Locate and assess the value of other natural features of the site, including rock ledges, boulders, interesting terrain fluctuations, and so forth.
- Take the measurements required for elevational drawings. The height to the eaves, distance from eaves to gable peak, height of windows, second-story features, and anything else not recorded by previous measurement might be included. Take photographs.
- Note the direction of prevailing summer and winter winds.
- Study the site's terrain. Plan for a topographical survey if more accurate study is necessary. (See Chapter 4, "Studying the Land Forms.")
- Note all good off-property views worth retaining. Measure the distance of that viewing horizon along the property line. Note objectionable views in the same manner to prepare for screening.
- Move off the property and look into it from all directions. Make notes and measurements in preparation for screening others' views into the property.
- Note the need to screen out noise, dust, car headlights, or other possible nuisances.

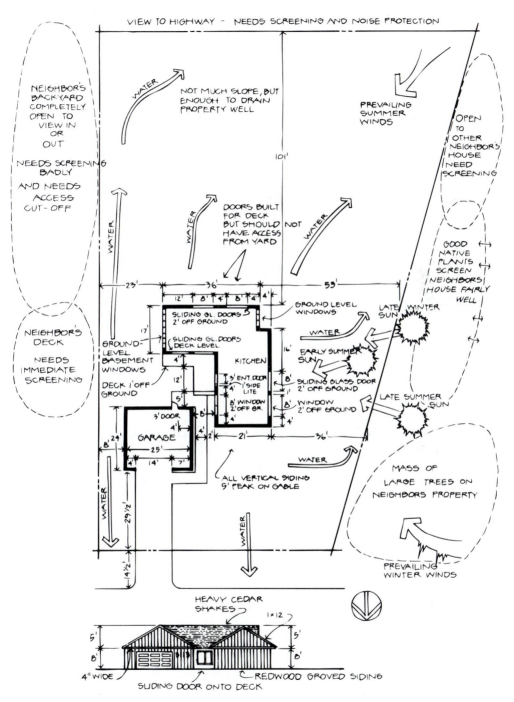

Figure 2-2. A quick, on-the-site diagram provides the designer the measurements and informational notes needed for work at the drawing board.

- Make notes about existing macroclimate and microclimate.
- Check the soil for depth, rock content, and so forth. Probe the soil and take samples for a soil analysis, if needed.

By the time site analysis is completed, the landscape designer should be prepared to utilize the worthwhile features of the site and deal with the problems presented. This site analysis and measurement process should not be hurried. By allowing plenty of time, a more accurate assessment of the site can be made, and design ideas begin to form. Following a prepared list of site-analysis criteria often prevents costly and unnecessary return trips.

All possible avenues to site study should be explored on the site. Views from each window of a house should be studied from all angles. The location of various rooms and traffic patterns within the house should be noted.

Taking several instant-developing photographs aids recall of site and building features. The same photographs also document improvements made by landscaping efforts for before-and-after remembrances.

ANALYSIS OF PEOPLE'S NEEDS

Be it residential, business, public, rental, or any other type of property, the needs of those people most involved in its use must weigh heavily. A property that cannot be used as people wish has little value. The landscape designer must determine the uses to be made of the property, preferred styles, and so forth, and then integrate these facts with the information gathered during site analysis to find suitable solutions.

Making a sound analysis of people's needs requires thorough questioning of clients. These questions are usually asked orally, although they can be written or even standardized on a form. Regardless of the method, the landscape designer must carefully obtain all information pertinent to that particular group of people. In order to receive the most judicious answers to questions, adequate time must be given to the respondents. The first answer to a designer's query will often be revised upon further thought. Some of the most valuable information given by the clients will be volunteered as ideas are exchanged.

Some typical topics to be broached during an analysis of people's residential needs follow:

- The ages, sex, and hobbies of all family members; how each would like to use the property.
- All personal plant preferences, including both likes and dislikes among varieties or general types; any plant allergies.
- How much time will be spent in maintenance of the landscape each week by family members; the maintenance capabilities they possess.
- Whether the property owners consider the house to be a permanent residence or just an interim home. (This fact is not always known; when available, it provides a valuable design guideline.)

- If driveways and parking surfaces are already in place on the property; whether they are satisfactory or need adjustment. Even if they are not already in existence, the same information is required for their design. Find out:

    the number of cars that generally will be parked in drives and parking spots each day;

    the number of cars that might be parked for parties or special gatherings and the frequency of such occasions;

    the availability and safety of off-property parking in close proximity;

    the adequacy of existing lighting and any further need for functional lighting in those areas;

    any preference the people may have for style and type of surfacing.

- Whether patios or decks already present are satisfactory. If not, or if designing new patios or decks is in order, find out:

    how patio areas are to be used (for example, for entertaining, outdoor dining, sunbathing, or just relaxing);

    the number of people who might use the patio areas at any one time, both normally and occasionally; the frequency of heavy usage;

    the time of the day when patio areas will be used and in what weather, so it can be determined whether solid or partial roofing, screening, and so forth, are required; nighttime and all-weather uses;

    the amount of furniture planned for patio areas and the approximate sizes of those pieces of furniture;

    the needs for patio storage units;

    the type of outdoor cooking facilities needed and the corresponding electrical services;

    whether built-in benches might be used in patio areas;

    the client's preferences for patio or deck surfacing materials.

- The suitability of existing walks and paths and any further need for circulation elements.

- Any plans for swimming-pool installation, now or in the future. If a swimming pool is planned, find out:

    the desired size and shape of the pool;

    the need for additional storage associated with the pool;

    the type of fencing preferred for pool-area enclosure and the size of the fenced area;

    the lighting requirements for nighttime use;

    the timing of installation, so access to the site to excavate and build can be planned;

    if the client is familiar with liability and insurance requirements.

- The need for other activity areas:

for lawn sports (including such games as badminton, tetherball, basketball, croquet, horseshoes, shuffleboard, football, putting, and
tennis)—find out how frequently these games may be played to
determine the need for special hard surfaces;

a children's play area and what elements might be included (for
example, sandbox, playhouse or fort, slide, swing set, or wading
pool) and the space required for each; whether the area needs
immediate shade or fencing;

specialty garden areas—for vegetables, roses, cut flowers, herbs, or
other plants; sizes and special storage requirements for these gardens.

- Service-area requirements, including the concealment of clotheslines, compost bins, greenhouses, cold frames, dog runs, trash containers, or other
utilitarian elements; size requirements and supplemental storage needs.

- Special parking or storage needs for recreational vehicles, boats, trailers,
and the like; the size, access needs, and frequency with which these units
are used.

- Any special accessories desired in the landscape—a broad subject area that
might include sculpture; water features; bird feeders, houses, or baths;
boulders; and dramatic garden lighting fixtures. (This information is
designed to indicate preferences but not to limit accessories to those listed.)

Although this list is long, not everything that might be considered for each family can be included. By quizzing clients about specific areas, the designer can generate more thought among family members concerning their needs, so more
information will be volunteered. Some needs not mentioned in the above list
might be discovered, and all deserve equal attention.

Information gathered from site analysis and the analysis of people's needs
can now be pooled for a feasibility study. It is not unusual for compromises to be
made. Family needs might require more space than is available. Spaces then
must be made suitable for multipurpose uses, or some uses can be eliminated.
Maintenance requirements should also be clarified at this time, making sure family desires do not conflict with their willingness or ability to provide the maintenance. It is better to spell out such discrepancies at this stage in the design
process than to proceed with a landscape that is unreasonable for the people
involved. This stage in the planning process often involves compromising
between the ideal and that which actually suits a family's budget and abilities. A
well-conducted analysis of people's needs often helps people to discover the limitations of their landscaping desires.

The length of anticipated ownership is very important. If a family considers
a house to be an interim residence until they relocate or buy a different house,
the landscaping might best be arranged to suit a general population. This does
not mean that individual family needs become unimportant. It just means that

the landscaping should be designed with a definite period of maturity in mind, and the landscaping should be designed to suit a general buying public instead of just one family. The designer might select plants that mature more quickly, or use larger plants in beginning plantings, to facilitate the sale of the house. Highly imaginative or unorthodox landscaping might cause a house to remain on the real-estate market for a longer period of time.

A family's needs often change. Families with young children, for example, have a need for playground equipment that might be completely unnecessary in a few years. The landscape design for such a home might offer alternative uses for that playground area when the family outgrows that need.

When a house is considered to be a permanent residence, the landscaping need not be arranged for its sales value at a future time. Other considerations, including total landscaping budget, yearly installation budget, expectations of maturity, and installation scheduling, should be studied. It does little good to design a landscape well if it cannot be implemented smoothly. The design-analysis stage is the first opportunity for the homeowner and the landscape designer to make decisions leading to smooth project completion.

Each design of landscaping for uses other than residential requires specialized design analysis. Business landscaping, for example, offers different challenges, from a design-analysis standpoint, than does the design of landscaping for an apartment complex. The design stages that follow design analysis are also quite different, so design analysis for special landscaping applications will be discussed later (in Chapter 12, "Special Landscape Problems").

Design analysis may well be the most critical step toward designing a successful landscape. As indicated earlier, landscaping is largely a problem-solving activity, and the first step in solving any problem is to identify that problem. By the time the design analysis is complete, the designer should know the site and its occupants well enough to anticipate problems not even discussed. Many of the design concepts necessary later in the planning process already will have begun to take form.

POINTS TO REMEMBER

- Design analysis consists of both a site analysis and an analysis of people's needs.
- Design analysis identifies problems to be solved during the landscape designing process.
- Landscape problems can originate with the site, its buildings, or the people most involved in its use.
- All property and building measurements are taken during the site analysis and are recorded on paper, along with notes about both good and bad property features. Measurements must be very accurate.

- All easements, building setbacks, and other elements covered by regulations that affect the site are checked during site analysis.
- Taking soil samples for analysis and taking instant-developing photographs while making the site analysis often prevent expensive return trips to the site.
- The analysis of people's needs can be as varied as the people themselves. A good designer will stimulate their thoughts so that they will volunteer as much information as possible.
- A comprehensive analysis of people's needs includes, whenever possible, their plans for the future as well as the present.
- A feasibility study at the conclusion of the design analysis allows property owners to judge their own capabilities. Compromises between the ideal and the practical often can be made before the design process continues.
- A good design analysis may well be the most critical stage in landscape design. Identification of all landscaping problems is the first step toward their solution.

REVIEW QUESTIONS

1. List as many of the steps in a good site analysis as you can.
2. Name the conditions requiring screening during landscape design.
3. Name as many of the considerations to be made during the analysis of people's needs as you can.
4. Why is it often impossible to do an analysis of people's needs that is accurate, both for the present and for ten years hence?
5. Is determining the necessity for a service area in the landscape a function of the site analysis or the analysis of people's needs?
6. Is the location of underground utilities a function of the site analysis or the analysis of people's needs?

PRACTICAL TIP FROM A PRACTICING DESIGNER

When I begin working for a client, I label a manila file folder with the client's name, address, phone number, and information about the initial appointment. I record the site measurements on the outside of this folder, along with information gleaned from my first meeting with the client. A plot plan, if obtained from the client, site photographs, a copy of the cost estimate, and a copy of the billing information are placed into the folder, which becomes a complete record of my activities involving that client.

Chapter 3

AREAS AND CIRCULATION

In this chapter, you will learn how a good landscape designer determines how spaces should be utilized in the property being considered. Then, having determined the area division, the methods for determining the makeup of circulation routes from one area to another will be studied. The sizes, shapes, and physical construction of circulation structures will also be studied.

By the time all information gathered during design analysis is digested, the landscape designer should be prepared to divide a property into usage areas. When the areas within a landscape are useful as well as aesthetically pleasing, the landscape functions as it should. Part of the problem of making those areas useful is the design of functional circulation routes around the property.

During the initial design processes, the areas within the landscape may be considered only on the basis of their use. Later, as environmental and aesthetic factors are applied, it helps to think of areas within the landscape as "outdoor rooms," complete with walls, ceiling, and floor; then the boundaries of each area can be more specifically designated. At this stage, then, area designation might be compared to working a jigsaw puzzle. The approximate sizes and shapes required by design analysis criteria are maneuvered back and forth to find the most logical available positions.

The areas required for each landscape depend upon the uses to be made of that particular property. In most residential landscape applications, the property will first be cut into three general use areas: the public area, the private living area, and the service area (see Figure 3-1). The *public area* is that part of the landscape that is open to the public's view at all times. The front yard and portions of side yards are normally included in the public area. The *private living area*, also called the *outdoor living area*, is cut off from public view and accessibility. It is intended for the private use of family members and their guests for recreation, relaxation, dining, or similar activities that generally are not shared with the public. Normally found in the backyard and in portions of side yards, this area might include a swimming pool, patio and deck surfaces, game areas, and children's play areas. The *service area* provides for utilitarian functions that must take place on the property but are best left unseen. Vegetable gardens, compost piles, clotheslines, trash containers, dog runs, and garden storage buildings are just some of the elements found in the service area. Often cluttered and sometimes emanating unpleasant odors, the service areas are usually concealed from both the public area and the private living area. Side yards and portions of the backyard are the normal locales for service-area functions.

It is important to realize at this point that while *most* residential properties are divided into these three general use areas, this arrangement is not essential. Individual circumstances should rule. The front of a house need not always be displayed to the public, for example; it can be secluded for use as additional outdoor living space or buffered by plantings so the house can be "discovered" by guests, rather than openly displayed (see Figure 3-2). Similarly, many properties no longer require service areas. Trash is collected in garages, clothes are dried in machines, burning is prohibited by law, and vegetable gardens are more frequently accepted as part of other landscaping areas. The designation of public, private, and service areas should be done as design-analysis criteria dictate.

No law states that a property must have only one public area, one private area, and one service area. If it best suits family needs, three distinct service areas can be created. The designer's task is to make those areas blend with surrounding

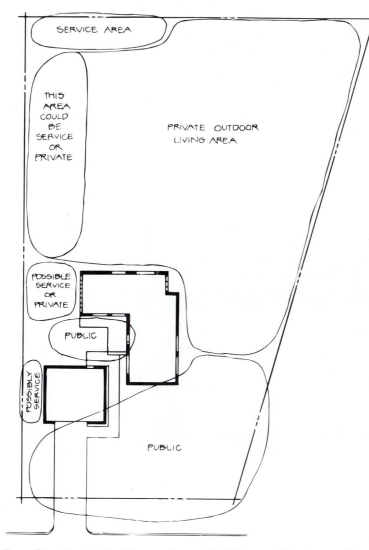

Figure 3-1. Most residential properties are divided into public, private, and service areas.

areas for a total effect that is aesthetically pleasing, yet useful. This is a difficult task, since many urban lots are small.

DEFINING AREAS IN THE LANDSCAPE

Making a list of areas required by site analysis and desired in the analysis of people's needs helps the designer begin to evaluate area designation. The sizes

Figure 3-2. Though most houses are on public display, one that is almost completely hidden by landscape elements can be very intriguing.

and general shapes required for these areas should also be noted, as should those functions that might be combined into the same area. For example, the following sizes are required for lawn games:

- Shuffleboard 45′ × 6′ (hard surface)
- Basketball 40′ × 40′ optimum (hard surface)
- Croquet 30′ × 60′ (grass)
- Badminton 24′ × 54′ (grass or hard surface)
- Horseshoes 10′ × 40′ (clay pits and pegs required)
- Tetherball 20′ diam. circle (hard surface or frequently moved)
- Football 50′ × 30′ minimum (grass)
- Tennis 100′ × 40′ minimum (36′ × 78′ doubles court plus margins; hard surface)

To complete the list, notes are made about the type of surfacing required. The designer may then be able to utilize one area for several similar functions. For example, a lawn area 60′ × 40′ could be used for football, badminton, and croquet, as desired. A tennis court could serve for badminton, shuffleboard, tetherball, and basketball. Driveways and parking areas can also be utilized for some of the hard-surface games. Advance planning results in a much more organized and comprehensive use of space.

Similar lists should be made of other required uses of space. As indicated on the analysis of people's needs, the swimming pool, any accompanying storage area required and the sizes of dog runs, vegetable gardens, and any other element occupying space should be listed for study. Again, the designer is wise to look for those elements that might be combined to share the same space in the landscape.

Fitting all of these units together into limited space frequently presents a challenge. Two methods can be used to aid the designer in this space designation. First, by overlaying a scaled drawing of the property and its buildings with tracing paper, the designer can make *bubble diagrams*—rough blocks or "bubbles" that approximate the size and shape required for each necessary element (see Figure 3-3). Several patterns might be tried in different bubble diagrams to find the one that makes the best use of available space. To test the circulation between areas, the designer draws lines between bubbles. Infrequently traveled routes are marked by light lines or broken lines, whereas those used most often are marked by heavy lines. Drawing these circulation lines indicates to the designer what it will be like for the property owner to move from one area to another. The bubble diagram that makes the most use of available space, while providing the easiest access to heavily traveled areas, is the one that should be chosen.

The second method, much like bubble diagramming, is to cut out areas, using various colored construction paper, at the same scale as a drawing of the property and buildings. These colored blocks of paper, each representing a particular use area, are then manipulated on the drawing of the property until a reasonable solution is reached. Again, the circulation routes for each arrangement are studied by drawing lines between areas or by connecting strips of black paper. In either case—bubbles or cut-outs—several combinations of areas and traffic patterns should be examined before settling on one.

During this process of defining areas and traffic patterns, the topography of the site must be kept uppermost in the designer's mind. On a reasonably flat lot, topography might not be a factor in area determination. On a sloping lot, however, it might completely dictate the location of areas (see Figure 3-4). When topography is a factor in area determination, a topographical survey is required, which results in the creation of a topographical map that can be studied as areas are designated. The study of topography is a specialized area of site analysis that is detailed in Chapter 4, "Studying the Land Forms."

When public, private, and service areas are segmented in the landscape, the situation of the house on the lot often dictates their positioning. Most urban

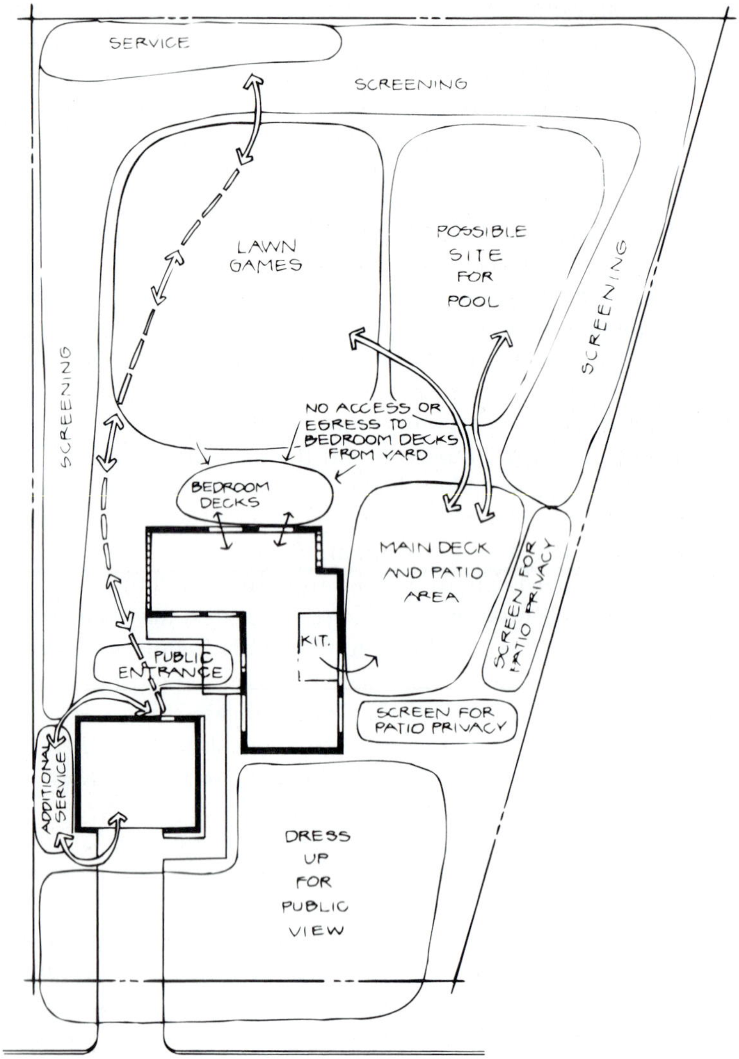

Figure 3-3. "Bubble diagrams," like the one shown here, are a good way to rough-out use areas and circulation patterns.

homes are aligned with the front door facing the street, narrow side yards between homes, and backyards facing other backyards. The only logical public area is the front yard, since most of the back is already secluded by the house and by other structures on surrounding properties. Side yards can be either public or private depending on their treatment, and backyards are best suited to private use, although additional screening is required to make them totally private. The

Figure 3-4. Sometimes the topography of an area dictates configurations for landscape areas.

placement of service areas, while partially determined by the need for screening them from both the public and private living areas, is often more dependent on logical traffic patterns. Activities in those areas might require frequent trips through a garage via a back door, for example. Access for service personnel might be required. To situate service areas far from those who need access is to negate their usefulness.

The proportions of individual areas are important. Generally, an area within the landscape looks best if it is more wide than it is deep. A deep, narrow backyard, for instance, looks better if it is cut into pieces that appear wider than they are deep. This principle can be applied during the area-designation portion of the design sequence, then further implemented later as planting beds, walls, fences, or mass plantings are projected across, dividing these areas. When selecting general areas by uses, though, just keep in mind that areas are best when proportionately wider than deep (see Figure 3-5).

CIRCULATION

Circulation has been mentioned several times already in this chapter as a part of area designation. However, circulation deserves much attention on its own. Two types of circulation occur on residential properties: *pedestrian* and *motor*. Making adequate provision for each is one of the landscape designer's duties.

Figure 3-5. The arrangement of masses and voids in the landscape functions and looks best if areas appear wider than deep.

Driveways and parking areas constitute motor-circulation areas on a residential property. These elements often are already present when the landscape designer first sees a property. Even so, these elements should be studied and their sizes and shapes related to information gleaned from the analysis of people's needs so that any necessary adjustments can be made. Though builders sometimes do consider the appearance of a driveway, they are likely to be more cognizant of its construction cost. Beyond that, unless a home is custom-built, the builder is ill equipped to anticipate fully the needs of the ultimate homeowner. The landscape designer should always be prepared to suggest reconstruction of these elements, or additions to them, if necessary.

Driveways necessarily must accommodate the size and turning radii of numerous makes of automobiles. They must be located for easy access to the garage and parking spots, and their size should be kept to a minimum for reduced cost. Beyond providing for these needs, the driveway and parking areas should be made as inconspicuous as possible. Large expanses of hard surface contribute little to the aesthetic appearance of a property. The illustrations in Figure 3-6 give the proper design criteria for various driveway and parking elements.

Pedestrian circulation involves planning for *primary* and *secondary* walks, garden paths, and open traffic ways in the lawn (see Figure 3-7). Primary walks are those most used. They service the main entryways into the house. A walk leading from the street to the front entrance, for example, would be a primary walk, as would a walk from the driveway/parking area to the front door. These walks should be wide enough to accommodate two people walking side by side,

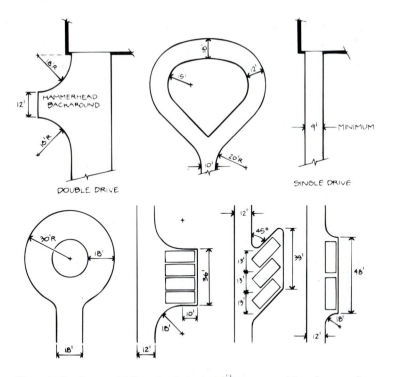

Figure 3-6. Some guidelines for designing driveways, parking places, and turnarounds for driveways are shown here.

or a minimum of 4' wide. Because they are used frequently, in all types of weather, by people wearing all sorts of footgear, these walks must have a solid, secure surface that is easily cleaned.

Secondary walks are those that are necessary on the property but that are not used as frequently as the primary walks; they are more likely to be used by only one person at a time. Because of the single usage, these walks need only be 2-1/2' to 3' wide. In fact, the appearance of these walks is less obtrusive in the overall landscape if they are kept to a minimum width. A walk connecting the backyard with the front yard or connecting two patios might be considered a secondary walk. Although these walks are also used with enough frequency to require a hard surface, more flexibility is available than for primary walks. These secondary walks serve well when made from separate stepping stones or poured-in-place concrete blocks of various sizes.

The garden path is used infrequently. It often serves as an ornamental function in the landscape as much as a circulation function. Therefore, it will often be made from stepping stones, wooden rounds, or other broken pieces of some design. The garden path may be used to border a planting bed or to divide an expanse of lawn. Infrequently used, and normally used most by the property owner, these paths need not be so obvious as other walks.

Figure 3-7. Walks are of great importance to both the utility and the beauty of a landscape. The lines they contribute are important to the landscape's appearance, but they must also follow a logical route of travel if they are to be useful. A brick walk of straight-line design and a curved concrete walk are illustrated in these photos.

When designing the pedestrian circulation elements in the landscape, the designer should always remember that circulation is their primary purpose. If they do not serve to carry people from one location to another, they fail. Since people prefer the most direct route from one place to another, the walks should reflect that preference. A wildly curving walk may look pleasant on paper, but it never serves its function adequately because people refuse to take the additional steps required by the curve. A walk need not exactly connect two points by a straight line, but it should not obviously take its users far out of their way.

DECKS AND PATIOS

Decks and patios are circulation elements, connecting the outdoors with interior rooms. At the same time, they serve as outdoor dining rooms, party rooms, or just places to relax.

Figure 3-7 (continued)

Patios are constructed at ground level, usually out of a solid-surfaced material such as concrete, bricks, or flagstone. Many surface variations are possible. They offer solid support, easy cleaning, ground-level access, and the potential for permitting overflow onto an adjacent lawn area (see Figure 3-8).

Decks tend to be more self-limiting in size than patios because they are usually surrounded by railings or benches. Since the deck is often elevated above the ground-level patio, the ability of the lawn to accept the deck's overflow is also limited (see Figure 3-9).

One of the major reasons decks are popular is that they can be built where patios cannot because of uneven terrain or high-level access to a building (see Figure 3-10). Decks serve essentially the same function as patios but generally at higher cost. Wooden decks are cooler than patios in the summer because they do not reflect heat as do lighter-colored patio surfaces, and because air can circulate through the deck's floor. The floor of a deck is more cushioned than patio surfaces, but because of the slotted spacings between decking boards, they can be difficult for women wearing high-heeled shoes.

Given the information from the analysis of people's needs and from the site analysis, the designer can project family uses for patios or decks. Decisions between decks and patios are based on the topography of the site and family preferences. Decks and patios often are used in combination, forming a pleasing partnership that satisfies requirements for outdoor dining, sunbathing, entertaining, or just relaxing (see Figure 3-11).

Figure 3-8.   Some of the many patio surfaces and designs.

Figure 3-8 (continued)

Figure 3-8 (continued)

Figure 3-9. Some of the many types of possible deck designs.

Figure 3-9 (continued)

Figure 3-9 (continued)

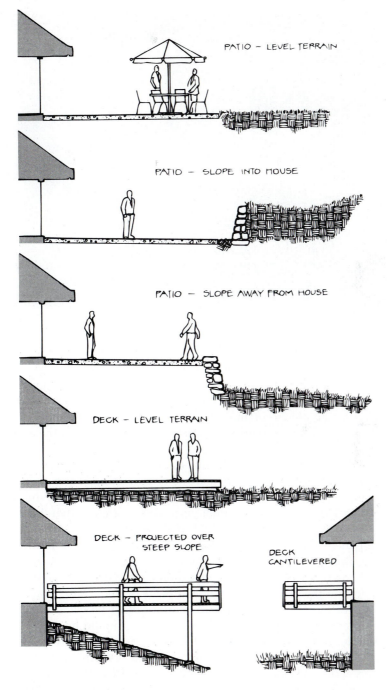

PATIO — LEVEL TERRAIN

PATIO — SLOPE INTO HOUSE

PATIO — SLOPE AWAY FROM HOUSE

DECK — LEVEL TERRAIN

DECK — PROJECTED OVER STEEP SLOPE

DECK CANTILEVERED

Figure 3-10. While patios are best suited to level terrain, decks can be extended over almost any terrain by being cantilevered from a building or supported by posts.

Figure 3-11. Patio–deck combinations are interesting and useful.

Planning patio and deck areas might be compared to planning an indoor room (see Figure 3-12). The size of the room is dictated by the number of people likely to occupy it at any given time, the amount of furniture to be used, and the space needed for ample circulation through and about the room. The shape of the patio or deck is based in part on all of the above, but also on the ground patterns to be established later in the planning process.

A patio designer has certain advantages over an interior designer. By allowing a patio to flow onto open lawn space, the perimeters of this outdoor room can be expanded to accommodate occasional overflow. The fact that a family might entertain 100 guests at an annual party does not mean that the *patio* must accommodate 100 persons comfortably. It does, however, mean that areas adjacent to that patio should allow space for the overflow. The patio itself should be designed to suit the family's normal needs and more frequent party size.

If it is known, the furniture to be used on a patio or deck can be measured to help determine the required size for the patio or deck. Next, the number of people who will most frequently use the surface must be balanced against the maximum number likely to use it. How much space should be allotted per person is debatable. There is an old standard allowance of 125 square feet per family member, but that figure varies from family to family. One that uses a patio daily might require more space per person; in other cases, the surface may hardly ever be used for either family or entertainment purposes. To design maximum space

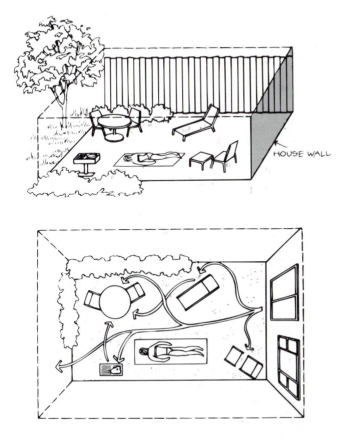

Figure 3-12. Sometimes it is helpful for the designer to consider the patio as a boxlike "room," complete with walls, during the planning process, allowing the space necessary for furniture and circulation as the space is planned.

for the latter would be wasteful, just as to limit the space for active outdoor people who like to entertain would be a failure to serve their needs.

Perhaps the best way to plan a patio's size is to rope off an area for testing. Place furniture—or cardboard pieces that cover approximately the furniture-sized areas—in the area to be tested, and then have the family move around in the area, testing its possibilities. Adjust the space as needed, then wait until ground patterns can be established before selecting the final form.

The landscaping features surrounding a patio or deck can contribute to its size (see Figure 3-13). If a fence is required to screen or enclose one side of a patio, its positioning will affect the way that patio "feels." Tightly quartered against the patio, the fence will make the surface seem small and tight, but spaced back away from the patio with a lawn or planting bed between, that same fence will contribute spatially to a feeling of openness, effectively enlarging the area.

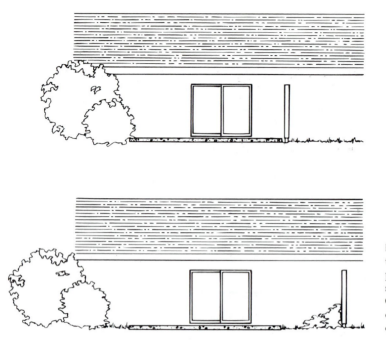

Figure 3-13. The elements that enclose the edges of a patio can greatly affect the spatial feeling of that patio. Generally, it is best not to diminish that space with confining "walls."

Patios can be built out of concrete, brick, patio blocks, flagstone, slate, or other materials. Borders and dividers of contrasting materials are often used to give diversity to their appearances.

Decks are built out of redwood, calcium-chloride, arsenic (CCA) treated wood, or woods that have been sealed, stained, or painted. The design of a deck is limited only by the necessary understructure. The addition of various railings, benches, and other trim elements allows much flexibility in deck design (see Figure 3-14). In Figure 3-15, a deck and boardwalk are used to connect two patio areas that are separated by a considerable distance.

THE CIRCULATION ELEMENTS

At this stage in the design process, it is necessary for the designer to determine the location and size of circulation elements. Final outlines and surfaces should not be determined until later in the design process, because to do so is to limit potential ground patterns within the landscape.

An open trafficway in the lawn is often preferable to a structured walk or path. The open lawn area usually contributes to a more graceful overall

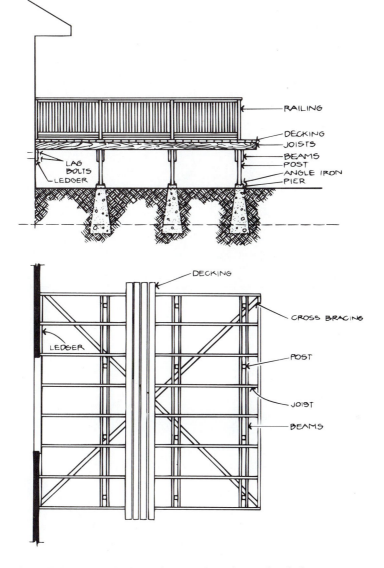

RAILING
DECKING
JOISTS
BEAMS
POST
ANGLE IRON
PIER
LAG BOLTS
LEDGER

DECKING
CROSS BRACING
LEDGER
POST
JOIST
BEAMS

Figure 3-14. Typical structural components of a wooden deck.

appearance. Even if time proves that a solid walk will eventually be necessary, it can be added at some later date; it is more difficult and expensive to remove a walk that is used so infrequently as not to be necessary. The general rule for walks, then, is *less is better*. Make sure a walk is justified before planning it into the landscape.

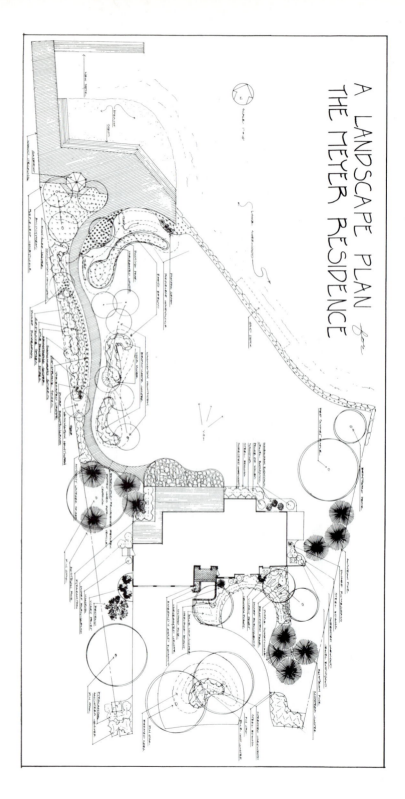

Figure 3-15. A residential plan featuring a boardwalk from the patio to the lakeshore, where a large deck ties together a gazebo, a boat dock, and a sandy beach. Gentle low earth berms with colorful plantings accompany the boardwalk. (Leroy G. Hannebaum, designer, Blackburn Nursery & Lawn Service, Topeka, KS.)

A LANDSCAPE PLAN for THE MEYER RESIDENCE

THE OUTDOOR ROOM

Having determined the best arrangement of areas for use and circulation, the designer can then begin to think of each area as an "outdoor room" (see Figure 3-16), planning the walls, ceiling, and floor of each room to suit best its intended use, environmental requirements, and appearance, tying all of the individual spaces together in a harmonious fashion. Provision for the walls and ceiling will be discussed, beginning in Chapter 6, "The Walls and Ceiling," following the study of land forms and the necessary manipulation of those landforms to make the areas and circulation elements work.

POINTS TO REMEMBER

- The areas to be provided in each landscape are dependent on information supplied by the site analysis and the analysis of people's needs.
- The feasibility of areas within a given landscape is determined by the property's topography, size, and shape.
- Most residential landscapes, though not all, are made up of three general-use areas: public, private living, and service.
- Making a list of the areas desired, with corresponding sizes, shapes, and required surfacing, helps the designer determine the amount of space required, coordinating multiple activities in one area to the extent possible.

Figure 3-16. Thinking of outdoor spaces as "rooms" with floor, ceiling, and walls is helpful during the design process.

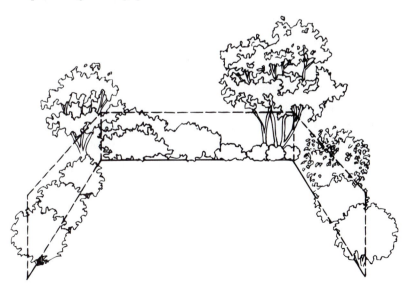

- "Bubble diagramming" and cutting out to-scale pieces of colored construction paper are two ways to compare different area arrangements.
- Circulation between areas should be of prime importance when locations for those areas are determined.
- Proportions should be a factor at all times as general areas are designated. Areas should be more wide than deep for the best appearance.
- Circulation elements should be provided in the landscape for both motor and pedestrian traffic.
- Driveways should be designed for easy use, regardless of car size, but generally should be as inconspicuous as possible. Parking must be arranged for the needs of the individual property owner.
- Primary walks are those most often used, usually by more than one person. They should be at least 4' wide to accommodate two people walking side by side, be of solid surface, and directly connect two points.
- Secondary walks need to accommodate only one person at a time and should be provided only when absolutely necessary.
- Decks and patios should be designed for the normal, daily amount of traffic, with overload capability built into surrounding areas.
- Choices between decks and patios, the sizes of these elements, and their importance evolve from design-analysis information.

REVIEW QUESTIONS

1. Name the three most common use areas in the landscape.
2. Is it always necessary to divide a property into three use areas? Why?
3. What is a "bubble diagram"?
4. What physical feature of a property might dictate how use areas are designated?
5. Generally, should designated use areas in the landscape be more deep than wide, or more wide than deep?
6. Describe the planning process for driveways on a property.
7. How do secondary walks differ from primary walks?
8. Why are decks often more self-limiting in size than patios?
9. Identify the factors to be considered while designing decks and patios.
10. How can the landscape features surrounding a deck or patio affect the way it "feels"?
11. What is the general rule for determining how many walks to use in the landscape?

PRACTICAL TIP FROM A PRACTICING DESIGNER

When a client can't tell me, or I can't decide, whether a secondary walk is necessary, I'm inclined against including it in a design. On many campuses or other public places that have heavy pedestrian traffic, secondary walks around new buildings are included only after lawn wear indicates that a sufficient trafficway exists. Not a bad idea, because it saves money should a walk not be necessary, and avoids directing people where they do not wish to travel.

Chapter **4**

STUDYING THE LAND FORMS

In this chapter, you will study topography and the rules of drainage. You will also learn how to conduct a topographical survey, how to map the results of that survey, and how to read topographical maps.

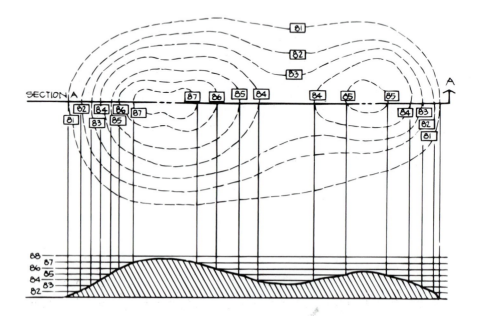

Nature has blessed us with a terrain that sheds excess water and adds much interest to the landscape of the countryside. It is the landscape designer's duty to work within the boundaries of nature when altering the land forms in any way.

DRAINAGE

The land is seldom flat. Areas that appear to be level usually do slope in one direction to at least a minute degree. Some slope is necessary to allow excess water from rain and snow to drain. Only where swamps or lakes occur does the terrain flatten, and then only for a short span. When these lakes or swamps overflow, that water becomes a part of the natural drainage system again.

When people make adjustments to the natural terrain for development purposes, the drainage patterns of the area are greatly disturbed. The natural vegetation and geological factors that would ordinarily prevent erosion are disrupted, allowing the land to be carved. Additionally, many of the changes people make (among them parking lots, streets, and driveways) speed the flow of surface water, causing natural drainways to become glutted, overflowing their former bounds. Erosion progresses at a more rapid rate. Flooding occurs, further destroying the terrain and reducing its defenses against other types of erosion. The impact of such floods is well known, both from an economical standpoint and from that of the physical safety of people and animals (see Figure 4-1).

Figure 4–1.   The construction of a large parking lot often redirects and speeds the flow of surface drainage. If not controlled by landscape elements, severe drainage problems might result.

Careful land development, then, is necessary, beginning with the architects and engineers, continuing with the construction contractors, and ending with the landscape development. Drainage patterns must be carefully planned, properly executed, and meticulously maintained to prevent major disturbance of the natural drainage systems.

The Rules of Drainage

The rules of drainage are simple. Water always runs downhill, and the steeper the hill, the faster the pace of the drainage. In a depressed area, water will stand, causing natural swamps and lakes. Rivers and streams occur at the lowest points of surrounding terrain, where decreasing relative heights, in coordination with the earth's gravitational pull, cause the surface water to flow.

When people design drainage patterns, they create hills and valleys that will function in harmony with surrounding natural patterns. By using the minimum slope to drain a steep site, spreading the drainage over a wide base, and protecting the surfaces of the drainage areas well, the designer minimizes the erosive effects of drainage.

Analyzing Drainage Needs

The best way to study the drainage of a given area of land is by reading a *topographical map* (see Figure 4-2). A topographical map indicates the relative levels of all parts of an area of land by means of *contour lines*. Contour lines are lines that connect all points of an equal elevation. Although these lines are invisible on the property itself, they can be mapped. Existing valleys, hills, ridges, and slopes are all graphically depicted on a topographical map by the arrangement of contour lines. Contour lines are numbered in accordance with their height relative to another known point. If the *sea-level elevation* of one point on the land can be ascertained, all other elevations can then be expressed in terms of sea-level elevations—their height in relation to the nearest ocean. Often, though, the sea-level elevation may be unknown. Contour lines then are established by assigning an arbitrary elevation to one spot; all other elevations on the land to be studied then relate to that elevation by being higher than, equal to, or lower than that assigned elevation. Small land masses, such as a residential lot, do not need to relate to sea level but only to all property surrounding the land. *Relative elevations* are used in these cases, all relating to an arbitrarily designated spot in the area.

Contour lines are represented on a topographical map by means of freehand broken lines. A *proposed contour* (a grading change suggested by a designer) is indicated by a solid line on the map. Contour lines are usually numbered both at the points where they cross the boundaries of a map and intermittently as needed for clarity. Numbers are written on the high side of the contour line. The vertical distance between the contour lines is known as the *contour interval*. This interval may be one foot, five feet, or several feet, but a constant interval is used on each map.

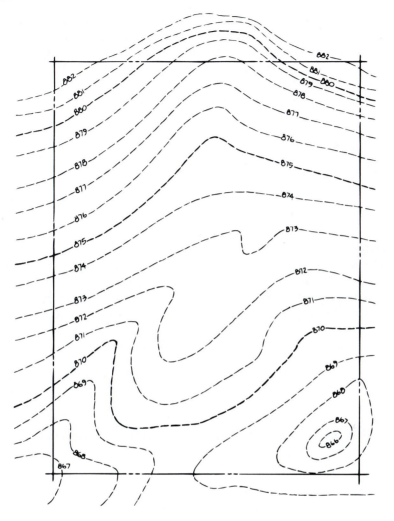

Figure 4-2. Each contour line is indicated on a topographical map by broken lines. In this example, the contour interval is one foot, and every fifth contour is darkened for easy interpretation.

SURVEYING

The determination of the relative levels of a land mass for the purpose of making a topographical map is accomplished by taking a survey. Essential to the survey is the extension of a level line from one point over all other points on the property. This level line can be a line of sight, or it can be a physical line by string or board. As measurements are taken from this level line to the ground at various points, the changes in ground elevation are recorded.

The simplest type of survey can be accomplished by the use of a stringline and a stringline level or a carpenter's level and a straight board (see Figure 4-3). The string or board is placed on a selected spot and extended over an area of lower elevation. Using the stringline level or carpenter's level to establish a level line, the distance from the string or board to the ground at the lowest elevation is measured. This type of survey is impractical for large areas, but it works well for localized spots where other surveying equipment is unavailable.

Surveying Equipment

For larger areas, more specialized surveying equipment is required (see Figure 4-4). Normally, either a *builder's level* (engineer's level) or a *transit* is used to sight targets on a *target rod*. An engineer's level is a telescopic device, which, when mounted on a tripod, rotates a full 360 degrees. Leveling screws provide adjustment in the instrument's sight line. The balancing of bubbles in a fluid medium indicates when the instrument is level. This allows the instrument to retain a level line of sight as it is rotated completely around. The target rod is graded in either tenths of a foot, inches, or metric measurements. As the target rod is moved around on a property, the stationary builder's level is aimed at the rod, and sightings of numerical value appear through the instrument's telescope. The changing elevations of the ground surface as the target rod is moved from place to place cause varying numerical readings, since the sight line always remains level.

A transit is a more sophisticated surveying instrument that can also be used to measure angles and distances, but, like the builder's level, it will also serve as

Figure 4-3. A simple survey can be completed using a string, stringline level, tape measure, and carpenter's square or plumb bob. Though not as accurate as more sophisticated methods, this type of survey works well for small areas.

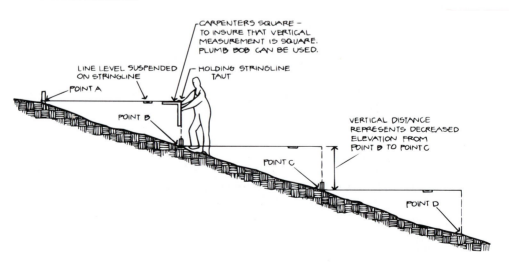

Figure 4-4. Surveying tools. The builder's or engineer's level, mounted on its tripod, and the target rod are used in tandem.

a level sighting device. A third type of surveying instrument is the hand-held *sight level*. A bubble level within this small telescope's sights indicates a level sight line. Because it is hand-held, and the telescope is not as powerful, this instrument is not as reliable as the transit or builder's level. It is most helpful for spot checking elevations during construction processes.

Establishing a Grid System

A reliable topographical map can be developed without surveying each and every square inch on a plot of ground. Instead, sightings are taken on a *grid system* devised to cover the plot of ground at pre-set spacings (usually from 5' to 25'), and the elevations that occur between the sightings are judged to follow the patterns set by those sightings (see Figure 4-5).

A grid system originates from one corner of a property, with an X axis extending the length of one boundary and a Y axis extending along the other boundary from that point of origin. Perpendicular lines extend from each axis straight across the property at the predetermined spacing. Intersecting lines from both axes form a grid, identifying a sighting position at each intersection. Lines are numbered on each axis to serve as the coordinates for future identification (for example, "X-11, Y-5" would identify a spot where the eleventh line on the X axis intersects with the fifth line on the Y axis, or, if preferred, the lines on one axis may be identified by letters of the alphabet and the lines on the other axis by numbers, as shown in Figure 4-5).

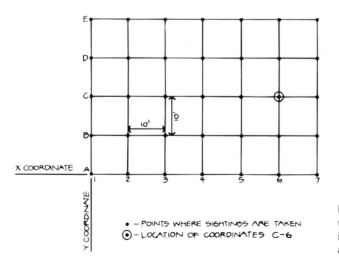

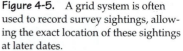

• – POINTS WHERE SIGHTINGS ARE TAKEN
⊙ – LOCATION OF COORDINATES C-6

Figure 4-5. A grid system is often used to record survey sightings, allowing the exact location of these sightings at later dates.

The distance between sightings on a grid system is determined by the degree of variation in the terrain. If changes occur rapidly and often, the grid system should be of close spacings, so less elevational change would escape the survey. Conversely, the grid system for an area of gradual and uniform changes in slope might be arranged on 25′ spacings for expediency with little loss in accuracy. A grid system need not be of equal spacings so long as all sighting points can be relocated exactly.

The use of a grid system ensures even coverage of the piece of land by the survey. It also provides records that can be used to relocate sighting points at a later date.

Survey Procedure

After a grid system is established, a *benchmark* is selected. This benchmark is a spot of permanent, unchanging elevation to which all other elevations can be related. Usually, this position is on a concrete surface that will not settle or erode.

The surveying instrument is positioned so that the benchmark spot and other locations on the grid system can be sighted. After the instrument is located and leveled, a sighting is taken at the benchmark. This sighting is called the *height-of-instrument*. All other positions on the grid system are then sighted and recorded. Additionally, all special features of the property are sighted and located within the grid-system map. Included in these special features might be existing trees, patios, sidewalks, driveways, and other permanent features whose elevations need to be known.

In an open plot of land, all sightings can be made while the instrument remains at one location—unless the change in levels is so great that some sightings extend over the top or under the bottom of the target rod (see Figure 4-6).

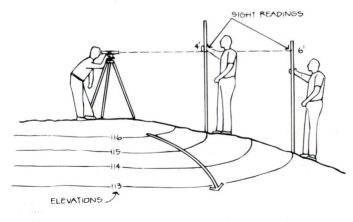

Figure 4-6. The relationship between the surveying instrument and the target rod as the latter moves about the land surface is illustrated here. Note that as the elevation of the land decreases the sight readings taken on the target increase in numerical value.

When this occurs, the instrument must be moved to a new location, making possible sightings to the remaining locations. Similarly, if a house or other building impedes the sighting at some point, the instrument will have to be moved before the survey can be completed. During the movement of the surveying instrument, the height-of-instrument changes also, since it is unlikely that the tripod will be placed on ground of exactly the same elevation as before. Provision must be made to synchronize the readings taken from the new instrument position with those of the old position or the two portions of the survey cannot be related.

To make a *turnaround* (moving the surveying instrument in mid-survey), one grid intersection is selected that can be sighted from the old instrument posi-

Figure 4-7. When the target rod is no longer visible along the level line of sight projected through the surveying instrument, a turnaround, as illustrated here, must be performed. It is necessary for at least one point on the property to be sighted from both the old and the new instrument positions so that all sightings will relate to one another.

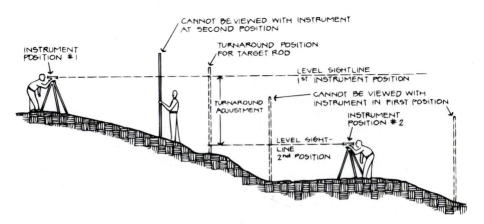

tion as well as from the new one (see Figure 4-7). This location is known as the *turnaround position*. The difference between the sighting values from the old and new positions is then either added to or subtracted from every sighting taken at the new instrument position in order to synchronize the readings to the original height-of-instrument. For example, if a sighting from the original instrument position reads 5.4', and a sighting to the same spot reads 4.4' from the new instrument position, it may be concluded that the instrument is situated exactly one foot lower in elevation than it was originally. (Since the target rod has remained in the same position, a lower sighting on that rod indicates that the level sight line from the instrument has to be on a lower plane.) Therefore, in order to synchronize the new sightings to the old, one foot must be added to each new sighting. The survey can then be completed, with each new reading synchronized to the old height-of-instrument. A survey can include as many turnarounds as necessary, but each time the instrument is moved, the sightings must be adjusted to match the *original* height-of-instrument.

MAPPING SURVEY RESULTS

Conversion of Sight Readings to Relative Elevations

The number read on the target rod increases as the rod moves to a position of lower elevation. Conversely, as the elevation increases, the numerical value of the sight readings decreases. When sight readings are converted to relative elevations by the following formula, the changes in elevation are made to correspond to numerical values:

$$HI - S + BME = RE \qquad \text{where} \qquad \begin{aligned} H &= \text{height-of-instrument} \\ S &= \text{sighting} \\ BME &= \text{benchmark elevation} \\ RE &= \text{relative elevation} \end{aligned}$$

Ordinarily, an elevation of 100' is assigned to the benchmark when the sea-level elevation is unknown. Each sighting can then be subtracted from the height-of-instrument (the sighting taken at the benchmark), which results in either a positive or a negative value that is then added to the 100' benchmark elevation. A negative value will result in an elevation of less than 100', whereas a positive value will be added to the 100'. For example, assume that the height-of-instrument is 9.6' at the benchmark, which has been designated as being 100' in elevation. A second sighting at a grid intersection is 4.6', and a third sighting is 11.8'. The following two calculations will convert these sightings into relative elevations:

$$9.6' \ (HI) - 4.6' \ (S) + 100' \ (BME) = 105.0' \ (RE)$$
$$9.6' \ (HI) - 11.8' \ (S) + 100' \ (BME) = 97.8' \ (RE)$$

The sight reading conversion illustrated on page 69, demonstrates the fact that higher sight readings indicate lower relative elevations, whereas lower sight readings indicate higher relative elevations. When all sight readings have been converted to relative elevations, any survey made at a later date will correspond to the data, regardless of the surveying instrument positioning. Since the benchmark remains constant, and the grid system allows exact relocation of the surveyed spots, new sightings can also be converted to the same set of relative elevations.

Contour Interpolation

Seldom will the relative elevation at each grid intersection be a whole number. More often, the whole-numbered contour will occur somewhere between these grid intersections. To complete a topographical map from a grid-system survey, it is necessary to find the location of the whole-numbered contours and connect these points with contour lines. The location of a contour between two sightings is derived through a process called *contour interpolation* (see Figure 4-8). The formula for this process, which may be used between any two points on a grid system where a whole contour exists, is as follows:

$$\frac{v}{V} \times d = x$$

where

v = the vertical distance from the lowest elevation to the nearest contour

V = the total vertical distance between points

d = the total horizontal distance between points

x = the distance from the lowest point to where the contour will occur

For example, assume that one grid-intersection sighting converts to an elevation of 102.7′, and an adjacent one converts to 103.7′. The intersections are 10′ apart. The whole-number contour 103′ falls somewhere between the two intersections. The lower of the two elevations is 102.7′, so v (the vertical distance from the lowest elevation to the nearest contour) is .3′ (103.0′ − 102.7′). The total vertical distance between points (V) is found to be 1.0′, and d (the total horizontal distance between points) is 10′. The formula now can be used as follows:

$$\frac{.3'(v)}{1.0'(V)} \times 10'(d) = 3'(x)$$

The whole number contour 103.0′ can now be located by measuring 3′ from the lowest point of elevation (the grid intersection with an elevation of 102.7′) toward the highest point (the grid intersection with an elevation of 103.7′). If two or more contour lines are located between two of the grid intersections, the procedure is repeated for each one, always measuring from the point of lowest

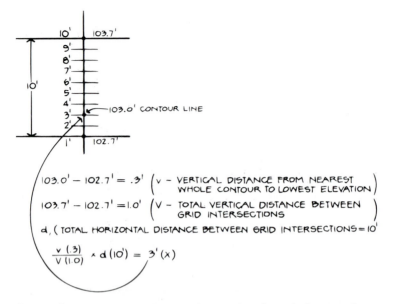

Figure 4-8. Contour interpolation is a process that allows the location of whole-numbered contour positions between the elevations recorded on a grid system.

elevation, not from a preceding contour line found between the same two points. If no contours are located between two grid intersections, no interpolation is needed. When all contours have been interpolated, the contour lines may be drawn, resulting in a topographical map of the area surveyed.

Reading Topographical Maps

A few rules are helpful in the interpretation of a topographical map (see Figure 4-9).

Studying Contours by Sectional Drawing

By drawing sectional views of contour maps, the topographical features along that section line become visible in side view (see Figure 4-10). Sectional drawing is accomplished by drawing a perpendicular line through the middle of a group of contour lines. This line is called the *section line*. A second line, drawn parallel to the section line and below it, is called the *horizontal base line*. At the intersection of each contour line with the section line, another line is drawn straight down, perpendicular to the horizontal base line and connecting with it. All contours are connected with the horizontal base line from the section line in the same perpendicular fashion. Starting with the lowest contour represented, the distances are then measured vertically up from the horizontal base line to represent the vertical increase in each contour interval. A dot is placed to represent the height of

CONTOUR LINES NEVER CROSS, EXCEPT IN THE UNUSUAL CASES OF AN
OVERHANGING CLIFF, OR AN ARCHED
OR PIERCED ROCK.

CONTOUR LINES NEVER SPLIT.

CONTOUR LINES ALWAYS CLOSE ON THEMSELVES, ALTHOUGH THIS MAY
OCCUR OUTSIDE THE BOUNDARIES OF THE TOPOGRAPHICAL MAP.
A CONTOUR LINE THAT CLOSES ON ITSELF WITHIN THE BOUNDARIES OF A
TOPOGRAPHICAL MAP DEPICTS EITHER A SUMMIT OR A DEPRESSION.
IF THE CONTOURS IN THE CENTER OF THE CLOSED AREA ARE THE LOWEST
IN NUMBER, A DEPRESSION IS INDICATED, BUT A SUMMIT IS INDICATED
WHEN THE CLOSED CONTOUR LINES IN THE CENTER OF THE CLOSED
AREA ARE THOSE OF THE HIGHEST NUMERICAL VALUE.

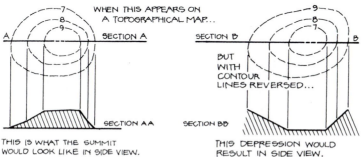

THIS IS WHAT THE SUMMIT
WOULD LOOK LIKE IN SIDE VIEW.

THIS DEPRESSION WOULD
RESULT IN SIDE VIEW.

EQUAL HORIZONTAL SPACINGS BETWEEN ROUGHLY PARALLEL CONTOUR
LINES INDICATE A UNIFORM SLOPE.

WHEN COUNTOUR LINES LOOK LIKE
THIS ON A TOPOGRAPHICAL MAP

A UNIFORM SLOPE WILL RESULT

WHEN THE HORIZONTAL SPACING BETWEEN ROUGHLY PARALLEL
CONTOUR LINES ARE CLOSE TOGETHER AT THE HIGHEST NUMBERED
CONTOURS, AND WIDER-SPACED AT LOWER-NUMBERED CONTOURS,
A CONCAVE SLOPE IS INDICATED.

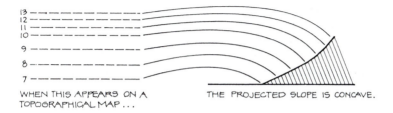

WHEN THIS APPEARS ON A
TOPOGRAPHICAL MAP . . .

THE PROJECTED SLOPE IS CONCAVE.

Figure 4-9. Ease of reading and understanding topographical maps is greatly
increased if a few rules are remembered.

WIDER HORIZONTAL SPACINGS BETWEEN ROUGHLY PARALLEL CONTOUR
LINES OF HIGHER NUMBERS, WITH NARROWER SPACINGS BETWEEN
CONTOUR LINES OF LOWER NUMBERS, INDICATE A <u>CONVEX SLOPE</u>.

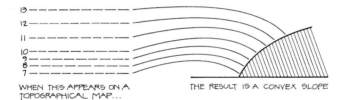

WHEN THIS APPEARS ON A   THE RESULT IS A CONVEX SLOPE
TOPOGRAPHICAL MAP...

WHEN THE CURVE OF A GROUP OF PARALLELING CONTOUR LINES POINTS
TOWARD THE CONTOURS OF HIGHEST ELEVATION, OR UPHILL,
A <u>VALLEY</u> IS INDICATED

CURVE POINTS
TOWARD HIGHER
ELEVATIONS

VALLEY

WHEN THE CURVE OF A GROUP OF PARALLELING CONTOUR LINES POINTS
TOWARD THE CONTOURS OF LOWEST ELEVATION, OR DOWNHILL,
A <u>RIDGE</u> IS INDICATED.

CURVE POINTS
TOWARD LOWER
ELEVATIONS

TWO PARALLELING CONTOUR LINES OF THE <u>SAME ELEVATION</u>, THAT
DO NOT CLOSE ON THEMSELVES WITHIN THE BOUNDARIES OF THE MAP,
INDICATE THE BOTTOM OF A <u>VALLEY</u>, IF LOWER IN NUMBER THAN
SURROUNDING CONTOURS, OR THE TOP OF A <u>RIDGE</u>, IF SURROUNDING
CONTOURS ARE HIGHER.

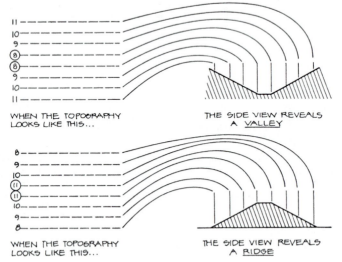

WHEN THE TOPOGRAPHY   THE SIDE VIEW REVEALS
LOOKS LIKE THIS...   A <u>VALLEY</u>

WHEN THE TOPOGRAPHY   THE SIDE VIEW REVEALS
LOOKS LIKE THIS...   A <u>RIDGE</u>

Figure 4-9 (continued)

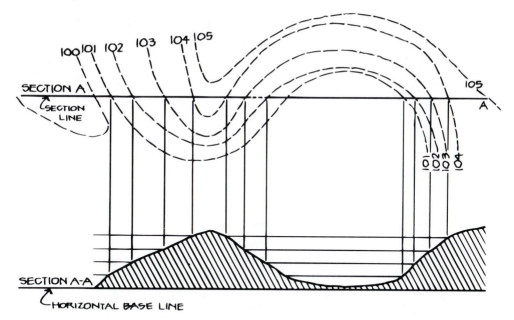

Figure 4-10. Sectional drawings provide a two-dimensional, cross-sectional view of the topography represented on the plan view.

each contour line. When these dots are connected, the line formed represents a two-dimensional side view of the slope at that section line.

It is important to remember that a sectional view represents only the slope at the exact point of the section line. It will not represent the slope 5' to the left or right, unless the contour interspaces are exactly the same as those at the section line.

Points to Remember

- The development of a topographical map for a property is a specialized part of site analysis.
- Changing elevations on land are indicated on a topographical map by freehand, broken lines called *contour lines*.
- The changes in elevation on a plot of ground are discovered by performing a topographical survey.
- Simple site surveys are performed by using the builder's level or the transit to provide a level sight line at a target rod. The different sightings that result as the target rod is moved around indicate the changes in elevation.
- A grid system can be established to perform survey sightings at established intervals that are indicative of the changes in elevation occurring between sightings.

- The *benchmark* is a spot of permanent, unchanging elevation. All other elevations relate to this sighting as being either higher or lower in elevation. The *height-of-instrument* is a survey sighting taken at that benchmark.
- A *turnaround* is a procedure that allows the surveying instrument to be moved to a different elevation but that also allows all subsequent sightings taken to relate to those taken before the move.
- Survey sightings are converted to relative elevations so numerical values will correspond to relative heights and so subsequent survey sightings can be related to original sightings even though the instrument's position changes.
- *Contour interpolation* is a mathematical process for locating a whole-numbered contour line that falls between two sightings on a grid-system survey.
- A topographical map results from interpolating all whole-numbered contour lines located within the grid system of a survey, then connecting lines between all contour points of equal number.
- Several rules exist that facilitate an easy understanding of topographical maps, including: contour lines never split; contour lines that close on themselves indicate either a summit or a depression; and so forth.
- A two-dimensional side view of the slope of an area of land results from the drawing of a sectional view that represents a portion of a topographical map.

REVIEW QUESTIONS

1. What surveying procedure does the term *turnaround* describe?
2. What do solid contour lines indicate on a topographical map?
3. When two survey sightings, taken from the same instrument position, vary, was the higher of the readings taken at a higher or lower elevation than the lower reading?
4. Does the benchmark change after a turnaround is performed?
5. Why is a grid system used to record survey sightings?
6. What is required to perform a survey of any given site?
7. When a contour line splits into two, what is indicated?
8. When a contour line closes on itself, what are the two possible terrain features?
9. Does water drain parallel to contour lines or perpendicular to contour lines?

PRACTICAL TIP FROM A PRACTICING DESIGNER

When trying to assess the changing elevation of a sloping area next to a house, the lowest edge of house siding can often be used to figure the slope closely.

Normally, the base of this siding can be considered to be level. If a house is cloaked in horizontal siding, the width of individual panels of siding also can help determine the total slope of an area next to a house. A telephone pole or some other vertical element can also be used somewhat effectively as a "target rod" when no real target rod is available.

If an area appears to be flat, and you do not have any surveying equipment—a carpenter's level or so forth—you can pour water into a cakepan, let it settle, then measure the depth of water in each end. The end with the deepest water will, of course, be the direction in which drainage will flow.

Chapter 5

PLANNING THE ALTERATION OF LAND FORMS

In this chapter, you will learn how to manipulate the topography of a site to its most useful form and how to represent the proposed changes on a contour map. You will also study how the various types of retaining walls and terraces are used to manipulate contours and how they are designed. You will learn how to calculate cut and fill volumes, as well as the formulas for determining the amounts to cut and fill to establish proper surface drainage. Subsurface draining will also be studied.

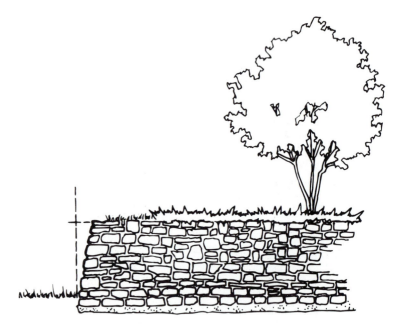

Intensive study of the topographical map developed for an area of land reveals its physical features in detail. This enables the designer to rearrange that land form as necessary for development purposes. Such alterations in land forms are performed by grading. *Grading* is a process by which the land forms are molded to the physical configuration necessary for a given set of circumstances.

DESIGNING FOR GRADING

By designing for proper grading, the designer provides for adequate drainage of surface water; provides areas for building construction, lawn space, or other uses requiring a fairly level space; and provides for circulation routes for pedestrian and motor traffic on the property (see Figure 5-1).

Grading involves any degree of soil movement. It can be so minor that it may be accomplished by shovel and rake, or it can be by major earth movements involving giant machines. The principles are always the same, and all soil movements are directed by a grading plan completed from information supplied by the topographical map of the area.

In residential and small commercial applications, grading design is usually most concerned with drainage and the development of usable spaces. Terracing a lawn to allow more usable space is a good example of a grading application in landscape design. Some degree of grading is involved in the construction design of retaining walls, decks, patios, drives, and walks. The topographical map guides the landscape designer toward feasible solutions for the problems presented by these elements.

Surface Drainage

Surface drainage is considered first in grading design. The designer inspects the topographical map developed for a project to see that excess surface water will drain adequately in all areas. If not, he or she manipulates the

Figure 5-1.   Grading operations are undertaken to create reasonably flat areas, provide drainage, and allow proper circulation.

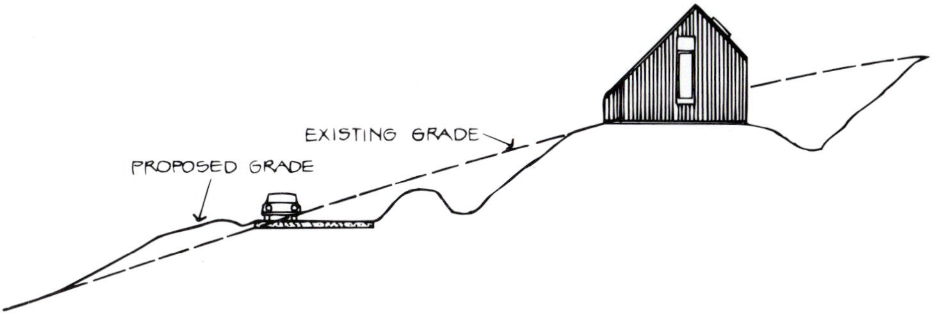

contours on paper so drainage is possible, while simultaneously planning other land form changes.

The amount of slope on the surface for a given area can be expressed in two different ways (see Figure 5-2). The *gradient* is an expression of the relationship between the horizontal distance covered by a slope and its vertical distance. It makes use of the following formula:

$$V{:}H = G \quad \text{where} \quad$$
V is the vertical distance of a slope
H is the horizontal distance of a slope
G is the gradient

If a slope rises 10' in 100' of horizontal distance, the gradient would be determined as follows:

$$10'{:}100' = 1{:}10 \text{ slope}$$
$$(V)\,(H) \qquad (G)$$

The amount of slope in a given area can also be expressed as a percentage. As such, it is calculated as follows, using the same 10' of rise in 100' of horizontal distance:

$$\frac{V}{H} = \text{slope or} \quad \frac{10'}{100'} = 10\ \%\ \text{slope}$$

Normally, percentages are used to describe the minimal slopes, while slopes greater than 1:1 are expressed in gradients; for example, 4:1, 3:1, or 2:1. In any case, these expressions of the amount of slope can be used by the designer to evaluate and project grading possibilities. If given the horizontal distances of a plot of ground and the necessary degree of slope for its proper drainage, the designer can calculate the amount of vertical change necessary for adequate drainage. For example, assume that a span of land is 100' in length, and the desirable degree of slope for proper drainage is 3%. The designer can use these figures to calculate the amount of vertical decline necessary to drain the area from its highest point by using the following calculation:

$$100'\ (H) \times 3\%\ (\%\ \text{slope required}) = 3'\ \text{vertical drop required}\ (V)$$

As the result of this calculation, the designer knows that if the highest contour of the area above is 75.0', then the lowest contour at the other end of the land must be 72.0' or less to provide the minimum of 3% slope needed for drainage. By a similar calculation, the level of any spot between the high and low points can be calculated (see Figure 5-3). This is essential during grading operations.

Using the same formula, a designer can also determine the possibility of achieving a minimum amount of slope within the confines of a given area. For

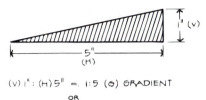

$(v) 1'' : (H) 5'' = 1:5\ (G)\ GRADIENT$

OR

$\dfrac{1''\ (v)}{5''\ (H)} = 20\%\ SLOPE$

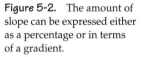

Figure 5-2. The amount of slope can be expressed either as a percentage or in terms of a gradient.

example, assume that the elevations are known to be 102.0' at the highest point in a residential backyard and 99.0' at the street curb in front. Assume further that the only possible escape for backyard drainage is over the curb in front and that a minimum 2% slope is necessary. The formula for percentage of slope can then be applied in the following way, ascertaining the maximum length that can be drained with that amount of vertical drop:

$$\frac{3'V}{2\ \%\ (\%\ \text{slope})} = 150'\ \text{slope}\ (H)$$

This shows that 150' (*H*) is the horizontal length that can be accommodated by that amount—3'—of vertical drop at 2% slope. If more than 150' of horizontal length must be drained, less than 2% slope will be realized, but if less than 150' of horizontal length is being drained, a slope of greater than 2% will be realized.

Figure 5-3. During grading operations, it is often necessary to calculate the desired elevation at a given spot mathematically so that soil at that spot may be cut or filled over as necessary.

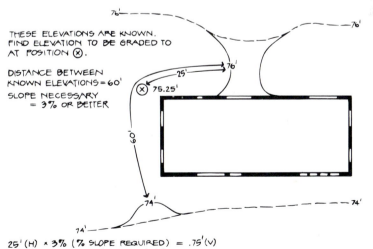

$25'\ (H) \times 3\%\ (\%\ SLOPE\ REQUIRED) = .75'\ (v)$
$SO...\quad 76.0' - .75' = 75.25'\ (\otimes\ ELEVATION)$

Small valleys are used to collect and direct the water toward a release point. These small valleys are called *drainage swales* (see Figure 5-4). Their cupped or V-shaped bases decrease in elevation at a consistent degree of slope, so excess water moves off the property at a steady pace without puddling. Any puddling of water for a significant length of time creates a waterlogged soil beneath, which ultimately results in unhealthy grass or plantings and in water leakage into basements. Constantly waterlogged soils cause the death of plants by eliminating the oxygen supply to their root systems.

In addition to making sure all areas on a property will drain adequately, it is best to make sure that drainage is not too rapid. Rapidly flowing surface water on a steeply sloping lot erodes the soil and can temporarily clog storm-sewer systems by the sheer volume of water.

Manipulation of the Contours

The manipulation of contours for surface-drainage purposes is simplified by keeping in mind a few rules of topography (see Figure 5-5).

To indicate proposed grading on a plan, the designer draws a solid contour line that deviates from the dotted, existing contour lines at the point where the alteration is to originate (see Figure 5-6). By *bending* the contour lines that are shown on the topographical map into new locations, the designer indicates changes that are to be made in the level of the land at that location.

Cuts and Fills

Grading is accomplished by either cutting into the existing grade or filling over it. A *cut* is the removal of a prescribed depth of soil within the space between an existing and a proposed contour line. A *fill* is the addition of a prescribed amount of soil over the existing contour in the space between existing and proposed contours (see Figure 5-7).

Figure 5-4. Drainage swales control the movement of water over the ground's surface. Three typical configurations of swales are shown here.

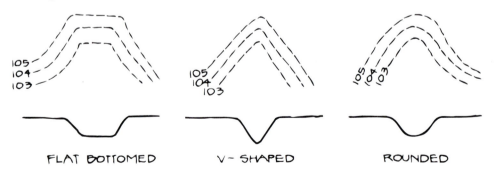

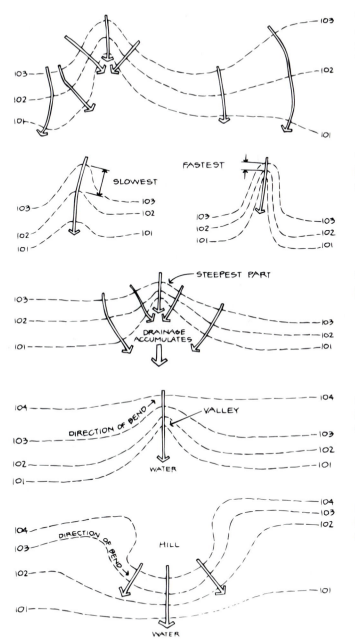

Water always flows at right angles, or perpendicular, to contour lines, from the lines of highest elevation toward the lowest.

The shorter the horizontal space between contour lines, the faster the surface water will flow.

Water always seeks the steepest possible slope.

Contour lines that bend toward contour lines of higher elevations indicate a valley.

Contour lines that bend toward contour lines of lower elevations indicate a hill or ridge.

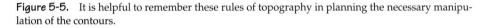

Figure 5-5. It is helpful to remember these rules of topography in planning the necessary manipulation of the contours.

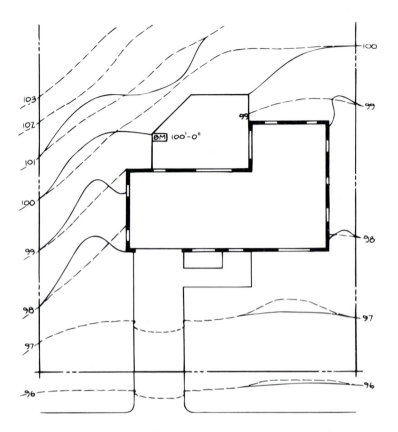

Figure 5-6. When topographical changes are planned, they are indicated by solid lines that deviate from existing broken contour lines.

Proposed cuts and fills on a grading plan can be recognized at a glance by remembering two rules:

- When a proposed contour line bends toward an existing contour of a higher number, the proposed grading change is to be accomplished by cutting.
- When a proposed contour line bends toward an existing contour of a lower number, the proposed change involves filling.

Cuts and fills are measurable quantities. Each cut or fill made is to be measured in three dimensions: length, height, and width (see Figure 5-8). The height of a cut or fill is calculated by the number of contours included times the interval between contours. Length is a measurement of the length along the contour lines included in the area to be cut or filled. The width of the cut or fill is the distance the grading change extends toward other contour lines. Measurements are normally taken in feet, with cut or fill volumes figured in terms of *cubic feet* of soil by the following calculation:

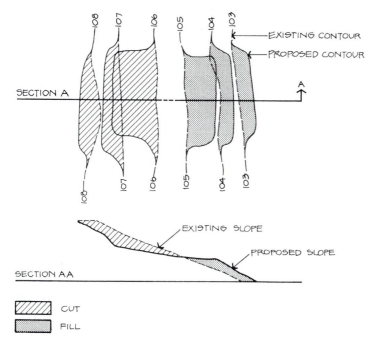

Figure 5-7. Proposed cut or fill grading operations are more visible in sectional view and are often planned in that mode, then transferred to plan view.

$$\text{Length (in feet)} \times \text{Width (in feet)} \times \text{Height (in feet)} = \text{cubic feet}$$

Cubic feet are often converted to *cubic yards*, primarily because the volume capacities of most construction equipment are measured in cubic yards. A typical dump truck, for example, might haul from 8 to 16 cubic yards of soil per load. One cubic yard of material equals 27 cubic feet (3' × 3' × 3'). So, if a cut or fill is calculated in cubic feet, it is necessary only to divide that total by 27 to convert it to cubic yards. For metric conversions, see the metric conversion table on page 425.

GRADING METHODS

Grading may be accomplished entirely by fill, entirely by cut, or by a combination of cut and fill (see Figure 5-9). Each method offers advantages and drawbacks.

Grading by Cut

Grading entirely by cutting offers the advantage of greater soil stability. Since the remaining soil beneath the cut remains in place, it is already well compacted, with soil particles knit closely together. Both erosion and settling are minimized.

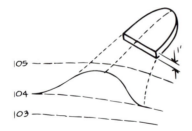

Figure 5-8. Each proposed change on a grading plan represents a three-dimensional volume of soil that is either to be cut away from or to be filled into the existing grade.

The primary disadvantage to grading entirely by cut involves disposal expense. All of the cut soil must be hauled away—an expensive proposition at best. Loss of topsoil, with the resulting exposure of nonfertile soils, is another disadvantage. Deep cuts expose soils that are not well suited to growing vegetation, having been buried below organic-activity levels. The stockpiling of topsoil during cutting operations for later respreading over the new surface provides a profile suitable for vegetative growth, but erosion-control advantages are lost.

Grading by Fill

Grading entirely by fill is the method used to raise a low spot when no other method will successfully drain surface water. This method is usually reserved for localized spots. Sometimes areas of significant size and depth are

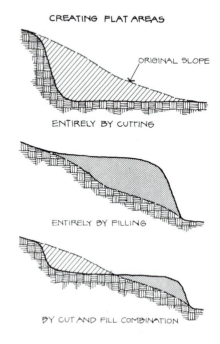

CREATING FLAT AREAS

ORIGINAL SLOPE

ENTIRELY BY CUTTING

ENTIRELY BY FILLING

BY CUT AND FILL COMBINATION

Figure 5-9. A designer must choose from one of three grading possibilities.

filled to raise an area, but it is most difficult to compact large areas of fill in such a way that further settling will not occur. Also, since the soil in a fill has been disturbed, the soil particles are not well knit, and erosion occurs more readily. The cost of locating, acquiring, and transporting the fill soil is also a major disadvantage of grading entirely by fill.

Combining Cut and Fill

The most economical grading method often involves both cut and fill in equal measure. This combination prevents the introduction of foreign soils into the area being graded and makes heavy transportation expenses unnecessary. Soils newly introduced into an area often cause problems with plant growth if they differ greatly in structure, fertility, pH, or other qualities from the native soil.

Though the combination of cut and fill seems advantageous, other circumstances sometimes have an adverse effect. It might not be possible to arrange spaces suitable to the needs of clients or the property by balancing cut and fill. Aesthetic considerations might influence the choice toward either cutting or filling exclusively.

When a ready market exists for selling volumes of cut soil or for purchasing fill inexpensively, those methods become more feasible. But unless arrangements are made well before the start of grading operations, extensive unbalanced cut or fill operations should be considered expensive.

Measuring Proposed Cuts and Fills

Since the proposed cuts and fills in an area are seldom precisely cubic in nature (that is, the depth of the cut or fill varies considerably over the entire area), volumes must normally be calculated in increments of cut and fill. One way to measure increments is by sectional drawings, on which the existing slope can be depicted as well as the proposed grade. The spaces between existing and new grades will give a two-dimensional look at the volumes of cut and fill. The height and width of each cut is then visible and can be blocked into cubic increments. Only the length of each cube remains to be determined. Since a sectional view represents only the length that *exactly* intersects the section line, virtually no length is represented by that sectional view. (Even slight differences in the horizontal distances between contour lines on either side of the section line represent a different slope than that intersected by the section line.) By carefully placing section lines in an area of *similar* spacing between contour lines, indicating that a *similar* grade exists in those areas, the designer can consider that area of similar grade as being identical for purposes of estimating cut and fill volumes. The lengths of contour lines representing the similar grade are then measured and become the length, or third dimension, for cut and fill calculations (see Figure 5-10).

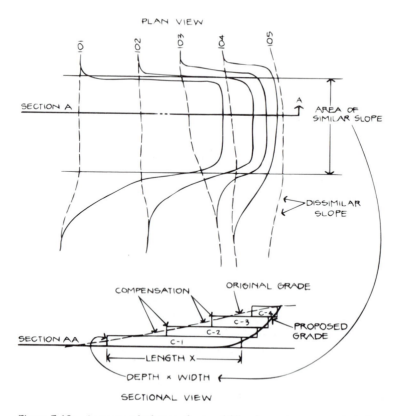

Figure 5-10. Accurate calculation of cut and fill volumes is necessary to test the feasibility of grading plans. Working simultaneously with sectional and plan-view drawings often facilitates accuracy.

DESIGNING TERRACES

Sectional views are also helpful when designing landscape features that relate to the topography of the land. Representing portions of the terrain where similar slope exists lets the designer work from both a side view, through the sectional picture, and a top view, as indicated on the topographical map. The sectional view allows the designer to draw the possible "triangles" of cut and fill that result from manipulation of various contours, showing the resulting terraces created in side view also. The topographical view allows the designer to work within the framework of lines suitable to other landscaping features, architectural features, and property lines, with a better overall view of the dimensions of spaces created. The more graphic the representation available during this design process, the easier and more accurate the design will be (see Figure 5-11).

Calculations of cut and fill volumes, so necessary for the estimating of costs for the completion of a grading project, are also facilitated by working from plan

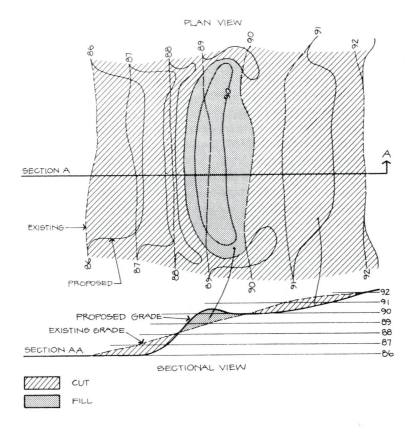

PLAN VIEW

SECTION A

EXISTING →

PROPOSED →

PROPOSED GRADE

EXISTING GRADE

SECTION AA

SECTIONAL VIEW

CUT

FILL

Figure 5-11.   A grading design for the proposed terracing of a slope, in both sectional and plan views.

and sectional views simultaneously. The depth and height measurements necessary for the calculation of soil volumes are obtained from the sectional view, with the length of each contour forming the third dimension from the plan view of the topographical map. As each cut or fill increment is measured, it can be marked with a colored pencil, ensuring that each increment is not measured twice. Subsequent totaling of all cut volumes, for comparison with the total fill volumes, reveals the excess cut or fill required.

When calculating cut and fill volumes, it is best to figure that the amount of cut plus 10% is required to balance as fill. The 10% approximates the wastage that occurs during the transporting of cut material to its position as fill. Therefore, if a project requires 100 cubic yards of fill, approximately 110 cubic yards will have to be cut elsewhere to supply the need adequately.

Terracing permits the creation of more usable areas on a sloping property. It can also help to control water drainage on the surface by diverting water to the sides of a lot instead of allowing it free run down a slope; terraces control erosion in this way. However, it must be remembered that in order to minimize the slope on one portion of a sloping property, it is necessary to magnify the slope elsewhere. The same total amount of vertical decline still exists on the property. It is merely managed differently.

Terraces can be created by controlled grading alone or by the use of retaining walls. In a sense, a retaining wall might be considered a vertical slope. The contour lines all run through a retaining wall, just as they would a steep slope, but since the retaining wall is vertical, the contour lines fall directly on top of one another and so only the top and bottom contours are seen on the topographical map. Being vertical, retaining walls offer the advantage of creating the largest amount of usable space between terraces. Terraces formed without retaining walls are limited to the spaces needed to allow for the soil's *angle of repose*. For each soil there is a maximum angle of repose—the steepest gradient at which the soil will remain in place (see Figure 5-12). Beyond that gradient, the soil will slide to the base of the slope until the angle of repose is reached. Whenever soil is piled loosely, it seeks its own particular angle of repose, which is affected by the moisture content of the soil as well as the soil type. Without retaining structures for support, terraces must be limited by the angle of repose that governs that particular soil. It follows that the lower the angle of repose for a particular soil, the more space a terrace would occupy, leaving smaller interspaces between terraces.

Regardless of the type of terrace designed, water should be diverted behind the terrace, not over its top. This is particularly true if the terrace is made up entirely of soil, leaving an erosion-susceptible slope vulnerable. But even when retaining walls are used, surface water draining over the walls' tops may weaken them and possibly cause their collapse. At the very least, erosion behind the retaining walls will occur. Drainage swales, which collect water behind the terrace and carry it to the terrace ends, are in order.

DESIGNING RETAINING WALLS

Retaining walls retain soil. By doing so, they allow the maximum usable space between changes in level, while at the same time controlling the surface-water drainage. Retaining walls also make possible a wide range of material selection, adding to the aesthetic value of a property by the use of color, texture, and form. The many materials available for use in retaining walls offer a variety of strengths, construction costs, and appearances.

Figure 5-12.   Each material, when piled loosely, assumes its own maximum angle of repose.

Retaining walls may be categorized as being either *solid* or *porous*. The solid walls are either made of solid concrete or are mortared at the joints of the construction material. Porous walls, on the other hand, allow water to escape between the joints in the construction materials. Brick, concrete, mortared rock, and concrete-block retaining walls are all of the solid type, whereas dry rock, railroad ties, landscape timbers, post walls, and wooden walls are all porous.

Solid walls require *footings*. Footings are underground foundations made of poured concrete that extend below the frost line for the geographic area in which they are constructed. They add strength to stabilize the wall, preventing the movement that would otherwise accompany the expansions and contractions of the soil caused by alternate freezing and thawing. Reinforcing steel rods, called *rebars,* strengthen concrete footings, keeping the concrete from cracking and breaking. Good footings are wider at their bases than at their tops and wider than the retaining wall itself, preventing settling by spreading the weight of the wall over a broad base. Footings are poured before the wall's construction and are allowed to cure and harden before the wall's weight is placed upon them (see Figure 5-13).

Footings are also required for some of the porous walls, but they serve mostly as a support function. Because porous walls are not cemented together, they are in no danger of cracking. Modified footings are used in the construction of post walls and wooden walls, adding structural strength.

Figure 5-13. Construction details for solid retaining walls.

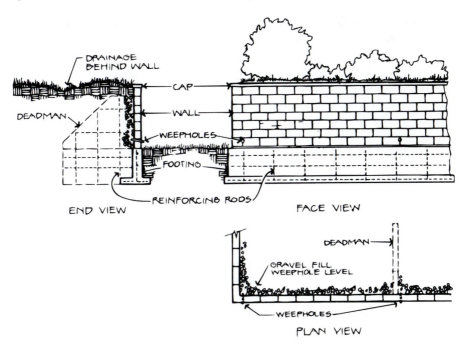

Individual Construction Details

To design retaining walls, it is necessary for the designer to be familiar with the individual construction methods of each type. This familiarity is also required to draw construction details and make estimates of cost. A brief description of each is in order.

Solid Walls

Because they are solid, water pressure builds up behind concrete and mortared walls. If it is not relieved, the pressure eventually becomes so great that it forces the wall forward, causing it to break or collapse. Intermittent *weepholes*, drilled through the bottom of solid walls, allow this excess water to exit. These weepholes are placed every 6' to 8' along the base of the wall.

The face of a solid wall is usually vertical. To add support and keep the wall from leaning beyond the vertical, perpendicular supports extend back into the grade behind the wall. These supports, usually of poured concrete, are called *dead men*. The number of dead men and the size of each depends on the height of the wall and, consequently, the amount of soil it must retain. On average, a good solid wall might have a dead man extending 6' back into the grade every 12' to 15' along the wall's face. Like the footings, dead men should be well reinforced with steel.

Dry Rock Walls

Dry, in this case, simply means that the wall is not held together by any cementing agent. Rocks are stacked in overlapping layers. Since no cementing agent is used, the rocks are free to move by minute amounts during the expansion and contraction movements of the soil. Excess water is released through the cracks between the rocks, so weepholes are unnecessary. Although footings are not required, it is advisable to place the base of the wall in a shallow trench, preventing the rocks from sliding forward.

The face of a dry rock wall needs to lean back toward the soil being retained. This lean is known as *batter* and is normally specified as 2" to 3" of batter per one foot in height. The back side of the dry rock wall must be either vertical or have a slight batter toward the front. A base wider than the top provides better support and a hedge against settling. The batter on the face of the wall shifts the weight of the rocks back against the soil, holding it in place. In turn, the soil stabilizes the rocks. A symbiotic relationship between rocks and soil contributes to the success of this type of retaining wall (see Figure 5-14).

Packing gravel immediately behind the retaining wall facilitates drainage of water that might otherwise build up pressure behind the retaining wall. This *gravel pack* will also fill in cracks between rocks and aid in leveling individual rocks. When a gravel pack is used properly, surface water can safely drain over the top of the wall without concern.

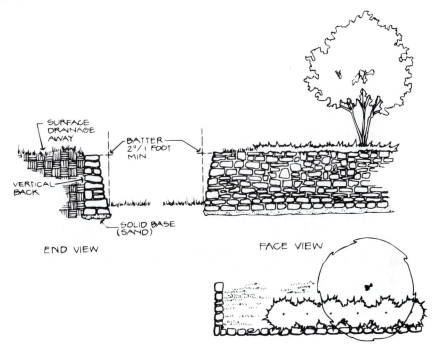

Figure 5-14.   Construction details for dry rock retaining walls.

Figure 5-14 (continued)

Figure 5-15. These walls are made of Pyzique blocks, a concrete block textured and colored to look like stone.

Dry Block Retaining Walls

Concrete blocks, colored and textured to look like rock, are becoming increasingly popular for retaining walls. Some types have an interlocking system while others stack like rocks. Several sizes, shapes, and colors are available.

Dry block walls are built using the same principles as those for dry rock walls, using the gravel pack system and tilting the face of the wall back (batter), as described earlier. The only footing required is a solid gravel base just below the ground's surface. Once a level first course is established, these walls lay up rapidly, because the blocks are of equal thickness. Courses are laid so the seams between blocks are staggered. Because of that, some blocks at the end of the wall must be cut, which is accomplished by cutting partially through the block with a masonry blade, then breaking the block (see Figure 5-15).

Railroad-Tie or Landscape-Timber Walls

Railroad ties became popular for retaining wall construction years ago, when they were plentiful and inexpensive. Though scarcer and more expensive now, they remain popular because of their versatility of color and texture. Horizontal ties make excellent walls and do not require a footing. Like dry rock walls, the base ties should be based beneath grade. Layers of ties are staked together with lengths of rebar or long spike nails. When rebars are used, starter

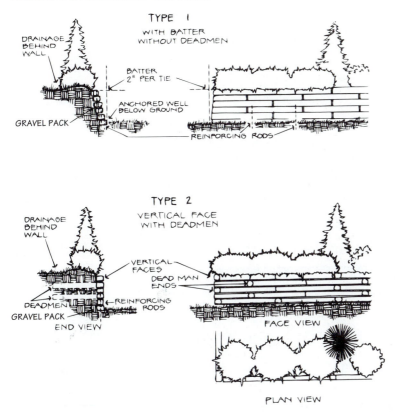

TYPE 1
WITH BATTER
WITHOUT DEADMEN

DRAINAGE BEHIND WALL

BATTER 2" PER TIE

ANCHORED WELL BELOW GROUND

GRAVEL PACK

REINFORCING RODS

TYPE 2
VERTICAL FACE
WITH DEADMEN

DRAINAGE BEHIND WALL

VERTICAL FACES

DEAD MAN ENDS

DEADMEN

REINFORCING RODS

GRAVEL PACK

END VIEW

FACE VIEW

PLAN VIEW

Figure 5-16. Construction details for railroad-tie or landscape-timber retaining walls.

holes must be drilled into the top tie through which rebars can be driven, penetrating the next layer and the third layer of ties below. Each 8' to 10' tie is anchored in three places—at each end and in the center.

Further support for railroad ties is provided by one of two means. These walls can either be constructed with batter (as described for dry rock walls) or by extending portions of railroad ties back into the grade at intervals to serve as dead men. Often, both batter and dead men are used, especially in walls over 3' tall. If batter is used, individual layers of ties are stepped back 1" to 2" from the vertical so that the face of the wall is stair-stepped (see Figure 5-16). A gravel pack, as described for dry rock retaining walls is also suggested for tie or timber walls.

Landscape timbers are treated wood timbers, approximately 4" × 5" × 10', which are used in a fashion similar to railroad ties. Smaller and finer in texture than ties, they require a different means of support when laid horizontally. The best way to support them is by placing vertical timbers in the ground in front of the wall, like a post anchored with a concrete collar. Timbers are nailed to one another with post nails and are also nailed to the upright timbers, which are spaced some 4' to 5' apart (see Figure 5-17).

Figure 5-17. A typical timber retaining wall and retaining walls constructed with landscape timbers.

Post Walls

Exciting variety is available in post wall construction. Available materials are diverse; they include railroad ties and landscape timbers. Posts of any kind are cut and placed side-by-side in a trench. The trench is then filled with concrete, with an equal collar of concrete on each side of the wall. The portion underground

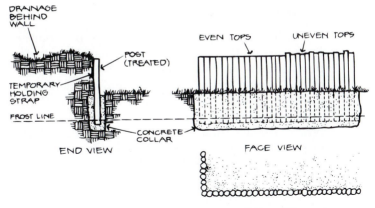

Figure 5-18. Construction details for post walls.

Figure 5-19. A typical post wall.

varies with the wall's height. Generally, as much post should be placed underground as above, to a depth of 3' to 3-1/2'. Post walls are usually vertical, with higher walls requiring larger-diameter posts. Posts may be cut off evenly or unevenly on the top, depending upon the appearance wanted. Weepholes are advisable, even though some excess water escapes between the posts (see Figures 5-18 and 5-19). A gravel pack facilitates pressure release behind the wall.

Wooden Retaining Walls

Although there are many types of wooden walls that can be built, their construction methods are similar. Wooden wall boards are attached to posts and anchored in concrete collars. The wall boards must be at least 2" thick. Thinner boards are sometimes nailed to these wall boards, creating different designs. Redwood or CCA-treated lumber, which resist decay organisms and do not require paint or stain, are commonly used for this type of construction. Regardless of wood type, though, all surfaces that are to remain in contact with the soil should be treated with creosote or some other preservative material. Galvanized bolts and nails resist rusting (see Figures 5-20 and 5-21).

Posts must be closely spaced to absorb the entire stress of soil against the wooden wall. Unless a post of more than 4" in diameter is used, wooden walls should not exceed 3-1/2' to 4' in height. Posts should be spaced from 3' to 4' apart, with the closer spacing used at the maximum height. A gravel pack is recommended.

Choosing the Type of Retaining Wall

With so many types of retaining walls available, choosing one type can be difficult. There are criteria to guide this choice, however; some of them are discussed below.

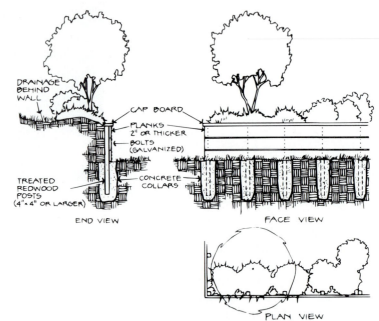

Figure 5-20. Construction details for wooden retaining walls.

Figure 5-21. One type of wooden retaining wall. The boards on the outer face of this wall are nailed to the structurally sound 2″ × 12″ boards behind them. Much flexibility is made available by good design.

Height and strength requirements eliminate some walls as possible choices. If a wall must be higher than 4′, most wooden walls, small-diameter post walls, and walls made of landscape timbers lack the strength to endure the pressure. Solid walls of all types, dry rock walls, and horizontal railroad-tie walls all serve well as tall walls.

The height and horizontal length of a wall will also, to an extent, dictate the choice of material. Smaller materials look best in shorter walls. Proportion is always important. A long, tall dry rock wall is best built with large rocks, for example, whereas a shorter dry rock wall will look best if thinner rocks are used.

The *surface drainage behind the walls* is a factor in choosing wall materials. As mentioned before, it is best that surface drainage be diverted behind and around the ends of retaining walls (see Figure 5-22). At times, though, it may be necessary, because of space limitations or extreme angles of slope above and behind a wall, to permit drainage over the top of the wall. Solid walls will work in this case only if they are reinforced well, are anchored by many dead men, and contain many weepholes. Post walls and wooden walls usually work well for this situation, although they occasionally need additional backfill as soil washes through them.

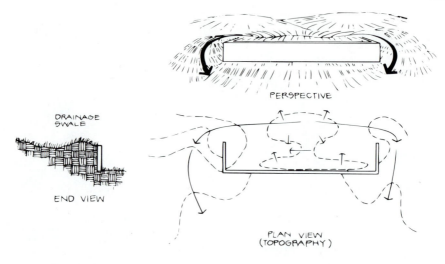

Figure 5-22. For maximum stability, heavy surface drainage should be controlled well behind retaining walls so the water runs around the wall's ends instead of over its top.

Materials used in other features on the property dictate some coordination of color and texture. Rock walls, for example, may not work well with a brick house. Rustic railroad ties may not be a good choice for blending with a formal house or landscape. Conversely, a formal brick wall might not be suitable with a rustic house.

Textures can vary considerably between two walls made of the same materials. Dry rock walls and post walls provide good examples: the smaller the rocks or posts, the finer the texture of the wall. The height/size relationship also comes into play again. A 4' retaining wall built with 3"-diameter posts will appear finer in texture than a 2' wall built with the same 3" posts, because the extra height gives a different proportion to the posts.

The *shape of a retaining wall* affects the materials chosen for it (see Figure 5-23). Horizontal railroad ties cannot be bent, for example, and so do not lend themselves well to curving walls. If it will be necessary to step the top of a wall down at intervals, mortared walls, railroad ties, posts, landscape timbers, and wood all suit the purpose well. A dry rock wall, however, because it depends on its soil backing for support, does not work as well.

Availability of materials is an important factor in choosing the type of wall. Within geographic locations, the availability of materials varies. Beyond that, the availability of specific materials varies at times. If scarce, materials are likely to cost more than normal. It is the responsibility of the designer to be sure the materials to be used in a wall can be obtained at a price reasonable for the client's

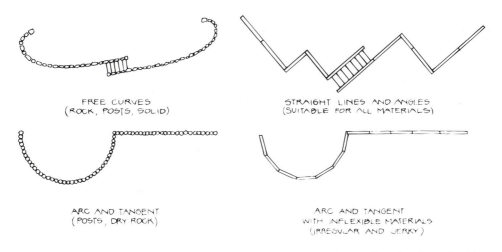

FREE CURVES
(ROCK, POSTS, SOLID)

STRAIGHT LINES AND ANGLES
(SUITABLE FOR ALL MATERIALS)

ARC AND TANGENT
(POSTS, DRY ROCK)

ARC AND TANGENT
WITH INFLEXIBLE MATERIALS
(IRREGULAR AND JERKY)

Figure 5-23. The type of material used in the construction of a retaining wall is often determined by the shape required of the wall.

budget before specifying them on a plan. Similarly, if specialized craftspeople will be required to construct a wall, the designer must ensure their availability.

The *cost* of each type of retaining wall is also important. Some aspects of cost have already been discussed. Beyond that, cost will vary with the contractor. If cost is to be a deciding factor, it is wise to preestimate two or more different types of walls, determining the most economical type before making final plans. Limestone retaining walls are included in the landscape plan represented in Figure 5-24.

BERMS IN THE LANDSCAPE

The point has been made that natural features in the landscape should be utilized to their fullest advantage. An attractive rock ledge, a rolling knoll, or an interesting terrain undulation can provide interest in a landscape, providing it is, or appears to be, natural. A hill or knoll existing on the property might function for wind protection, screening, or implied enclosure. It can also provide excellent background for focal points to be established by the design.

When creating mounds, or *berms*, the designer must carefully avoid an artificial look (see Figure 5-25). A berm of any significant size requires large quantities of soil and, so, can be expensive to create. Skimping on the size, though, will result in a berm more resembling a leftover pile of soil than anything seen in nature. As such, it will draw an inordinate amount of attention, accomplishing little else.

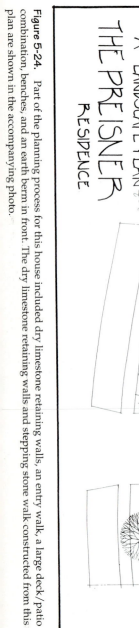

Figure 5-24. Part of the planning process for this house included dry limestone retaining walls, an entry walk, a large deck/patio combination, benches, and an earth berm in front. The dry limestone retaining walls and stepping stone walk constructed from this plan are shown in the accompanying photo.

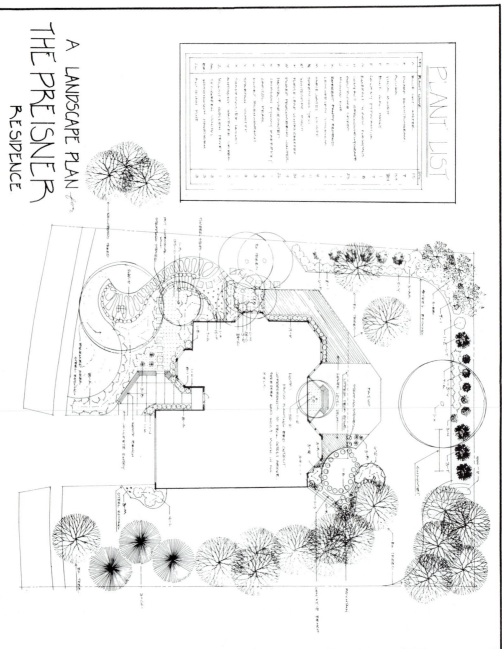

A LANDSCAPE PLAN for

THE PREISNER
RESIDENCE

PLANT LIST

Figure 5-24 (continued)

Figure 5-25. In order for earth berms to look natural in the landscape, they must blend with the surrounding terrain.

Figure 5-26. Gentle undulations along the sides of a constructed earth berm lend a more natural appearance.

Regardless of the surfacing planned for a berm, it must be maintained in some way—a fact that must be remembered during its design. The angle of repose for the soil used in a berm dictates its maximum slope, but it might be judicious to use less than the maximum angle on occasion, particularly if the berm must be mowed. For easy and safe mowing, a slope should not exceed a 1:3 gradient (33% slope), but it may be steeper in small areas for special effects. The gradient on a berm's side should ordinarily fluctuate in order to repeat characteristic forms found in nature (see Figure 5-26). Consistently uniform slopes are often boring. To the extent possible, the flow of terrain in a landscape should repeat the characteristic land forms surrounding the property. For that reason, rounded berms of soil might look out-of-place in mountains or the Arizona desert.

When designing a berm or a series of berms, the designer should consider both the source of soil to be used and the drainage of the area. On a new construction site, it might be possible to use soil that otherwise would need to be hauled away, or the height of building foundations might be adjusted downward, providing the necessary amount of soil. Otherwise, berm construction demands grading entirely by fill, often requiring truckloads of expensive topsoil.

Improperly placed berms act as dams, restricting surface water drainage. Surface water always must be allowed to flow out of an area. Sometimes the soil cut to form a needed drainage swale may be used in berm construction, at least partially balancing the cut and fill.

Properly used, berms provide interesting land forms that offer immediate size and shape interest and high-density wind and sound protection. Young trees and shrubs can be positioned on a berm's sides or top, making them more imme-

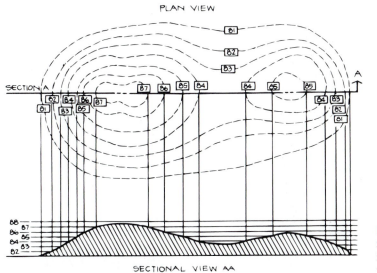

Figure 5-27. A sample plan for a proposed berm, shown in both sectional and plan views.

diately useful and visible in the landscape. For these reasons, berms should be considered along with other landscaping alternatives. (See Figure 5-27 for a sample plan for a berm.)

A final note about berms. Berms alter the microclimate of an area. On a sizeable mound of soil, those slopes facing the south and west warm more quickly in the spring and stay warm longer in the fall. At the same time, the east and north slopes of the berm have a shorter growing season than usual. Even on berms 4' or 5' in height, grass will become green a week or two earlier on the sunny slopes than on the shadier ones. Consequently, the plant material selected for use on berms depends on that microclimate; the designer should find this an advantage, because it permits a wider selection of plant material than would be possible if the exposure in an area were to remain constant. However, ignoring these microclimatic effects results in misplaced plant material that grows poorly.

FINAL NOTES ABOUT GRADING

Circulation structures (walks, drives, and so forth) look best and are usually easiest to use if they follow the contours of the land, gradually rising from one elevation to the next higher one, rather than being placed perpendicular to them (see Figure 5-28). A steep, sloping driveway, for example, is more difficult to care for and harder to use than one that winds its way along the slope. The size of the lot, however, often limits this practice.

A walk is comfortably used as a ramp at slopes up to 20% (1:5). Beyond that gradient, steps should be included in the walk. Steps are composed of vertical *ris-*

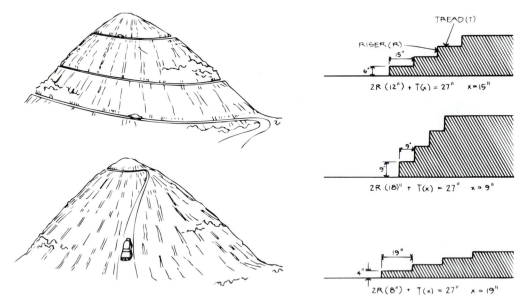

Figure 5-28. Although the shortest distance up a slope is a straight line, traffic most often finds it easier to climb with the contours.

Figure 5-29. The most comfortable steps are planned using this standard riser-plus-tread formula.

ers (*r*) and horizontal *treads* (*t*). As a rule, the formula, 2*r* plus *t* = 27″, can be used to fashion comfortable steps (see Figure 5-29). In other words, for a 6″ riser, the tread width should be approximately 15″: 2*r*(6″ + 6″ = 12″) plus *t*(15″) = 27″. The comfortable range for risers is generally between 4″ and 9″. The determining factor in riser height is the degree of slope on which the steps are placed. Steps are most easily planned in sectional view, so they can be drawn in on the slope as existing.

When grading plans encounter existing trees that are to be retained on the site, often the level of the ground must be changed around them. But the vital roots in the top 6″ of soil under trees can be neither cut nor buried. If cutting is planned around a tree, it is then necessary to construct a retaining wall or otherwise terrace the ground around the tree so that it remains at the original level. If filling is to be done around the tree, a dry well must be constructed around the tree. If possible, the area retained at its original level should approximate the circle covered by the tree's canopy because most of the feeder roots extend to that boundary. Examples of these special treatments for trees existing in areas to be graded are shown in Figure 5-30.

SUBSURFACE DRAINAGE

Water drains underground as well as on the surface. As water moves over the surface, much of it is absorbed into the soil, ultimately causing saturation. At saturation, the excess water must be released through subsurface drainage channels.

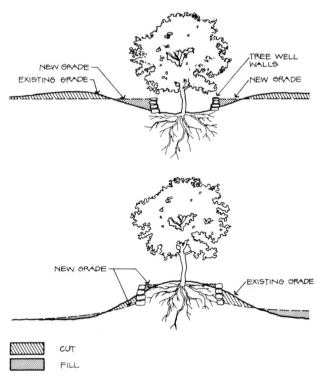

Figure 5-30. When the soil around existing trees is to be regraded, it is necessary to construct tree wells to protect existing roots from physical damage, exposure, or deep burial (which limits oxygen availability).

Natural channels exist between rock layers or variable soil layers, allowing this excess water to join the underground aquafers that supply the water we pump through our wells. Those channels may, instead, continue to a point where the water is released back onto a surface drainage system by means of springs.

Sometimes soil disturbance during building construction will alter the composition of the subsurface so that normal subsurface drainage channels are closed off. When normal releases for this excess water are closed off, pressure builds, forcing the water to the nearest available release point. Often that release point is the seam between the foundation walls and floor in a basement, or cracks in the basement wall.

Whenever this problem of blocked drainage channels can be anticipated, it is wise to design artificial subsurface drainage systems that relieve the pressure by allowing the excess water another exit from the soil. Tile or pipe drainage systems, installed around the base of foundation footings, serve this function well (see Figure 5-31). Loose tiles or perforated pipes are installed around the footings and surrounded by gravel. As the gravel becomes saturated, excess water moves into the pipe or tile, which is extended to a place where the water can again be absorbed by a rapidly draining soil or released back into the aboveground drainage systems.

If an area to be drained is lower than all surrounding terrain, or if the maximum available vertical drop will not accommodate surface drainage, subsurface

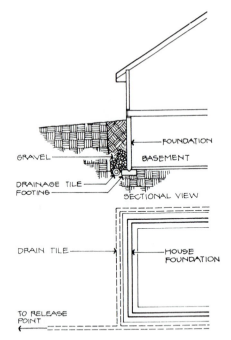

Figure 5-31. A typical foundation drainage system to relieve the pressure built up by increased ground water.

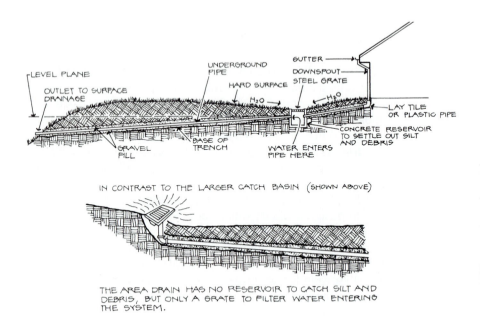

IN CONTRAST TO THE LARGER CATCH BASIN (SHOWN ABOVE)

THE AREA DRAIN HAS NO RESERVOIR TO CATCH SILT AND DEBRIS, BUT ONLY A GRATE TO FILTER WATER ENTERING THE SYSTEM.

Figure 5-32. Subsurface drainage systems.

drainage systems must be devised (see Figure 5-32). The simplest type of subsurface drainage involves the use of a perforated pipe or open tile, surrounded by gravel for the foundation drainage system. In this case, the gravel extends to the surface of a narrow trench, allowing surface water to percolate through the loose aggregate and into the pipeline. The underground line slopes just enough to allow water to run away. Because the pipe is smooth and even, a grade of .5% is sufficient for drainage. Again, the water collected must be drained to a point where it can be released into more porous soil or back into a surface drainage system.

When subsurface drainage is heavy in volume or moves at a rapid pace, large amounts of debris will collect. *Area drains* or *catch basins* are then used to replace the gravel at the point of origin. An area drain is a square or rectangular concrete box fitted with a metal grating to keep debris from following water into the underground pipe and thus causing clogging. The larger catch basin includes a deep pit beneath the entrance to the subsurface pipe. Silt and other sediments settle out in the bottom of the pit instead of entering the pipe. Catch basins are particularly useful in areas where soil erosion might occur, causing large quantities of soil to enter the drainage system. Collected soil is periodically cleaned out of the catch basin.

Because subsurface drainage systems are expensive to install and can be difficult to maintain, they should only be used when surface drainage cannot be accomplished. Well-coordinated piping from the point of origin to the point of release is essential. Generally, the amount of slope in a subsurface drainage system should be minimal (2% or less), because as the distance increases, deeper trenching is required, magnifying costs.

POINTS TO REMEMBER

- Grading allows a reasonable amount of land form manipulation to provide adequate surface drainage, create useful areas, and provide for circulation around a property.
- The gradient is an expression of the vertical change in elevation related to the horizontal distance covered by the vertical change.
- Percentage of slope is often used to express vertical/horizontal relationships up to a 1:1 gradient.
- A drainage swale is a cupped or V-shaped valley designed to confine and conduct surface water.
- The manipulation of contours for landscape purposes is always dependent on the rules of topography, for example, water follows the steepest route, flowing at right angles to contour lines; and so forth.
- A cut is the removal of a prescribed amount of soil from an area.
- A fill is the addition of a prescribed amount of soil to an area.

- Cut and fill volumes are cubic in nature and are usually expressed as cubic feet or cubic yards.
- Grading may be accomplished entirely by either cut or fill, but it is usually best done by balancing cut and fill.
- Calculation of proposed volumes of cut and fill is facilitated by designing both in plan view and in sectional view of the topography.
- Terraces provide a more level space or series of spaces. They can be built with or without retaining walls.
- The angle of repose for a particular soil is the vertical angle its slopes will seek when the soil is dumped loosely in a pile.
- Terraces with retaining walls allow the maximum useful space because of the vertical structure of the walls.
- Retaining walls may be either solid or porous, depending on whether or not their components are joined by a cementing agent.
- Solid walls require footings, dead men, and weepholes, in addition to steel reinforcing. Porous walls may require footings and dead men for support.
- Height and strength requirements, surface drainage behind walls, materials found elsewhere on the property, the desired shape of the wall, availability of materials, and cost are all factors in the choice of a retaining wall.
- Berms must look natural, not contrived, and must be in keeping with terrain features found around the property.
- Well-designed berms provide land forms of immediate size and shape interest that can provide screening, wind protection, and a higher platform from which to start young trees and shrubs.
- Supply of soil and subsequent costs, maintenance considerations, and effects on surface drainage are all factors in berm design.
- Circulation structures should follow the contours to the extent possible. Steps should be planned when the slope exceeds 20%.
- Existing trees in an area to be graded must be protected.
- Subsurface drainage is usually called for only when surface drainage systems cannot solve a problem. Accurate planning keeps drains functioning properly, while restricting costs.
- Area drains and catch basins are specialized collection devices for subsurface drainage that filter the water entering the drainage system.

REVIEW QUESTIONS

1. Name three accomplishments of proper grading design.
2. What is the difference between *gradient* and *percentage of slope*?
3. What is a drainage swale?
4. What is being compared when contour lines bend toward other contour lines of higher elevation?
5. What grading operation is indicated when a proposed contour line bends toward existing contour lines of a lower number?
6. If an area 10′ wide by 100′ long is to be filled to an average depth of 2′, how many cubic feet of fill soil will be required? How many cubic yards?
7. By what three methods may a flat area be created on a sloping site?
8. Why does a solid retaining wall require a footing?
9. Why do dry rock walls not require weepholes?
10. What is the formula for comfortable steps?

PRACTICAL TIP FROM A PRACTICING DESIGNER

If, after developing a contour map of a property, you still have difficulty developing a plan for manipulating the contours, try making a model, using one layer of either posterboard or thin foam to represent each contour. Then you can actually cut the model where you might propose to cut into the soil, insert model retaining walls, and gauge the amount of fill required (if any). Sometimes, three-dimensional modeling clears the fog.

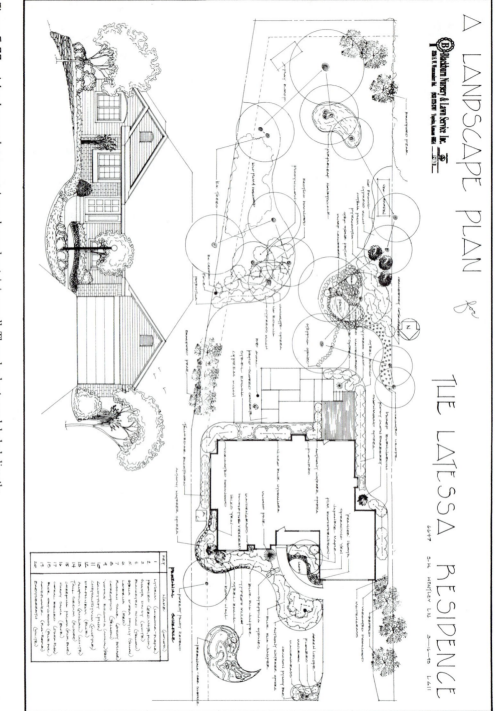

Figure 5-33. A landscape plan proposing a dry rock retaining wall. Though plants are labeled directly on this plan, a separate plant schedule is used for perennials, to avoid cluttering the plan.

THE WALLS AND CEILING

In this chapter, you will begin to study the concept of creating "outdoor rooms" in the landscape by looking at the makeup of the walls and the ceiling of these "rooms." Providing environmental comforts through screening, wind protection, and shade will be discussed by studying the uses of fences, walls, and shade trellises, along with the use of plants in the walls and ceiling of the landscape.

The walls of outdoor "rooms" give dimension to their spaces. A ceiling (the sky) is always present, as is a floor (the ground), but without the walls created by landscape design, these spaces might just blend together into one vast area. The ceiling and floor are seldom left as is, because by adjustment they can better suit landscaping purposes. In fact, the environmental adjustments possible through landscaping occur because of changes in these three dimensions of the outdoor room.

To a degree, the final appearance and function of the walls, the ceiling, or the floor of landscaped "rooms" result from adjustments made to the other two. The location, size, and shape of the walls, for example, determine in large part how the floor of the landscape will look. The height and structure of the ceiling will vary the appearance of both the walls and the floor. So, though the walls and ceiling are discussed somewhat separately in this chapter, and the floor is covered later, all relate to one another. Whenever elements are planned for one dimension of the room, consideration must also be given to their effect on the other two dimensions.

Of all the virtues of good landscaping, the environmental alterations it makes possible might be most important. Good landscape design prepares a property to become more comfortable as a people habitat. These environmental adjustments are provided primarily through the structure of the walls and ceiling.

Among the adjustments possible through wall manipulation are:

- Screening out undesirable views
- Screening the view into the landscape from outside the area
- Framing good off-property views
- Screening out dust and other pollutants
- Screening out noise
- Protecting and insulating from the wind
- Filtering breezes into the property
- Providing enclosure

The ceiling can provide:

- Shade from a hot summer sun
- Solar heat from the winter sun's rays
- Protection from the elements (rain, snow, etc.)
- Screening from dust and other pollutants

Many other functions also are served by the walls and ceiling of the landscape—a number of them are aesthetically oriented. Choices exist for the construction of walls and ceilings; they can be built from structural hard materials or from plant materials. At first, it is best to consider only what these elements are required to do in the landscape, selecting materials as all walls and the ceiling are combined.

THE WALLS OF THE LANDSCAPE

Earlier in the design process, general landscape areas were plotted by bubble diagramming or other means. The feasibility of circulation routes was determined. Topographical studies, if necessary, were performed, and the land forms were manipulated to accommodate the areas of use desired and the necessary surface drainage. Compromises in area usage were made where land forms could not be adjusted sufficiently to follow the original bubble diagram. Now the size and shape of the outdoor "rooms" is known, and although minor adjustments will still be made, it is possible to construct the walls (see Figure 6-1).

The purposes of the walls were generally decided during the design-analysis stage. At that time, the designer determined the prevailing wind directions, the sources of polluted air, the noise sources, and the need to enclose certain areas to keep children or pets in or to keep others out. Now it is time in the design process to apply that information.

The landscape is made up of exterior and interior walls. The exterior wall extends around property perimeters and is most likely to carry out the environmental functions. One section of that wall may be asked to perform several duties simultaneously. For example, one exterior wall might have to supply wind protection, define the property boundary, and provide screening. Additionally, for the design to be complete, the wall also has to contribute to the aesthetic appearance of the landscape as a whole. With so many considerations to be made, along with the vast choices from available hard materials or plants, the design of that wall can seem an almost overwhelming task. Because of that, it helps to think first of each wall only in abstract terms—how high it must be, how dense, and so forth, building a set of specifications that can later be translated into real materials for construction.

One way to take an abstract look at the duties a particular wall must perform is to draw that segment in vertical elevation. Measure a segment of wall on the site plan that was prepared during site analysis. Draw a horizontal line on a piece of tracing paper to exactly the same scaled distance, then consider the empty space above the line to be the space that will lie outside the wall when it is constructed. Next, visualize whatever lies beyond the landscape wall. Is there something there that you wish to screen from view? If so, how tall is the element to be screened when you stand next to the wall? How tall is that object when you move further back? How far does the screening need to extend horizontally? Does that wall have to restrict traffic as well? Does it have to block or filter the wind or maybe filter out dust or other windblown articles? Does the wall need to be of sufficient density to absorb noise from outside the site? How about the view into the property from different angles? Are there portions of the view into the yard that need screening? Can that wall help insulate the site from cold winter winds or maybe block intrusive car headlights from windows or private living areas at night (see Figure 6-2)?

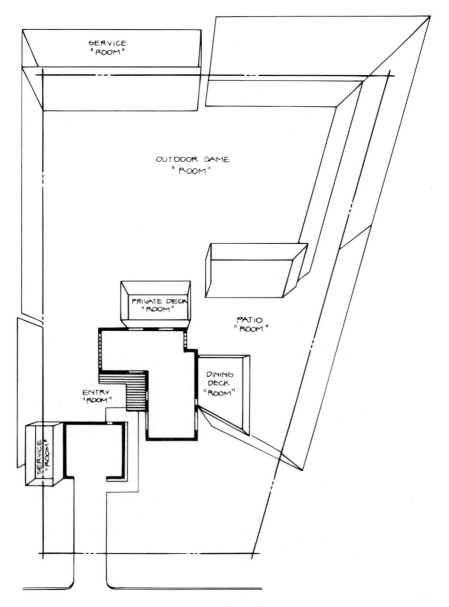

Figure 6-1. The exterior landscape can be pictured as a group of spaces, or "rooms,"
bounded by "walls" that function much like the interior of a house.

The systematic answering of questions like these helps the designer form
impressions of the general size, shape, and density needed for each wall in the
landscape. Such thorough examination might require a return trip to reexamine
the site and the elements outside it. However, with experience, designers learn to

Figure 6-2.   Before làndscape "walls" can be designed on paper, the designer must determine the size, form, and structure most suitable for each wall.

observe with more perception during site analysis, making appropriate notes so that this questioning procedure is actually completed while the site measurements are being taken (see Figure 6-3).

Wall units surrounding a property's boundaries are each considered in turn until the designer has worked out the abstract height and width units required of each segment of the exterior walls and made the necessary notes about the density required for each. Later, as the units are blended into one complete harmonious composition, some compromise will be made. In order to blend one unit into another, some units may have to be taller than otherwise necessary, for example, or denser than actually required at that point. More design consideration is necessary.

Interior walls might be used to screen service areas from living areas, to separate living areas from public areas, or merely to divide use areas from one another. In some cases, interior walls may merely divide the lawn into more proportionate shapes—for example, making a backyard seem more wide than deep. In other cases, the interior walls might do no more than add an air of mystery, keeping all the landscaped areas from being discovered simultaneously. Interior walls might also best be considered by abstract sizes and shapes at this point in the design process, with particular emphasis placed on the density aspect. Many of the interior walls need not be dense at all. In fact, they might not even really be walls, but just dividers to be seen through or over.

A closer look at each of the wall's functions is in order so that criteria can be established for their planning.

Screening

As mentioned before, screening includes blocking the views both into and out of the property as well as noise absorption and control of dust and other airborne pollutants. The type of screening provided depends on what is being

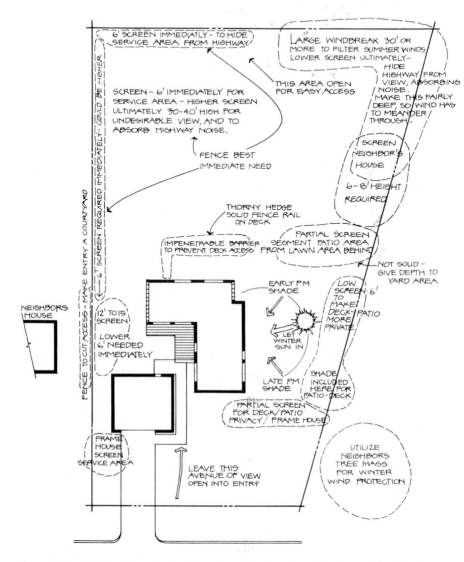

Figure 6-3. Making plan-view notations about the size, shape, density, and functional requirements for each wall unit helps a designer see the overall view of the common functions of wall units.

screened. Screening out sights, for example, only requires enough solidity to prevent clear vision. The screening out of sounds, on the other hand, requires a thickness or density that will absorb that sound. Airborne particles must either be stopped cold by a solid surface or be filtered through a dense wall. Therefore, the first decision about screening walls requires the assessment of the structure needed for that type of screening.

Our sight is like a funnel, with the small end next to the eye and the large end at the farthest extension of our view. The farther away the view, the wider the large end of the funnel becomes (see Figure 6-4). In designing a view-screening wall, then, it is important to decide how far away one is likely to be when the screening is needed and from how many positions the screening is necessary. The closer the screening wall is, the narrower the funnel of vision and, hence, the lower the screening wall required. By the same token, the farther away the object needing screening is, the smaller it will appear to be, so the lower the screening wall can be. When several different locations in a yard must be screened from an objectionable view, the one farthest from the screening wall must be the one considered, because it requires the highest screening unit.

Enclosure

Enclosure can be either *absolute* or *implied*. A solid fence or wall that one cannot penetrate is absolute. A low hedge that divides areas but could easily be stepped over implies enclosure without absolutely preventing entrance or egress (see Figure 6-5).

Absolute enclosure confines pets and children, keeps out intruders, and provides safety on a property. To be absolute, it must prevent passage both in and out. Walls may be designed to provide screening and wind protection as well as enclosure, but they do not necessarily have to do so. Enclosure then serves the entire function of defining spaces as well. That function is extremely important by itself. Few of us would enjoy sitting on chairs in an open field for any length of time. We are accustomed to having the spaces we occupy defined by walls or dividers. Enclosure structures or plantings help to provide that definition.

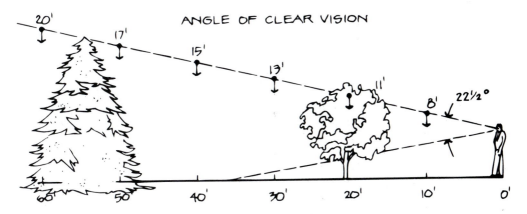

Figure 6-4. A clear focus of vision exists in the center of our view. The farther away from which we view, the broader the spectrum of clear focus becomes. Our vision, then, is like looking through the small end of a funnel into the distance.

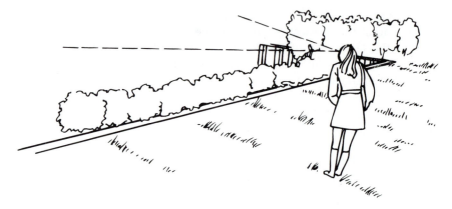

Figure 6-5. Enclosure can be either implied or absolute, depending on the degree to which vision and access are blocked.

Wind Protection

On the average residential lot, *wind protection* is not synonymous with *windbreak*. A windbreak is designed to lift the wind entirely over its top. Ultimately, that wind reaches the ground's surface again. A too-narrow windbreak of limited height, then, allows the wind to reach the ground again too soon, so by excluding the wind from one section of the residential lot, it merely transfers it to another section of the same lot. To be of sufficient height and depth to lift the wind high enough to clear the entire property, too much of the property would be occupied by the windbreak plantings (see Figure 6-6).

Wind protection on a residential lot, then, usually is best provided by breaking the wind's force as it moves through the landscape elements. For that reason, fences and walls by themselves do not function well as wind protection units. Because of their limited height, the wind merely moves over their tops, swooping back quickly to the ground on the other side. When combined with plantings, though, those same elements work well, breaking the ground force of the wind and allowing the plant foliage to break its force further.

Predominant seasonal wind directions exist in most parts of the country. In the plains, for example, prevailing winds blow from southwest to northeast during the spring and summer, and from northwest to southeast in the fall and winter. The landscape designer must be familiar with the local pattern so that the microclimate of the landscaped area can be made more comfortable at all times of the year.

Though evergreen foliage might provide the best winter windbreak, even leafless deciduous trees will slow the wind's force as it circulates through branches. A solid evergreen planting close to a driveway can create severe drifting on the leeward side in snow country.

As wind protection is planned, it should be remembered that cooling breezes during hot summer evenings are desirable and necessary (see Figure 6-7).

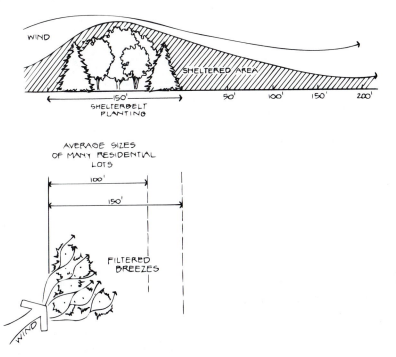

Figure 6-6. Whereas a shelter belt has the height and depth required to lift the wind completely over a sizeable distance, most residential lots are too narrow to accommodate such extensive plantings. On residential properties, the wind is more often channeled through plants, slowing rather than completely eliminating it.

To eliminate these breezes completely from a landscaped area not only makes the area uncomfortable, but also creates ideal conditions for the fungus diseases that can affect plants.

Framing a View

Off-property views can be enhanced by the creation of a frame in the enclosure elements of the landscape. Supplying a frame around an already good view helps focus attention on it, making it seem an integral part of the landscape. Using off-property views in this manner makes a property seem larger. A proper frame also enhances the view by adding more depth perspective.

To design a view frame, it is best to repeat the dominant characteristics within that view. A view of rolling hills, for example, is best framed by predominantly horizontal units, whereas a view of mountain peaks is best framed by more vertical, pyramidal forms. Proportion is very important. The farther away the view, the smaller its components will seem. It is also essential that the framing units be small so as not to overwhelm the view. The frame should seem to pull together the elements in the view, making them a part of the landscape wall.

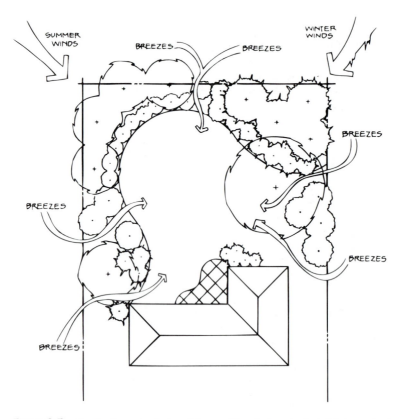

Figure 6-7. As plantings are designed to provide wind protection, it is important to provide channels for filtered breezes, allowing good air circulation in the protected areas.

CHOOSING BETWEEN STRUCTURAL AND PLANT MATERIALS

The walls of the landscape can be built of many materials. The choice of these materials depends on the specifications detailed during the abstract planning process, and on other criteria. Basically, choices are made between hard materials and plants; specific forms within each realm are then selected.

Landscape walls can be made up of fences, walls, hedges, massed plantings, or earth forms. Combinations of these elements are frequently found to work best, both functioning well and looking pleasant.

Fences and Walls

Where only limited space is available, fences and walls can provide height for screening or enclosure functions. The widest of walls might only occupy one foot of space while reaching some 6' to 8' in height, whereas even the narrowest hedge would need to be much wider at its base to stay full at those heights. Informal plantings would, of course, occupy even more space. Another advantage of fences and walls is that, unlike plant materials, these constructed elements start out at their full sizes. A wide range of appearances are available through use of fences and walls, and they will absolutely enclose the landscaped area better than plants.

Fences are much more commonly found in the landscape than are freestanding walls. Primarily, this is a matter of expense. Fences range greatly in price and use, from the inexpense chainlink fences that provide enclosure and security without screening or wind protection, to elaborate wooden and wrought-iron fences of many designs. The primary limitations to the use of a fence for enclosure stems from height limitations and the fact that, by itself, a fence of any design becomes boring if not combined with other landscaping elements. Wind pressure against the side of a solid or semi-solid fence limits the cost-effective sizes of most fences from 6' to 8', unless very substantial wood or metal posts are used (see Figures 6-8, 6-9, 6-10, and 6-11).

Freestanding walls are supported by strong, broad footings. They can be built of a wide range of masonry products, including bricks, rock, concrete blocks, or patterned concrete. Some are solid; others are built so that partial views can be seen through their patterns (see Figures 6-12 and 6-13). If well built, these walls can be the most maintenance-free choice for walls in the landscape, but again, when used exclusively, they can become boring.

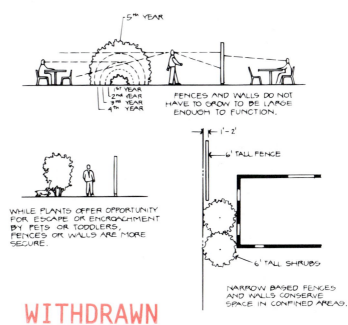

Figure 6-8. There are distinct spatial and time-related advantages, in some cases, to using constructed fences or walls in the landscape instead of plant "walls."

WITHDRAWN

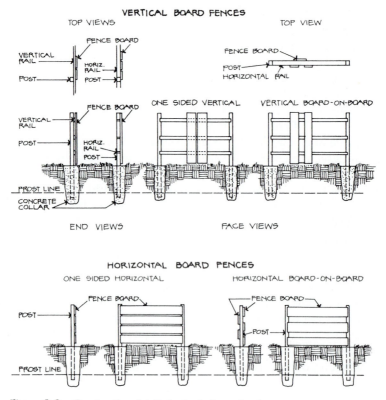

Figure 6-9. Construction details for typical wooden fences.

Plant Materials

Monotype plantings consist of only one variety of plant. These plantings may exist side by side in the informal shape that is natural for them or they may be pruned into hedges. These plantings make excellent walls in the landscape, offering great versatility in height and density for screening and wind protection. Particularly when trimmed regularly into formal hedges, these monotype plantings require more maintenance than fences or walls, and they, too, can be boring if used exclusively.

Mass plantings of many different varieties is a popular choice for many walls in the contemporary landscape (see Figure 6-14). Often called shrub borders, these plant masses usually contain trees as well, providing change in texture, color, and form. More variation in height, thickness, and density is available in this type of wall structure than in any other.

Combining Structural Elements and Plant Materials

To use only one of the possible structures available for landscape walls is to limit the effectiveness of that wall, inviting boredom at the same time. For these

Figure 6-10. Several of the many styles of wooden fences that can be used in landscape "walls."

Figure 6-10 (continued)

Figure 6-11.   A living fence, consisting of wooden posts and rails with wire mesh to support vine growth.

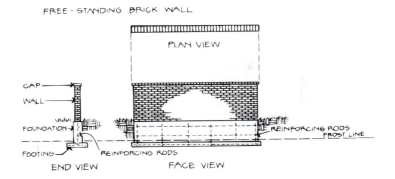

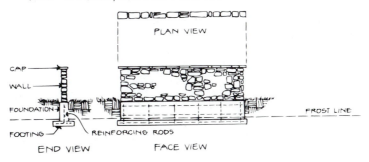

Figure 6-12.   Construction details for freestanding constructed walls.

Figure 6-13. One type of freestanding wall constructed of mortared rock.

Figure 6-14. Mass plantings of various shrubs and trees compose this landscape "wall."

reasons, the walls are normally composed of combinations of two or more types (see Figure 6-15), and greater effectiveness of both function and appearance is realized. A fence or wall, for example, looks best if partially faced with plantings or backgrounded by taller plants. Similarly, a mass of plantings can be enhanced by the varying colors and textures of fence and wall materials. When plants are placed in front of a fence or wall, they should be selected to grow to either 1/3 or 2/3 the fence's or wall's height for good proportion.

Specific Wall Designs

To make specific decisions about the materials to be used in landscape walls, it is best to return once more to the vertical elevations of wall units drawn earlier, where sizes and shapes were specified. Now the designer can draw actual forms on these elevations, indicating combinations of fences, walls, and plantings that carry out the functions required while pleasing the senses.

Before proceeding to design specific wall forms, though, more information is necessary. In its final forms, landscape design must conform to some principles of artistic composition. These principles will be discussed in Chapter 7, "Principles of Planting Design." Meanwhile, the specifications for building walls are complete, so the designer can turn his or her attention to the ceiling of the landscape.

Figure 6-15.   This landscape "wall" is made up of plantings and a fence, combined for good effect.

THE CEILING OF THE LANDSCAPE

The sky is always there to provide a ceiling. However, it is often better to change that ceiling, lower it in places, texture it, and provide protection against the elements that issue from it. Probably the most frequent alterations made in the landscape's ceiling are those that provide shading. The reverse of shading—allowing solar-heating sun rays in during the winter—is also very important.

Shade

The design and placement of shading units must be precise. To accomplish this, it is necessary for the designer to know the sun's exact path over a property at all times of the year (see Figure 6-16). In the northern hemisphere, the sun moves high in the sky as it passes from east to west during the summer. During the winter, it drops to a lower, more southerly path across the sky. This change in angle is important, because it allows the designer to utilize the sun's heating rays in winter while still effectively blocking them in the summer. Since the path of the sun varies with geographic location as well as with the situation of a house on a lot, it is important for the designer to scrutinize thoroughly the sun's journey over each property landscaped. Shade then can be provided for maximum benefit.

It is also essential to study the angle of the sun's rays as they enter areas at critical times of the day. Shade for a patio area, for instance, might be needed most during the outdoor dining hours between 5 P.M. and 7 P.M. Knowing the angles at which the sun penetrates the patio area at those times each day is essential for placing shading units properly. If that same patio is used earlier in the day, when a totally different shading unit is required, that angle of penetration must also be known.

As needs for shade are determined and the sun's path and critical angles of penetration become known, the designer must begin to make choices about how to provide that shade. Once more, the basic choice is between hard, structural elements and plants. We ordinarily think of large shade trees in this context, but a wide range of shading trellises and roofs is available for various purposes. Before making a choice, the designer must also evaluate the other uses to be made of the area to be shaded.

Does the area requiring shade also need:

- protection from rain and snow?
- lighting for night use?
- protection from insects?
- artificial heating or cooling?

If the answer to any of these questions is yes, then the shading problem is best solved by a structural shade rather than by trees.

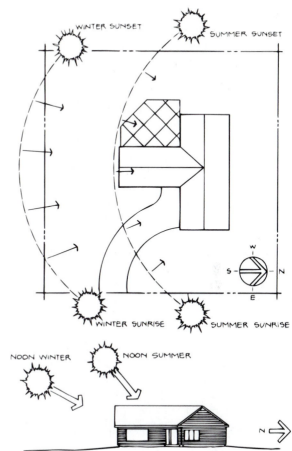

Figure 6-16. The angle of the sun's rays into a property changes with the seasons. To design a landscape ceiling, the designer must be aware of the differing paths the sun takes seasonally, as well as the directional positioning of the house on the lot.

If shade must be provided immediately, the construction of a structural shade might be indicated, because shade trees usually must grow before they are large enough to do the job. However, either the size of the area needing shade or cost factors might prohibit structural shade. Mature shade trees can span large areas with their canopies at relatively little expense when compared to structural shading units.

Structural Shading Units

There are a variety of types of structural shade. Solid roofs provide the most absolute shade, also offering the advantage of waterproofing, alternatives for lighting, and enclosing the walls to make the area insect-proof or to heat and cool the area artificially. Lattice-type roofs can be designed to provide varying degrees of shade, depending on the amount of area covered by the lattice boards as compared to the amount of open space between them. A 50% lattice shade, for example, contains equal amounts of structure and open space, thereby removing half of the potential sunlight from an area, whereas a 40% lattice leaves 60% open space. At the other end of the spectrum, the arbor is a minimal structure over which vines are allowed to grow. These provide maximum shade during the hottest time of the year, when foliage covers them, while allowing full sun during the colder times when the vines are without leaves (see Figures 6-17 and 6-18).

A solid roof must necessarily be supported by a much stronger understructure than a lattice roof. Snow loads in the winter can demand even greater strength. If the walls beneath the solid roof are open or screened, wind circling under the roof lifts against that roof, placing more strain on it. The open spaces on a lattice or arbor allow snow to filter through, and such structures do not resist the wind as a solid roof does. When a solid roof is used, then, the posts and beams supporting the structure must necessarily be bulkier.

Structural shading is often misused. An overhead trellis does a fine job of shading early in the day, for example, but often allows the lower sun rays to

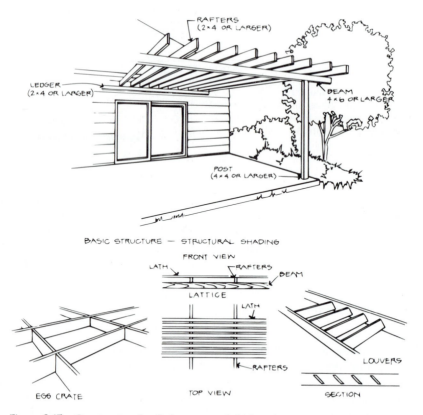

Figure 6-17. Construction details for structural shade units.

Figure 6-18. An arbor trellis, with vines growing over its top for maximum shading during hot summer months, and a shade structure of wood laths.

penetrate under the roof late in the day. All too often, a patio that is used primarily for evening cookouts is covered by a trellis that provides shade only in early afternoon. Once more, it is vital that the sun's path and critical angles of penetration be considered along with the times of day shading is required (see Figure 6-19).

Trees for Shading

Even most ornamental tree varieties reach heights of from 15′ to 25′. Certainly trees of that size can provide some shade, so, although we customarily think of shade trees as being large, all trees can be utilized for shading purposes.

Figure 6-18 (continued)

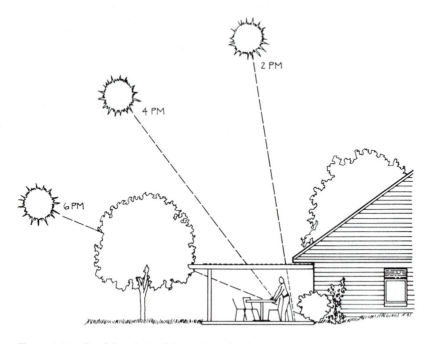

Figure 6-19. Careful analysis of the sun's angle of penetration at various times of the day and at various times of the year is essential before effective structural shading units can be designed.

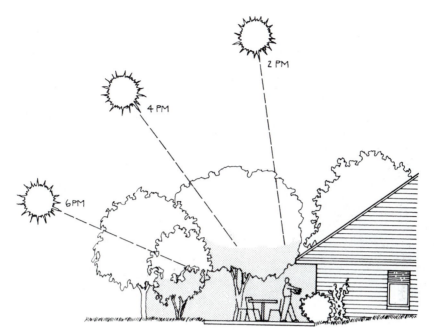

Figure 6-20. In addition to the angle of the sun's penetration at various times of the day and at various times of the year, the size and shape of the tree canopy needed and the distance from the area to be shaded should be considered when placing trees for shading purposes.

Smaller trees are often preferable because they do not take up as much space as trees that reach heights of 60′ and more. Since small residential lots allow for few large shade trees to be used, smaller trees must be used wisely, also.

The placement of trees for shade is critical (see Figure 6-20). Not only must the shading function be carried out, but the trees must be placed so as to avoid the creation of other landscape distortions. For example, placing a variety of tree that has low weeping branches in the center of a lawn area may interrupt that lawn area by breaking the view across its expanse. Another variety, one with upward-sweeping branches, the lower of which are trimmed sufficiently high, would not distort the view of an open lawn area. Instead, the trunk only provides a foreground, adding depth to the view. Small trees used for shading are usually best included in other planting masses, since their canopies are low enough to restrict both the view and the movement through an area. Because they are shorter, these trees have to be placed closer to the area needing shade.

Selecting trees for shading purposes requires consideration of their width as well as their height. Some trees develop good breadth in relation to their height, whereas others maintain a narrow shape. The shade requirements of an area determine the canopy type most suitable in each case. The structure of tree branches, limbs, and foliage should be carefully evaluated, also. Some trees provide an extremely dense shade because they have many leaves, their leaves are larger, or they have many branches. Others, with small, compound leaves, open

Figure 6-21. The configuration and density the tree canopies will reach when the landscape becomes mature should be considered even when the landscape is being designed.

and sparse branching structure, and a smaller number of leaves, offer more of a filtered sunlight than a dense shade. Selecting from the wide range of shade densities available is like determining the percentage of shade that can be provided by a structural shade trellis. It depends on the circumstances. While the open, more sparsely shading trees offer advantages for growing grass or other plants beneath their canopies and easier leaf clean-up in the fall, the densest of the trees provide the most cooling shade (see Figure 6-21).

In a climate where a particular tree is to provide shade in the summer, but where the warming effects of the sun are desired during late fall and winter, the trees with the shortest growing seasons generally work best. Normally, those trees are native to that area. Even though leaves are absent in fall and winter, the bare branches and trunks will still cut the sun's rays somewhat. Their placement should always take into account the sun's path in winter and summer to avoid any interference with warming winter rays.

Whenever trees are used for any purpose, both overhead lines and structures and any underground lines, sewerage laterals, and so forth must be avoided. Many tree canopies have been mutilated needlessly because of poor placement under power lines, and many root systems have encroached into porous sewerage laterals when the problem could have been avoided.

When trees serve as part of the landscape ceiling, the air in that area is improved. In addition to the cooling effects, oxygen is given off as a by-product of photosynthesis, and many impurities are filtered out of the air as it circulates through the leaves. Tree foliage is an excellent filter for removing airborne dust.

Although temperature control is the most important consideration of shade in the landscape, the aesthetic effects of the light and shadow patterns created by various ceiling arrangements should not go unnoticed in the design scheme (see Figure 6-22). Trellis structures form patterns of light and shadow different from those of trees, for example, since they are much more formally structured. Varying heights in the ceiling structure are also important, contributing to the overall feeling of proportion in the landscaped rooms (see Figure 6-23).

A final consideration of the ceiling structure in the landscape is that often those elements used in a backyard can also be seen in the front yard. As they mature, shade trees often grow tall enough to be seen above a house. Because of this, these trees affect the landscape arrangement in an area that may be completely unlike the area in which they are situated. Their effects on other areas must be considered when their location is planned.

SPECIAL CONSIDERATIONS: WALLS AND CEILING ARRANGEMENTS

Passive solar heating has been discussed here as a function opposite to that of shade in the landscape. But the advent of solar heating by active storage methods creates some other factors for consideration. When active solar heating units are used, extra care must be taken not to place shading elements where they will

Figure 6-22. The mature trees in a landscape not only provide shade, wind protection, and so forth, but also cast interesting patterns of light and shadow on the ground or on other landscape elements.

Figure 6-22 (continued)

Figure 6-23.   Ultimately, the trees planned for backyard functions grow tall enough to be seen above the front of the house. If appropriately positioned for balance, they will make an effective background for the house, making house and landscape seem more harmonious.

interfere with collector panels. Furthermore, if storage units are to be located in the yard and away from the house, an extra space must be created for them by the landscape designer. Not a lot is known about this area of fledgling technology. Perhaps in the future landscape designers will design berms containing rock heat storage units that also conceal collector units.

One thing is certain—the walls and ceiling of a landscape have great impact on climatic controls within a given property. One of the best illustrations of that fact is the following extract from *Cost Effective Site Planning*, a book published by the National Association of Homebuilders, which is reprinted here with their permission.* It illustrates the concern builders are giving to proper site development and landscaping.

Basic Tips for Climate Modification

As can be seen, the home builders of America are vitally concerned with the same areas of energy conservation and climatic modification as are the landscape designers. Most of the points made in this list of valuable tips are concerned with the walls and ceiling of the landscape.

POINTS TO REMEMBER

- The walls, ceiling, and floor are the dimensions of the outdoor "room." A ceiling (the sky) and floor (the ground) are always present, though they might require modification. The walls are created as part of the landscape design.
- The structure of any one of the three dimensions mentioned above may affect the appearance and/or function of the other two.
- The landscape's walls are responsible for screening, wind protection, framing of off-property views, enclosure, and so forth.
- The ceiling of the landscape provides shade, protection from weather elements, passive solar heating, and so forth.
- Layout of the landscape's walls results from thorough examination of needs during design analysis, followed by general area layout during bubble diagramming or similar processes.
- By first thinking of walls only in abstract vertical sizes and shapes, the designer takes a systematic approach that eliminates confusion.
- Screening, depending on the type, requires walls of certain sizes and densities.
- Enclosure may be either absolute (impenetrable) or implied.
- Wind protection is usually best accomplished on residential sites by slowing the wind and breaking its force, rather than by blocking it entirely. A complete blocking just lifts the wind, which subsequently must return to the ground surface.

*National Association of Homebuilders, *Cost Effective Site Planning* (Washington, D.C.: N.A.H.B., 1976), pp. 46 and 47.

evergreens and
ridge provide
winter wind break,
slope faces southeast

road alignment
channels
summer breeze

houses follow the
flow of the topo and
are set into the grade

deciduous trees
provide shade,
allow free flow
of summer breeze

winter W.&N.W. winds

garages and
ridge line
block cold wind

snow accumulation
& protected entry

deciduous trees
allow winter sun
to warm house,
shade in summer

cold air moves
through swales
and valleys

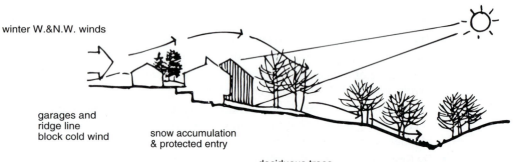

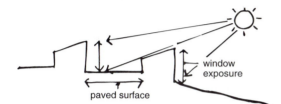

TO MAKE IT WARMER:

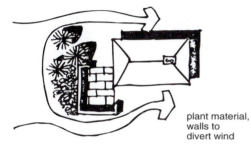

prune lower growth for increased air circulation

TO MAKE IT COOLER:

plant material, walls to divert wind

TO MAKE IT LESS WINDY:

overhead planting slows evaporation adds transpiration

TO MAKE IT MORE HUMID:

COOL & TEMPERATE ZONES

To make it warmer:

- Maximum solar exposure
- Paved areas, rock or masonry surfaces, southern slopes for increased absorption of radiation
- Structural or plant "ceilings" to reflect back outgoing radiation at night
- Sun pockets
- Wind breaks and cold air diverters

To make it colder:

- Shade trees and vines
- Overhangs, awnings, canopies (cooler in day time, warmer at night)
- Planted ground covers
- Pruning of lower growth for increased air circulation
- Evaporative cooling (sprinklers, pools, ponds and lakes)

To make it less windy:

- Wind breaks, baffles, diverters (plant material and structures)
- Berms, land form
- Semi-enclosed outdoor living areas

To make it breezier:

- Pruning of low branches of trees
- Minimum of low plant growth
- Creation of breeze ways (structural and planted)

To make it more humid:

- Overhead planting (slows evaporation and adds transpiration)
- Low windbreaks
- Planted ground covers
- Pools, cascades, sprinklers

To make it drier:

- Maximum solar exposure
- Maximum ventilation
- Efficient drainage system
- Paved ground surfaces

- An off-property view is best framed by landscape wall sections that repeat the dominant lines in the view itself in proper proportion to the view's components.
- Structural walls for the landscape include many types of walls and fences. They offer the advantages of full height from the start, limited ground coverage, and variety of materials.
- Monotype plantings are those of one variety only. They may be allowed to grow in their own natural form or they may be clipped into formal hedges.
- Massed plantings, sometimes called shrub borders, consist of a mixed variety of shrubs and trees. Though more varied than other types of landscape wall materials, they occupy more space.
- The most satisfactory landscape walls often combine both structural and planting materials.
- The principal concern with ceiling structure in the landscape is for shading purposes. Shade may be provided by structural roofs, awnings, arbors, or the like, or by shade and ornamental trees.
- Good shading units depend on accurate recognition of the time of day when the shade is necessary, the path of the sun over a property, and the angle at which the sun penetrates the area during the time that shade is needed. Further recognition of the density of shade desired is also necessary.
- In designing shading units, decisions also must take into account other needs, such as protection from rain and snow, lighting for night use, elimination of insects, and use of artificial heating or cooling.
- Tree placement must be based on above- and below-ground utility structures that might be affected by—or affect—the tree's branches or roots.
- The light and shadow patterns created by the landscape's ceiling structure are extremely important aesthetically.

REVIEW QUESTIONS

1. Name six of the eight landscape adjustments that can be facilitated by designing good landscape "walls."
2. Name four provisions of the ceiling of a landscape "room."
3. What types of screening are possible through the use of landscape "walls"?
4. What is meant by *absolute* and *implied* enclosure?
5. Why might a fence be preferable to plant material for a given landscape "wall"?
6. When planning shading elements in the landscape, why is it necessary to consider different times of the year?
7. When does a landscape designer begin planning for the "walls" and "ceilings" in a given landscape?

8. Differentiate between structural and planting materials in their use in landscape "walls."

PRACTICAL TIP FROM A PRACTICING DESIGNER

To view individual sections of the landscape "wall" from the property itself, it is sometimes helpful to hold your hands up and forward, using your thumbs and forefingers held at right angles, effectively making three sides of a picture frame. Such a frame allows you to consider only that portion of the landscape wall as seen within the frame. It also gives you a better feeling for the scale of that segment of wall. Artists use such a frame to size a landscape painting. The landscape designer similarly sizes the wall, then imagines the elements that would best fill it.

PRINCIPLES OF PLANTING DESIGN

In this chapter, you will begin to study the principles of artistic design as applied to plant materials. Both the physical properties of plants (color, texture, and form) and how those features are used to compose a unified design will be discussed in detail. The process of first designing in elevational view, then transferring the design to plan view, will be discussed.

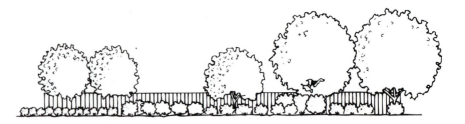

As practical as it is, planting design is an art. Having determined what functions are necessary to it, the designer's next task is to apply the principles of planting design in artistic composition. Up to this point, only size and general placement have been considered. Now it is time to furnish the design with real forms that can be sensed, felt, and seen.

Plant materials have many sensory qualities. We can see their various forms, textures, and colors. We can feel their textures. We can smell their fragrances. We can even taste their foliage, blooms, and fruit. But in order to create a pleasing landscape design, we must coordinate the functional uses of plants with our sensory perceptions.

THE PHYSICAL PROPERTIES OF PLANTS

Form

An obvious physical property of any plant is its form. Planting designers are usually concerned with the mature silhouette of a plant, but its intermediate shapes should also be considered, particularly when a plant develops slowly.

Most plant forms are rounded and more horizontal than vertical in shape. Rounded or horizontal shapes are less dramatic than those with vertical emphasis because they are more expected and they follow the shape of the terrain more naturally. Vertical shapes demand attention, even startling the viewer at times.

Native plant forms usually conform to land forms (see Figure 7-1). In mountainous regions, vertical shapes prevail, reflecting the sharp peaks and jagged rock configurations of the area. Horizontal plant forms are most common on the plains, and in rolling or hilly terrain rounded plant forms predominate. Landscape designers do well to remember this, using the natural plant forms of an area in a design and reserving the unusual forms for emphasis.

Although the form of each plant is unique, there are general classifications of forms. Trees can be round, columnar, vase-shaped, weeping, pyramidal, or oval (see Figure 7-2). The outline of a tree depends on its branching pattern. Narrow crotch angles at the point where lateral branches separate from the trunk cause upright forms; the more rounded forms are caused by wider angles.

Shrubs may be round, oval, pyramidal, or oblong; they may be prostrate or creeping (see Figure 7-3). Part of a plant's form is the result of the growth habit of the plant. In some evergreens, for example, the branches overlay one another. The plant's form takes on an irregular line because of this layering. Growth habit should always be considered to be an element of form.

The best way to study plant forms is to visit a park, arboretum, or other area where mature plants are in plentiful supply. Compare the forms closely to classify specific plants and note the minor differences within classifications. Visits to a nursery are helpful for studying the forms of young or intermediate growth stages of plants.

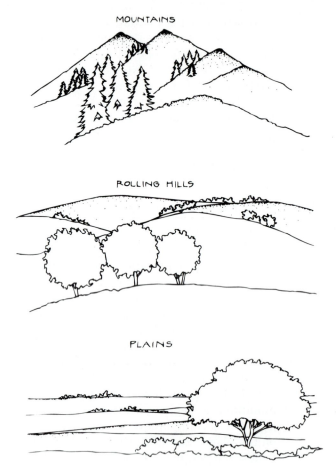

MOUNTAINS

ROLLING HILLS

PLAINS

Figure 7-1. Plant forms tend to reflect the natural terrain of the areas to which they are native. Good design calls for the use of these predominant forms to blend with the natural surroundings.

The silhouette formed by a group of plants is probably the most important contribution of form to landscape composition (see Figure 7-4). The form of plants in silhouette must allow for function (shade, screening, wind protection, enclosure, and so on), while providing pleasing lines at the same time.

Texture

Stems, leaves, bark, and buds are the physical features that determine the texture of a plant. Textures ranging from fine through medium to coarse are visible because of the size and shape of these features and the way light and shadow play off them.

Larger leaves, stems, and buds usually create an effect of coarseness. But the number of branches and leaves and the spacing between them also affects the texture. Thick, tight foliage results in finer texture, while widely separated foliage gives a coarser texture. Patterns of light and shadow depend more upon individ-

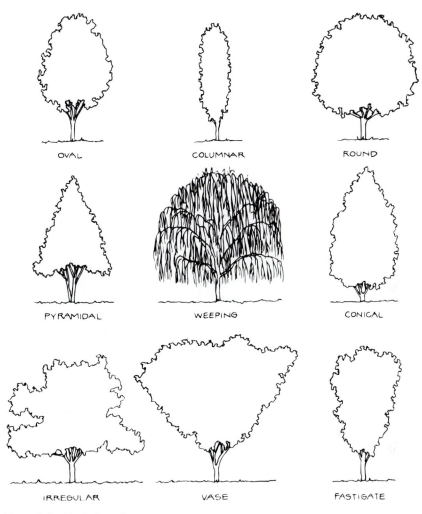

OVAL   COLUMNAR   ROUND

PYRAMIDAL   WEEPING   CONICAL

IRREGULAR   VASE   FASTIGATE

Figure 7-2. Typical tree forms.

ual leaf surfaces in a tight, dense shape; in a loose structure, the masses of leaves and corresponding voids dictate light and shadow, causing a coarser texture. Leaf style and shape also affect texture. Simple leaves will appear coarser than compound leaves of even larger size, and leaves with deep cuts in the margin, like oak leaves, show a finer texture than other leaves of similar size (see Figure 7-5).

Plant texture can be felt as well as seen. One good way to study textures is by closing your eyes and feeling the plants. The leaves, branches, bark, and buds of various plants all feel distinctly different. Some are smooth, some prickly, some downright thorny; each sensation is a part of the plant's textural character.

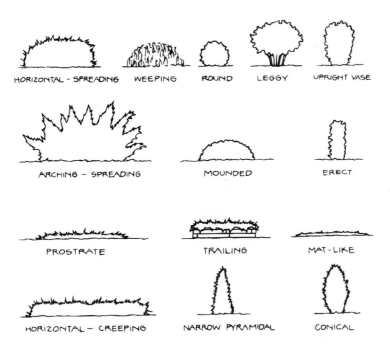

Figure 7-3. Typical shrub forms.

The farther one stands from a plant, the finer its texture will appear. For that reason, the distance of view must be considered during the textural study of planting design.

Color

Color results from light penetration, absorption, and reflection. Light rays of variable lengths enter a plant leaf to be either absorbed or reflected. If all light rays are absorbed, none are reflected back to the surface; the result is the absence of color—or black. If all rays are reflected back to the surface in equal amounts, white results. In most cases, the light rays reflected are a mixture of different color rays, which results in a color hue (see Figure 7-6).

Figure 7-4. The silhouette of a mature massed planting is of more primary concern to the designer than the individual forms of plants in the grouping.

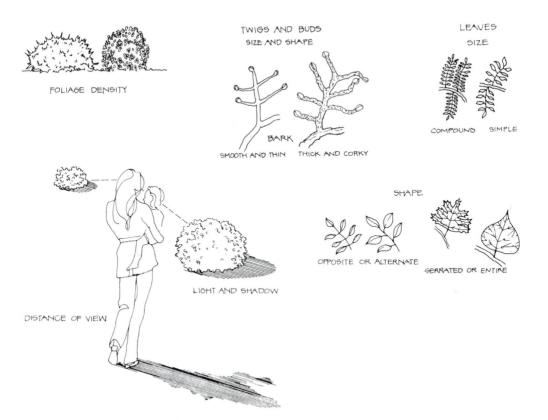

Figure 7-5. The individual physical characteristics of plants, the way light strikes them, and the distance from which the plants are viewed determine individual plant textures.

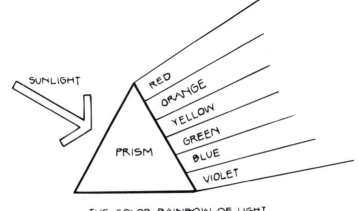

Figure 7-6. As sunlight enters a prism, the rays are separated, and a rainbow of colors is emitted from the other side. The colors of various plants are determined by the light rays each absorbs and the light rays each reflects.

Light rays produce red, orange, yellow, green, blue, and violet colors. Blends of these color rays produce all of the primary, secondary, and tertiary hues we see. Intensity is a measurement of the quality of the basic color in the blend. Bright greens, for example, are said to be intense. Another measurement of color is its value, which indicates the amount of light reflected. A small amount of light reflection produces a dark color; a large amount of light reflection produces a lighter shade. Plants with a dark blue-green foliage are reflecting small amounts of light, and those with yellow foliage reflect large amounts of light. The foliage of most plants is dominated by the green hue, meaning that green light rays are reflected in the largest quantity.

Plant foliage colors range from black-green (grayish) to blue-green to the bright greens to red-greens and finally to yellow-greens. The green predominates because of the presence of chlorophyll in the leaves. Some leaves turn to yellow or red-orange shades in the fall because chlorophyll is replaced by the pigments anthrocyanin (red), carotene (orange), and xanthophyll (yellow) in varying amounts. The presence of these pigments causes light rays to be bent and reflected differently, so the leaves change color.

Colors are warm or cool, depending upon their hue. Warm colors are those ranging from yellow through orange and into the red hues. Colors ranging from green through blue and into the violet color hues are cool. Warm colors are bright, inviting, and lively; cool colors are restful and receding, and they are not as conspicuous. Landscaping moods relate most directly to color hues (see Figure 7-7).

It is usually the color of a plant's foliage that is considered most in the design process, because the foliage is present during most of the year. But flowers, fruit, bark, and seeds also produce colors worthy of consideration. While the colors in a landscape do not usually clash, good design provides for a better blend.

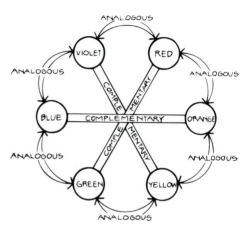

Figure 7-7. The color wheel, showing analogous and complementary colors.

UNITY IN DESIGN

Unity in landscape design describes the harmonious combination of various parts to create a feeling of oneness. It was earlier established that a landscape is made up of problem-solving units in different locations on a property. A good landscape design combines all of these functions into a unified composition (see Figure 7-8). The viewer is allowed to view components in context with the whole.

Unity in a landscape design is achieved by the successful combination of six ingredients: simplicity, variety, emphasis, balance, sequence, and scale. These ingredients are applied to the physical selections of form, texture, and color to achieve a harmonious design. Each ingredient warrants specific attention.

Simplicity

Simplicity breeds elegance. Simple lines, forms, and functional designs are always more interesting than complex, hard-to-digest designs that do not allow a

Figure 7-8. Designing a unified composition requires the careful mixing of the right ingredients.

proper focus of attention. Simplicity does not mean dull design, though. It means subtle combinations of ingredients to create appeal while solving a functional need.

The most important factor in creating simplicity of design is repetition. Repetition can apply to form, texture, or color as well as to specific plants. Different plants with the same texture can contribute to simplicity by repeating that characteristic throughout the plan. In the same way, plants with the same colors, though of different varieties, can contribute to simplicity. Repetition of a plant form allows our eyes to move comfortably over a landscape, secure in the vision of something familiar. Repeating the same plant variety in a landscape contributes to unity by allowing that plant to have more impact. If a flowering shrub appears in a mass planting in one place in a landscape, it should generally reappear elsewhere (see Figure 7-9).

To prevent monotony, repetition must be carefully restrained. Variety is used to control repetition and spark the viewer's interest.

Variety

Variety can apply to form, color, or texture. Variety adds spice and allows the designer to control the mood of the planting design. By varying the forms,

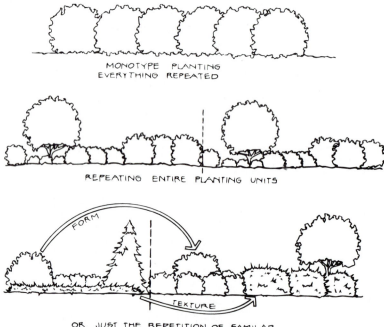

MONOTYPE PLANTING
EVERYTHING REPEATED

REPEATING ENTIRE PLANTING UNITS

FORM

TEXTURE

OR, JUST THE REPETITION OF FAMILAR
FORMS, COLORS, AND TEXTURES IN
DISSIMILAR PLANTING UNITS.

Figure 7-9. The repetition of familiar forms, colors, or textures from one planting unit to another reassures the viewer, helping unify the units into a total composition.

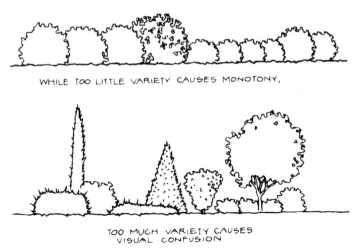

WHILE TOO LITTLE VARIETY CAUSES MONOTONY,

TOO MUCH VARIETY CAUSES
VISUAL CONFUSION

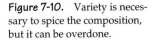

Figure 7-10. Variety is necessary to spice the composition, but it can be overdone.

textures, and colors in a landscape, the designer prevents boredom, giving the viewer a reason to look further.

Careful balance between repetition and variety is essential. While too much repetition causes monotony, too much variety can result in confusion (see Figure 7-10). Since variety creates strong contrast, it should be used sparingly.

Emphasis

Emphasis is a means of drawing attention to important features while allowing less important features to take a subordinate role. For example, it is normally desirable in a residential design to attract the viewer's attention to the front door of the house. This is often accomplished by emphasizing that entrance by the use of outstanding plants that offer strong variety in color, texture, or form. The plantings surrounding the accent plant support its role, strengthening the emphasis.

Emphasis requires variety, because that which is to do the emphasizing must draw and hold the viewer's attention longer than anything surrounding it (see Figure 7-11). Accent plants have especially strong features, causing people to pick them out of a landscape and look at them for longer periods of time.

Balance

Subconsciously, we look for balance in everything we view. Balance can be *symmetrical*, with the elements on either side of an axis exactly alike, or it can be *asymmetrical*, with unlike elements of equal weight on each side (see Figure 7-12). Weight can be either physical or visual.

Symmetrical balance is achieved by using the same plants on both sides of a doorway, both ends of a house, or both back corners of a lot, so that one side

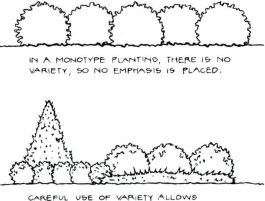

IN A MONOTYPE PLANTING, THERE IS NO
VARIETY, SO NO EMPHASIS IS PLACED.

Figure 7-11. The addition of variety to a planting unit creates emphasis, but only if the variety is controlled.

CAREFUL USE OF VARIETY ALLOWS
EMPHASIS TO BE PLACED WHERE DESIRED.

forms a mirror-image of the other side. This type of balance is formal and should not be used in an informal design situation. Because most of our landscape needs and the buildings we occupy are of an informal nature, few landscaping situations call for symmetrical balance.

Asymmetrical balance can be created by using balancing forms of unequal size. One tree might balance three small shrubs, for example. Balance is not only seen, it is felt. Color can influence balance by adding visual weight to a scene. For example, a brightly colored plant on one side of a planting unit might have to be balanced at the other end of the planting unit by several plants of the same or nearly the same size that have less visual weight. Texture also contributes to balance. Coarse textures are heavy visually, and the finer textures are light. When texture is changed within a planting unit, more of the finer-textured plants are required to balance those of coarser texture.

Balance also applies to the depth of a view; it must be preserved between the foreground, middle ground, and background of a view. If the landscape is unbalanced, one of the views will dominate, causing the others to be lost to the composition.

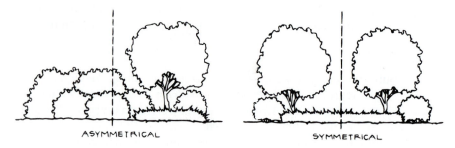

ASYMMETRICAL

SYMMETRICAL

Figure 7-12. Symmetrical and asymmetrical types of balance.

Sequence

For the viewer's eyes to move over a landscape in an orderly fashion to each point of emphasis, a sequence must be established. This sequence can be created by a progression of form, texture, or color (see Figure 7-13). It can also be made up of combinations of each. However, if all three physical properties are altered at once, sequence is lost, because too much variety is introduced. One example of a sequence commonly used in landscape design is holding the color constant and changing the plant forms slightly, causing the eye to flow with the increasing height of the plant silhouettes. At the same time, subtle textural changes might occur, moving from fine through medium or medium-coarse as the plants increase in height to a point of emphasis. All changes in form, texture, or color should be gradual and subtle in order to make a sequential change. Anything startling in the sequential progress will create a point of emphasis, thus ending the sequence.

Sequence might be thought of as the rhythm of the landscape, causing the eye to progress to a point of emphasis then move away gradually to rest on another point of emphasis.

Scale

A landscape plan is drafted to a prescribed scale. One such scale is 1/8" = 1', meaning that by drawing a line 1/8" long on paper, we are representing a span 1' long on the property. This type of scale is known as the *absolute scale*, because one unit in size represents a measurable quantity.

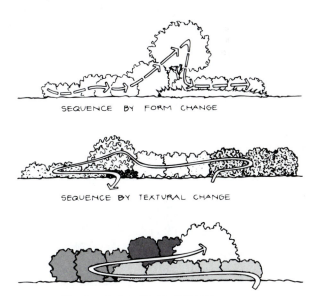

SEQUENCE BY FORM CHANGE

SEQUENCE BY TEXTURAL CHANGE

SEQUENCE BY COLOR CHANGE

Figure 7-13. Types of sequential change within planting units.

156   CHAPTER 7

Relative scale might be thought of as proportion (see Figure 7-14). Instead of being determined by absolute measurement, relative scale is a feeling about the way one unit relates to another in size. Human beings tend to relate the size of an object to their own forms. Objects that relate well in size to the human form are considered normal. Larger-than-normal scale tends to frighten us, while smaller scale is subservient—we feel that we are in command. Imagine how a child feels in an adult world. Is it any wonder she or he craves security? Yet if given a doll-house with small-scale people, that child feels in control. She or he will discipline the small people, soothe their pains, and totally dominate their activities. Many adults, when visiting a large metropolitan area for the first time, feel insecure because the skyscrapers are in such monumental scale compared to that which they normally expect.

By controlling the proportionate scale of landscaping features, the designer evokes emotions. Since it is usually desirable to make people comfortable and relaxed, most landscaping is done on a normal scale to which people relate easily. There are exceptions to this rule. Japanese gardens, because they are designed on a very intimate scale, allow a tiny yard space to seem much larger. On the other hand, if we frame a panoramic view with landscaping, we sometimes can make that view seem more vast, yet at the same time better defined.

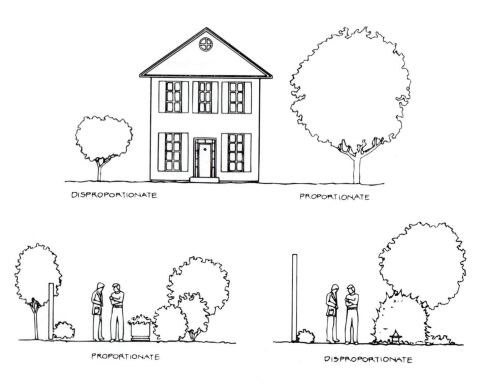

Figure 7-14. Relative scale is more accurately called proportion.

APPLYING PRINCIPLES TO DESIGN

Earlier in the design process, basic sizes for screening, wind protection, and enclosure, among other functions, were established. Now, it is necessary to apply the principles of design so that color, texture, and form can be unified into a pleasing composition. The general choices between hard construction elements and planting materials also have been weighed, so they now may be combined (see Figure 7-15).

By the time a designer reaches this point, the purpose and intent of each planting unit in the landscape should be known. Rough size and shape have been worked out for each unit, and the designer knows all the pros and cons of using structural materials versus plant materials in each application. The task at hand is to combine all of the elements in these units so they will perform their individual functions but still comprise a unified whole.

Since such terms as "a unified whole" can be tossed about somewhat gratuitously, maybe the following will clarify what is meant by a unified composition. A landscape is made up of many units, each performing the specific duties already discussed. Because of these separate functions and the different locations of units within the landscape, the size, shape, and visual importance of each unit varies, but when walking through a landscape, the average viewer should be unaware that such distinct differences exist. His or her eyes should be led to points of emphasis, resting on each for a time, then moving on to another through a pleasing sequence of change in color, texture, or form. At no time should the viewer detect any disproportion, nor should he or she be led to feel that nothing in the landscape relates to anything else. It should be possible for the nonprofessional to view the landscape and easily discern the most important features, without necessarily knowing why. There should be enough variety in that landscape to stimulate the viewer, yet enough familiar objects to make her or him feel comfortable. All told, each space in the landscape should seem "a place to be" all by itself. It should give all who visit the landscaped area a sense of being in a place where all is right. That does not just happen. It has to be planned. The principles of unity must be applied to the three physical features: form, color, and texture.

The landscape must continue to be designed as a collection of separate units, because our eyes are only capable of viewing so much at one time. Within each unit, then, balance, scale, emphasis, sequence, variety, and repetition have to be considered. All elements do not have to be used in each unit, however. For example, consider a unit composed entirely of a monotype hedge. Since all the plants are alike, there is no variety, and, hence, there is no sequence within the unit and there is no point of emphasis. But balance exists, and certainly repetition is practiced, and the planting must be proportionate to its surroundings. The same could be said for any unit occupying enough space to prevent our eyes from perceiving anything else at the same time—a solid fence or wall, for example. But whenever something does change within a unit, variety is introduced,

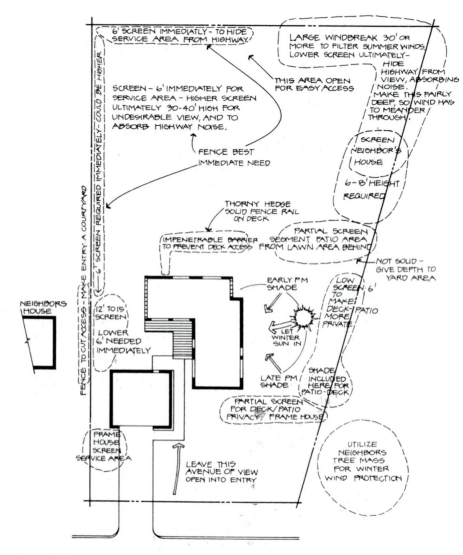

Figure 7-15. Before a planting unit is designed, it is helpful to review the plan-view notes made earlier in the design process about the unit's size, form, density, and purpose.

causing emphasis to be made. It is not possible to combine two items that differ in form, color, or texture without one of the items having a stronger visual attraction than the other. It is possible that two people might each perceive a different item as having the stronger visual attraction, however. For that reason, it is better that the designer, when introducing variety into a unit, intentionally creates a point of emphasis, a *focal point*. By intentionally creating enough visual variety with that focal point, the designer controls the viewer's attention. Everything else in the unit then supports that emphasis by sequencing attention to it and then away from it to another unit. Avoiding too much variety, the designer is able to focus the viewer's attention where it is warranted, preventing the elements in each unit from competing for attention. The viewer comes away more satisfied because he or she is able to move from one unit to another comfortably, feeling that he or she has enjoyed it all and that it was all part of the same composition (see Figure 7-16).

To control the design, it is best that the designer take a systematic approach, unit by unit at first, then adjusting units to fit together. By doing this, the designer resists the impulse to use all favorite plantings and hard materials that do not tie together well. Many designers work out all planting units in plan view, although vertical elevations or perspectives must form in their minds first. For others, especially the inexperienced, it is better to work out planting units in vertical elevation and then transfer them to plan view. This way, a physical picture, as well as a mental one, is formed.

The physical feature most dramatically represented in an elevational view of a planting unit is form. The silhouette formed by combined plant materials and hard elements can be represented most graphically on an elevation, even though specific plant varieties should not crowd the designer's mind at

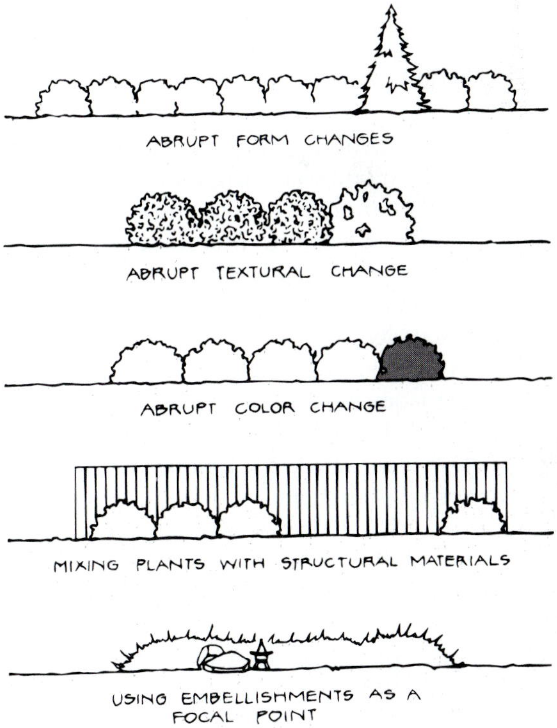

ABRUPT FORM CHANGES

ABRUPT TEXTURAL CHANGE

ABRUPT COLOR CHANGE

MIXING PLANTS WITH STRUCTURAL MATERIALS

USING EMBELLISHMENTS AS A FOCAL POINT

Figure 7-16. Different ways to create emphasis within a planting unit.

that time. Instead, stylized representations should be used. Texture can be depicted on elevational drawings, but some skill is required to make these representations accurately. Color cannot be drawn on paper with any accuracy, for only the most talented artist can capture the subtle changes in plant foliage colors. So, while a combination of drawing silhouettes in elevation and showing symbolic area coverages in plan view aids the designer in the planting-design process, much of the designing must be accomplished through mental imagery. Familiarity with various foliage colors and textures is a must, so that those physical features can be conjured up again and again in the designer's mind. As decisions are made about the colors, textures, and forms to be used within planting units, a set of specifications is built for the final selection of materials (see Figure 7-17).

As each unit within the landscape is designed, a decision must be made about that unit's importance in the entire scheme in relation to all other units. If the unit is to be one of major importance, the degree of emphasis placed on it must be greater than on other units. As the plants within a unit support the one accent plant or group of plants with the greatest emphasis, so should less important planting units support the ones deemed to be most important to the overall landscape plan. Some units, for example, might exist simply to provide needed screening, wind protection, or enclosure without warranting special attention. These units should be less emphatic than those that frame a desirable view or direct attention to an entrance.

The *accent plant* has been mentioned as a means of creating emphasis. An accent plant is one with extremely strong visual features—so strong, in fact, that one plant of a variety can command enough attention to make it stand out in a large grouping containing many other plantings. The visual strength of an accent plant may originate in any of the three physical characteristics or in a combination of two or more. In other words, a plant may become an accent plant just because it has a stronger color than others. Vicary privet and redleaf barberry are good examples; placed close to a large group of plantings of predominantly green hue, one bright yellow-green or red-green plant commands a great deal of attention. For another example, the sharply pyramidal form of upright junipers attracts a great deal of attention because it is drastically different from most plant forms. This is one of the reasons for that particular plant form's being misused so often. Commonly used at building corners, the plant draws an inordinate amount of attention, but it fails to accomplish needed landscaping functions.

Not all accent plants need to be as strong as those just mentioned. A simple change in form from predominantly horizontal plants to a single rounded one, for example, can be enough to create emphasis on the rounded plant. Similarly, a change in texture that is more abrupt than the sequence through the other plantings in a unit can cause the eye to focus on a particular plant. Changing from more muted blue-green foliage to a brighter emerald green can draw attention.

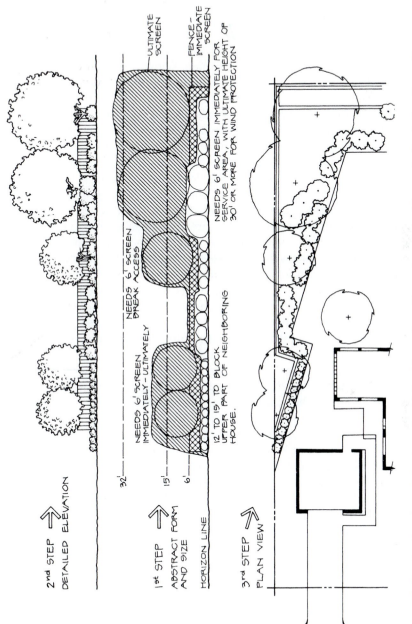

2nd STEP ⟹ DETAILED ELEVATION

1st STEP ⟹ ABSTRACT FORM AND SIZE

HORIZON LINE

32'

15'

6'

NEEDS 6' SCREEN BREAK ACCESS

NEEDS 6' SCREEN IMMEDIATELY - ULTIMATELY

12' TO 15' TO BLOCK UPPER PART OF NEIGHBORING HOUSE.

ULTIMATE SCREEN

FENCE - IMMEDIATE SCREEN

NEEDS 6' SCREEN IMMEDIATELY FOR SERVICE AREA, WITH ULTIMATE HEIGHT OF 30' OR MORE FOR WIND PROTECTION

3rd STEP ⟹ PLAN VIEW

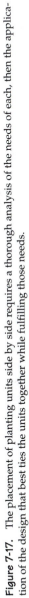

Figure 7-17. The placement of planting units side by side requires a thorough analysis of the needs of each, then the application of the design that best ties the units together while fulfilling those needs.

Besides accent plants, there are two other general groups of plants that are grouped according to their visual qualities. Most plants do not have the strong visual qualities of accent plants. These plants are best suited to group plantings made up of three plants or more. These are called *massing plants*, and they look best when grouped in odd numbers. Normally, they are spaced so that, when mature, they will grow together—or mass. They lose their individual identities then, and the mass effect is seen in the landscape. Plants in the other group stand alone, as do accent plants, but they are usually completely removed from other masses of plantings. These plants are called *specimen plants*.

Specimen plants have strong visual qualities, but they also have a characteristic symmetry that allows them to be planted alone, removed from other plants. Most specimen plants in the landscape are trees, because there is little reason for a single shrub to stand alone. Colorado blue spruce is the prime example of a specimen tree (see Figure 7-18). Allowed to grow by itself, it will usually grow to nearly perfect form. Its physical characteristics are strong and attract much attention. For this reason, some care must be taken not to place it where little attention is desired. A specimen tree may be used in a planting unit where all the other plants are shrubs. In this case, the specimen tree does stand alone, but it also serves as the accent for that planting unit (see Figure 7-19).

A planting unit, then, usually consists of an accent plant and supporting mass plantings. Within the mass plantings, a sequence is built. The viewer's eye is normally attracted to the accent first and then is gradually led away by the sequence within the plantings to another unit and another point of emphasis. When two or more units can be seen at the same time, the viewer's brain instantly recognizes the emphasis that is more important, and the eye rests on that point for a period of time. That is why the designer must decide which of the units is more important than the others, placing the emphasis more strongly on that unit. Remember that emphasis can be strengthened by increasing variety in color, texture, or form, or with a combination of these physical characteristics.

Emphasis does not have to be created by plant materials, nor do the supporting portions of a unit have to be made up of plant materials. All types of hard elements in the landscape have a part in the scheme of unity. For example, a solid fence contributes to a unit by repeating the same form, creating a visual weight for balancing the unit, sequencing to a point of greater attention as a visually stimulating plant is placed along the fence, adding variety to an otherwise largely planted landscape wall, and contributing to the scale of elements in the landscape—if it is properly sized. The same can be said for any other constructed elements. The colors, textures, and forms of these materials must be combined by using the same guidelines for creating unity that are applied to plant materials.

Anything special and different in the landscape creates emphasis by its greater variety. Water features, sculptures, boulders, benches, and lighting are just a few of the landscape accessories that can be used to emphasize areas. These special elements are commonly called *landscape embellishments* and are discussed separately in Chapter 11. Because these elements are so drastically different in

Figure 7-18.   The Colorado Blue Spruce is one of the most dramatic of the specimen plants. It needs no help from subordinate plantings to make a statement in the landscape.

form, color, and texture from everything else in the landscape, they normally become focal points and, as such, must be carefully planned (see Figure 7-20).

As all planting units are designed, both hard construction elements and plant materials are incorporated into an elevational view and then arranged on the ground in plan view. Parts of this process remain to be discussed—the combination of architecture and plantings, which involves some special principles outlined in Chapter 8, and the arrangement of ground patterns for the entire landscape. Although discussed separately from this chapter's principles of planting design, these other principles must be applied simultaneously (see Figures 7-21 and 7-22).

As is the case when drawing symbols in plan view, elevational plant forms should always be drawn at or near mature-size representation. By using mature sizes at the appropriate scale, the designer is assured of seeing a proportionate picture of the way a landscape unit will ultimately appear.

Figure 7-19. A specimen plant can serve as an accent in a planting unit. Here, the unusual white bark and triple stems of the birch accent the doorway to the house. Further accent is provided by the vining sarcoxie euonymus climbing the wall on the opposite side of the door.

The elevational views selected as being most appropriate for each planting unit graphically depict the form of the plants. Not yet having selected specific plants, the designer can select from a number of varieties that are of the size and form specified in the elevational drawing. At this time, the designer should indicate colors and textures, which further narrows the list of plants from which to make final selections.

Although important, the colors and textures of a plant's flower, fruit, seed, and bark usually play a smaller role than the colors and textures of the foliage. The foliage is present for a longer time and so plays a stronger role than flowers, fruits, or seeds. Bark is less obvious than foliage.

POINTS TO REMEMBER

- The physical characteristics of plants are form, texture, and color.
- The plant forms in native vegetation tend to conform in general shape to the natural land forms of that area.

Figure 7-20. When too much variety is introduced, emphasis is confused. In this photo, the sculpture on the wall, the flagpole, the vines massing on the wall, the railing by the steps, and the light fixture in the foreground all compete for attention.

Figure 7-21.   This specimen multistemmed Redbud accents a doorway while also masking a sharp corner on the building.

- The silhouette formed by combined groups of plants in vertical elevation must accommodate all of the landscape wall functions (screening, wind protection, and enclosure) while at the same time providing pleasing lines.
- Textures of plants range from fine through coarse. Texture is created by the stems, leaves, bark, and buds and can be seen and felt.
- Color results from light penetration, absorption, and reflection. The more light rays are reflected, the brighter the color; the more absorbed, the darker the color will be.
- Color hues are the result of light rays of variable lengths being reflected in mixtures.
- Simplicity, variety, emphasis, balance, sequence, and scale are all applied to the composition of a unified landscape planting.
- Whenever variable elements are used in a planting unit, emphasis is created. The designer's job is to place greater emphasis where it is warranted.
- Good balance may be either symmetrical or asymmetrical. Balance must exist not only from side to side, but also from foreground to background of the view.

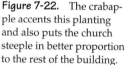

Figure 7-22. The crabapple accents this planting and also puts the church steeple in better proportion to the rest of the building.

- As planting units are designed, all possible viewing angles should be considered. The principles of composition must apply from typical viewing points as well as when moving through the landscape.
- A point of emphasis in a planting unit is often called a focal point. It may be created by means of an accent plant, a specimen plant serving as an accent plant, a hard element, or a landscape embellishment.

- To control a landscape design, each unit must be designed within itself, since the viewer is incapable of viewing the whole, but units must also relate favorably to one another to tie the landscape together.
- Trying design ideas simultaneously in elevational view and plan view is a good way for the designer to form accurate mental images. Plants should be represented at mature size.
- Individual plants may have qualities that make them suitable for accenting, massing, or as specimen plants.
- Designing in elevational and plan view simultaneously, without considering individual plant varieties, results in the building of a set of plant specifications without prejudice towards favorite varieties.

REVIEW QUESTIONS

1. What are the three physical properties of plants that are of concern to landscape designers?
2. How is color produced in plants?
3. What does "unity" in landscape design mean?
4. What six ingredients influence the feeling of unity in landscape design?
5. What does variety do in the landscape?
6. Differentiate between *symmetrical* and *asymmetrical* balance.
7. What is the difference between *relative* and *absolute* scale?
8. Differentiate between suitable *specimen* plants and *massing* plants.
9. Why is it good to plan a landscape in both *plan* view and *elevational* view?

PRACTICAL TIP FROM A PRACTICING DESIGNER

The practice of "doodling" plant forms while designing planting units can be helpful in a couple of ways. First, it helps you visualize in vertical plant forms by allowing the vision of the "silhouette" formed by a group of plants in various arrangements. Second, it enables you to practice drawing plant forms—developing an all-important sketching ability, which can be applied to elevational views or perspectives that are generally enlightening for clients (see Chapter 8).

Chapter 8

PLANTINGS AND ARCHITECTURE

In this chapter you will learn about architecture and how it is affected by landscaping features. You will see how to use trees for enframement, to mask awkward architectural features, and as backgrounding. You will also learn how to make elevational and isometric drawings.

Buildings do not blend easily into the natural landscape. While most natural terrain is rolling and predominantly horizontal, buildings are necessarily made up of sharp angles and straight lines. It is true that the architecture can be designed to suit its surroundings better. On a wooded lot, for example, an architect might choose rustic materials, like heavy shake shingles, rough wood siding, or a rock veneer, using rock from the site to make the house seem more a part of its surroundings. The exterior lines of a house can help adapt it to its surroundings, also. An A-frame house, with its sharp, pyramidal form, looks good in mountainous surroundings because it repeats the jagged mountain peaks and pyramidal forms of native conifers. In another locale, a two-story house might be fitted with a hip roof of a more gentle angle than the normal gable roof, molding the house more snugly into a rolling terrain (see Figure 8-1).

Unfortunately, architectural design considerations are often neglected, particularly in tract houses and small-business buildings. Harmony between architecture and landscape is then left to the landscape designer.

Figure 8-1.   When architecture suits its surroundings, the landscape designer's job is easier. Too often, though, such is not the case.

To design the plantings adjacent to buildings, it is helpful to take photographs for reference, then draw simple elevations on which the landscape can be planned using forms first. One simple method involves taking slides and projecting them on a wall covered with tracing paper. Design ideas can then be tested by drawing them on the tracing paper on which the slide is projected. This method allows the designer to keep all architectural color and textural contrasts in mind as design concepts are formed. The drawing of elevations is quicker, though, unless one is prepared to process slides immediately.

ELEVATIONS OF ARCHITECTURE

To draw elevational views of a freestanding landscape wall, as discussed in the previous chapter, one starts with a horizontal line representing the scaled distance the unit will cover. However, when architectural features already exist in the background, the elevation must include these features before design can begin.

To draw an elevational view of a building it is first necessary to plot exact measurements of the building's face in plan view (see Figure 8-2). The measurements of all windows, doors, siding changes, and other pertinent features should be noted. Above the plan view, a horizontal line is then drawn, representing the base from which all vertical lines on the building will originate. This line is the same length as the plan-view section of building wall, and it parallels the plan-view wall.

Next, perpendicular lines are drawn upward from the plan view at the juncture of each major change shown on it. For instance, where a window is shown on the plan view, a vertical line is extended upwards from the plan view, through and beyond the horizontal base line of the elevation. Similar lines are extended upwards at each corner of the building, wherever there are door margins, at each change in siding material, and so forth. These lines mark the vertical positioning of those elements on the elevational view at the same scale used on the plan view.

Using the same scale as the plan view, the height of each major vertical element marked by the lines is then measured from the horizontal base line. If a window is 4' high and its base some 3' off the ground, these measurements are scaled out on the elevational drawings, and horizontal lines are rendered, framing the complete window. In the same way, the rooflines, tops of doors, steps on porches, and roof peak are measured. When these measurements are completed, the building is completely outlined.

With the major outline of a building elevation completed, the designer can study the building a bit before textural details are drawn in. At this stage, the dominant lines of the architecture become more evident. Be they primarily horizontal, vertical, or pyramidal, these lines of dominance should be reflected in the planting design. By repeating the dominant architectural lines in the planting design, the architecture and the landscaping complement and strengthen one another (see Figure 8-3).

3rd STEP — FILL IN DETAILS TO FINISH ELEVATION.

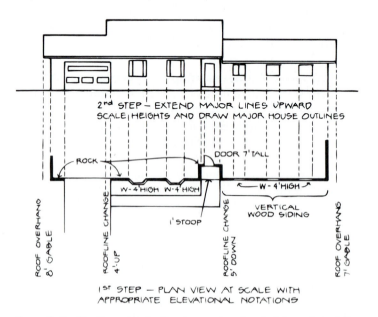

2nd STEP — EXTEND MAJOR LINES UPWARD
SCALE HEIGHTS AND DRAW MAJOR HOUSE OUTLINES

ROCK

DOOR 7' TALL

W-4'HIGH W-4 HIGH

W - 4'HIGH

I' STOOP

VERTICAL
WOOD SIDING

ROOF OVERHANG
8' GABLE

ROOFLINE CHANGE
4'-UP

ROOFLINE CHANGE
5' DOWN

ROOF OVERHANG
7' GABLE

1st STEP — PLAN VIEW AT SCALE WITH
APPROPRIATE ELEVATIONAL NOTATIONS

Figure 8-2.   The three steps in drawing an elevational picture of a building.

Now, having determined the dominant lines in the architecture, the designer can complete the elevational drawing of the building by drawing in textural
features. The roofing pattern, siding patterns, window trim, and any other trim
features on the building should be indicated. Photographs are most helpful at
this stage if the designer is working away from the site.

BALANCING STRUCTURAL AND PLANT MASSES

When all textural and trim elements have been added, further study of the elevation
by the designer might reveal that the building is made up of various masses. These
structural masses may be caused by variable visual weights of siding or trim elements. They may also be caused by vertical lines separating one part of the building
from another, changes in height of building structure, or forward extension of one
part of the building. Garage doors usually segment one portion of the normal house
from other parts because of their heavy visual weight (see Figure 8-4).

Figure 8-3.   The low berm with horizontal blue chip junipers just behind accent the horizontal line of the eave, while the rounded form of the redbuds emulates the arched entry roof, also accenting the entry to the house.

As the number and relative proportions of these structural masses become apparent, the designer can begin to form two-dimensional planting elevations against the building elevation. Better proportion is gained between plantings and architecture by *reversing* the structural masses found in the architecture in the planting masses that are seen in front of the building* (see Figure 8-5). If the structural mass of architecture on the left-hand side of the building's elevation is box-like, while at the other extreme the mass is more horizontal, the landscape design will place a horizontal planting at the boxlike end of the building and a boxlike planting at the horizontal end of the building. The same reversal of structural mass can occur at either side of an entryway door. Overall balance and proportion are facilitated by following this general rule. Once more, it is better that the designer

Figure 8-4.   Identification of the distinct structural masses of a building.

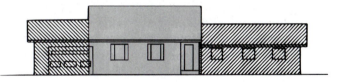

*Nelson, William R., *Landscaping Your Home*, Urbana, IL: University of Illinois, 1975.

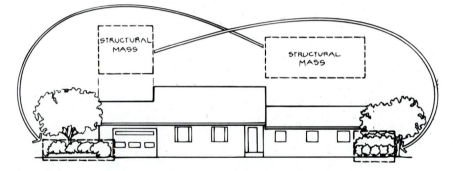

Figure 8-5. When the structural masses found at each extreme of a building are reversed in the landscape, the building and landscape are better balanced.

be concerned only with abstract outlines or general plant silhouettes at this point, not locking the design into specific varieties until all factors have been considered.

As a general rule, the shrub plantings at each corner of a house should not extend higher than two-thirds of the distance from the ground to the eaveline on the house. If a low horizontal mass is indicated, these corner plantings may be lower. Although the plantings seen in conjunction with the front of a building (often called foundation plantings) always appear to be planted immediately in front of the wall, they need not be. Even when planted in islands separated from the building by a strip of lawn, they still appear immediately in front of the building in an elevational drawing. The designer should always consider the view in depth perspective, however.

ENFRAMEMENT

Buildings look best when framed by corner plantings. Although the shrub plantings on each corner become a part of that frame, it is trees that really perform the framing function. Trees placed in front or to the sides of corner shrub plantings are not subject to the two-thirds rule. In fact, to do an adequate job of framing, the trees must be at least as high as the building, though, for good proportion, not much higher. Trees at the corners of a house will minimize its height if they are too large; they will make the house seem insignificant if they are too small. If well proportioned, they set the house in a frame, snugging it into the landscape.

The placement of trees for enframement depends on the predominant viewing angles at which the house is seen. Passersby seldom view a house from the head-on view depicted in an elevational drawing. Instead, as drivers or pedestrians move past a house, they view predominantly toward their front, so they see the building at an angle to the right or left, depending on their line of approach. Visitors also are afforded these angular views as they arrive, but they are treated to a more head-on view as they enter through the drive or front walkway.

Enframement trees should be situated so all three of these predominant angles of view are accommodated, then, unless only one or two such angles exist (see Figure 8-6). Sometimes only one angle exists—for instance, if a house is situated at the end of a cul-de-sac.

In addition to snugging the house onto the lot (see Figure 8-7), enframement trees can soften harsh lines in architecture by masking them. They contribute to the balance and proportion of house and landscape together, often making the house seem larger because the sharp lines at the ends of the building cannot be readily seen and the viewer's mind can imagine that the walls actually extend further.

FOCAL POINTS

Several features may compete for attention on a building. Windows, garage doors, and trim elements all demand attention, as do the various types of siding, paints, and attached lighting. It is necessary to use the landscaping on the front

Figure 8-6. When positioning trees to enframe the front view of a house, all possible angles of view must be considered.

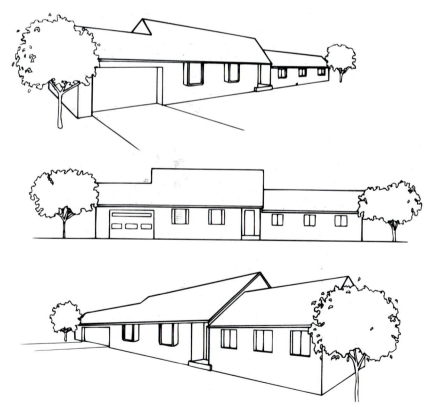

Figure 8-7. Enframement trees snug the house comfortably into the lot.

of a building to help the viewer differentiate among features, drawing his or her attention to the most important area. In most residential building landscapes, that primary attention is best guided toward the front entryway. Even in cases where the front of a building is concealed from public view, the entryway is normally accented so that visitors may discover it and be led into the building easily.

Since the building features mentioned already command much attention, designed plantings should only accent those areas that warrant further scrutiny. Do not frame windows with plantings—they are already framed. Do not place strong accent plants next to a trim element with a strong visual attraction unless there is a reason for people to jerk their heads quickly about in order to focus on that area. Generally, the landscaping should flow in a steady sequence toward the area where a focal point is desired, which is usually the entryway.

To achieve the proper focus of attention in a front foundation planting, an approach called *funneling* is often used (see Figure 8-8). From corner plantings extending up to two-thirds of the distance from ground to eaves, the plantings along a foundation gradually decline in height until, near the doorway, plantings are less than one-third of the height from ground to eaves. This declining silhouette of plantings then "funnels" the viewer's attention toward the doorway. At the doorway itself, one plant may rise higher suddenly, providing the needed variety for accent. Color and texture can also be altered to place more emphasis gradually at the doorway, but it is best that all three physical qualities of the plants not be altered at once.

It is not necessary for plantings to be stair-stepped to achieve the funnel effect. Nor is it necessary for all of the foundation to be covered by plantings. If the siding on a building is pleasant-looking, extending all the way to the ground, plants may be unnecessary in transition zones between corners and doorway. It

Figure 8-8. The funnel approach is a method of directing the viewer's attention to a front entryway by arranging for the heights of the plants to decline gradually from the corners toward the doorway.

is the general sequence of decreasing heights in foundation plantings that provides the funnel effect for emphasis.

The funnel effect is not the only way to spotlight an entryway. At other times, it might be best to rely strictly on the strong emphasis provided by variation in plant texture, color, or form to create a focal point. Corner plantings and other foundation plantings can be maintained at lower levels of visual weight. A strong bed formation leading to a climax by the front doorway often will suffice to turn maximum attention to that point. Sculpture, boulders, driftwood, and other nonliving landscape embellishments can also be used to draw the eyes to the appropriate place.

BACKGROUND

The trees planned for a backyard landscape eventually become tall enough to show above the roofline of a building, becoming a part of the front landscape as well (see Figure 8-9). This background is an essential part of the incorporation of building and land into one unit. It is also a factor to be considered in balancing the composition of landscape and building.

The trees that provide background usually function to provide shade, wind protection, or screening elements in the backyard. Because those functions require specific locations, it might not be possible to locate the trees for optimum backgrounding effect. The designer must consider all of the trees designed for backyard functions that will eventually become part of the foreground and make

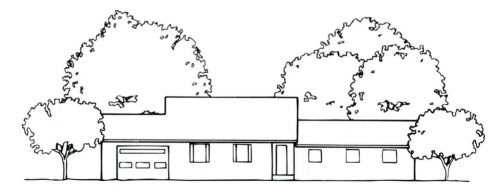

Figure 8-9. Though backyard trees usually serve for shade, wind protection, screening, and so forth, the designer must remember that these trees ultimately become tall enough to background the front view of the house. That background, therefore, must be carefully balanced.

adjustments for proper balance. The trees in the background may be balanced by other trees in either the backyard or the front yard and may have no other purpose than to provide visual balance. Of course, this balance need not be symmetrical.

TREES FOR MASKING

Besides not blending well with natural surroundings, the sharp angles and lines in architecture often do not blend well within their own composition. The transition of a roofline from one segment to another may be awkward, or architectural masses may seem too separated and disjointed. Trees can be used to mask these awkward lines, creating a better overall appearance (see Figure 8-10). Careful positioning of a tree so that its canopy ultimately hides the building's awkward lines from view may be accomplished without disturbing the rest of the landscape. A large shade tree works well for many of these purposes, especially when the masking is for a roofline feature and the lower branches may be trimmed up high enough so only the tree's trunk is in the viewing range of lower landscaping elements.

BERMS AND ARCHITECTURE

Berms have already been discussed as a means of providing visual screening, wind protection, noise screening, and additional interest to the open landscape. They can also be utilized effectively at times to help tie architecture and land together, but they must be used carefully. Remember, to be effective berms must be constructed in good proportion relative to their surroundings. They must look as if they are part of a naturally rolling terrain. Any artificiality in appearance will distract from the rest of the landscape.

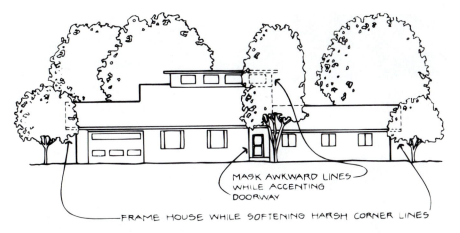

MASK AWKWARD LINES
WHILE ACCENTING
DOORWAY

FRAME HOUSE WHILE SOFTENING HARSH CORNER LINES

Figure 8-10. In addition to their other duties, trees can be used to mask architectural awkwardness.

Berms can be used to transform a flat property in the midst of a rolling area into that same type of undulating plane. The effect will be to make the property seem larger because the surrounding land will seem to be a part of it.

Remember that berms can generate a lot of attention by themselves. They should not be placed where attention is unwarranted if they are to have a strong visual appearance. On the other hand, if the berms seem a part of the natural terrain, they will not stimulate undue emphasis. Drainage and appropriate maintenance considerations always must accompany berm design.

TEXTURE AND ARCHITECTURE

Architecture has its own textures. Rough-sawn woods show a coarser texture than do finely milled woods. Brick is finer than most rock veneers. Painted siding is usually finer in textural appearance than is a stained or natural wood surface. Within each building, then, is a textural range to be considered as the landscape is designed.

The plantings adjacent to buildings should complement the textural range of building materials rather than compete with them for attention. Placing extremely fine-textured plantings in front of a coarse rubble-rock wall, for example, causes strong contrast. Unless sparingly used to create a focal point, the landscaping will constantly battle the architecture for attention (see Figure 8-11).

Fences, walls, shade structures, patios, decks, and other structural elements in the landscape all have textures to be blended into the design. These textures are present in the materials used, and they may be affected by the construction patterns.

Figure 8-11. When plants stand in front of a building wall, the textures of both wall and plant become more evident.

Colors and Architecture

The colors used in planting units can magnify some of the colors in the architecture (see Figure 8-12). For example, brick sidings are often multicolored. A careful designer can pick out the colors best suited to that particular building, then accent those colors in the landscape. If the best colors in a particular brick are deemed to be in the blue-gray range, then plantings of primarily blue-gray foliage might be used to accent and strengthen that hue. A house with pale green or yellow siding might best be enhanced by plantings found in the yellow-green to green range.

While colors can be used to draw attention to a focal point, those colors should never clash. Bright green foliage commands attention when placed next to a yellow house, and so does a bright red foliage. But, while the green foliage complements the yellow, the red might look gaudy. Colors should not be contrasted dramatically where attention is not desired, and a contrast need not

Figure 8-12. The white in the birch trunks brings out the white in the bricks on this house, helping to blend the landscape and architecture.

be dramatic to work. Subtle contrasts are dramatic in themselves if color is tightly controlled throughout the rest of the plantings in the immediate area. Subtlety of color combinations contributes to simplicity in the landscape. Remember—simplicity breeds elegance.

VISUAL INTEREST: ARCHITECTURE OR PLANTINGS?

A correlation exists between the amount of visual interest present in the building architecture and the amount required of the landscaping. Simply stated, the more visual weight contained in the architecture, the less visual weight is required of the landscaping (see Figure 8-13). Conversely, simple architecture, with little trim, requires heavier visual weight in the landscaping. Additional color, texture, and form variation is then in order.

Figure 8-13.   Restraint is often essential to good landscape designing. In these two photos, the architecture is visually strong and well accented by existing trees that were saved from construction damage. It was only necessary to provide ground surfacing; additional elements only would have cluttered the landscapes.

Figure 8-14. Two essential nonliving ingredients, a fence and a walk, are well incorporated into this landscape. While the walk is open and useful, the plantings make it less obvious, incorporating it into the total picture, including the house.

An increase in the number of nonliving elements in the landscape, such as walls, fences, and embellishments, reduces the need for visual contrast in the plantings. A delicate balance must exist, for if great variety is present in nonliving as well as living elements, confusion reigns (see Figure 8-14).

FINAL POINTS: DESIGNING PLANTINGS WITH ARCHITECTURE

By working with planting design and architectural elements in elevational view, the designer can combine forms very graphically. Colors and textures must be visualized in the designer's mind to a large extent. Later, the elevational view can be transferred to a plan view as ground patterns are determined.

It is important to recall that an elevational view is static. All elements are seen head-on and do not represent the way they would appear to someone moving through an area. Since people do move past and through the landscape, though, all possible angles of view must be considered.

Unless one is adept at sketching views in perspective, it is difficult to draw exact imitations of a planting unit from various angles. Depth is always lacking in elevations, but it is possible to use elevations to represent angular views of a planting unit by drawing them in *isometric* form (see Figure 8-15). To draw an

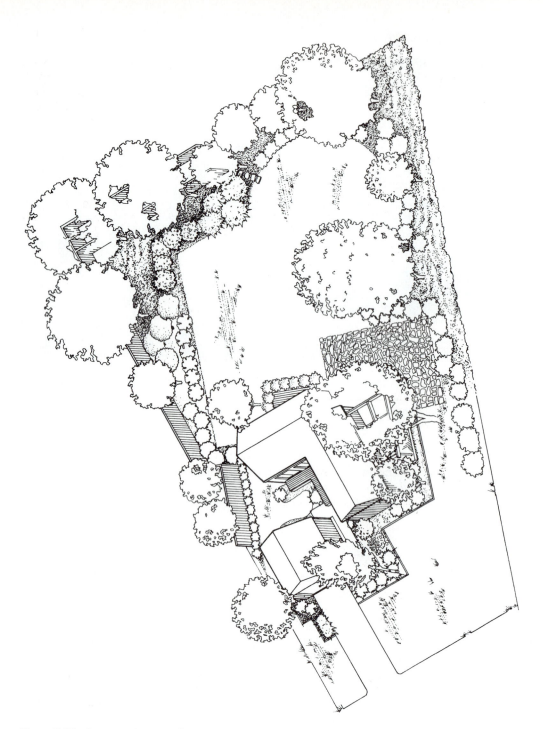

Figure 8-15. Isometric drawings, like the one shown here of the plan view in Figure 1-8, are really elevations without perspective. They are made by turning the plan view at a 30° angle on the drawing board, overlaying the plan view with tracing paper, and drawing elevational views of all components at the same scale as the plan view.

isometric elevation of a planting unit, the designer places a plan-view drawing in the drawing board at a 30° angle, overlaying that plan view with a sheet of tracing paper. Then, as all features on the plan view are measured upwards vertically at the same scale as in the plan view, the plants and other features will appear as they would from an angle, but in elevation form. The correct sizes and forms will be represented, although they will still lack depth perspective.

Isometric drawings, like regular elevational drawings, are often useful in communicating design concepts to property owners. The owners, more than anyone, are likely to have trouble visualizing the landscape from a plan-view representation. In Figures 8-16 through 8-19, elevational views and perspective views are shown.

POINTS TO REMEMBER

- Buildings are not natural elements, so landscaping help is required to tie the buildings to the land.
- Though buildings can be designed to match their natural surroundings, often the landscape designer must work with mismatched architecture and site surroundings.
- Elevational drawings are helpful, as the designer can use them to overlay building features with projected landscape concepts. In elevational view, the designer can determine the dominant lines in the architecture as well as its structural masses.
- Reversing structural masses in planting units helps to balance and strengthen the building-landscape relationship.
- Shrub plantings at the corners of a house should not exceed two-thirds of the distance between the ground and the eaveline of the house.
- Enframement trees help tuck the house into the landscape. They must be placed with all viewing angles in mind. The enframement trees must be proportionate to the size of the building.
- The funnel effect is a means of directing attention to the doorway of a house by a general diminishing in size of foundation plantings to a dissimilar accent plant placed by the door.
- A focal point may be created at an entryway by a sequence of color or texture or both. Embellishments may be used for accent, or ground-pattern lines may direct attention appropriately.
- Background trees usually have other, more critical functions. Trees must often be placed specifically to balance those in the background.
- Trees may be used to mask awkward angles and lines in the building without distorting other landscaping features.
- Berms can successfully make a flat building lot seem more a part of the larger, rolling countryside, effectively making a property seem larger.

- Textural coordination between plant materials, building materials, and other nonliving landscape elements results in better composition.
- Complementary colors in subtle combinations are usually better than stark contrasts that command too much attention.
- The more elaborate the trim elements in the building or other structural parts of the landscape, the simpler the planting design should be, with less contrast in color, texture, and form—and vice versa.
- Isometric views are elevations shown at an angle but without depth perspective. They help show the effects of landscape units at angular views.

REVIEW QUESTIONS

1. What is an elevational view of a building?
2. What is meant by *dominant lines* in architecture?
3. When planning trees for enframement, is only the straight-on view important? Why?
4. What does the term *funneling* mean in landscape design?
5. To be effective, what considerations must be given to berms in the landscape?
6. Why does subtlety of color combinations help make the landscape more elegant?
7. What is an isometric view, and how does it differ from an elevational view? How does it differ from a perspective view?
8. What is a focal point?

PRACTICAL TIP FROM A PRACTICING DESIGNER

When I draw a quick elevational sketch to show proposed landscaping as it will appear in front of a house, I like to extend lines up from a plan view in nonphoto blue lead. Then I draw landscape elements in before I ink in the final lines of the house. By avoiding drawing the house lines that are ultimately covered by landscape elements, I avoid lost time spent with the eraser.

Figure 8-16.   Although not rendered in correct perspective, this modified elevational view provides a sense of the forward extension of the retaining wall and landscape bed.

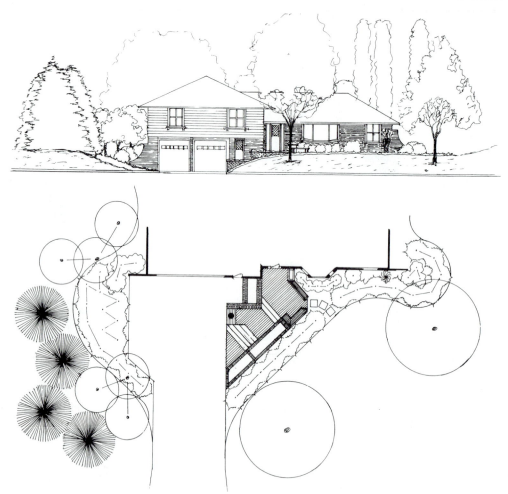

Figure 8-17. Although the elevational view in this drawing is rendered without perspective, it still shows the changes in elevation of the ground from side to side, and front to back.

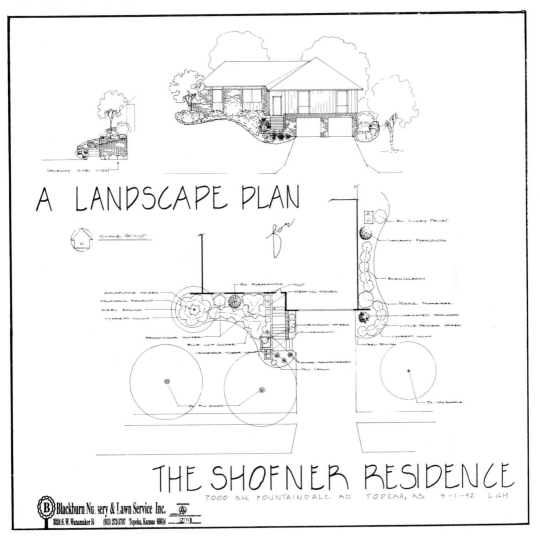

Figure 8-18. On this plan, two elevational views are included to give both primary views into the entrance stairway.

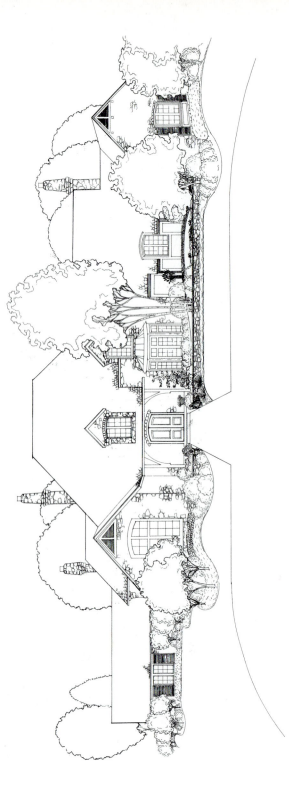

Figure 8-19. Although the perspective in this drawing might not be technically correct, it serves to demonstrate the depth of the court yard behind the short wall, as well as indicating that the left-hand portion of the house is recessed. To speed the rendering, just enough detail was included to show the house's characteristics.

Chapter **9**

MATCHING PLANT MATERIALS TO DESIGN CRITERIA

In this chapter, you will study the many factors affecting plant selection for a landscape design, including hardiness, nomenclature, and sun requirements.

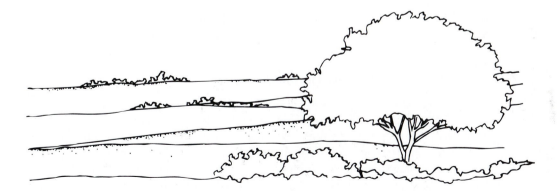

When decisions concerning sizes, forms, colors, and textures are made, and all other design criteria have become available, the selection of specific plant materials become possible. Various selections may come to mind easily enough for the experienced designer, but for the novice this systematic selection process is the result of eliminating varieties on plant lists. By building specifications for plant selection, even inexperienced designers can make prudent choices.

SPECIFICATIONS FOR PLANT SELECTION

The list of criteria for plant selection is as follows:

- Climatic adaptability and hardiness
- Soil requirements
- Sun or shade requirements
- Size and form
- Texture
- Color of foliage
- Growth and development rate
- Insect and disease susceptibility
- Flower and fruit production
- Commercial availability and price
- Special use considerations
- Nomenclature

This list of criteria is long, and it is not essential that it be followed in the order listed. To select the best possible plant for each landscape use, all factors must be considered. This is why it does not work well to design a landscape with specific plant varieties in mind. For those plants to match all criteria would be a stroke of luck. It is fine for the designer to give full consideration to the client's favorite, however, while making sure they match criteria before using them.

Climatic Adaptability and Hardiness

The plant selection process should begin with the plant materials that are climatically adapted to the area. This weeds out those plants that cannot feasibly be grown. It is true enough that a misplaced plant might exist happily for years in a particular area, but if it is not climatically adapted there, it ultimately will be killed or damaged by unfavorable weather. A large void appears in the landscape when a plant with several years' growth suddenly succumbs to climatic factors. Usually, such a void cannot be filled immediately.

Climatic zone maps (see Figure 9-1, for example) indicate adaptability ranges. Numerical ratings on plant lists are keyed to such maps, and they indicate a plant's range of suitability within these zones. Usually, a plant may be used in a warmer zone than that for which it is rated but not in a cooler zone.

While plant hardiness is largely determined by the temperature extremes within these planting zones, other factors include the amount of yearly rain, wind, and snowfall; the frequency of ice storms; and the microclimate of the specific planting area. For example, in dry climates temperature extremes are magnified, so thin-barked trees that dessicate badly may not grow successfully. The exposure of a specific location on a planting site might alter the microclimate enough to place it effectively in another climatic zone. A north- and east-facing slope will be much cooler than the norm for a given area, while a south- and west-facing slope might be a zone warmer. Similarly, the shade of a building or its reflection of light affects climatic adaptability. Weak-wooded, brittle plants should not be considered hardy in areas of high wind, heavy snowfall, or frequent ice storms.

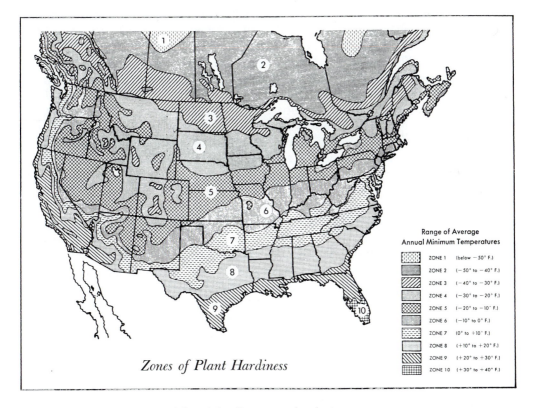

Zones of Plant Hardiness

Range of Average
Annual Minimum Temperatures

ZONE 1   (below −50° F.)
ZONE 2   (−50° to −40° F.)
ZONE 3   (−40° to −30° F.)
ZONE 4   (−30° to −20° F.)
ZONE 5   (−20° to −10° F.)
ZONE 6   (−10° to 0° F.)
ZONE 7   (0° to +10° F.)
ZONE 8   (+10° to +20° F.)
ZONE 9   (+20° to +30° F.)
ZONE 10 (+30° to +40° F.)

Figure 9-1.   The U.S.D.A. map of climatic hardiness zones for plants.

The anticipated longevity of individual plants is also a consideration that can be taken into account along with climatic adaptability. Many of the factors that affect longevity are climatic in nature; they include diseases, insects, and the natural life span of the plant. General life expectancies for particular plants are often included in plant lists or are available from other sources. Keep in mind, again, that it is difficult to replace a plant of some maturity without distorting the landscape.

Soil Requirements

During site analysis, soils on the planting site should have been sampled for analysis and fertility testing. The plant materials used should now reflect those findings.

Factors involved in soil suitability for plant growth include moisture retention capability, pH, and fertility. Soils contain minerals, water, humus, living organisms, and air. It is the combination of these elements that dictates the structure, drainage ability, fertility, and pH—in short, the suitability of the soil for plant growth.

Minerals found in soil are sand, silt, and clay. The amount of each determines the relative compaction of the soil and, hence, its capacity for air and water retention. Humus, which is the organic material present in various stages of decomposition in the soil, determines fertility. The higher the humus level in the soil, the greater will be its population of bacteria, protozoa, and fungi, which are required to cause organic decomposition. The proportions of minerals and humus in a soil determine its air capacity, vital to the soil's capacity for growing healthy plants. Air is essential, and the soil must retain moisture while allowing excess water to escape. The combination of minerals and organic humus is critical.

The pH of a soil indicates its relative acidity or alkalinity. A pH of 7.0 is neutral; the lower values are more acid, and the higher values are more alkaline. When a soil's pH strays far from the neutral range, plant selection is severely limited, unless adjustments are made to bring the pH closer to neutral.

Lime can be added to an acid soil to raise the pH, or sulphur materials can be used to lower it. Organic materials can be supplemented by the addition of peat moss or compost. Sand or other inert materials can be added to loosen a tightly compacted soil with a heavy clay content, although large quantities are usually required. Gypsum has a loosening effect on some soil types. Cultivation alone can loosen a tight soil significantly if performed under appropriate moisture conditions, but it will only compound the problem when the soil is wet. Though limited in usefulness and often expensive, soil amendments can be used to good advantage when the advice of a reputable soils laboratory or other local expert is sought and followed. However, whenever any soil amendment is added, it is imperative that it be thoroughly mixed with the original soil. Layering of amending materials does more harm than good, as the movement of water, air, and nutrients is restricted.

The color of a soil is dictated by its ingredients. A dark soil absorbs more heat than a light-colored soil and, so, will warm more quickly in the spring. High humus content darkens the soil, helping it carry heat more readily through the season. Sandy, light-colored soils will always be cooler, as more of the heat rays are reflected.

Slope of terrain, building shadows, wind channels, and any other effects of the site microclimate can greatly alter the soil temperature. An otherwise tight soil might drain well on a berm, while a sandy soil that usually retains moisture adequately might fail to do so when facing the southwest on a slope.

Sun or Shade Requirements

For optimum health and vigor, different plant varieties need varying combinations of sun and shade each day. Some plants enjoy exposure to the sun's full rays, while others prefer to bask in the protection of partial shade. A few tolerate shade during the entire day.

Placing a shade-loving plant in the full sun can cause injury or even death because it causes a too-high transpiration rate. At the same time, a plant that likes full sun will be sparsely foliated and malformed when planted in a shady location. Winter sun deserves as much thought as summer sun. A sunny winter day promotes transpiration in evergreens, and the lost water cannot be recovered from frozen soil. Winterburning, a browning of the leaves, results. Unless wrapped for protection, thin-barked trees often suffer from winter sun-scalding on the southwest exposure of their trunks. Rapid temperature changes in the bark cause expansion and contraction, resulting in a splitting of the bark.

Color production is affected by the amount of sunlight a plant receives, too. Most bright-colored varieties need sunlight to produce vivid colors. Lacking that exposure to sunlight, they revert to a tinted green cast.

Size and Form

During the abstract design process, tentative decisions about mature sizes and forms were made. However, many varieties can be found throughout the country that can match the size and form specifications for one plant. By eliminating those not climatically suitable, those that will not grow satisfactorily in a site's soil, and those with sun or shade requirements that cannot be met, the list is pared substantially. Now the designer can determine the suitability of those that remain on the list.

There are several special considerations that should be taken into account in selecting plants of a specified size and form. Overhead power lines, roof overhangs, and similar structures must be noted during tree selection. Some individual plants might be favored over others because of unique root structures that would affect nearby sewerage laterals, septic tanks, or open-jointed sewer lines. Some water-loving trees, such as willows, cottonwoods, and poplars, are more likely to become a menace growing near those structures than are the deeper-rooted hardwoods. The mature size and form are always considered, although intermediate shapes may be given thought if they are different from the mature shapes.

Secondary uses for plantings should also be reviewed. Trees used for shading in the backyard ultimately grow high enough to be seen in front, for instance. Although the forms chosen are based primarily on the shading need, auxiliary uses should be reconsidered at this time.

As plant varieties are eliminated throughout the selection steps, it is always possible that the remaining available varieties will not afford the right combinations of sizes and shapes. Adjustments may have to be made to the design of some planting units as a result. But normally, given the vast number of plant varieties that can be grown successfully in each geographic location, such adjustments are unnecessary.

Texture

Plant varieties not eliminated by the selection procedure above are compared for textural match-ups with the specifications made earlier during the abstract design procedures. Because only those conforming to size and shape requirements are left, once again adjustments may have to be made.

Seasonal textural changes must be given some thought. Whereas a narrowleaf evergreen changes little from one season to another, many deciduous plants present a very different texture without leaves. In some cases, texture may not be as important during one season as another. For example, the outdoor living area is often not used to any extent during the winter season, so textural differences are only important as they are seen from a distance at that time.

Viewer proximity, which should have been considered as part of the abstract design process, should be reviewed when plant varieties are chosen. The further away a viewer is, the finer a plant's texture appears—conversely, the closer the plant, the coarser its texture. The effects of light and shadow on texture should also be reconsidered as plants are chosen.

Color of Foliage

From adaptable plants that conform to all other specifications, the colors determined to be best during the abstract design processes are matched. The narrowing list of possible plant selections might be so limiting as to necessitate adjustments again.

It is well to remember that colors change with the seasons and that color changes occur with alteration in the viewing distance or amount of light available to the plants. Flower and fruit colors should not be a factor at this time, since only the foliage is present more of the year.

Growth and Development Rate

People often lack the necessary patience to wait for plants to mature. However, the varieties that grow fastest are often the most brittle and tend to be more susceptible to damage by insects, diseases, and weather factors. The slower, stronger species are often best used. It is also a fact that many of the fastest-growing varieties, particularly among trees, grow to the largest sizes. That fact in itself removes many of them from consideration. Fast-growing varieties of shrubs often become leggy without frequent prunings.

The landscape designer's task is to identify the species that grow and develop well, while also fitting into the framework established by all other plant specifications. In cases where only a slow-growing variety will work, it is the designer's duty to inform the client of that fact. A landscape that grows and develops rapidly but that lacks quality will not suit the client's needs in most cases.

Growth and development rates relate to longevity and hardiness, as discussed earlier. Those that are unsuitable because they are soft and brittle will probably be eliminated at this stage.

Insect and Disease Susceptibility

Although considered as factors in the longevity and hardiness of a plant variety, insect and disease susceptibility are discussed separately here because these pests often affect the plant a lot less than they affect the property owner. At times, insects and diseases infect healthy plants only temporarily, disappearing before any significant damage occurs. In such cases, no control measures are warranted. But the homeowner, not knowing that the plant will survive the onslaught, becomes anxious for the plant's safety at the first sign of attack. Reassured that the plant will be all right, he or she relaxes until the infestation recurs the next year at the same time. Whenever possible, designers should recognize this, choosing less susceptible plants.

Flower and Fruit Production

Flower and fruit production are major assets to landscape design. These elements of beauty contribute seasonal embellishment through sight, smell, and, in some cases, even taste. The timing of their production, duration, colors, textures, and sizes should all weigh in plant selection.

The various flowering times of the plants in a landscape can be arranged to provide continuous bloom during the growing season. Spreading the blooming dates across the growing season provides renewed interest at all times.

If the blooming dates of different varieties coincide, or if fruit is produced on one plant simultaneously with the flowers on another plant, it is best to select complementary or contrasting colors. Careful coordination of colors prevents clashes that can be distasteful or, at least, distracting.

Small, ornamental fruits, while very useful in the landscape, must ultimately drop from the plant. This fruit drop can create quite a maintenance problem. Most of us are all too familiar with the appearance of smashed, unsightly fruit drop and its accompanying odors.

The blooms of plants should also be carefully analyzed for allergy considerations. Many people are allergic to specific tree or shrub pollens. If that information can be gleaned from the analysis of people's needs, those pollens should be avoided.

Commercial Availability and Price

It does little good to specify plant materials that are unavailable for purchase, yet that very thing is done often by landscape designers who do not take the time to research plant availability (see Figure 9-2). It is one thing to say that a particular plant should be available for purchase because it merits use in the landscape, but it is quite another thing to specify one that is unavailable, frustrating property owners and contractors alike in their attempts to secure it. In this regard, many landscape designers who are employed by commercial landscape nurseries have an advantage over independent landscape architects. The majority of the plants they use come from the firm's stock, so availability is easily determined.

Size availability should also be checked. If a plant is available only in sizes that are miniscule in comparison to all else being planted in the landscape, it would probably be poor judgment to use that variety at all. It might take years of growth, if ever, for that smaller plant to catch up with all other varieties planted.

Figure 9-2. The availability of plant materials should be confirmed before plans are finalized, thereby avoiding the embarassment and inconvenience of not being able to obtain the materials to install a landscape.

When plant sizes are selected for the initial plantings, proportionate, mature sizes are often also included. In the funnel approach to a foundation planting, for example, the mature corner plantings are larger than those near the entryway to "funnel" the attention towards that entryway. However, the sizes of both the plantings installed at corners and those near the door are often the same at purchase and initial planting. It is far better in such cases to select initially larger-sized plants for the corners so that a better proportionate representation of the finished product is visible from the beginning. To do this, the designer must make sure the required sizes are available at planting time.

The individual plant prices should be a minor influence compared to other factors involved in plant selection. Only when more than one variety is found to be equally suitable for a specific purpose might price become a factor in design. It is the cumulative price of all the plants in the landscape that is of great importance to the homeowner.

Special-Use Considerations

Plants of one individual species may be asked to perform in several different ways in the landscape. That individual use often dictates which potential plant varieties are selected. For example, a hedge might be required to reach a mature height of some 10' to 12' and still maintain a narrow base. Some of the normal varieties used for hedging might be ruled out in that case because they will not grow to that height or because at that height full foliage at the hedge's base cannot be maintained. Hedging plants may need thorns to promote impenetrability or evergreen foliage for year-round screening.

Special functions, such as tight massing for windbreaks, eliminate some varieties from consideration. Because of some special growth requirements beneath a necessary shade tree, a lacy, open-canopied tree might be indicated. Special effects, like topiary or espaliered plantings, limit variety selection (see Figure 9-3). Specimen plants, which need to stand entirely on their individual merits, must be of varieties that consistently develop strong form and color characteristics. Any number of other special plant functions can create plant-selection criteria.

Nomenclature

When plant selection is completed, it is important to know that the names used to identify plants convey the same information to everyone involved. Common names are often unreliable. To use one example: *Vinca minor* is a groundcover plant used widely in landscape applications. In various locales, it is commonly called Vinca, periwinkle, and myrtle. There is also an annual flower in the genus *Vinca* that goes by the name periwinkle. In various parts of the country, other plants are called myrtle, including the shrub crapemyrtle. Finally, there is another groundcover, larger in size and leaf, with the botanical name *Vinca major*. To identify specifically the low-growing groundcover with small,

Figure 9-3. Sometimes the plants in a landscape require special treatment, such as the topiary pruning performed on this plant.

dark-green leaves and tiny blue violet flowers, one must refer to it as *Vinca minor*. It is the only plant variety in the nomenclature with that particular genus and species name. Sometimes, many cultivars exist within a species. In such cases, for accuracy the name used must include the genus, species, and cultivar name.

The plant-selection criteria enumerated here present a weighty volume of information through which to sort. However, with experience, designers make many decisions simultaneously, sifting out inappropriate selections quickly. Thorough knowledge of climatically adapted plant materials for an area and specific knowledge of various plant uses come with experience. Regardless of the designer's experience level, though, plant choices must be made carefully. To do otherwise might result in the ruin of a carefully conceived design. Making the appropriate choices results in a long-lasting landscape that functions as intended.

PLANT SIZES AT PURCHASE

The landscape designer is often involved in guiding the customer's initial purchase of plants for the landscape. By suggesting appropriate sizes, the designer can partially control the client's initial reaction to the landscaping installation. In many cases, it is this initial reaction that constitutes the client's entire feeling for the landscape. That is because we are a relatively mobile society, and the original purchaser is often not around to see the landscape mature. For that reason, during the time the client is exposed to the immature plantings, those plantings should be as nearly representative of the final product as is possible.

This should not be construed to mean that the largest possible sizes should always be suggested. Instead, the proportions between plants should determine sizes at purchase. Shade trees should be started at larger sizes than ornamental trees. Shrubs that will ultimately reach larger sizes than some other shrubs should be purchased at a larger initial size. Making the immature landscape more nearly imitate the mature landscape is the goal.

Plants are sold primarily in size groups. Shrubs, both evergreen and deciduous, are sold in ranges by inches or by feet. Typical size ranges for shrubs include: 9"–12", 12"–15", 15"–18", 18"–24", 24"–30", and 30"–36", and 2'–3', 3'–4', and 4'–5'. Small trees are sold in ranges of height measured in feet. Typical sizes include: 2'–3', 3'–4', 4'–5', 5'–6', 6'–8', 8'–10', and 10'–12'. After trees reach a certain stage of maturity, though, the caliper (the diameter of the trunk 6" above ground level) becomes a better gauge of their sizes and ages (see Figure 9-4). That is because the spacing at which they are grown in the nursery row determines their height more than does their age or maturity. Trees grown at close spacing in the nursery row will stretch tall more rapidly than those grown at wide spacings. A 15' tree, then, might not be any older than one that is only 10' tall, if the caliper of each is the same. Typically, caliper measurements begin at 1", except for fruit trees, which are usually measured at caliper for even the smaller sizes. Some frequently used caliper measurements include: 1"–1 1/4" cal., 1 1/4"–1 1/2" cal., 1 1/2"–2" cal., 2"–2 1/2" cal., 2 1/2"–3" cal., and so on, in 1/2" increments.

Although trees are always measured in terms of height or by their caliper, shrubs are measured by their dominant pattern of growth. When a shrub variety customarily grows more tall than wide, the measurement given for its size at sales time is an indication of that height. A shrub with predominantly horizontal growth habits will be measured by that width for sale. Container-grown shrubs are sometimes measured by the size of that container. Such a plant might be listed as a 1-gallon, 2-gallon, 3-gallon, 4-gallon, 5-gallon, or 7-gallon plant. When

Figure 9-4.   On larger trees, the caliper of the trunk is a more accurate gauge of size than is the tree's height. These two Rosehill Ash trees, each 2 1/2" in caliper as measured 6" above the ground, were photographed from exactly 25' and were enlarged exactly the same amount when the photos were printed, so an accurate height comparison can be made. The taller of the two was grown in a closely populated nursery row, while the shorter tree with the well-developed branching grew in a more open section of the nursery. The trees are exactly the same age.

size is determined by container volume, though, it is best also to measure the height or spread of the plant, making sure it matches other materials selected.

Roses and some groundcovers are sold by numerical groupings. A number 1 rosebush, for example, is the premium in size and quality; it is followed by number 1 1/2, number 2, number 3, and so forth. Groundcovers use the same numerical grades, if bare-root, but are usually sold by pot size when container-grown. Typical groundcover pot sizes include the 2" pot, 2 1/4" pot, 3" pot, 4" pot, 6" pot, 1-gallon pot, and so forth.

Plant sizes are regulated by the *American Standards for Nursery Stock*, published by the American Association of Nurserymen. Every landscape designer should become familiar with these standards, and give advice to his or her clients that is based upon those standards.

PLANT CONDITIONS AT PURCHASE

Plant condition refers to the way a plant is prepared for sale. Container-grown plantings, for example, are sold in the same container in which they are grown. The abbreviation "pot" refers to any container-grown plant. Plants that are dug from a nursery field may be prepared for sale in several ways. If dug without soil on the roots, they are called *bare-root* plants, abbreviated as *br-rt*. When an earth ball is left around the core root system, they are called *balled* plants.

Balled plants may be wrapped tightly with burlap, in which case they are referred to as *balled and burlapped* (*b&b*), or they may be enclosed in a container and called *field-potted*.

Bare-root plants are sometimes packed into artificially made balls of peat-moss and called *peat-balled*, or they may be enclosed in a moisture-conserving mulch and wrapped in plastic, becoming *packaged* plants.

Knowing these conditions is important to the landscape designer. For most species of plants, there is a preferred condition for transplanting. For some plants, the preferred condition of transplanting changes with the time of year, while others are always best transplanted in one specific condition. Some conditions lend themselves to seasonal planting better than others. For example, since the root system is not disturbed to any extent when a container is removed from a root ball, container plants may be transplanted at most times during the year. Bare-root plants, on the other hand, are practically suited only for dormant spring planting. Balled-and-burlapped plants must be harvested in a fairly dormant condition for greatest success, although they may be held for long periods of time in that condition. A landscape designer's responsibility often extends in aiding the client's choice of appropriate conditions for their plants at planting time.

Landscape designers often work for commercial nurseries, garden stores, or landscape operations that sell plant materials. There is a possibility that a designer will not select appropriate materials simply because his or her firm offers only a limited number of plant varieties. To limit plant selection in this manner is, of course, not fair to a client or to the design. To do a good job of designing is to eliminate any and all prejudices during the selection process. Fortunately, many of these commercial firms carry a wide variety of plant materials that are judged hardy for their region, suitable for the various landscaping requirements, and in demand by customers. Since these firms usually offer a guarantee that their plant materials will live and grow, climatic suitability is automatically screened. Given a broad selection of suitable materials for sale, a commercial designer should never be faced with a conflict between good plant-selection practices and the selling of company-owned plants.

POINTS TO REMEMBER

- Plant selection should always be based on specifications built during the design process and without consideration of personal prejudices.
- Plant selection should begin with only those plants climatically adapted to the area in which they are to be planted.
- Plant hardiness is determined by temperature extremes, yearly precipitation, wind velocities, snowfall amount and type, icestorm frequency, and microclimate of the planting area.
- Using plants that are climatically well suited and long-living prevents unfillable voids from being created by the death of an established plant in the landscape.
- The moisture-retention capabilities, pH, and fertility of a soil determine its capacity for growing healthy plants.
- Soils contain minerals, water, humus, living organisms, and air. It is the combination of these ingredients that determines the soil's suitability for plant growth.
- When soil amendments are made, the amending materials must be mixed with existing soil in a thoroughly homogeneous mixture.
- Optimum sun and shade combinations for plants should always be known so that they can be combined with site features, preventing sun-related plant injuries and bringing out the best in plant growth, form, and color.
- Selection of plants for specified size and form includes consideration of overhead and underground structures, secondary uses of plant form and size, and variation of size and form within a variety.
- Seasonal variations in texture changes with viewer proximity and effects of light and shadow are all part of choosing the right texture.
- The designer must consider the fact that a plant's color changes with the seasons, alteration in viewing distance, and the amount of light available as he or she selects plants for their color contributions to the landscape.

- The selection of plants that grow and develop quickly must be tempered by considerations of wood strength, longevity, and eventual size.
- In addition to selecting plants that are unlikely to be severely injured or killed by disease or insect invasion, consideration should be given to the client's peace of mind. Repeated minor infestations that do not significantly harm the plants might so disturb the property owner as to make their selection unwise.
- Colors and textures in the fruits and blooms are less important than these physical characteristics in the foliage, because leaves are present during more of the year.
- When it is possible to spread a sequence of blooms throughout the season, color clashes are avoided, and blooms have a longer-lasting effect on the landscape.
- Maintenance problems caused by fruit drop should be given plenty of thought.
- Before specifying a plant variety for use in a landscape, the designer should always make sure the plant is commercially available and there are sizes appropriate for the use to be made of it.
- The selection of proportionate sizes makes the initial planting represent the mature landscape in good scale.
- The specific use being made of a plant in the landscape must be considered during its selection. In many cases, the special uses dictate the varieties.
- Whenever there is any doubt about a plant's name, its botanical genus, species, and cultivar name should be used.
- The designer should guide clients to choose appropriate sizes and conditions for planting in the landscape. Initial reactions of clients towards the landscape often shape their lasting feelings about it.
- For a commercial landscape designer to select materials that are unsuitable because they are part of his or her firm's inventory is wrong. The best solution is for a landscape company to carry plants for all purposes in their inventory.

REVIEW QUESTIONS

1. List the twelve plant selection criteria used in landscape design.
2. Name some factors influencing plant hardiness.
3. When soil amendments are made during planting, what is necessary?
4. What are some considerations to be made regarding plant textures during the plant selection process?
5. Name several special-use considerations that might be made during the plant selection process.
6. List some considerations to be made of the size to be specified in plant materials.

PRACTICAL TIP FROM A PRACTICING DESIGNER

One of the more valuable contributions of computer-aided-drafting systems specializing in landscape design are the plant libraries included in such software (see Chapter 15). Many of these allow plants to be grouped by one of several criteria. For example, the plant libraries are organized by hardiness zones, but groups can be selected out by flower color, flowering time, berry color, or many other characteristics. Of course, this can help with the plant selection process.

Chapter 10

COVERING THE GROUND

In this chapter you will learn about the selection of groundcovering materials for the landscape, the arrangements of those materials, and the boundaries between them. Bed edgings will be discussed, as well as plant arrangements, seeding and sodding methods, and living and nonliving groundcovers.

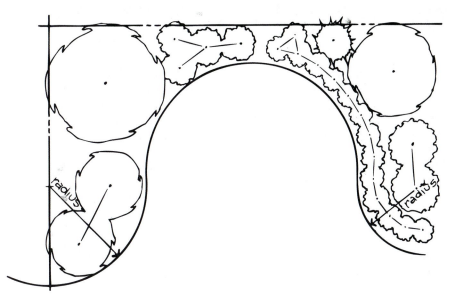

When all plantings have been designed in vertical elevation, whether on paper or in the designer's mind, the final arrangement of plants and other elements in plan view can be completed. It is important to remember at this point that the circles and other symbols used represent real items, and a plan view tells installers exactly where to place landscape elements. It is easy for a designer to become so involved in the on-paper arrangement that he or she forgets plant functions or vertical views. The designer should remember constantly that the plan view only represents positioning for real, three-dimensional items in the landscape. The plan-view representation is seen in its installed form only by those who might hover above the property as in a helicopter. Although it is important for the plan-view drawing on the plan to look attractive, it is more important that it represent those three-dimensional elements that make the landscape work and look attractive.

Plantings can be arranged in straight lines, in triangular or boxlike groups, in staggered lines, or in curved lines. In fact, there are really few rules that guide the physical arrangement of plants. Always consider their mature sizes and arrange the plants so as to accomplish what has already been planned for the planting unit. For a monotype hedge of formal design, the plants will be aligned in straight lines. Informal mass plantings are more likely to be arranged in triangular or boxlike formations (see Figure 10–1).

Spacings for massing plants of the same variety are usually calculated to allow the individual plants to merge as they near mature sizes. Upon merging each loses its individual identity, with the mass itself becoming a part of the planting unit. Accent plants are usually separated from other plants in the unit by more than what normal mature spacing would indicate. In that way, the accent plant never merges with other plantings and retains its individual identity.

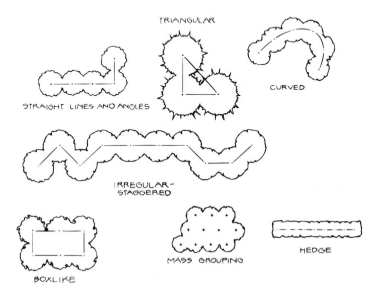

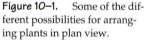

Figure 10–1. Some of the different possibilities for arranging plants in plan view.

Within a mass of identical plants, spacings are sometimes reduced in order to achieve a look of maturity more quickly (see Figure 10–2). For example, the normal spacing for mature massing of a group of Andorra junipers is 5'. But to hasten the appearance of carpetlike maturity and to secure the ground under the plants more quickly, the designer might choose to reduce the spacing between them to 3', causing them to merge in less than half the time. Although this practice does cause greater competition between individual plants for water and nutrients, the reduction in massing time eliminates much maintenance in caring for the spaces between plantings, so the plants' branches and surface roots are disturbed less.

Though plants can be successfully spaced more closely within individual varieties for quicker imitation of their mature appearance, the spacings between different varieties should never be decreased. Mature coverages should always be used between varieties to avoid that dreadful condition—overplanting. Overplanting is inexcusable. To remove healthy plants because some designer either did not have the patience to wait for maturity or wanted to sell more plants is wasteful and often results in a distortion of the landscape at a time when it should look its best.

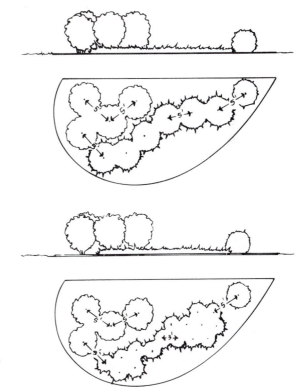

Figure 10–2.   Between plants of the same variety, spacings may be reduced to give the group a mature appearance more quickly; between different plant varieties mature-size spacings should always be maintained and overplanting avoided.

Figure 10–3. A swimming pool has a great effect on the ground-surfacing pattern in a landscape.

As bad as overplanting is, though, underplanting may be worse. To underplant is to neglect landscape needs. Problems will remain unsolved. *Every single element in a landscape design should have a function.* If it does, and if there are no problems left unsolved, and if the total design is unified, the landscape will be neither overplanted nor underplanted.

GROUND PATTERNS

Ground-surface patterns appear in plan view as the variations in the floor of the landscape begin to take shape. Patios, driveways, sidewalks, planting beds, masses of plantings, groundcover beds, and lawn all cause changes in the ground-surface pattern of the landscape. Whenever the surface changes from one type of surface to another, a line is created. As individual planting units are shaped, the ground-surface patterns take form (see Figure 10–3).

Ground patterns are made up of lines and spaces. The spaces are those created in accordance with design-analysis needs. The lines are determined by the designer at this point in the design process. These lines are of great importance because they give definition to the areas, and they invite viewers' eyes to follow them. When such an invitation is made, it is important to make the journey pleasant and rewarding. Additionally, the eye's journey should lead to something worthwhile. By carefully arranging the lines bordering the ground-surface elements, the designer can guide the viewers' eyes in beneficial directions.

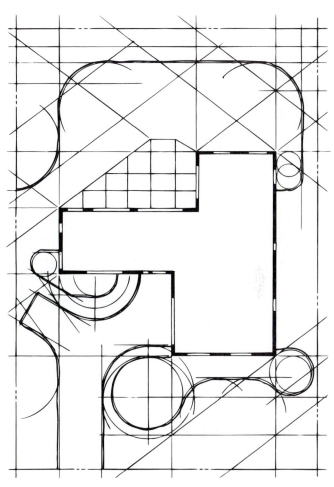

Figure 10–4. By extending all of the lines found in the plan-view diagram of a house and lot, then adding parallel lines in both directions, the entire lot becomes a series of lines in all directions. From that network of lines, bed lines can be chosen for ground-surface patterns that will blend well with house and lot.

Three basic choices for the line patterns in a landscape are straight lines and angles, curves, and arc-and-tangent patterns. Many variations of each pattern are possible, and each has its place.

Straight-line patterns are the easiest of the three to use successfully. Because straight lines repeat the lines in architecture and property boundaries, they are a natural blend. Straight-line patterns can be composed entirely of right angles, making all areas rectangular in configuration, or they can consist of angles of equal degree or angles of variable degrees.

A good way to get a feel for the possible bed patterns in a particular landscape is to extend all of the lines in a plan-view diagram of the property and building (see Figure 10–4). A tracing-paper overlay, positioned over the plan-view diagram of the building and property, allows the designer to diagram these lines without worrying about neatness. At each turn of the building's walls,

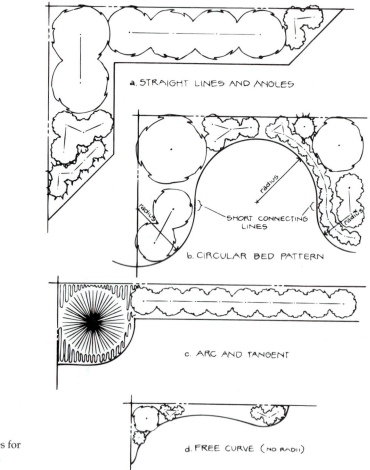

a. STRAIGHT LINES AND ANGLES

radius

SHORT CONNECTING LINES

radius

radius

b. CIRCULAR BED PATTERN

c. ARC AND TANGENT

d. FREE CURVE (NO RADII)

Figure 10–5. Possible choices for lines in the landscape's ground pattern.

juncture of wall with windows or doors, or wall ending, straight lines are extended across the property to a point past the property line. When all lines have been extended, patterns begin to form. Study of the lines will reveal that some appear to become more prominent, in better proportion to the building itself and the surrounding property lines. The bubble diagrams, completed earlier, can be overlaid for comparison, and lines can be selected that fit the architecture and property but also divide the areas as desired. Final straight-line patterns are then developed as a compromise between those that best extend from the architecture, those that separate areas as needed, and those that incorporate designed planting units in good proportion (see Figure 10–5a).

Curved lines are more difficult to work with because they do not naturally blend with the lines in architecture. They do, however, conform to the lines found in nature, so when they are well designed they can be quite effective (see Figure 10–5b). It requires some degree of skill and feeling to establish harmony between the straight lines of architecture and curved lines in the landscape. Still, curved lines are often worthwhile because they flow in relaxing fashion from one point to another. Curves give a sense of informality, a calming casualness to the landscape that straight lines and sharp angles do not.

Curved lines can be arranged in either *circular* or *free-curved* patterns. Circular curves originate from a central point on a radius. They are drawn with a compass or a circle template. A circular curve need not maintain the same radius throughout, though. The radius may be varied, causing the arc of the curve to fluctuate. Free curves are drawn without a radius, alternating the arc more freely. Though free curves are probably more popular, they are commonly done incorrectly.

Curved-line patterns work best when they are developed from the more normal straight-line patterns. Therefore, it is best to begin by extending the lines of the architecture and property boundaries once again, choosing those lines in best proportion to property and buildings as was done for straight-line patterns. Having accomplished that, the designer can then begin to mold those straight lines into pleasing curves where sharp angles once existed. The area shapes are retained in more or less the same size. This type of planning results in strong, firm curves. *Curved lines in the landscape must always be strong and bold.* Busy, squiggly lines that snake hither, thither, and yon are distracting, unable to hold the viewer's interest. Furthermore, they create maintenance problems because of the extra trimming required while mowing.

Arc-and-tangent lines combine the straight lines of architecture with the freedom of curves (see Figure 10–5c). Once more, skill is required of the designer who would use these patterns to make a successful transition from stiff lines to flexible curves. The extension of lines from architecture and property lines again serves as a good starting point. In the final process, some lines and angles are left as they are, while others are bent into pleasing curves. Though free curves can be used (see Figure 10–5d), arc-and-tangent patterns more often include circular curves of consistent radii.

The combination of angles and curves allows for greater contrast within the surfacing pattern, thereby helping to place emphasis at various focal points. Combining the sound practice of repeating architectural lines in the landscape while utilizing the freedom of curves, arc-and-tangent patterns result in a most dramatic surfacing pattern. Caution is in order again, though. The curves must be bold and strong and in good proportion to the lines forming the tangents (see Figure 10–6).

Regardless of how they are constructed, the ground-surface patterns must always be designed with the ground-level view in mind. The way these lines lead the eye through the landscape as the viewer moves through it matters more than the bird's-eye view that is depicted in plan view.

Figure 10–6.   The lines used in the ground-surfacing pattern of a landscape should always be strong, bold, and crisp, like the edge of the groundcover bed shown here.

FLOORING

The floor of an outdoor room is walked on, played on, laid on, and occasionally crawled on by the youngest inhabitants. Water must be allowed to drain over this surface in all places, with drainage concentrated in some areas. As we move about in the outdoor rooms, our direction is influenced by the covering of their floors.

The ground patterns that we see result largely from the mix of groundcoverings selected. As with the carpeting in an interior room, these groundcoverings help set the moods of the outdoor rooms.

Among the choices for covering the ground are lawn grasses, living groundcovers, nonliving groundcovers, and bare soil. Many landscapes incorporate more than one, sometimes utilizing all of these types.

Lawn Grasses

Lawn grasses come to mind first for surfacing the landscape. Grass is often chosen for the greater part of the ground area because it is traditional, but there are other sound reasons for its selection (see Figure 10–7). Some of these are list-ed below:

- Grass provides an ideal play surface for most outdoor games.
- Grass is durable—the most durable of any living groundcover.
- Grass provides a cool surface that is pleasant to walk on and to sit on.
- Grass provides an attractive foreground for plantings and flowers.
- Grass adds spaciousness to an area, helping develop depth of view.
- Grass contributes interesting color blends with some landscape elements while contrasting favorably with others.

Football, baseball, soccer, badminton, croquet, and other such games can be contested on a battlefield of grass, with the lawn returning to its normal serenity shortly afterwards. Grass has an amazing capacity to bounce back.

Because of the water coursing through it, grass is a cool and comfortable surface to walk, sit, or lie on. No other surfacing material has that "barefoot" quality. On cool fall days, the dark-green grass helps retain the warmth of after-noon sunshine.

In the majority of landscapes, expanses of lawn provide a feeling of spa-ciousness, giving both width and depth to our view. The lawn helps provide a feeling of good proportion in a landscape as we walk around in its spaces. The texture of a lawn—coarser in the near view, finer in the longer view—adds per-

Figure 10–7.   For most purposes in the landscape, it is difficult to choose a better surface than well-established lawn grass.

spective to our views in the landscape. The gentle roll of grassy terrain is pleasing to view, regardless of whether the undulations are natural or created by a landscape designer.

The green color of lawn grasses harmonizes well with all other colors in the landscape, adding vividness. A lawn's low, smooth plane leads our eyes easily to other landscaping elements, enhancing other plantings instead of distracting from them as other groundcovers sometimes do.

Although grass is commonly thought to be expensive and difficult to maintain, the reality is that, especially for large expanses of surface, it is probably the most reasonable surface to maintain over a long period of time. It is a matter of comparison. Areas covered by grasses are generally large and subject to heavy traffic and so other types of groundcoverings might require even more maintenance. Grass holds well against erosion, slowing the water flow while cleansing the water as it filters through grass leaves. Lawn maintenance is surely time-consuming, but considering everything, the lawn is well worth it.

Lawn-establishment practices are important to the landscape designer, who often is expected to advise clients. In fact, the lawn is such an important feature in most residential landscapes that prudent landscape designers make sure the client is at least given the information necessary to get a good lawn started. Appropriate maintenance suggestions also help keep the lawn in good condition, so the landscaping will also look good.

Grass can be planted by seeding, sodding, sprigging, or plugging, depending upon the type of grass used. Choosing the appropriate propagation method is part of the task of advising clients. Some grass varieties can be propagated by any of the four methods, but most are more limited. The propagation method available and their individual costs are factors in the selection of the appropriate variety.

Each lawn grass belongs to one of two general groups, the warm-season grasses or the cool-season grasses. *Warm-season* grasses grow well in warm, sunny climates but will not tolerate extremely cold winters. Therefore, the warm-season grasses are primarily grown in the southern portions of the United States. Included in this category are the Bermuda grasses, zoysia, centipedegrass, and St. Augustine. These grasses are generally low-growing and highly resistant to wear, affording good coverage for high-traffic areas.

The *cool-season* grasses include the bluegrasses, tall fescue (including the new turf-type fescues), creeping red fescue, chewings fescue, ryegrasses, and bentgrasses. These grasses are better adapted to the cooler growing seasons in the middle and northern portions of the United States. Cool-season grasses generally grow for a much longer season than warm-season grasses, retaining their green color much of the year in many locales.

All of the turfgrasses mentioned can be propagated by sodding, which is the quickest establishment method since it involves moving turf intact. Often called *instant lawn*, sodding is usually the most expensive method of turf establishment. It also might be the most difficult method for homeowners to attempt on their own, unless plentiful help is available. Sod is a perishable product, so timing is critical in its placement.

With a few notable exceptions, grasses can also be propagated by seed, which is probably the most common method used by homeowners. Seeding is the least expensive propagation method, although it may also be the riskiest, since the bare seedbed is exposed to erosionary elements for a period of time.

Those grasses with aggressive *rhizomes* or *stolons* can be propagated by sprigging or plugging. In ether case, it is the lateral movement of these special-ized stems that generate new roots, stems, and leaves that causes the grass to spread and cover. Plugs are round or square pieces of sod that are transplanted at prescribed spacings and allowed to grow toward one another. Sprigs are pieces of rhizomes or stolons that are planted without soil; given adequate water, they will generate new growth. More establishment time is required for either one of these methods than for seeding or sodding. In certain cases, though, seed is not reliably produced by a grass or is not viable, and sodding may be too expensive. Then, plugging or sprigging becomes a realistic approach. There are also some cases of a superior grass variety being introduced that does not reproduce truly by seed. Then the only way the variety can be propagated so as to retain its superior qualities is by sodding, plugging, or sprigging.

Grass variety selection depends on the climatic zone, microclimate of the site, propagation method, uses to be made of the grass, and its cost. In any case, it is wise to solicit the sound advice of experts in each local area before making a final grass selection. Extension publications and personnel, local seed merchants and landscapers, among others, are good sources of appropriate advice about varieties, propagation methods, and seed or fertilizer rates to use. Broad-based recommendations spanning large geographical areas are of little use, since each area has climatic or other quirks.

Since seeding is so popular, it deserves a few special comments. Though the seed type should be locally recommended, only the highest quality seed should be used. If two or more seed types are to be mixed in a lawn, they should be purchased separately. Mixtures of seeds of unequal size and density are unsatisfactory because the smallest, heaviest seed always settles to the bottom of its container, destroying the mixture. However, two or more varieties of the same grass—for instance, bluegrasses—may be blended without worry about their settling.

The seeding of lawns involves cultivation, fine grading, fertilizing, place-ment of seed, packing, and watering. Essentially, the ground must be cultivated to loosen the soil and provide for the other operations, graded to establish prop-er drainage and a smooth seedbed of equal firmness, and packed to provide the close contact necessary between seed and soil. Given proper attention to all other procedures, germination still will not occur satisfactorily without adequate moisture, which usually must be artificially provided.

There are three rules for proper seed placement. So long as the objectives of these three rules are met, good germination is possible:

Figure 10–8. Good equipment makes lawn-seeding operations more successful.

- The seed must be evenly applied at the correct seeding rate.
- The seed must be covered with soil to the correct depth.
- Soil must be snugly packed against the seed so the soil is in close contact with the seed on all sides.

In whatever manner these three rules are followed, the potential for a good lawn is established, leaving weather and watering practices to determine its fate. The use of appropriate, high-quality equipment facilitates good seeding operations (see Figure 10–8).

Like any other surfacing element, grass will serve best if combined with other types of surfaces. The capacity for developing interesting surface patterns is extremely limited with only one type of surfacing element, which tends to be boring as well.

The selection of ground-surface materials depends largely on the use to be made of each specific area and the appearance desired. As indicated, in play or high-traffic areas grass is hard to beat. In a planting bed, it is usually wise to use another groundcovering between and close to the plantings. The constant mowing and trimming that grass undergoes endangers close plantings, which are constantly being bumped, bruised, and cut by the lawnmower. Grass also saps vital nutrients and water needed for the growth and vigor of landscape plantings. Maintenance time increases with the constant need for trimming around and between plantings. The contrasting height, color, and textures afforded by additional types of groundcovering also create additional interest in the ground-sur-

Figure 10-9. The shorter living groundcovers contrast well with other plant materials and soften the junction of building and ground.

facing patterns of the landscape. Though single trees or groups of widely spaced trees are attractive with grass underneath, it is best to use other types of ground-coverings under massed plantings.

Living Groundcovers

A large number of living groundcovers are available, ranging in size from 4" to 4' in height, widely variable in spread, and suitable for all kinds of soil conditions (see Figures 10-9 and 10-10). Deciduous, broadleaf evergreen, and narrowleaf evergreen foliages are all represented. Many flower, and some produce ornamental fruits. A complete listing of available groundcovers can be found starting on page 403.

Living groundcovers offer many distinct advantages, some of which are following:

- *Natural color and form*—The foliage blends well with other plantings in the beds, and changing seasonal colors and textures add variety.

Figure 10–10.   Taller living groundcovers are efficient in erosion-prone areas and areas where mowing is undesirable.

- *Air-cleaning qualities*—Like other living plants, groundcovers filter the air in our environment.
- *Heat absorption*—Living groundcovers absorb heat instead of reflecting it back into the air. They transpire water back into the air, helping to cool it.
- *The stability of the root system*—Each plant's root system acts to bind the soil. This is particularly important where mowing is not possible and inherent dangers of erosion exist.
- *Contrast in heights*—Unlike most other surfacing materials, groundcovers are available in many heights, aiding the formation of strong surfacing patterns. Masses of groundcovers can also be used to imply enclosure.
- *Catches and holds debris*—While this might be a disadvantage in some cases, it is an advantage when blowing paper and other debris is best held on the property. Commercial applications are most likely here.
- *Provides a wildlife habitat*—Living groundcovers can provide an excellent haven for all types of wildlife, especially those with flowers for bees or fruit for birds and animals.
    Some disadvantages of using living groundcovers are following:
- *Establishment time*—It can take up to several years for small groundcover plants to become established and to cover an area. Intimate appearance and function are not immediately realized.

- *Degree of maintenance*—Although many of these groundcover plants are considered to be relatively low-maintenance items, most require regular watering and weeding, at least. Other maintenance might include pest control, cultivation, and erosion repairs until the root systems are thoroughly established.

- *Wildlife habitat*—This is the flip side of the advantage listed earlier. Groundcovers provide habitats for rodents, snakes, and other animals that property owners might consider undesirable.

- *Accessibility*—Some of the larger living groundcovers are so tall and thick that they are nearly impenetrable. This need not be a disadvantage, providing a careful selection of materials is made for any area requiring access. But regardless of their size, living groundcovers do not provide a good surface for extensive traffic. None of these plants will stand being trampled to any degree.

- *Vining qualities*—Many of the plants used as groundcovers will also vine, which can be a maintenance problem if they are used under trees and shrubs. The vines will continually climb into other plantings, often detracting from their appearance and sometimes hampering their health.

Nonliving Groundcovers

The nonliving groundcovers include a wide variety of either organic or mineral derivation. Organic materials include bark mulches, peanut hulls, cottonseed hulls, and pine needles, to name a few. A multitude of rocks and gravels are derived from mineral sources. Inert manufactured materials made of clay or shale are also included among these nonliving materials.

Nonliving surfacing materials are used extensively in planting beds adjacent to foundations or patios because of their immediate effect and the fact that they will accept a degree of traffic. Because of the latter, those materials serve well to increase effectively the usable area of a patio when the beds surrounding the patio are covered with them.

Most planting beds that are surfaced with rock, bark, or similar materials are bordered with a secure edging material (see Figure 10–11). This helps retain the shape of the bed, preventing the material from escaping the bed's confines. Edging also keeps grass from encroaching on the bed. Commonly used as edgings are redwood and other treated woods; sturdy flat steel, plastic, or PVC-manufactured edgings; bricks; and rock. Lightweight aluminum and other metal edgings are also used, but most fail to hold their form well and will not resist bending underfoot. Concrete edgings are also used, though they are expensive to install. Railroad ties and landscape timbers serve as edgings in many cases.

Beds for these nonliving materials are excavated so that the material is flush with the soil level outside the bed when the bed is complete. Usually, at least a 2″ thickness of the nonliving groundcover material is required. Black plastic film is often used under these materials to prevent unwanted weed and

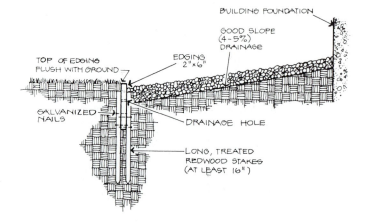

Figure 10-11. Proper edging installation on a nonliving ground-cover bed makes a landscape more impressive and easier to maintain.

grass growth. There is some evidence now that this may not be a good practice, since it also encourages shallow rooting of all plants in the bed. When plastic is used, it must be carefully tucked against all bed edges, for even the tiniest of spaces will allow for unwanted growth, and slits must be cut in the plastic around all plants to allow water to percolate into their root systems.

Landscape fabric, often called *weedmat,* is a porous material used in place of plastic. It is recognized as being better than plastic for plant growth, since its porosity allows penetration of water and air in the root zone. Some users complain, however, that the material also allows root penetration, so seeds can germinate in the mulch layers, sustaining growth by rooting through the fabric.

Preemergent weed control chemicals are often used under mulch, either by themselves or in conjunction with the use of landscape fabric. Several types are available, and one must always follow label directions to the letter.

Like other ground-surfacing materials, nonliving groundcovers offer many unique advantages to suit particular situations (see Figure 10–12). Some of these follow:

- *Immediate results*—With any of these materials, the appearance at installation time is as it will be thereafter. In other instances, as with bark chips, a weathering process must ensue but usually takes place within a short time and can be speeded along by artificially watering the material.

- *Low maintenance*—Without need for watering, fertilizing, or other maintenance practices common to living materials, the maintenance is understandably lower.

Figure 10–13 is a well-edged landscape bed that uses sedum as a living groundcover and shredded hardwood mulch as a nonliving groundcover.

- *Will withstand traffic*—Most of these nonliving materials can be walked on regularly, although some are more comfortable underfoot than others. The softer organic materials and waterworn or otherwise rounded pebbles are most conducive to traffic.

Figure 10–12. A nonliving groundcover, edged with 2" × 6" redwood, mulches these plantings, at the same time contrasting well in color.

- *Reasonable cost*—This does not always hold, but many of these materials are quite reasonable for area coverage, particularly in light of their low maintenance costs over a period of time.
- *Color variety*—These nonliving surfacing materials offer a multitude of color possibilities, many of which are unavailable by other groundcovering means.
- *Textural variety*—Like color, the textural range afforded by nonliving ground-surfacing materials is wide and diversified. Many of these textures are very unlike any of the living materials, creating interesting contrasts.

Unfortunately, there are some disadvantages to using these nonliving surfacing materials as well:

- *Excessive mobility*—Some of the lightweight materials are buoyant, so they can float or blow out of position. Bark chips, for example, will float, and shredded bark mulch will blow when dry. The heavier, denser materials in this group create no such problems.

Figure 10–13. This landscape bed is slightly crowned in the center for visual appeal. Steel edging defines a sharp, crisp edge, and both living and nonliving groundcovers are used, the latter to serve until the living groundcover spreads to completely cover the bed.

- *Missile effect*—The larger, heavier pebbles in this group can be thrown with enough force to cause damage. A wayward or careless youngster might be tempted to use them as a weapon or throw them through windows.
- *Color variety*—Yes, this was listed as an advantage, and it is, but it must be used carefully. The contrasting colors can be misused, creating a gaudy planting bed not in keeping with other landscaping elements.
- *Drainage problems*—This really should not be a disadvantage—and it will not be if beds are carefully designed and installed. But most planting beds are excavated to accommodate nonliving surfacing materials, and unless drainage is a prime consideration, these beds can become holding pools for surface water that ultimately finds its way into basement cracks.

Bare Soil under Plantings

In lieu of other surfacing materials, the ground under plantings is often left bare. Bare soil in a planting bed can be used to good advantage, primarily in the following ways:

- *Good growing medium*—The plants in a planting bed could probably ask for no better surface than cultivated soil underneath. Cultivation ensures good moisture retention and eliminates competition from other plants for water and nutrients. The dark color causes the soil to warm earlier in the spring, extending the growing season a bit.

- *Color contrast*—The dark soil contrasts well with plantings, affording a good appearance in the planting bed.
- *Low cost*—There is no surface that is less expensive.
- *Availability for growing other plants*—Bare soil allows for growing seasonal flowers or other annuals or perennials in the bed, although this is not a recommended practice unless those additional plants are used like a temporary groundcover. Mixing flowers or other plants in among the plants in a planting bed causes confusion, eliminates emphasis on particular features, and generally distorts the desired effects of the planting.

The disadvantages of using cultivated bare soil as a planting-bed surface include:

- *Erosion susceptibility*—Bare soil, especially when cultivated, is more subject to washing or blowing than surfaces that are covered in another manner.
- *Higher maintenance*—Although total maintenance time is not high, a planting bed with a bare soil surface must be cultivated frequently to keep weeds and grass out. The surface does not look good from a textural and color standpoint unless it is freshly cultivated.
- *Mud*—When it is wet, cultivated soil becomes mud. Mud can be a problem, particularly when there are young children in the family.

Ground-surfacing materials are chosen on the basis of colors, textures, usage, cost, aesthetic appeal in combination with other landscaping elements, and availability. During the selection process, the advantages and disadvantages of each should be considered. Often, several types of surfacing materials are used in the same landscape.

The availability of surfacing materials varies geographically. Nonliving ground-surfacing materials are often expensive to move long distances because of their weight, which generates high freight costs. Thorough and continuing research of the area in which a landscape designer works is necessary to keep abreast of availability and costs.

POINTS TO REMEMBER

- Plants may be arranged in a straight line, triangular, boxlike, or almost any configuration so long as they serve the purposes intended.
- For massing, plant spacings should allow plants to merge as they near maturity, losing their individual identities.

- Within a group of plants of the same variety, spacings can be reduced considerably to reduce the massing time, but to do so with plants of different varieties constitutes overplanting.
- Ground-surface patterns in the landscape are formed by such hard surfaces as patios, driveways, and sidewalks, combined with planting beds, masses of plantings, groundcover beds, and lawn surfaces.
- Lines that form the definition of ground spaces invite the viewer's eyes to follow them, so they should lead to something consequential.
- The three choices for lines in a landscape are straight lines and angles, curves, and arcs and tangents.
- Straight lines most easily blend with architecture. Curves most naturally blend with the natural landscape. Arcs and tangents combine elements of both.
- Whenever curved lines are used, they must be strong and bold.
- Grass is used more than any other surfacing material because it is ideal for play, for temperature control, as a foreground to a view, as a contrast to other materials, and because it is durable.
- Giving advice about lawn-establishment and maintenance procedures often falls within the realm of a landscape designer's duties.
- Living groundcovers offer multiple sizes, colors, and foliage types. They help cool an area, cleanse the air, provide a habitat for desirable wildlife, and stabilize slopes that cannot be mowed.
- Living groundcovers sometimes vine into other plants, prevent good accessibility by foot into some areas, and take considerable time to become established. Furthermore, they must be weeded and watered while they become established.
- Nonliving groundcovers include all rocks, barks, and so forth. They add various colors and textures to the landscape, require little maintenance, and become established immediately.
- While lightweight nonliving groundcovers might blow or wash out, the heavier ones can be thrown at people or windows, doing damage. The bright colors of some of these materials must be carefully used, and drainage must always be thoroughly planned.
- Bare soil provides a great growth medium for the plants in a bed and also provides a medium for growing seasonal plants. It is the least expensive ground surface, and it provides good color contrast with plantings.
- Bare soil surfaces are most susceptible to erosion, get muddy when wet, and must be kept cultivated to look good.
- The availability and cost of ground-surfacing materials vary considerably with geographical location.

REVIEW QUESTIONS

1. What constitutes the ground-surface pattern in the landscape?
2. What are the three basic line patterns that can be used in the landscape?
3. What is the difference between *circular* and *free-curve* patterns?
4. Why is lawn grass usually chosen for surfacing the bulk of the landscape ground area?
5. Name and describe four lawn planting methods.
6. List at least five advantages of using living groundcovers (besides grass).
7. Give at least five advantages of using nonliving groundcovers as a ground-surfacing agent.

PRACTICAL TIP FROM A PRACTICING DESIGNER

When I arrange a group of plants of the same variety on a plan, I like to use a circle template. Choosing a circle of a diameter appropriate for the ultimate spread of the plant, I draw light circles, just overlapping, with either nonphoto lead or pencil. Then, when I've achieved the arrangement I want, I ink in the outline of the mass with the appropriate symbol.

Chapter **11**

EMBELLISHMENTS

In this chapter you will learn about embellishments—those items used in the landscape that give it a special flavor. Embellishments can include such things as sculptures, boulders, flowers, or landscape lighting, and their proper use can greatly contribute to a landscape's individuality.

The landscape can be greatly enhanced by the addition of elements that appeal strongly to our senses. The elements are called "embellishments." *Landscape embellishments* include flowers, specially treated or unusual types of plants, ornamental structures, sculptures and statuaries, water features, dramatic lighting, musical devices, and other art and collected materials. Most of these command attention by strong visual attraction, but they can appeal to our senses of hearing and smell as well.

Individual tastes weigh heavily in the selection of these embellishments. They add dimension and individuality to the landscape but they must not be overused or a hodge-podge results. Although embellishments are considered here towards the end of the design process, sometimes the development of a planting unit begins with an embellishment serving as the focal point. Many times the use of an embellishment arises from the analysis of people's needs, when the designer finds the property owner wants to use a special object.

FLOWERS

Flowers are included as embellishments because their colors are so visually strong that they must be very carefully used in the landscape. Since flowers are so seasonal, they are not to be considered permanent landscape fixtures. Annuals, perennials, and roses are all included under the umbrella heading of "flowers."

Well-designed flower borders are beautiful. It is no mystery why people love flowers so much. Brilliant, cheerful colors, rich fragrances, and the option of cutting them for indoor use make flowers a tempting addition to the landscape. But all too often, flowers are misused. When wrongly placed, they distract from other landscape elements, negating the entire appearance. The development of a constantly picturesque flower border is very demanding from both a design and a maintenance standpoint.

Flowers should never be used where intense attention is not warranted (see Figure 11–1). For example, the sprinkling of flowers among shrubs in a foundation planting is an incorrect and overused practice. Because the flowers are separated by shrubs, our eyes dart back and forth, never settling on any one grouping. The sequence intended in the shrub groupings is destroyed wherever it is interrupted by the flowers. The common practice of grouping flowers at the front corners of a house is usually not desirable either, unless it is the designer's intent to draw attention to those corners. Normally, the focus should be near the front entrance to a house, where such attention is warranted. Small, well-organized color masses in that location can enhance the foundation plantings rather than competing with them for attention.

Flower plantings always look best if massed in color groups, using variable sizes of complementary or contrasting colors. Bands or blocks of the same colors can be "staged" from front to back, with the tallest varieties in back. This layer-

Figure 11–1. The flowers in this picture are misused. because they attract attention at the wrong places, confusing the emphasis in the landscaping.

ing effect allows all colors to be seen at once. The same principles that govern the design of ornamental planting units also apply to flower-border design except that color must necessarily be given more attention.

Flowers show up best in the landscape when they are provided with a background. The green foliage of a mass shrub planting serves as excellent background for flowers, making the flower colors more vivid. The flowers become part of the mass-planting unit and are not missed so badly when they are out of season. Fences or walls can also provide interesting contrasts as background for flower borders, but without shrub plantings the absence of the flowers in the off-season is more pronounced. Flower borders work best on the incurve or the inside angle of planting beds, backed up by something less influenced by the season.

Flowers are a high-maintenance addition to the landscape. They should never be utilized where maintenance cannot or will not be provided. Flowers that are poorly maintained look worse than no flowers at all.

NONESSENTIAL CONSTRUCTION FEATURES

This broad category of garden garnishments includes anything built to beautify the landscape that does not serve an environmental function (see Figure 11–2). Included in this category are such things as ornamental walls, raised planters, seats and benches, ornamental fences, and decorative flower boxes and planters.

Figure 11–2.   The raised brick planter in this picture is a nonessential embellishment because the brick wall could exist without it. But the blue rug junipers draping over the planter wall contribute to a softening of the wall, minimizing its height, while mixing soft materials into an area otherwise dominated by hard materials.

Notice that many of these items are useful but do not function as the walls, ceiling, or floor of the landscape.

These structures contribute by adding textures, colors, and forms, especially in consideration of their many individual design possibilities. These features can often be combined. A raised planter 16" to 18" tall, for example, can double as a bench. An ornamental wall may also be used as part of a raised planter.

Unlike flowers, constructed embellishments need not be so visually demanding as always to create emphasis. A decorative rail fence, for example, can lead the eye to a point of emphasis, much as does the clean line on the edge of a planting bed, only with vertical as well as horizontal dimensions.

Ornamental fence panels provide interest in a narrow space, add variety in materials and construction, and serve as an excellent backdrop for special plant features. Rail fences add ornamentation, with the added advantage that elements on each side of the fence can be seen. In this case, the plant materials provide background for the fence, highlighting the interesting lines in the fence itself. Rustic split-rail fences work well in a naturalistic landscape, while formal rail fences should be reserved for more formal landscaping.

Raised planters combine the visual strengths of their construction with the plant materials that are grown in them. The change in height adds interest on a flat space through abrupt vertical emphasis. A raised planter can help to set off a

Figure 11–3. Statuary and sculpture work well in the landscape as long as proper scale is maintained and formality is not mixed with informality.

special plant by "putting it on a pedestal," but such a plant must be worth the attention created.

Flower boxes are little used with contemporary architecture, but when a window or a series of windows is too tall in proportion to their width, flower boxes might be used to correct the imbalance by extending the width a bit. Flower boxes can also be used to line the edges of a concrete landing or a large, bland concrete patio. Combining colorful blooms and construction materials in the planter box with the concrete itself creates a more interesting appearance.

Seats and benches supplement the furniture used on patios and decks and occupy little space. These are especially useful for parties or larger-than-normal gatherings, and many designs are possible. Wood, metal, or plastic construction patterns and styles are available, and colorful pads can be added for comfort and beauty.

SCULPTURE AND STATUARY

The historic use of various types of sculpture, statuary, and other art forms as landscape embellishments is well documented. Though more frequently used in the formal gardens of earlier times, they continue to decorate contemporary gardens. They are not always easy to use correctly because of their strong visual interest and the difficulty encountered in bringing them into scale with other landscaping elements. Many of the commonly used concrete statues are extremely small when compared to their surroundings in the landscape. Skillful design is required to integrate them at the right proportions (see Figure 11–3).

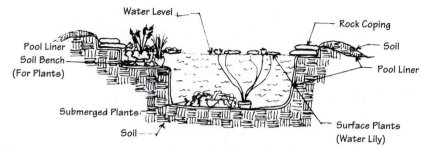

Figure 11–4. A side view of a flexible liner pool, showing the rock coping and a soil bench to hold plants.

The very nature of sculpture and statuary demands that they become focal points. Therefore, as with flowers, the designer must make sure that the attention is warranted and that it is properly placed. A statue or piece of sculpture placed alone in the middle of an open lawn merely detracts from the impact of the embellishment and, at the same time, from the other landscape features. To be really effective, these items must be displayed against a background of neutral plantings or panels of fencing, and attention should be gradually led to them, then away.

Finally, sculptures and statuaries should match the mood of the landscape and the architecture around them. Very formal, symmetrical shapes should only be used in formal landscapes, and informal pieces in informal landscapes.

WATER FEATURES

Water can do things in the landscape. It can add serenity or motion. It provides great visual impact and, if it is moving, pleasant listening. See Figure 11–4. For many, moving water is the greatest source of relaxation. For others, a quiet reflecting pool that mirrors surrounding landscape elements is best.

Water can be used as a setting for other landscape-enriching items. Statues are often placed in or around water features, as are water lilies and other specialized plant items. Pebbles and boulders take on a new look when placed in water; their colors change, as, to a degree, does their texture.

While water features are normally used as focal points, they can also be used effectively to divide areas. The use of water to separate areas began with the use of moats around ancient castles. Water also alters the local environment by increasing the humidity of an enclosed area, cooling the air as breezes blow across the surface of the water.

Designing Water Features

A water feature in the landscape may consist of a single pool, multiple pools connected by a stream, or pools with waterfalls or fountains. Ranging from formal to naturalistic, water features are highly individualistic undertakings, each requiring the presence of only one common element—water. Add water plants to the feature and you have a water garden. Add the appropriate number of fish and you have a biologically balanced water garden.

Location of the Water Feature

To be appreciated, the water feature must be positioned to be seen, but not necessarily from all points within the landscape and not necessarily at all times. If a pool is to become a focal point in a backyard, easily viewed from a patio area or from the back windows of a house, that pool should be located at a low elevation in the yard, far enough from the house to be seen from all desired viewpoints, but not so far away that details are lost from view. Sometimes, though, a water feature may be concealed from many views within the landscape, so that it may be discovered as viewers move through the landscape. Discovery might occur when they see the water feature or when they first hear moving water. When discovery is desired, the landscape's design must provide the impetus that makes people move in the right direction. This is often accomplished with a path of some sort, which leads first the eyes, then the feet, to the water feature.

A water garden should receive 4 to 6 hours of sunlight a day for best water management. Too much sunlight heats the water to undesirable levels, while too little sunlight limits photosynthesis by water plants.

Photosynthetic activity releases oxygen, which is necessary to support a fish population. Fish are just as essential to pond management as are plants, because during respiration they emit carbon dioxide, a necessary raw ingredient for photosynthesis, and fish waste includes nitrites and nitrates for plant food. Achieving a balance between the number of fish and the number and types of plants is essential for control of algae, which, if uncontrolled, render the water thick and soupy.

Selecting Pool Type

Generally, garden pools are of three types: masonry pools, preformed plastic or fiberglass pools, and pools made with flexible liners. Concrete pools are costly and difficult to build. Preformed pools are easily built and relatively inexpensive, but they are limited in size and shape. Because they are the least expensive and most easily constructed, pools built with flexible liners are a popular choice. To an extent, the desired shape of a pool dictates the construction possibilities. Concrete pools (see Figure 11–6) can be molded to virtually any shape desired, as can those using flexible liners. Preformed pools are rigid, so the shape and size selected is dictated by the inventory available for purchase.

The shape selected for a garden pool also influences the mood affected by the pool. Even-radius curves or straight lines and angles tend to be more formal than free curves of uneven radius. The type of finishing used around the pool's edge also has an impact. Cut-stone coping looks more formal than does irregular fieldstone with or without mortar. An irregular, graveled edge is probably the most naturalistic look. (See Figure 11–5 and Figure 11–7.)

Figure 11–5. A backyard pond with small patio and bench … a nice place to while away relaxing minutes watching the fish play.

Figure 11–6. This pool and fountain represent only two of the ways water features can be used in the landscape, appealing to the senses of sight and sound.

Figure 11–7.   A placid pool reflects landscape elements in a tranquil scene.

Because flexible liner pools are so popular, we will discuss some construction aspects of this type of pool here. It is necessary to understand the construction methods in order to design such a pool.

Construction of Flexible Liner Pools

The size, shape, and depth of a flexible liner pool is determined by the hole dug for it. The liner snugs up against the edges of that hole when the pool is filled with water.

The depth of most pools should vary. If fish are to spend the winter in the pool, at least part of the pool's bottom must be deeper than the deepest ice penetration during the winter. As long as there is free water with enough oxygen under the ice, goldfish will survive the winter without food, because when the water temperature falls below 50° the goldfish's metabolism nearly ceases. In many places frost levels during severe winters go as deep as 30" or more, so life-sustaining pools must exceed that depth.

The root system of many aquatic plants must be submerged, while the top should remain above the waterline. Accordingly, flat soil benches are carved 9" to 10" below the top of the pool's edge. These soil benches may be as wide as desired—they may even extend completely across the pool. These shallows also provide ideal areas in which fish can feed or hide under the foliage.

The sides of the pool should be close to vertical, with bottom portions on various levels being flat. Any protruding roots or rocks must be removed, and the sides and bottom must be left smooth. If rock coping is to be installed, a shelf is cut around the top edge of the pit to accommodate the number of layers desired. See Figure 11–4.

When the excavation is complete, the hole is lined with moist sand, clay, or some other cushioning material that will protect the liner from sharp rocks or roots that might work their way to the surface. The hole is then ready for the liner.

To determine the size required of a liner, use the following formula: Twice the deepest depth of the hole plus the length of the pit, by twice the deepest depth of the pit plus the width of the pit equals the size of the liner. Thus, if a pit measures 10′ by 6′ and is 2′ deep at its deepest point, the liner's length would be calculated at 14′ (2′ x 2 + 10′). The liner's width would be 10′ (2′ x 2 + 6′).

The liner is first stretched over the hole, then pushed down into it. The liner must be kept taut along the bottom. Rocks are placed around the outside edges of the liner to keep the tension as it is pulled down. As the liner settles into the hole, wrinkles will appear along the sides. These wrinkles should be carefully and neatly folded before the pool is filled with water. The water's weight will pull the liner snug against the bottom and walls of the pit. Some excess liner will extend out of the hole, under the rock coping and up, high enough to prevent water from leaking out under the coping. Excess liner then should be trimmed away, and the pool will be finished.

Establishing the Water Garden

As indicated earlier, both plants and fish are necessary for a successful management of a water garden. Developing the right balance between flora and fauna can be tricky, but it is essential. This is because of the rapid development of algae in water-clouding populations, whenever temperature and sunlight conditions favor their growth. Fish consume algae, and plants can aid in algae control by shading portions of the water's surface. Generally, at least half of a pool's surface should be shaded by plants for successful algae control, and it should hold 1″ of fish per square foot of pool area.

Because the chemicals in most water supplies can be harmful to both plants and fish, it is best to allow a newly filled pool to stand for four days or so before adding either type of life form. This also allows the water temperature to stabilize. Chemicals can be used to neutralize chlorine if one is in a hurry, however.

It is best to introduce fish a few at a time, allowing the nitrogen cycle to be initiated before the entire fish population inhabits the pool. Float new arrivals in the pool, still in the waterbag they come in from the pet shop for an hour or two, or until the water temperature in the bag equals the temperature of the water in the pool. Otherwise, shock can kill new fish as they are dumped into colder pool water.

Although goldfish and the more exotic Koi are colorful and fun to watch, one type of fish that can be valuable in the water garden is neither colorful nor interesting. Grass carp are dark and sluggish and they generally stay close to the bottom of a pool, but they consume large volumes of algae. Because of that, they are welcomed by many pool owners.

Figure 11–8.   A waterfall and stream without water. An arrangement of boulders and river gravel suggest the presence of water features at lower initial cost and minimal maintenance.

Snails can also be used well in the ongoing war against algae. Two snails per square foot of pool surface will adequately clean plants and rocks of surface-coating algae.

At night, water features can be lighted dramatically for interesting effects. Blue and green lights work particularly well with water features. Special water-tight lighting fixtures can be placed directly in the water without danger of electrical shock to highlight the use of water.

When water features are planned, it is necessary to remember the requirements for underground wiring. Most pumps used in water fountains and water-falls today are self-contained, so plumbing is unnecessary to provide the source of water. However, pumps and lights do require an outdoor electrical outlet. Wires leading from the house to such outlets are usually buried underground, encased in metal conduit for protection.

When using water is impractical, the presence of water can be suggested by rocks and gravel, as in Figure 11–8.

COLLECTED EMBELLISHMENTS

Many of the most enriching items are found in nature. Interesting pieces of drift-wood and boulders are the most commonly used natural embellishments. Colorful river pebbles, washed clean and smooth, are sometimes used to high-

Redwood constructed features surrounding this swimming pool serve as retaining walls, deck, benches, and planter boxes. The fence at the back-right conceals the pool equipment and a large catch basin which leads into a 16" and a 12" drainage tube that reroute a drainage creek around and beyond the pool.

A small birch forest gives depth to the landscape.

The strong but gentle curve of this walk leads our eyes as well as our feet to the entry.

This fence and walk complement one another well because they flow along the same line and the square stepping stones repeat the lines and angles in the lattice.

Intense areas of color contrast are effectively used here. The slope is controlled by a rock garden planting.

In most instances, an area inside of a walk might be devoid of grass, but a small, sharply defined crescent of grass provides interesting contrast.

Slight elevation of a landscape bed allows elements within the bed to be more effective at smaller sizes. The crisp, clean edge of this bed is facilitated by the use of stell edging.

The principle of repetition is illustrated in this photo, where the repetitive character of the wall is duplicated by the landscaping.

Good use of form, texture, and color enhance the wall and sign, directing attention to the lettering.

The rolling contour of the landscape bed inside of the entry walk offers greater interest than a flat or recessed bed.

Maidengrass and a massed planting of 'Francee' Hosta welcome visitors to this entry courtyard. The variation in form and texture is enhanced here by light, and at other times by breezes which create movement.

Water lilies and other plants do more than add beauty to the water garden. Together with fish, they provide the ecological balance necessary for successful water management.

A lively collection of annual and perennial flowers and grasses can brighten an otherwise drab day.

Place a bench among the colorful plantings which line a wooded creekbank, creating an inviting place for quiet reflection in the cool shade.

Two pools, one with the waterfall pictured below, are connected by a meandering stream which passes under two segments of a wooden deck.

A small waterfall adds motion and sound to the landscape. The photos on these pages demonstrate how small areas can be maximized by creative landscaping.

Sometimes, the landscape designer has only to take advantage of existing natural features, such as the interesting triple-trunk tree in this picture.

Inside the entry courtyard, the interesting color, form, and texture of the Japanese Maple provides a pleasing view to the entrant, and also to those who view it from inside the window.

The two pools are populated with plants and fish, and the shallow stream with its gently sloping gravel bottom, invites playful songbirds to bathe and frolic. A diverse group of plantings helps make this 10' by 70' area seem larger and more important.

The sight and sound of running water contributes mightily to a relaxing evening on the patio.

This deck/patio combination features a lower patio with a built-in sandbox. Later, when the children are grown, the sandbox will be converted into a reflecting pool.

Rugged boulders in a country setting are enhanced by the ever-renewing color of daylilies.

Rock steps follow the stream up the hill, allowing one to walk beside the water feature, enjoying the changing sounds as one leaves the waterfall area and follows the bubbling brook.

Mature trees add much to the landscape, including shade, backgrounding, enframement, and interesting shade patterns on the ground.

Native boulders from the site are incorporated into the flagstone patio, then extend into the stream.

Walks can be incorporated into the landscape to enhance the ground patterns, as this one does, while also serving as a bed edging.

Bright color invites guests to this pool entrance.

Three River Birch trees contribute to the "mountain cabin" look of this A-frame house. The low evergreen carpet of Blue Chip Junipers leads the eye toward the entry, with Goldmound Spirea providing a splash of color.

Small areas can have large impact with colorful perennial and annual flowers.

Figure 11–9.   Collected embellishments include a broad spectrum of items that can be successfully incorporated into the landscape. Unfortunately, these are the most frequently abused elements in the landscape. Here, for instance, the water pump commands all of the attention, detracting from the house and landscape. The pump probably should not be that important.

light particular areas, like the area beneath a small-scale bridge over a seemingly natural stream that has been constructed. Petrified wood and even portions of animal skeletons have been used to a lesser extent (see Figure 11–9).

Collected art forms of all types adorn landscapes. These allow the maximum individuality in the landscape. Again, the proportions must always be correct. Pieces of art that would be in good proportion to elements in an indoor room often seem sadly insignificant in an outdoor room (see Figure 11–10).

MUSICAL ENRICHMENTS

Sound is an integral part of the landscape. Although some kinds of outdoor sound must be screened from the property owner's ears (for example, traffic and factory noises), other sounds are welcomed. The pleasant sound of running water has already been discussed, and the company of songbirds is enjoyable. Another inviting sound is that of wind chimes or bells. Like moving water, the gentle rustling of a musical chime provides relaxation. Instruments should be chosen individually for their sound and appearance. It is possible to harmonize the sounds of several of these devices.

As with water effects, wind chimes or bells must be placed where they can be heard. A small bell at a remote end of a property may be insignificant unless the design calls for visitors to be lured to that corner, then surprised by the

Figure 11–10.   The selection of any item to be placed in the landscape, like the flower pot and furniture surrounding the pool in this picture, should always be made with great care and with an eye for proper proportion, texture, and style.

sound as they arrive. Conversely, extremely loud instruments, whose sound overwhelms listeners, should be avoided. Sounds should be muted, only adding background to other pleasant features in the yard.

LIGHTING

Lighting cannot be considered as only an embellishment. It is a necessity in the landscape, both to guide people safely through the circulation routes and to provide security for the grounds. There are, however, many ways that dramatic lighting can be used as an enriching item in the landscape.

Some of the major uses of lighting in the landscape are:

- To guide people through the circulation routes safely.
- To provide security for the area, discouraging prowlers.
- To allow greater nighttime use of the outdoor rooms.
- To aid in the creation of dramatic focal points in the landscape at night.
- To create unusual and charming nighttime views of the outdoors from inside the building.
- To create special effects for special occasions (Christmas, parties, etc.).

Although entire books have been written about outdoor lighting, a few of the major principles should be emphasized here. Lights should never be aimed directly at people's eyes or at windows; the direct glare of lights is not only discomforting, it also causes a temporary blinding to darker objects. Light that is aimed directly into the eyes destroys the intended illuminating effect. Lights that shine into windows make it impossible to look out of those windows. To be effective, lighting should always be placed either above or below eye level.

It is important to provide the correct amount of light. If that which is to be illuminated has a light-colored surface, less light will be required. Darker surfaces require more illumination, permitting greater contrast. For functional lighting of walks, steps, and other circulation routes, use more light close to doors or places where other strong lighting already exists (See Figure 11–11). The glare from the existing lighting tends to darken surrounding features.

For dramatic effects, always consider the shadows. Patterns formed by light and shadow are the essence of dramatic garden lighting. To highlight dominant lines formed by tree trunks, for example, the trunks should be lighted from

Figure 11–11. Functional lighting of the outside areas around a home is critical for safety and security reasons, but it can enhance the landscape as well. (Photo courtesy Westinghouse Electric Corporation)

Figure 11–12.   A good landscape lighting system invites viewers and users into the landscape at night while safely guiding the way and creating interesting light and shadow effects. (Photo courtesy Westinghouse Electric Corporation)

an angle. To light them head on is to wash out their features by reducing the contrast. Dramatic effects often can be achieved by lighting the background behind a tree, allowing the dark trunk and branches to show up against the lighted background. The illuminated background might be a panel of a fence, a mass of plantings, or any other fairly solid background.

Lighting effects in the landscape can be created in many ways. Floodlights in treetops cast interesting shadows on the ground surface below, as well as providing pools of illumination. Low floodlights can be washed over landscape features for interesting light-and-shadow effects. Ground-level lights can be aimed into treetops to create some very unusual shadow effects (see Figure 11–12). Sophisticated cross-lighting patterns can be created by washing light from two or more directions over landscaping features, multiplying the shadow effects. Interesting, sometimes eerie patterns can be achieved by backlighting landscape elements—highlighting the edges while leaving the rest of the object in muted darkness.

Colored lights are used for special effects and Christmas lighting. Timers and moving sequential lights also offer a realm of possibilities (see Figure 11–13).

There are almost endless combinations available for landscape enhancement through the use of embellishments. To a large extent, the individuality of

Figure 11–13. Dramatic garden lighting makes the landscape come alive at night, creating an entirely different mood than during the day. (Photo courtesy Westinghouse Electric Corporation)

each landscape is the result of these forms of adornment. They greatly enliven the landscape, stimulating discussion among those who see them.

As with any other prominent landscape element, there is an inherent danger of overusing these items of enrichment. Since they do command attention, too many such embellishments will disrupt the harmony of the setting. Selections should be made carefully, therefore, ensuring that the embellishments chosen will blend in good proportion with other landscaping features, accenting only those areas worthy of particular attention.

POINTS TO REMEMBER

- Embellishments serve the landscape as desserts serve to complete a good meal. Both enhance the flavor.
- Flowers may be considered embellishments, because although they are short-seasoned, they are so visually demanding that they must be used with extreme care so that they do not override other landscape features.
- Flowers should never be used where intense attention is unwarranted.
- Flower borders generally look best when backgrounded by solid plantings, fences, or walls.

- Flowers should always be planted in color masses of nicely contrasting or complementary colors. However, confusion is created by indiscriminate planting of separate plants of individual colors.
- Nonessential construction items, including ornamental walls, raised planters, seats and benches, ornamental fences, and flower boxes, can contribute additional colors, textures, and forms to the landscape.
- When statuary and sculpture are used in the landscape, extreme care must be taken to keep them in good proportion to surrounding elements.
- Water can provide additional sights and sounds in the landscape, as well as helping to alter the environment.
- When a water feature is used, provision must be made for an electrical supply and for lights and pumps.
- Collected pieces of art that would be in good proportion to elements of the indoor rooms are often quite disproportionate in the outdoor rooms.
- The sounds of running water, birds, and musical chimes or bells are usually welcomed as background in the landscape.
- Lighting is used functionally in the landscape to illuminate circulation routes and to provide security for the area.
- Dramatic garden lighting can highlight garden features while making the landscape more usable at night.
- Lights should always be placed above or below eye level.
- Dark surfaces require brighter illumination than light-colored surfaces but do allow greater contrast.
- Many special seasonal effects, such as Christmas lighting, can be created by dramatic lighting of the landscape.
- To a large extent, embellishments provide the individuality in each landscape.

Review Questions

1. Why are flowers considered to be embellishments, instead of being dealt with in the same manner as trees and shrubs?
2. What is a nonessential construction item? Give several examples.
3. What is the major problem encountered by using statuaries in the landscape?
4. How can water features benefit the landscape in ways other than visual?
5. List the six major uses of lighting in the landscape.
6. Why is the location of sound-making embellishments in the landscape of great importance?
7. Why are flowers best incorporated in front of shrub groupings in the landscape?

PRACTICAL TIP FROM A PRACTICING DESIGNER

Some might consider birdfeeders and birdhouses as landscape embellishments. Though they are not listed in this chapter as embellishments, there is no denying that the presence of these elements can make the home landscape environment more enjoyable. Birds contribute music and motion to what might otherwise be a static view. Of course, birds also create some minor problems as well. For example, sometimes they drop their food into the landscape beds, causing a weed prevention or elimination problem that can persist throughout the summer.

Chapter **12**

SPECIAL LANDSCAPE PROBLEMS: BUSINESS AND RENTAL PROPERTIES

In this chapter, you will learn of many specialized landscaping concerns that relate to business buildings, rental properties, and institutions. Understanding the basis of many of these concerns helps build a solid basis for selling to the owners of such concerns.

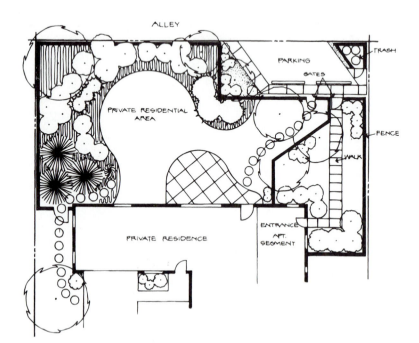

Throughout most of this book, landscaping has been addressed from a residential design standpoint. However, the landscape designer commonly encounters many other more specialized landscaping situations. The two most common of these involve small-business properties and rental properties. By addressing these two special needs, it can be pointed out that in all cases careful design means fitting the landscape to specific needs.

THE PROFIT MOTIVE

Profit is an absolute necessity to both the businessperson and the rental-property owner. Unless favorable returns on their investments are possible, neither can afford to risk his or her capital. There are generally safer investment possibilities for the funds of either investor, but profit is not necessarily the sole reason for selecting investments. Many other factors—including a desire to be one's own boss, an inclination to serve the public, a yen to be an employer of others, or the aspiration to provide goods and services of a superior nature—might also influence the decision to enter commerce. Some believe that their investments are always safer in rental properties because these properties are so tangible. Any number of motivations exist for owning a business or rental property. Nevertheless, none of the motives is satisfactory unless there is a potential for profit. People invest capital to realize a profit on it, not to lose it.

Although the principles of planting design remain the same in these special landscape-design problems, the approach to the design changes. The needs the landscaping must satisfy are altered considerably, and it is up to the designer to ferret out those needs. The changes in procedure begin during the initial design-analysis stage.

Design Analysis for Business-Building Landscaping

The landscaping of a business property requires many of the same site-analysis considerations as a residential property. Because of the special use of the property, though, many new needs also arise. Such factors as parking-lot size and access, sign locations, the need for daily deliveries (both in and out), and street traffic safety past business entrances and exits are among the new concerns for a business property.

People's needs change in a business situation, also. The needs of the business's owner, employees, and customers must all be ascertained. These needs are largely determined by the type of business to be conducted. Is it desirable for customers to browse about the building for long periods of time, or is it best for business transactions to be conducted quickly to make room for others? Must clients wait before being served, as in a doctor's office? Does the type of business conducted call for a particular image in the landscape? What security needs should the landscaping serve? Are there other business neighbors who deserve consideration because they might be affected by the landscaping of a business building? What major types of advertising will the business use? Can the landscaping strengthen and reinforce that advertising?

Maintenance is a major factor. Parking-lot cleaning, snow removal, and traffic control are all of concern.

All of the above are standard questions that apply to each business landscaping situation. In addition, each business will have its own unique needs. It would be difficult to use a form questionnaire to analyze business-building landscaping needs because of their diversity. The important thing is to study each business individually and become completely familiar with its unique problems. Then, the application of landscaping principles can enhance the profitability of the business's operation.

Design Analysis for Rental Property

Rental properties are very diverse. They range all the way from a basement apartment in a private home to vast ranges of apartment buildings. To a large extent, the design analysis for apartments is the same as that for residential properties. These are homes for people, after all. But there are special considerations. For a basement or in-home apartment, some thought should be given to providing a private entrance for renters. Good views and the necessary screening from apartment windows should be noted. The need for special patio areas or circulation routes should be determined.

In large apartment complexes, environmental adjustments have to be designed for all units as a whole. There are also many other group considerations; for example, the swimming pool, children's play area, recreational facilities, and other use areas are often combined for use by all tenants. Site analysis includes logical thought about the location and ease of access to these areas.

Producing private areas for each tenant is a special problem encountered during design analysis for a large apartment complex. Security problems are magnified in a rental situation, where access to buildings must be open to more than one occupant. In large apartment complexes and even in privately owned condominiums, the proximity of a larger number of people at all times sets forth new criteria for lighting and other security measures.

Maintenance costs are a major factor in determining the profitability of rental properties. The design of the landscaping probably affects these exterior maintenance costs more than anything else. The time to consider maintenance requirements is before the design is prepared, of course, so that profit-saving solutions can be found.

Sometimes the construction style and building materials change from one unit to another in an apartment complex, just as they do in condominiums. So, although the units are adjacent to one another, they must be landscaped as separate units would be. More details must be gathered during site analysis to prepare properly for these changes.

Once a specialized design analysis for a business or rental property is compiled, it is necessary to apply the appropriate solutions. The remainder of this chapter will be concerned with some of the most widely used of these solutions.

BUSINESS APPLICATIONS FOR LANDSCAPING

Some of the specialized demands of landscaping for businesses are listed below. Each will be discussed in detail, but they are presented as a group to give a better look at the vast ground they cover.

- Environmental considerations
- Advertising benefits
- Location enhancement
- Traffic control
- Customer comforts
- Buyer exposure time
- Security provisions
- Maintenance considerations
- Community service

Environmental Considerations

These days, environmental considerations have taken on a new importance. Energy shortages dictate that we find new ways to conserve all types of fuels. There is an ever-increasing desire to engineer and construct business sites to preserve the beauty of the natural habitat. In many cases, this conservation is manifested in zoning regulations.

Shade trees are desirable in a business location whenever possible. Even downtown areas, previously all concrete, are being altered to accommodate shade and ornamental trees to cool and beautify the areas. Sometimes, though, it is impossible to use shade trees in a business location. Unless the trees are well positioned, they may block the view of a sign or the visibility of the building itself. Business owners enjoy shade, and they know the savings these trees can generate in cooling costs, but they will not tolerate poor visibility of their buildings or signs. In addition, they must be considerate of their business neighbors. Blocking a neighboring businessperson's building or sign from view must be avoided. Shade trees should be so placed as to allow the winter sun to reach windows, providing passive solar heating while still blocking the sun in the summer. Also, flocks of birds tend to congregate in trees when there are few other roosts available. These birds can be a real nuisance, especially when the tree's branches extend over sidewalks.

The *screening* of unsightly views is important to the businessperson, especially when that screening can also be used to draw more attention to his or her building by providing background or enframement.

The use of trees, shrubs, fences, or other means of wind protection will increase the comfort of customers while reducing heating and cooling bills. Once more, neighbors deserve consideration. It is often possible to design shade, screening, and wind protection that suit adjacent properties as well, thereby benefiting neighbors and making a strong commitment to neighborhood unity.

Whenever possible, a business building should be constructed to blend with its natural surroundings (see Figure 12–1). For example, though it may be inconvenient at times, business buildings and parking lots can be constructed on wooded lots, which can be beneficial in many ways. By maintaining the natural landscape, the businessperson will attract much positive attention from the public; provide for the environmental needs for shade, wind protection, and screening; and be the possessor of an extremely attractive business site.

Advertising Benefits

Advertising is a term used to describe a vast array of means by which businesspeople attempt to attract customers and create suitable public images. Although we usually think of advertising in terms of slick commercials on television, catchy jingles on radios, and polished newspaper and magazine ads, the field encompasses many other areas. Virtually every business utilizes several types of advertising. Most firms have letterheads on their stationery, business cards, personalized bills and statements, signs on their vehicles and buildings, and yellow-page listings in the telephone directory. These are all forms of advertising (see Figure 12–2).

The attraction of customers to businesses is, in itself, a gargantuan enterprise. Billions of dollars are spent by businesspeople each year in an attempt to draw potential customers through their doors. And it works. Madison Avenue people are able to convince us that one type of painkiller is much superior to another when, in fact, both contain the same amount of aspirin. We become convinced that one brand of automobile is better than others because its seats are

Figure 12–1.   The landscaping of larger-than-residential-size buildings entails careful consideration of relative scale, or proportion, between plantings and building. These two photos show good proportion between trees and large-scale buildings.

Figure 12-1 (continued)

covered with a rich leather, or we buy another brand of car because it is as American as baseball, hot dogs, and apple pie. Products are continually touted as being "new" or "improved." Attractive people with pleasant voices are used in commercials and ads. The association between pleasant sights and sounds and desirable products is powerful. Similarly, a pleasantly landscaped business building will be associated with desirable products and services.

Landscaping can enhance a business building to the point of increasing traffic and trade in several different ways. Like a sign, good landscaping draws a great deal of attention. In fact, good landscaping magnifies the attention drawn to a sign. The most easily noticed signs are usually surrounded by attractive plantings (see Figure 12–3).

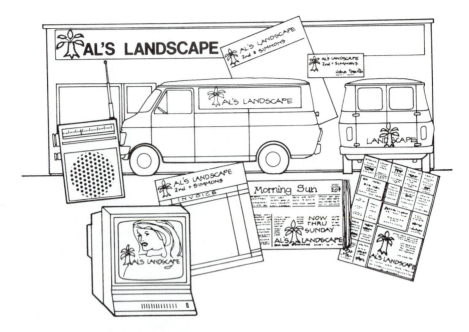

Figure 12–2. Some of the more commonly recognized methods of advertising used by businesses. Landscaping applications make just as good sense for businesspeople.

Figure 12–3. Bright lights, distinctive shapes, and neon letters on signs attract a lot of attention. However, such signs are so numerous that it makes sense to use distinctive landscaping to set them apart and attract still more attention.

Cities are filled with plastic and neon signs. Different sizes, designs, colors, and styles are used to provide variety and individuality. When looking down an avenue filled with such signs, though, it is difficult to pick one out from the crowd. The addition of color, texture, and plant forms by landscaping may provide more visual impact than the sign itself.

CHANGING THEMES.   Large national advertisers frequently change themes. When they do, the new themes must be used in all of their advertising media. The advertisements stressing that theme are then used for weeks, months, or years until the public recognizes the association readily. Then, suddenly, the advertising slogan changes, and a new theme is adopted. Advertisers do this to renew interest constantly in their products.

There are two correlations between advertising methods and business landscaping. First, the landscaping of a business need not be static. If the objectives of a business change or if they merely want to attract attention quickly, the remodeling of the exterior landscaping can have a great effect. The appearance of a building can be strikingly different with a new landscape. Such changes are undoubtedly less expensive than a complete overhaul of the building's exterior. Second, the landscaping can be used to reflect a change in policy within a business. Landscapes can create moods of many types, including conservative, progressive, colorful, and lively. The landscaping can also reflect the changing theme of a company.

IMAGES.   Images are of paramount importance to businesspeople. There is a special image most suitable for the objectives of each enterprise. Banks, for example, like an appearance of confidence, stability, prosperity, and dignity, while still looking progressive. Service-oriented companies must appear competent and reliable. Retail stores should be clean and inviting. The offices of doctors and lawyers must appear professional and dignified (see Figures 12–4 and 12–5).

The point of this is that the landscaping can and should reflect the image desired by a business. Customers would be reluctant to hire a pest-control company if they knew that the evergreens outside the company's office were festering with bagworms. A carpet-cleaning crew would not wish to arrive at a home in dirty trucks. Landscaping merely reflects the image we wish to project.

Many doctors and lawyers have resisted using conventional means of advertising, choosing to effectively project their image by other means. Selecting an architecturally pleasing, easily accessible office building, then landscaping it to create a truly beautiful setting, is one such means of projecting image. Ample parking, pleasant surroundings, and other client-oriented conveniences add to this image, effectively advertising services.

Retail stores must attract traffic. Prices, product quality, and service will carry them from that point. The exterior landscaping, if well maintained, can have a great influence on the store's ability to attract customers. Clean and inviting, remember?

Figure 12–4.   Places of business need not look different from residences to be effective. In this picture, the white birch trees on the left not only enhance the appearance of the building, but also mask the parking lot behind them without completely hiding its existence. Since these same trees can be viewed from inside this dental office, they also provide a restful view for anxious patients.

Figure 12–5.   Landscaping can create many moods—for example, the restful, quiet, dignified treatment of the entrance to this medical clinic.

Enhancement of Location

The location of any business is important, but perhaps it is most critical to retail stores. Location is often pointed out as the most important criterion for success in a retail venture. Many factors influence the value of a location. Traffic patterns and volume, ease of access, speed of access, and proximity to other businesses that draw large crowds are just a few of the influential factors.

With all of the above criteria relating to high traffic volume and easy access, why do we hear of retail businesses in remote locations that still do a tremendous volume of trade? Some of these businesses attract the traffic with extremely heavy media advertising. Others, though, are located in extremely attractive locations that, even though remote, are so well developed as to be "places to be" and "places to go" all by themselves. No other reward is necessary. Of course, once people get there, they are likely to make purchases. Landscaping helps to create such a "place to go or be" (see Figure 12–6).

Traffic Control

Both pedestrian and motor traffic must be controlled for efficiency and safety in business operations. Trees and shrubs can be planted in either cut-out or raised planters for effective diversions to direct traffic in the proper direction (see Figure 12–7). Small hedges or low plantings can indicate the

Figure 12–6.   When a business location is not ideal, the landscaping can help to make the premises "a place to be" on its own merits, thereby stimulating business by increasing traffic. This mobile-home sales lot provides a pleasant, "homey" look for models on display.

Figure 12–7.   Landscaping can be used to help direct traffic for greater business efficiency and customer safety.

direction in which traffic should flow. Plantings at the junction of sidewalks prevent corner-cutting by keeping people on the walks. Landscaping can be used to draw attention to signs that offer further traffic direction (see Figure 12–8). Hedges or other plantings can be used to separate parking lots that belong to different businesses. Lawn areas effectively divide parking lots and soften the space between parking lots and buildings. Living fences (hedges) or wood fences spiced by plantings can be used effectively to keep people out of areas not open to the public. Landscaped planters can also be used to slow traffic for safety purposes.

Customer Comforts

Customers should always be made comfortable while shopping or waiting in a place of business. Waiting rooms offer comfortable furniture, soft music, and reading material to accommodate clients. Interior landscaping, water fountains or waterfalls, and fireplaces are all used to create a comfortable environment for customers.

Often neglected, but no less important, is the view of the exterior landscaping from the inside of a business building. A pleasantly framed view of the exterior landscaping through large windows can do much to add to a customer's comfort (see Figure 12–9).

Figure 12–8.   Landscaping can integrate the necessary traffic control signs into the overall look of the buildings and grounds. Signs then become more effective and less obtrusive.

Figure 12–9.   When it is necessary for customers to wait for service, a pleasant view through waiting-room windows lessens their impatience.

The sound and sight of moving water is relaxing to most people; it has an almost hypnotic effect. Water, color, and lighting can be used effectively to help customers remain comfortable and make them eager to return.

Buyer Exposure Time

Landscaping can be used effectively to control the length of time a customer spends in a business establishment. If the landscaping makes a customer comfortable, he or she will spend more time in a store. This additional time might be desirable to a retail store, where impulse sales by browsers are important. Unusual areas of interest, created with waterfalls or fountains or other special features, can all serve to delay a customer's departure.

Sometimes, though, it is desirable for a customer to do his or her business quickly. Fast-food operations must necessarily move traffic quickly, since they have only short periods in which to conduct the maximum amount of business. A flowing sequence in the plantings will imply movement, causing the customers to flow in the same pattern. Traffic control is part of this sequence, since customers are ushered into and out of the store in an organized fashion. Strong areas of interest must be limited so that everything will move to a quick conclusion (see Figure 12–10).

Security Provisions

Locks, lighting, and fencing come to mind when we think of security. These devices, though necessary, will not attract customers—except to a bank or other storage facility for valuables. However, when combined effectively with good landscaping, safety provisions become attractive as well as functional.

Lighting, for example, can be quite attractive. Well-designed exterior lights enhance the appearance of a business building at night (see Figure 12–11). Combined with the landscaping, the lighting becomes particularly effective. Colorful lights, shining up into trees, create interesting patterns while still providing security. Lights and water combine for interesting effects in a fountain or waterfall.

Necessary fencing should not be hidden by the landscaping. Rather, the landscaping should enhance the fence, and vice versa. Trees of a friendly, climbable nature should not be planted so close to a fence that they allow access over the fence. Plantings in a security area should be low, preventing the possibility of their concealing prowlers.

A solid plant hedge can prove more impenetrable than the strongest fence, particularly if the plants have nasty thorns. A hedge can be allowed to grow higher than the limits of a fence, although it necessarily occupies a wider base.

Maintenance Considerations

Well-conceived business landscaping reduces maintenance requirements. Clear definition of lawn areas; the use of gravel, bark, or other low-maintenance

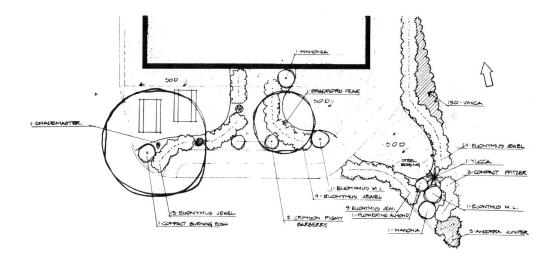

Figure 12–10. Plantings can help control the amount of time customers spend in a place of business. At this fast-food restaurant, the owners prefer that customers not linger beyond the time needed to eat. The sidewalks and landscape plantings were designed to "flow," so customers would be influenced by the subtle suggestion of movement While stimulating movement, the plantings also control the direction of that movement (Design by Marguerite Koepke)

Figure 12–11.   The night lighting of a business building, though designed primarily for security and identification might as well be attractive at the same time.

groundcovers; underground sprinkler systems; and the selection of plantings that stay within the size limitations afforded by each area are some maintenance considerations to be handled by a designer, but there are additional ones in some business situations (see Figure 12–12).

A constant trash problem in the parking lot plagues many businesses, particularly fast-food restaurants. There is a landscaping device to relieve this problem. It is desirable for the trash not to be allowed to blow off the property and for it to be easy to collect. If small hedges or other plantings are placed on the downwind side of the property the trash will accumulate next to them. Since the debris is then concentrated in these areas, it may be collected easily (see Figure 12–13).

Snow removal and cleaning of parking lots and driveways must be provided for by business landscaping design. A row of tall evergreens adjacent to the north side of a driveway in snow country for example will result in the accumulation of tremendous drifts during a blizzard. Furthermore if no provision is made for a place to pile this snow, its removal will result in injury to the plants surrounding the parking lot.

The number of maintenance applications in individual businesses is almost endless. A thorough study of the maintenance needs of each business is necessary as landscape plans are formulated.

Figure 12–12.   Maintenance of the landscape is vitally important in business surroundings. The impeccable lawn and plantings in this picture draw attention, and while the viewer is admiring them, he or she is also aware of the nicely blended, though conservative, sign.

Figure 12–13.   Far from being merely decorative, these island plantings divide and control traffic and also stop windblown debris, consolidating it for easy collection.

Community Service

The final, and perhaps most important contribution landscaping can make to a business operation is through community service and the recognition associated with it. Current environmental concerns have given the businessperson an opportunity to impress the public with his or her own contributions. A well-landscaped business site, contributing to energy conservation, clean air, and the preservation of natural surroundings, will score well for the company's image. Some communities, in fact, have given prizes or other forms of recognition to those businesses that make the largest contributions in environmental areas. In many places, zoning regulations require such efforts to be made. Regardless of requirements, businesspeople who take it upon themselves to make efforts in these areas will be well rewarded.

APPLICATIONS FOR LANDSCAPING RENTAL PROPERTIES

The goals of landscaping for a rental property often seem paradoxical. Ideally, the design should attract more renters at higher monthly rates but still be accomplished as inexpensively as possible. To make renters comfortable it is necessary for the landscape to be well maintained, yet holding down maintenance costs is one of the primary goals. In large complexes, the landscaping must encompass the whole building, tying together all units. But at the same time, each individual renter must be given privacy. In an in-home apartment situation, the landlord would often just as soon disguise the fact that an apartment exists. To make the renters happy, though, some special private areas, a nice view from within the apartment, and maybe a special dressing of the apartment's entryway may be in order.

The Apartment in the Residence

In most cases, an apartment in a residential building does not command treatment that would separate the house from other residential units in the same neighborhood. But the fact that the apartment is there should be given ample thought. If an entrance is to be highlighted for public view, for example, it should be the main entrance to the house. The entrance to the apartment might be given special treatment so the visitors can appreciate it more, but it still might be hidden completely from public view. The assumption is made that visitors to the apartment have been given adequate instructions for finding it (see Figure 12–14).

Views from apartment windows may be taken into consideration in the normal course of preparing the walls of the residential landscape. Perhaps a landscaping unit might be given more priority if it is constantly on exhibit from apartment windows.

Provision of a private living area for the occupants of an apartment can be considered during the creation of areas for the residence. In addition, special cir-

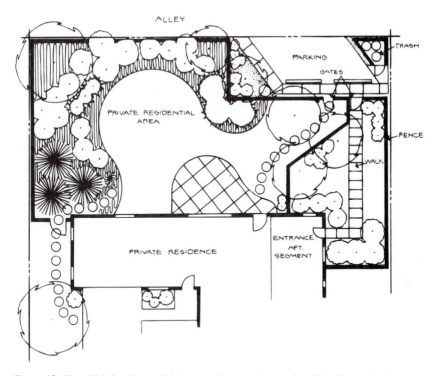

Figure 12–14. This landscape design provides a private and well-landscaped entrance for an in-residence apartment dweller without intruding on the private spaces allocated only to the homeowner.

culation walks must be designed to service the apartment entrance. Because of space limitations, the private outdoor area for apartment dwellers in a residential home is often located just outside the entry.

Apartment Buildings

The landscaping of an apartment building must be done primarily for the benefit of tenants but must still be suited to the budget and maintenance capabilities of the landlord. It is not possible, of course, to landscape to suit the individual tastes of any and all tenants. Certain requirements will fulfill the needs of the majority, though. Among these are the environmental requirements for shade, wind protection, and screening. Provision for adequate parking and good lighting for security and pleasant nighttime appearance are important. Individual privacy for tenants is appreciated, and, of course, a pleasant appearance helps rent apartments more quickly and at a higher rate (see Figure 12–15).

The landscaping of an apartment building should not hide the parking lot. Potential renters are impressed by the availability of ample parking, and guests

Figure 12–15. Condominiums and townhouses often present unique problems for the landscape designer, as building materials and styles change from one unit to another. In this photo, notice the vine growing up around the mailbox on the lefthand unit, softening the transition from one unit to another while allowing each its own identity.

should not have to search for it. Green spaces, filled with well-placed trees and shrubs, can soften and disguise the harsh, uninteresting materials used in parking-lot construction without hiding the parking lot from view. It is a matter of allowing people to view something pleasant instead of dwelling on the concrete. Landscaping can help to emphasize entrances and exits and also direct attention to other traffic-control signs.

Signs that indicate the name or address of an apartment building are necessary for advertisement and to help visitors to find the right place. These signs are more attractive and more effective if there are well-designed landscape units to attract attention to them. A well-placed ornamental tree or other plantings will often draw more attention than the sign itself.

Plantings designed for apartment buildings should be primarily low and nonconcealing so they will not hide muggers. If security fencing is used, the designer must take care to see that the trees selected will not provide easy access over that fencing as they mature. Outdoor lighting can effectively provide security and enhance the nighttime landscape simultaneously.

Finally, by utilizing only plant materials that conform to appropriate size requirements in each area, using gravels or other nonliving groundcovers under planting beds, and edging the beds with materials that afford easy trimming of lawn areas, maintenance of an apartment complex's grounds can actually be reduced. Lawn-sprinkler systems can be designed to contribute to the ease of maintenance. If regulated correctly, these sprinkler systems can also reduce the water bill for high-quality lawn care.

As a final consideration in landscaping rental properties, remember that the renters do not own the plants or other elements of the landscape. Because of that, many renters are careless, running through planting units or otherwise abusing them. The most durable materials must be selected if they are to withstand the extra abuse they will receive.

POINTS TO REMEMBER

- In special landscaping situations other than residential, the designer should always evaluate the special needs of the property and its users individually, then mold the landscape to fit those needs.
- The profit motive must be considered thoroughly in any commercial landscape design. Anything that can contribute to profits is valuable.
- Design analysis of a business building requires analysis of the day-to-day operations of the business itself.
- Good design analysis for a rental property involves sorting out the problems of tenants, then applying the goals of the landlord along with solutions to these problems.
- When providing for the environmental needs of a business property, the solutions must be secondary to the profit motive.
- Landscaping, if well done, serves the business need for advertising by drawing the maximum amount of attention.
- The landscaping of a business building should reflect the image desired by creating the appropriate mood.
- A poor business location can be enhanced by such good landscaping that it makes that location a "place to go" merely on its landscaping merits.
- Landscaping on a business property should contribute to both pedestrian and motor traffic control and safety.
- Pleasant views, sounds, and comfortable environments created by the landscaping can contribute to the comfort of waiting customers.
- The flow of the landscaping can effectively control the length of time a customer spends in a location, regulating the buyer exposure time on the basis of the needs of the business conducted.
- Landscaping elements, such as fences, also function as security devices. Lighting and other security measures can be incorporated beautifully into the landscape.
- Individual maintenance considerations should be taken into account for each business-building landscape.
- Although the landscaping of a residence with an apartment should primarily be designed for the landlord, careful design analysis provides many landscaping solutions that also benefit the renter.
- Good landscaping of a large apartment complex should provide visibility of the units, security for all, ease of maintenance, and individual privacy.

REVIEW QUESTIONS

1. What is the most important consideration business owners use when deciding upon a purchase of landscaping?
2. Give at least three ways the design analysis for a small business differs from the design analysis for a residential design.
3. List the specialized demands served by landscaping for business properties.
4. How can landscaping enhance the value of business signs?
5. Give some examples of landscape design influencing traffic control on a business property.
6. What are some examples of how specialized landscape design can benefit renters?
7. How can landscaping help a business with a remote location?

PRACTICAL TIP FROM A PRACTICING DESIGNER

Right or wrong, it seems that the landscaping of a business property is often not considered until the building's construction is complete or in the finishing stages. Then special consideration in the design process is necessary to ensure that required materials are available and readily obtainable for swift installation.

Chapter **13**

SPECIFICATIONS, ESTIMATIONS, AND BIDS

In this chapter, you will learn how to read and write specifications, how to do a takeoff in preparation for cost estimating, and how to make cost estimations and bids. The mathematical calculations involved in cost estimating are discussed. You will also learn about digitizers and planimeters and their role in cost estimating.

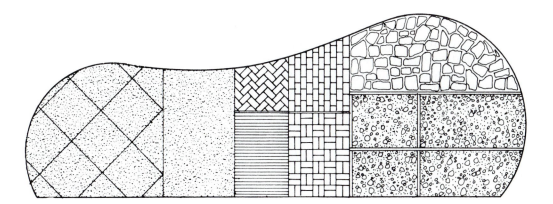

A property owner will usually need to know the anticipated cost of a proposed landscape before pursuing its completion. Whether budgetary guidelines were set at the initiation of the planning process or not, the end product will still have to be cost estimated in its final form. When the landscape planner is connected with a commercial landscaping firm, this cost estimate usually accompanies the presentation of plans to the client as a sales measure. But an independent designer might still be required to furnish a cost estimation before the plans go to contractors for bids. This allows the client a preview of the cost, preventing a fruitless request for bids on a proposed landscape not suitable to the homeowner's budget.

For cost estimation and bidding purposes, the communications afforded by the plan itself might not be adequate. Communication of all criteria for the completion of a landscape project often requires written instructions in addition to the plans. These written instructions are called *specifications.*

LANDSCAPE SPECIFICATIONS

Specifications are written to ensure a consistent quality in materials and workmanship regardless of the source of supply. There are identifiable quality standards for every material or type of task to be performed in a landscape installation. The written specifications identify those features so the desirable quality levels will be reached. For example, simply specifying that a particular tree should be of a given botanical name, 5' to 6' tall, and in a balled and burlapped condition will not assure the property owner of receiving the same quality tree from all bidders. To accomplish that, it is necessary to stipulate further that the tree should conform to standards desired for the number of branches, size of root ball, and caliper of trunk. Or, in the interest of brevity, it might simply be written that the tree must conform to existing specifications in the *American Standards for Nursery Stock* as published by the American Association of Nurserymen. Either way, the specifications will then outline a set of criteria by which plant quality can be judged, assuring the property owner of consistent quality from different bidders.

In order for specifications to be effective, they must be clearly written, reasonably complied with, and adequately enforced. Failure to write specifications in a clear, straightforward manner that can be easily understood can eliminate some potential bidders and encourage others who have no intention of following the quality guidelines. In either case, the property owner is the loser. Unreasonably strict specifications can have the same effect—those bidders who honestly want to comply simply will not bid, knowing the standards cannot be met. The property owner is then stuck with only those bidders who have no intention of complying. Enforcement of specifications requires strict inspection procedures with practical remedies for noncompliance. Once it becomes known that a designer regularly fails to inspect for compliance with specifications, his or her specifications are quickly ignored by many potential contractors and suppliers (see Figure 13–1).

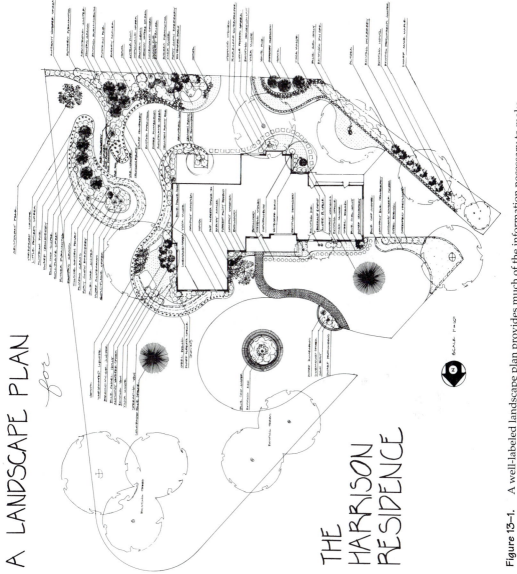

Figure 13–1. A well-labeled landscape plan provides much of the information necessary to make accurate estimates and bids. Written specifications offer information not given on the plan, as well as clarification. (Leroy G. Hannebaum, designer, Blackburn Nursery & Lawn Service, Topeka, KS.)

Specification Contents

Although specification contents vary, most of them encompass the following general areas. The arrangement of sections is also variable, except in a few cases, as will be noted when each section is discussed separately.

- Bidder's instructions
- Scope of work
- Material specifications
- Installation specifications
- Maintenance
- Guarantees and warranties
- Inspections and remedies
- Performance times
- Terms for payment

Bidder's instructions should come first in any set of specifications. In it, the qualifications required of the bidder are spelled out so that an unqualified bidder need not waste time reading further. In the interest of protecting a property owner, the designer might specify certain levels of experience or minimum size requirements to qualify a bidder. This type of requirement assures the property owner that the bidder has experience in performing the required tasks and that the business is of sufficient size to handle its financial obligations.

In most contracts, minimum insurance coverages must be guaranteed by potential contractors. These minimum coverages are stipulated in the bidder's instructions to insure the property owner against large claims for damages, particularly from a liability standpoint. Compliance is indicated as potential contractors supply insurance certificates stating their coverages (see Figure 13–2a).

A bid bond or other type of surety might be required in this segment, ensuring that bids submitted will be honored by bidders for a prescribed length of time. If the bidder then fails to stand behind his or her bid by signing a contract when the bid is awarded, the bond or surety amount is forfeited as compensation for wasted time and efforts and the bids are re-let (see Figure 13–2b).

Also included in the bidder's instructions are the day, hour, and place that bids will be accepted and opened and the manner in which the bids will be accepted. Sometimes bids will be accepted only in sealed envelopes by mail. At other times, bidders will be allowed to hand carry sealed envelopes to the place where the bids are opened and remain as the bids are read aloud. Normally, the bidder's-instructions segment also includes a disclaimer stating that any and all bids may be rejected. Thus, the property owner need not accept the lowest bid offered if he or she feels the low bidder will not meet all requirements. It also allows for the rejection of all bids should they be higher than the amount budgeted for the project.

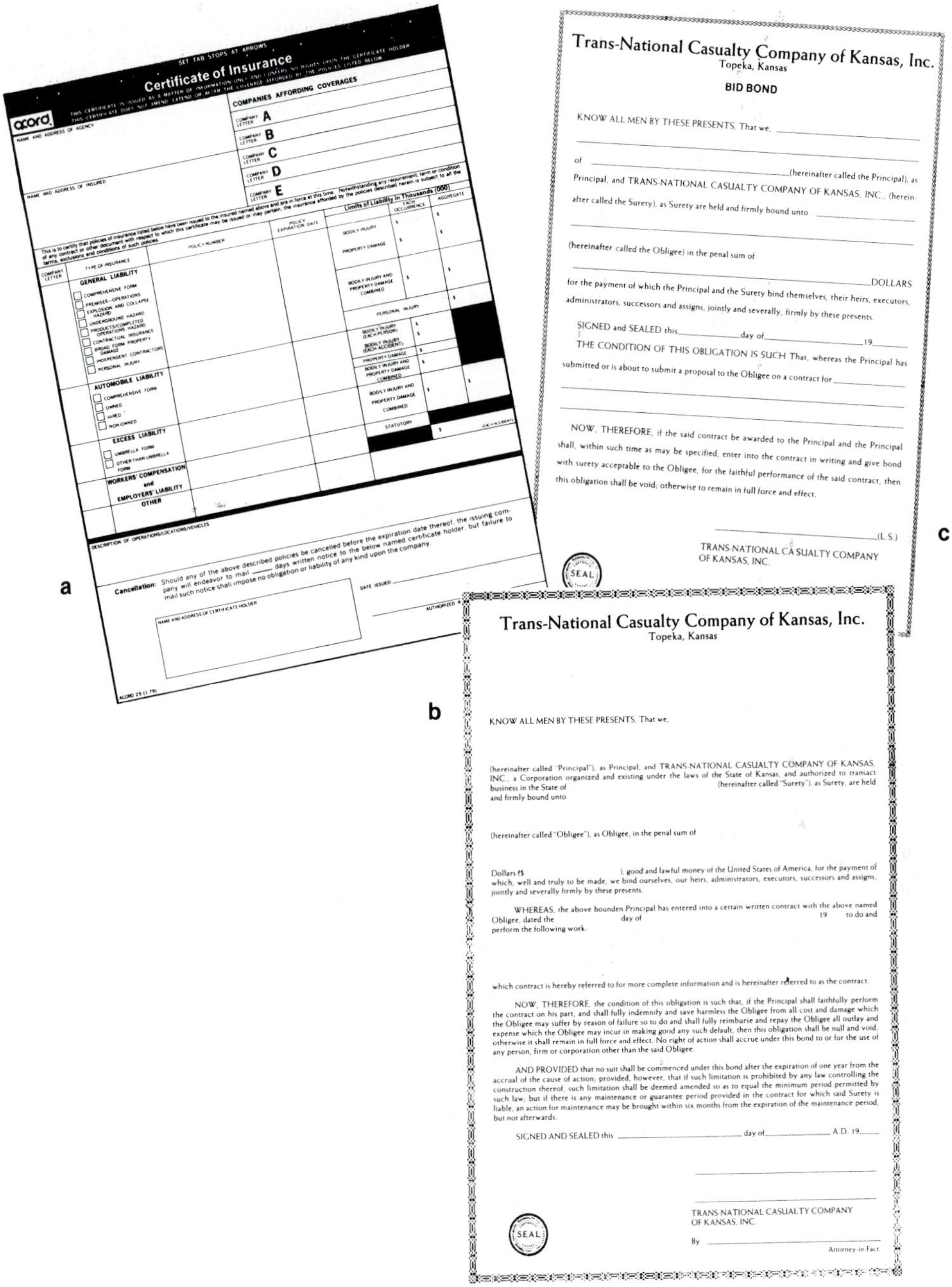

Figure 13–2. A certificate proving insurance coverage, a bid bond, and a performance bond are often required of the successful bidder on a landscape project.

Finally, the bidder's instructions stipulate the type of contractual agreement to be made between bidder and property owner, the time span within which those contracts must be signed, and the manner in which they are to be executed.

The *scope of work* section briefly sets out the limits of the project, including its location and a general description of the work to be accomplished. This section should tell potential bidders enough about the project so they can determine its suitability for their firms. This saves time for the bidders and helps to sort out those bidders not suitable for the project.

The *materials specifications* section specifies quality standards for all materials to be used in the completion of the landscaping project. Typically, a complete plant list, with names, sizes, quantities, and conditions, will appear in this section. Quality standards for plant materials will either be spelled out in detail or covered by a blanket statement that materials must conform to those set forth in *American Standards for Nursery Stock.* Individual standards for nonplant materials are similarly written.

This section usually provides for the inspection of materials before their installation. It also spells out any regulations for on-site storage of materials. Invoices received by the contractor will sometimes be required as evidence of material quality or quantity purchased.

Overall job quality and cost are greatly influenced by the *installation specifications.* Procedures for installations of exactly the type needed for each material are carefully set forth in this segment. To overspecify in this area is wasteful of the property owner's dollars. Certain soil types, for example, might dictate the excavation of extremely large planting holes, providing adequate drainage in tight clay soils, or replacing infertile soils. But if the soil type existing on the site is suitable, requiring excessively large holes or replacement of soil merely increases the cost of the project.

It is necessary, then, for a designer to know the conditions of each site before writing good installation specifications. Then, and only then, can the specifications be appropriate for that installation. Besides the added expense, overspecification irritates many contractors to the point where they refuse to submit a bid.

Procedures for setting plants in holes, backfilling, tamping, watering, staking, and guying, wrapping tree trunks, and pruning plants are all included in this section. Installation of edgings, gravels or mulches, groundcovers, and other landscape elements are also covered here (see Figure 13–3).

Often, provision is made for the designer to cooperate in staking out the entire landscaping project in advance. Then, nothing can be installed in an improper position without the designer's knowledge. The costly job of moving a misplaced element is thus prevented.

The seasonal timing of installations may be specified in this section or by itself. For landscaping installations, two time spans, for fall or spring planting, are commonly specified. Separate times will be listed for lawn installations, when included.

The contractor's *maintenance* responsibilities are spelled out in a separate section. This vital information has great bearing on the project's success. It is

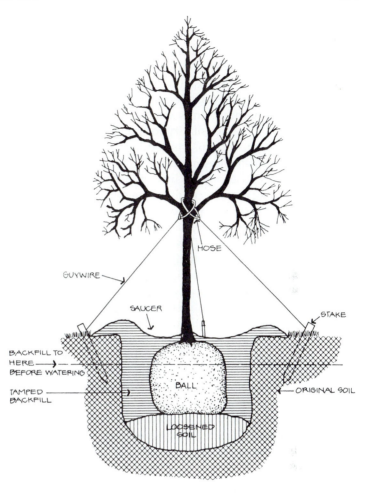

HOSE

GUYWIRE

SAUCER

STAKE

BACKFILL TO
HERE
BEFORE WATERING

TAMPED
BACKFILL

BALL

LOOSENED
SOIL

ORIGINAL SOIL

Figure 13–3. A typical planting and guying specification for trees.

also important in the bidder's cost determination. While more maintenance does mean higher total cost to the property owner, it also reduces the risk of the landscaping getting off to a poor start. In addition, it reduces the contractor's risk resulting from guarantees and warranties specified. Information written here tells the contractor how long he will have to maintain the new project after installation and what materials will be required to perform those tasks. The extent of maintenance is also covered. For example, one project might require complete maintenance of a lawn area, while another might not require mowing.

Guarantees and warranties help ensure that the materials installed are going to be long-lasting improvements. It is felt that if the plant materials live and thrive for a period of time after they are planted, they are of long-lasting quality and have been properly installed.

All conditions of guarantees and warranties—such as time span, extent of coverage, and responsibility for replacements—are covered here. Plants are often covered by a limited warranty. The contractor may be responsible for blanket coverage of a plant's health in some cases, but in most, the natural catastrophes are excluded. In these limited warranties, hail damage, drought, and other "acts of God" may be considered to be outside the realm of the guarantees. Length of coverage varies from six to twelve months. Also stipulated is the contractor's subsequent responsibility for guaranteeing plant replacements. Usually, it is felt that the contractor's extended involvement by guaranteeing replacement plantings generates more cost to the client than the extended coverage is worth.

Specifications do little good unless *inspections and remedies* are provided. The timing of inspections, along with the methods to be used, is spelled out separately and carefully. Normally, the contractor is responsible for notifying the owner's representative at certain stages of the project's completion so that inspections can be made. This notification may be verbal or written. The contractor is notified of the acceptability of inspected materials and workmanship. If they are found to be unacceptable, then the remedies will be applied. These remedies may require the work to be redone, a portion of the contract amount to be forfeited, or the work to be recontracted with another firm at the first contractor's expense.

Remedies are often provided by a performance bond obtained by the contractor as a part of his or her responsibility at the time of the contract signing (see Figure 13–2c on page 271). A bond equal to the amount of the contract is purchased by the contractor at the time contracts are signed. In case of contractor default, the amount of that bond is forfeited to the owner.

The *performance-times* segment of a landscape specification is not always necessary. It is used to specify the length of time in which the contractor must complete the entire job. Failure to complete the project within the allotted time, when compromise is not deemed a viable alternative by the owner, can cause the contractor to forfeit a performance bond or be liable for other remedies.

If subcontracting is to be allowed, the rules are spelled out in the specifications. Normally, the principal contractor must bear final responsibility to the client, regardless of subcontractors. Subcontractors are then responsible to the principal contractor by separate agreement.

The *terms for payment* section might be the single most important part of a landscape specification from the bidder's standpoint. This section spells out all details for partial and full payments from the owner to the successful bidder. Of course, these details are also included in the job contracts, but specifications precede contracts.

On smaller landscaping projects, the entire contractual amount might be due upon final acceptance of the work by the property owner's representative. Many times a *retainage* of 10 percent, or some similar figure, will be withheld pending the contractor's satisfactory fulfilling of all guarantee and warranty requirements. This means the contractor might have to wait an entire year's guarantee period before receiving the final 10% of the contracted amount. This increases the total amount of the contractor's bid, because interest must be included on that money for a year, but it also secures the guarantees and warranties, providing remedy in the event they are not upheld.

On larger projects, where work is expected to take place over an extended period of time, provision is often made for partial payments. At the end of a month of work, the contractor submits a partial billing, based on the portion of the contract completed during that month. Sometimes these partial payments even include payment for materials that the contractor has purchased but has not yet installed on the site. Nearly always, when such partial payments are made, a percentage will be retained by the owner until the project is complete or until the guarantees and warranties have been satisfied. The designer who writes specifications must carefully keep both the property owner and the contractor in mind when specifying payments, at once protecting the owner and being fair to the contractor.

Although specifications are written to ensure equal quality of materials and workmanship, that idealistic goal is seldom obtainable. Equal quality from separate bidders is not possible because of their differing capabilities. All can produce to a minimum standard, however, and this is what specifications seek. While one of the unsuccessful bidders might have produced a more satisfactory job, the one who meets the minimum standards set forth by specifications and submits a lower price will get the job.

OBTAINING PRICES FROM CONTRACTORS

A landscape designer's duties often extend to helping clients obtain prices from contractors and vendors. In the case of a commercially employed designer/salesperson, those prices are extended by the firm for which the designer works. In any case, the property owner will at least have to purchase materials and, if not inclined to do the entire installation, labor also. A designer with true interest in the final product—the landscape itself—gives the property owner guidance in purchasing and contracting as a logical extension of the design process.

There are three general ways in which prices are extended from a business to its customers: the time-plus-materials method, the cost estimation, and the bid. A firm using the *time-plus-materials method* of pricing merely tells its customers that careful records will be kept of all materials and labor used on the project, and those materials and labor will be priced by unit prices at the project's conclusion. No effort is made to estimate the total cost for the project. Many businesses use this pricing method because it is the safest. Their established prices generate a proper amount of profit, and by avoiding a total price, they eliminate the chance of incorrectly assessing the working conditions. The client has no chance to take advantage of an underestimated cost (in which he or she ultimately receives goods and services at lower-than-normal prices) when the time-plus-materials method is used. On the other side of the coin, the customer also does not have to be concerned that the contractor will overestimate costs, charging the full amount of the estimate and thereby increasing normal unit costs for materials and labor.

When *cost estimations* are given to customers, the materials and labor needed to complete the project are anticipated by the business. Cost estimations are presented as an *estimated* total cost or cost range. In effect, the business is saying: "This may not be the exact total amount we will bill you for these materials and labor, but it is a close estimation." Various circumstances that occur during the progress of the project can alter the final bill.

A *bid* is a firm price. Bids are preceded by the cost-estimation process, and the company finally settles on a firm price for the entire job. By this definition, the bid price may not be altered, regardless of the circumstances encountered during job progress. Bids are normally used when more than one firm competes for the same project. Given a set of landscape plans and specifications as a guide to the quality of materials and workmanship, the bidders prepare cost estimations and extend bids. All other factors being equal, the lowest bidder is awarded the contract.

Bids are usually bounded by the plans and specifications. Anything added to the job by the property owner or his or her representative that is not included in the original plans and specifications will be billed as extra work.

A bid does offer the client the security of knowing exactly what the project will cost. However, since the contractor has to honor that price, regardless of job contingencies encountered, the contractor might inflate the bid by a *contingency percentage* for protection. If no unusual circumstances arise during job performance, the extra cost of the contingency percentage is absorbed wholly by the property owner. In that case, the materials and services would have cost less by the time-and-materials method.

Individual circumstances must rule. Bids are a necessity if two, three, or more firms compete for a job. Anything other than a firm price cannot be measured against competition. A contractor might give a low price range, knowing that he or she is not required to stand behind it, just to get a job. Of course, there is no way of comparing prices by the time-plus-materials method, except for comparing individual materials and labor prices by units. Even when unit prices are compared, they are often meaningless. A firm charging several dollars per hour more than a competitor might be able to complete work of equal quality in a much shorter time span, ultimately becoming the less expensive of the two.

MAKING COST ESTIMATES

A cost estimation involves the anticipation of events to occur as a project is under way. In that sense, good estimations can be based only on adequate previous experience. The experience required can come from the estimator's own background or from the background of others with a longer time in the field. It might not be possible for an inexperienced estimator to anticipate accurately the length of time required to complete a given landscaping project, never having personally experienced such work, but if others from the same firm have had that experience and can pass it on to the estimator, it can be utilized in composing an estimate. Others' experiences must be evaluated carefully, though. To accept the time estimations of someone with experience with a different labor market or soil type would be foolish. Standardized, present time spans for completing different landscape tasks, regardless of conditions, simply must be inaccurate in many instances. Soil and weather conditions and the intelligence, experience, training, and aptitude of the work force, plus the availability of machinery, can all have a significant effect on the time required to perform landscaping tasks.

Any cost estimate can be broken down into two main ingredients—labor and materials. All materials are stated on landscape plans or specifications. The estimator must count the numbers, measure quantities, and calculate amounts, listing them precisely. Accurate numbers and measurements result from the estimator being absolutely meticulous. It helps to list these materials in the same order each time an estimate is made. This materials listing is called the *takeoff*, as the individual materials are "taken off" the plans and specifications. The order in which takeoff items are listed may vary among estimators, and the order itself is not important. *It is important, though, for an estimator to follow the same order each time so as not to forget anything.* One suggested order for the takeoff is listed below:

1. List all plant materials; their quantities, sizes, and conditions.
2. List all nonliving groundcovering materials.
   a. Measure areas to be covered and calculate volumes needed.
   b. Calculate amount of poly film or weedmat to be used under mulches.
3. Measure and list all edgings required. Calculate board feet if wood edgings are used.
4. Calculate and list volumes of required soil amendments.
5. Calculate and list all staking and guying materials, along with tree wraps and other materials necessary to finish plantings.
6. List any other hardgoods required for the job, such as stepping stones, statuaries, and boulders.
7. Calculate any landscape construction work to be completed as a unit.
   a. Itemize materials to be used and calculate quantities.
   b. Secure estimates for any necessary preliminary work to be subcontracted (for example, excavation by a bulldozer).
   c. Estimate time requirements for completion of the construction work.
8. Calculate time required to stake out plantings, beds, and other landscaping features.
9. Calculate the length of time required for bed excavation and preparation.

10. Estimate planting time.

11. Estimate the time required for installing nonliving groundcovers and edgings.

12. Estimate the time requirements for staking, guying, and wrapping trees.

13. Estimate the time required for pruning, removing tags, making saucers, and other finishing operations.

14. Estimate lawn establishment.

   a. Measure areas and calculate materials needed.

   b. Assess level of difficulty and estimate labor and machine work.

15. Estimate clean-up time at job's end.

16. Estimate maintenance for any specified period.

   a. Materials.

   b. Labor and machine work.

17. Log unit prices, multiply unit prices by number of units, extend total costs for each unit and total prices for all units.

18. Add the necessary sales taxes.

Estimators often use a standard takeoff form that has been devised to suit their individual needs (see Figure 13–4). Such a form encourages accuracy and saves time by listing many commonly used items. Then, the estimator only has to write in the numbers and costs. An estimate, however, can be prepared on any type of paper so long as every element of the project is accounted for, and the estimation sheet can be filed for future reference. Just remember, though, that to forget anything on an estimate could result in the loss of the entire profit planned for that job; or, if the estimate is just being prepared for the customer's benefit, the distortion could lead him or her to make the wrong decision. Estimations must be as complete and precise as possible.

CALCULATIONS IN ESTIMATING

Most of the calculations needed for landscaping estimations use simple arithmetic. As quantities of materials and laborhours are determined, the estimator multiplies unit quantities by unit prices, arriving at total prices. In addition, *area sizes* of pieces of land and *volumes* of materials must often be calculated.

To calculate the *area* of a piece of land, simply multiply *length* times *width*— after making sure that both dimensions are measured in the same units. The area of a landscape bed that is 20′ x 50′, for example, is calculated as shown below:

$$50' \text{ (length)} \times 20' \text{ (width)} = 1,000 \text{ sq. ft. (area)}$$

Area calculations are used in determining seed, sod, sprig, and plug material requirements for lawn establishment. They are also required for deducing

Client _____Address _____Ph. _____

Type of work: (circle) lawn seeding   lawn sodding   sprigging   plugging

Landscape: planting   groundcovers   gravel/mulch beds   edgings

Construction: fence   walls   deck   patio   walks   sprinkler system

Plant Materials

Name	Size	Quantity	Unit	Total	Name	Size	Quantity	Unit	Total

Total—plant materials _____

Hardgoods

Name	Size	Quantity	Unit	Total	Name	Size	Quantity	Unit	Total

Total—Hardgoods_____

Labor

Lawn: tractor____ hrs @ ____ = ____   Landscaping____ manhrs @ ____

labor____ hrs @ ____ = ____

machines_____   Construction____ manhrs @ ____

Total_____   Total labor_____

Total materials and labor_____

Figure 13–4.   An example of a standard takeoff that might be used by a landscape contractor to prepare a bid.

groundcover numbers when only the spacings are known and for calculating fertilizer amounts.

Volume is a cubic measure, calculated by the formula *length* times *width* times *depth* equals *cubic volume* (see Figure 13–5). To find the amount of gravel needed to cover a planting bed to a prescribed depth, the amount of soil-amending materials needed, or the volume of cuts and fills in grading operations, this formula is used. As an example, suppose that in the landscape bed used for the earlier area calculation (50′ × 20′) it is necessary to find the volume of soil to a depth of 2′. The calculation would be as follows:

50′ (length) × 20′ (width) × 2′ (depth) = 2,000 cu.ft. (cubic volume)

These calculations become more complex when not all dimensions are given in the same units of measurement. For example, if the volume of soil to be removed from that same 50′ × 20′ bed is to be 2″ instead of 2′, the three dimensions are no longer represented by the same units of measurement. Simply to multiply 50 × 20 × 2 would give a grossly overstated volume, because the product would be in cubic feet, as if the 2 represented feet instead of inches. It is necessary to convert all measurements into the same standard units for volume and area calculations. In the example given, the estimator has a choice between converting measurements so that either all are in inches or all are in feet. Since two of the numbers are already given in feet, it would seem logical in this case to convert the depth figure from inches to a fraction of a foot. Two inches is 1/6 of 1′ (12″ divided by 2″ = 6), so the volume calculation can be accomplished as shown below:

50′ (length) × 20′ (width) × 1/6′ (depth) = 167 cu.ft. (cubic volume)

The 2″ can also be converted to a decimal part of 1′ by dividing 2 by 12:

2″ ÷ 12″ = 0.1666667′

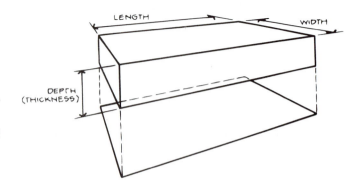

Figure 13–5. The cubic volume of any material is represented by the three dimensions of length, width, and depth.

The volume calculation is then completed as before, with the decimal substituted for the fraction. Either way, the result is the same:

50′ (length) × 20′ (width) × 0.1666667′ (depth) = 166.6667 cu.ft. (cubic volume)

The other possibility in this example is to convert all figures to inches. In this case, the depth (2″) is already in inches, so the other two dimensions must be converted from feet to inches by multiplying each by 12, the number of inches in a foot:

$$50′ \times 12″ = 600″$$
$$20′ \times 12″ = 240″$$

The entire volume calculation would look like this with the product expressed in cubic inches:

600″ (length) × 240″ (width)× 2″ (depth) = 288,000 cu.in. (volume)

Regardless of the standard of measurement used to calculate areas of volume, it must often be converted to another standard of measurement in the final calculation for pricing purposes. Most materials that are sold by volume measurements are priced by either the cubic foot or the cubic yard. It is necessary, therefore, for the estimator to be able to convert volumes from one standard to another. The relationships of one volume measurement to another are:

$$1 \text{ cu.yd (1 yd.} \times 1 \text{ yd.} \times 1 \text{ yd.)} = 27 \text{ cu.ft (3′} \times 3′ \times 3′)$$
$$= 46{,}656 \text{ cu.in. (36″} \times 36″ \times 36″)$$
$$1 \text{ cu.ft. (1′} \times 1′ \times 1′) = 1{,}728 \text{ cu.in. (12″} \times 12″ \times 12″)$$

In the previous example, then, where the cubic volume was calculated in cubic inches, that volume can be converted to cubic feet of volume by dividing the product of the calculation by 1,728, the number of cubic inches in one cubic foot:

288,000 cu.in. ÷ 1,728 cu.in./cu.ft. = 166.67 cu.ft.

That same volume can be converted to cubic yards of material by dividing the cubic-foot total by 27, the number of cubic feet in 1 cubic yard:

166.67 cu.ft. ÷ 27 cu.ft./cu.yd. = 6.173 cu.yd.

Any set of dimensions can be calculated in the same fashion, by converting all dimensions to the same increments of measurement. In the example used throughout for volume calculations, the 6.173 cubic yards might represent both the amount of soil to be removed from a planting bed and the amount of gravel to be installed in that bed following excavation.

Calculating Lumber Volumes

There is one notable exception to the rule of converting to the same units of measurement before making calculations for estimations. The need to calculate lumber volumes often arises in landscape estimating. Lumber is sold by increments called board feet. A *board foot* of lumber is any product of the three dimensions of lumber (length, width, and thickness) that multiplies to a total of 12 (see Figure 13–6). But unlike the calculation for volume for other materials, all measurements are not in like units. The length is given in feet, but the width and thickness of lumber are given in inches. The formula for calculating the board feet of lumber is as follows:

$$\frac{\text{length (in feet)} \times \text{width (in inches)} \times \text{thickness (in inches)}}{12} = \text{number of board feet}$$

As indicated, any three numbers that multiply to a product of 12 are equal to a board foot of lumber. Therefore, in the formula above, the product of length times width times thickness is divided by 12 to reveal the number of board feet in a piece of lumber or in several pieces of lumber with the same width and thickness. For an example, let us assume that the materials takeoff for a landscaping project reveals that a total length of 240 linear feet of 2″ × 4″ redwood is to be used for edging planting beds. The lumber is priced by the board foot, so it is necessary to calculate the number of board feet in the edging. Using the formula for board feet, the calculation would look like this:

$$\frac{240' \text{ (lin.ft.)(length)} \times 4'' \text{ (width)} \times 2'' \text{ (thickness)}}{12} = 160 \text{ bd.ft.}$$

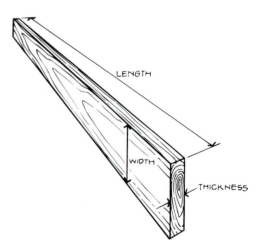

Figure 13–6.   The dimensions of lumber.

By and large, the calculations required for landscape estimations are not complicated. But it is of paramount importance to do them right, always double-checking the accuracy of the arithmetic. It is also wise to avoid assumptions not based on sound mathematical results. For instance, one might quickly assume that by halving the spacing of groundcover plants one would double the number of plants used. Not so. To demonstrate, assume that an area to be planted with living groundcover plants is 60' × 50', and that plants are to be spaced 1' apart. The following calculation would serve to estimate the number of plants required:

$$60' \text{ (length)} \times 50' \text{ (width)} = 3,000 \text{ sq.ft}$$
$$1' \times 1' = 1 \text{ sq.ft. of coverage per groundcover plant}$$
$$3,000 \text{ sq.ft.} \div 1 \text{ sq.ft./plant} = 3,000 \text{ plants}$$

Now, assume that the spacing is to be changed from 1' to 6" between plants. It would seem that by cutting the spacing in half, the number of plants would double—but again, by applying the formula:

$$60' \times 50' = 3,000 \text{ sq.ft.}$$

just as before, but 6" = .5', so

$$.5' \times .5' = .25 \text{ sq.ft. coverage per plant}$$

therefore,

$$3,000 \text{ sq.ft.} \div .25 \text{ sq.ft./plant} = 12,000 \text{ plants}$$

So the number of plants required when the spacing between plants is halved would be four times the number required at the original spacing.

For convenient reference, see the landscape-estimation data charts in the appendixes.

PLANIMETERS AND DIGITIZERS

A planimeter is a mechanical device that can be used to measure and record lengths, calculate areas and volumes, and can even function as a drafting aid, accurately measuring lengths of lines to be drawn.

The modern electronic planimeter consists of a cursor mounted on a tracer-arm, a processor, and accessories allowing the planimeter to become a drafting instrument. Figure 13–7 illustrates a modern planimeter.

To use a planimeter, the operator first selects the scale to be used, setting the processor accordingly. Then the operator systematically moves the instrument's cursor over the lines to be measured, and the distances are recorded by the processor. Calculations of areas and volumes are done by the processor as

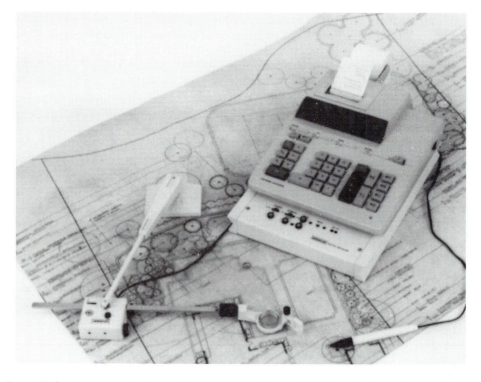

Figure 13–7.   A modern planimeter. (Photo courtesy of Lasico, 2451 Riverside Drive, Los Angeles, CA 90039)

demanded by the operator. Both accuracy and speed are facilitated by the planimeter. To convert the planimeter to a drafting aid, drafting attachments are employed.

Modern electronic planimeters, like Lasico's Model 42P, are able to make adjustments for changing terrain as they calculate areas and volumes. Because of this, a project estimator's takeoff can be more accurate with the use of a planimeter than when measurements are taken manually and calculations are made without the use of the constant correcting slope-influenced measurements. Cost or yield factors can easily be created and used by the processor during the takeoff to yield final cost numbers. If preferred, the planimeter can be connected to a computer by use of interface circuits. It can then automatically input data into a computer cost-estimation system.

A digitizer is an electronic instrument capable of the same functions as the planimeter—and more. The digitizer can also automatically determine X and Y coordinates for easy relocation of points on a plan. The digitizer generally has higher resolution, meaning greater accuracy in both takeoffs and drafting layout functions. Digitizers are often an integral component of computer-aided-drafting (CAD) or the computer-imaging system. (See Chapter 15.)

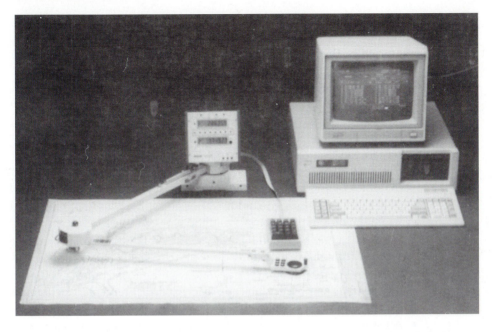

Figure 13–8. Lasico's Series 1280 digitizer, tied in with a microcomputer by means of a built-in computer interface. (Photo courtesy of Lasico, 2451 Riverside Drive, Los Angeles, CA 90039)

Many digitizers, like Lasico's Series 1280 have built-in computer interfaces (Figure 13–8).

POINTS TO REMEMBER

- Landscape specifications often accompany plans in an attempt to assure property owners that they will receive equal quality in materials and workmanship regardless of the source.
- In order to be effective, landscape specifications must be written in clear, concise language and must be reasonably complied with. Inspection procedures must be followed and remedies must be reasonable and well enforced.
- Bidder's instructions, spelling out the conditions of bidder qualification, should always come first so that those eliminated from the bidding do not waste valuable time reading further.
- Bid bonds are purchased by bidders to assure the property owner that a successful bidder will sign a contract to perform the work when the contract is awarded.
- Performance bonds are purchased by a contractor to ensure project completion after contracts are signed and work is begun.

- The specifications for postinstallation maintenance greatly affect a contractor's anticipated costs for guarantees and warranties and vice versa.
- Normally, the principal contractor on a project is also responsible for the performance of any subcontractors he or she hires.
- A retainage of part of the contracted amount for the time span covered by guarantees and warranties results in more expense to the contractor because of the interest charged against the amount of such retainage. It also insures the client against the contractor's defaulting on guarantees and warranties.
- Prices are quoted to customers by commercial firms using the time-plus-materials method, cost estimation, or bid. Only the bid is a firm price.
- Cost estimations precede bidding, but no estimations of cost are made when the time-plus-materials method is used.
- A bid is usually bounded by information on landscape plans and specifications. Additional work is only done at extra cost.
- The primary requirement for anyone wishing to become a good estimator is a systematic and meticulous approach to measurements, calculations, and other mathematical details so as not to miss anything.
- A listing of all materials required, along with labor and machine work necessary to perform a landscape project, is called a takeoff.
- The two calculations used most frequently to determine quantities during a landscape estimation are those for area size and for cubic volumes of materials.
- The formula for calculating the square area is length × width = square area.
- The formula for calculating the cubic volume of an area at a prescribed depth is length × width × depth = cubic volume.
- When making area or volume calculations, it is necessary for all dimensions to be expressed in the same units of measurement.
- Lumber volumes are calculated in terms of board feet as follows: (length [in feet] × width and thickness [in inches]) ÷ 12.
- It is very important not to make unfounded assumptions about quantities of materials. Unless you are sure of the outcome, sound mathematical calculations should always be used.

REVIEW QUESTIONS

1. What are design specifications, and why are they written?
2. What is usually included in the "bidder's instructions" part of written specifications?
3. How does a bid bond differentiate from a performance bond?

4. Why is a materials specification necessary when competitive bids are being taken for a landscaping project?

5. What is the difference between a cost estimate and a bid?

6. Why is it best that a contractor uses the exact same order of listing items on each cost estimate made?

7. Give the formula for calculating area.

8. Give the formula for calculating cubic volume.

9. Give the formula for calculating board feet of lumber.

PRACTICAL TIP FROM A PRACTICING DESIGNER

A great timesaving tool available to the landscape designer is the scaled plan measuring wheel. This device is particularly helpful when you want to measure edging, retaining walls, or anything else that is curved, because straight scale-sticks do not easily or accurately bend around the curves. As the wheel is rolled along the line that is being measured, the number of feet shows on the dial, given in various scales. Most wheels display architectural, engineering, and metric scales. Some of the more expensive devices give the number of feet measured in a digital readout. Electronic models can also calculate square area or cubic volume upon demand.

Chapter 14

THE ROLE OF THE DESIGNER/SALESPERSON

In this chapter, you will learn how to make sales to individuals, couples, committees, and businesspeople. You will learn about prospecting for potential clients, handling objections potential clients might make, and closing the sale.

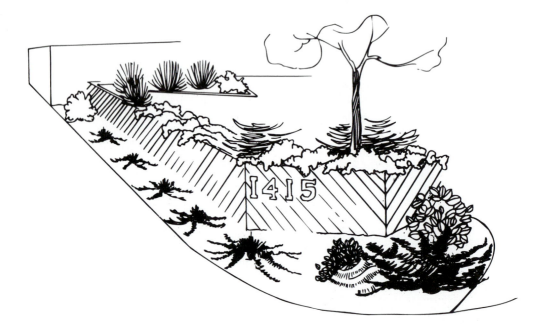

The sales process is a natural extension of the design process. After all, who is better equipped to explain a design to a client than the person who conceived it? Since only when a design is sold is the designer assured of its implementation, most landscape planners have a natural interest in making sales, and most designers, believing strongly in their work, demonstrate a keen interest in the ultimate installation of their creations. Most modern design/build landscape firms employ landscape designers who are capable of doubling as salespersons.

MOTIVATIONS FOR PURCHASING

For many, the term *sales* has harsh, mercenary overtones. In reality, though, a sale is a transaction between two parties that should benefit both. On the one hand, the landscaping firm sells goods and services, generating money to pay salaries, buy more goods to sell, pay operating expenses, and, it is hoped, leave a profit for the business owners. Purchasers are willing to pay because they need or desire those goods and services. It is those *needs* and *desires* for goods and services that motivate clients to purchase. When his or her needs and desires are satisfied, the client benefits from having spent the money.

We all buy food, clothing, heating fuel, and other essentials because of our need for them. Other purchases, for example a pleasure boat or golf clubs, might be made strictly because of a desire to own them. Sometimes both motivations may be present, making the impetus to buy even stronger. But without one or the other, purchases are unlikely.

Landscaping sales in particular are stimulated by both needs and desires in varying proportions. The public has become increasingly aware of the environmental, ecological, and other benefits afforded by private landscaping. This need for landscaping has also been greatly stimulated by our growing suburban population in their efforts to revegetate barren subdivisions. That landscaping is desired by the public is evidenced by the fact that increasing amounts of literature on the subject are readily snapped up.

The task of the designer/salesperson is to educate potential clients about their needs for landscaping, stimulating a desire for it at the same time. A good salesperson might be best considered as a teacher, always educating clients about needs for products and services sold.

THE SALES EDUCATION

Establishing Needs and Desires

Many of the needs for landscaping are discovered by property owners during the design process. In fact, in the initial stages of the design process, when the site analysis and the analysis of people's needs are completed, the designer is guiding property owners to discover their own needs for landscaping. Their

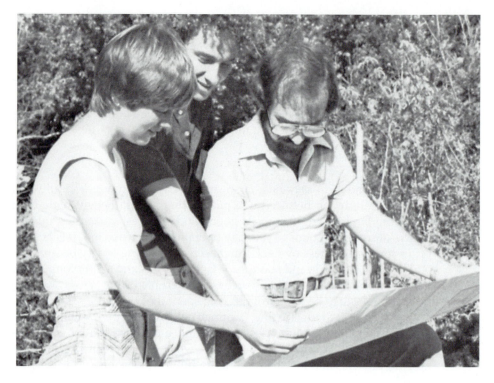

Figure 14–1.   A landscape designer/salesperson explains proposed landscaping to his clients.

basic needs for screening, wind protection, shade, and enclosure might not be apparent to them before that time, but as they discuss these factors with the designer, they become educated as to the value of a good landscape. The entire design process should be a learning experience for property owners, as long as the designer carefully maintains effective oral and written communications.

Whereas a landscape designer must question clients in order to establish design criteria, the designer/salesperson should also emphasize why those questions are being asked. When the designer thinks out loud, it not only teaches the client some of the principles of landscaping, establishing needs along the way, but it also reaffirms that the landscape is being designed for the client, not for the designer.

Communications

All through the design process, the designer should keep in touch with the clients, informing them of progress, asking further questions, or testing design ideas on them (see Figure 14–1). Nothing cools a client's interest faster than weeks of inactivity on the part of the designer. The client's interest is understandably high as the design process is initiated, but it will quickly wane if that process drags on and on without any contact from the designer. Sales from plans are more difficult if the client's desire fades, even though he or she may still recognize the needs.

Many designers first show their clients rough drawings of proposed landscape plans before spending a considerable amount of time to produce finished drafts. The idea is to gain acceptance of their ideas before that drafting time is expended. Another school of thought believes, however, that clients are less apt to accept the ideas in rough drawings than they are if those ideas are neatly and clearly represented in a finished drawing. Reasoning that the extra drafting time is worthwhile because it results in less redesigning, those same designers also believe that if great care is taken during the analysis and designing stages, the plans they initially present should be the best they can produce for that property.

Whichever approach is taken, it should be remembered that the landscape plan is a communication device. Supplemented by verbal explanation, and possibly by pictures of finished work or photographs of plants, the plan serves as part of the learning material for the client's sales education. If done well, that finished landscape plan will detail for readers exactly what is intended for the final landscape. Nevertheless, the designer should always remember that those who are unfamiliar with the reading of landscape plans may need help to absorb and understand all that is graphically represented.

The role of the designer/salesperson when landscape plans are first shown to a client is as an interpreter. Each and every symbol on the plans should be carefully explained to the client so that he or she can better understand the design intentions and, therefore, have a better grasp of the needs for proposed landscaping. Furthermore, the clearer the client's understanding of plans, the more his or her desire will be stimulated for the end product.

Sequencing Information

As a salesperson showing plans to a client, the designer should carefully sequence information, starting with one feature on the plans and following through all others. Environmental needs might be established first, with all shading, wind protection, solar heating, and insulation units being explained thoroughly. Next, area divisions might be covered, with the designer explaining how each area is to be used and how its size and shape conform to intended uses. During this explanation, the designer is always mindful of the fact that these usages were originally suggested by the client for his or her own needs during design analysis. Again, the needs are magnified, making the client's decision to purchase much easier. Circulation might be next on the agenda, with the designer showing the client how easily he or she will be able to get to every place in the landscaped grounds. Patio size, shape, and construction should be discussed here, as well as the arrangement of driveway, parking spaces, and walks.

Plantings have already been mentioned in connection with establishing environmental features, area dividers, and so forth. Now each plant can be discussed individually. This discussion should be of sufficient depth to allow the client to form a mental picture of each plant. Photographs of plants help, of course, but the verbal description must be strong enough to form images of the plant's main features in the client's mind.

Finally, the landscape's embellishments may be discussed. Many of these may have been included at the client's suggestions anyway, so he or she will be well equipped to understand and appreciate them. It is wise to point them out, though, making sure the client knows of their existence in the design and understands their purpose.

Descriptive Language

During the sales education, it is vital to use color-descriptive language. While color is only one of the physical features the designer works with, it is the most appealing feature to most clients. Form and size are important and are fairly easily grasped by the client, but color is the feature they remember the most. Texture is more difficult to explain and often just clouds the client's understanding.

After carefully going over the features of the landscape plan, both by "needs" groupings and by individual features, it is wise to review the plan's highlights. For example, if a shrub border has been designed to sequence blooms throughout the growing season, the designer/salesperson might review that flowering sequence. The client's desire for all of these flowers during the growing season will be stimulated. One of the nice things about selling landscaping is the fact that the product being sold is naturally beautiful and good for people. By merely pointing out the many uses of the products and emphasizing their natural beauty, the designer can easily stimulate the client's desire to purchase.

Questions and Objections

During the sales education, questions from the client should be encouraged. Questions indicate a real interest, and the answers tend to be remembered.

Objections to purchasing are commonly raised by clients during a sales education. Some of these objections are based on real doubts about an item's suitability to the plan and some by the client's budget. At other times, the client merely wants more affirmation of the need for something as it is shown. Regardless of their basis, these objections should never be viewed by the salesperson as negative reactions. Instead, they should be seen as the opportunities they really are. Each objection raised offers the salesperson a chance to make solid sales points by offering feasible, positive solutions. By offering solutions that counteract the objections, the salesperson more firmly implants the needs, stimulating desire in the client's mind.

Sometimes objections are made by a client simply as a means of reducing his or her own inhibitions about making the purchase. A positive, feasible answer by the salesperson allows the purchase to be made without qualms.

At some point in a sales presentation, prices must be given to the client. Prices often become a stumbling point for inexperienced salespeople, who feel uncomfortable with them. This is especially likely if the salesperson tries to guess at the amounts the client is able or willing to pay. It is very important for a salesperson not to try to anticipate the client's reaction to prices. Only the customer is in a position to make these judgments. Prices should always be simply stated, leaving decisions entirely to the client.

The tone of a sales education is important. A relaxed, conversational tone is best. Because a designer/salesperson is involved with a client over a longer period of time than other sales personnel normally are, it is easier for them to adopt the appropriate tone. But just the same, nervous chattering, dramatic changes in voice inflection, inordinate politeness, or wild claims should all be avoided. Any of these mistakes can quickly convert a sales education into a sales pitch, making the client wary.

QUALIFICATIONS OF A SALESPERSON

Although salespeople fit many molds, there are certain attributes that a person should possess or develop in order to be successful. These are described in no particular order of importance:

- A good salesperson will be knowledgeable about products and services sold. The ability to educate customers depends on knowing these products and services well enough to answer questions and objections. Certainly any qualified landscape designer should have little trouble meeting this qualification.

- A good salesperson must be a good teacher. The ability to teach a client about the goods or services offered allows the salesperson to establish the needs or desires that will eventually motivate the customer to buy.

- A good salesperson should be enthusiastically aggressive. Energetic pursuit of sales does not mean being obnoxious, however. Enthusiasm *with sensitivity* is the key.

- A good salesperson must be honest. Promises about price, delivery dates, quality, and so forth must not be broken. One broken promise has more lasting effect than ten that are kept.

- A good aspiring salesperson must be articulate. Clear and concise verbal communication is essential to help clients discover their needs and desires for products and services. Incorrect grammar and too much slang are distractions from the sales purpose.

- Cleanliness and good grooming are essential. Anything less is a distraction, and the salesperson's desire is to keep the client's attention on the landscaping under discussion. Clothing should fit the job. A business suit is unnecessary for landscape sales.

- A good salesperson will be sensitive to the feelings of clients. Although an initial negative reaction will not deter the salesperson from trying to complete a sale, care must be exercised not to become a pest. The salesperson must learn to judge the client's reactions.

- A good salesperson will always be grateful to clients. A sincere thank-you is always appreciated. Expressions of gratitude influence a client's opinion of a salesperson, in turn influencing what the client says to others about the firm's work.
- A good salesperson will never forget a client. That client may have need for further products and services or may have friends considering similar purchases.
- A good salesperson will be loyal to his or her employer. Customers easily recognize disloyalty and frown on it, figuring the salesperson could just as easily be disloyal to them.

There are no great secrets to becoming a successful landscaping salesperson. In most cases, as in designing landscapes, sales is a problem-solving activity. By discovering what people need and like, then fulfilling as much of that as is possible, sales efforts are essentially completed. In short, sales are made most readily by demonstrating concern for the client and the client's property, then devising the most suitable landscape for that property. The sales consummation occurs as clients are appropriately educated about design intentions.

DEVELOPMENT OF A CLIENTELE

Attracting potential clients is necessary for increasing a firm's sales volume. This process is often called *prospecting*, when a firm hunts for customers in the way a miner hunts for gold. Prospecting may be accomplished in many ways, with most businesses using a combination of them.

Advertising

Every landscaping firm uses some types of advertising to help attract clients. Advertising covers a broad spectrum of media, but essentially it is anything designed to put the company name before the public. We are accustomed to thinking of advertising as commercials on radio and television, advertisements in newspapers or magazines, and direct mailings sent to potential customers. But advertising also includes business cards, letterhead stationery, signs on buildings or vehicles, telephone directory listings, and any other means of displaying a company name. Advertising need not be generated by the firm it benefits. Word-of-mouth advertising is probably the strongest form available in the landscaping industry. When a satisfied customer recommends a firm to another person, the impact is strong. Most businesses use a combination of several—maybe even all—of these advertising means to attract potential customers.

Direct Contact

Some firms do most of their prospecting by directly contacting potential clients. This might be accomplished by simply ringing doorbells, briefly identifying the business and services offered, and asking if the firm might be of service.

In areas where door-to-door sales are restricted by law, direct contact often is replaced by a direct mailing or the use of a welcoming service, offering some incentive for the potential client to contact the business.

Direct-contact prospecting methods are usually most successful when no pressure is applied to the potential client. The salesperson simply lets the client know his or her firm's name and location, the products and services offered, and indicates a desire to be of service. It is helpful to leave a business card or brochure with the prospect so the firm's name, phone, and address will be at hand. This "soft-sell" method seldom offends and is a good way for the company to be assured that a potential client at least knows of the firm's existence.

SALES STRATEGIES

Attitudes

Two general sales attitudes are found within landscaping firms. An *active sales attitude* dictates that a firm pursues both customers and sales to customers energetically. Do not confuse this with high-pressure sales. Although active sales can be pursued with high-pressure methods, most firms opt for the soft sell instead. Being active simply means being enthusiastically aggressive about making as many sales as possible to as many clients as possible.

Passive sales attitudes also are used by some landscaping businesses. These firms might do some traditional advertising, by way of telephone directories, business cards, and other printed materials, but they do not actively solicit business by any other means. These firms have usually been in business long enough to have built a solid reputation and await customer contact before any sales efforts are made. They do little prospecting of any type.

Regardless of the individual firm's sales attitude, prospective customers must somehow become available before sales efforts can be fruitful. In a landscaping application the treatment of a client throughout the design and sales stages should be similar. For this reason, design and sales are often combined in modern landscape operations.

Group-Size Influences on Sales Methods

Sales methods will be dictated largely by the size and composition of the group to whom the sale is being made. Selling to an individual differs considerably from selling to a couple or a committee, and still another strategy is best for selling to a businessperson. Recognition of some of these basic strategies at the outset of a sales attempt can be helpful.

An *individual homeowner* offers only one set of likes and dislikes, one set of needs and desires. Successful selling to that individual involves the discovery of these needs and desires so that the selling points can be built around them. Objections made by the client to purchasing can then be countered more successfully.

Much can be learned about an individual client by observing his or her possessions. Does the person dress extravagantly or simply? Are the furnishings of the house practically oriented or are they more elaborate and decorative? Does the client's car indicate practicality or a desire for luxury or flamboyance? Although not a complete indication of that client's inclinations in landscaping, observation of these possessions might at least lend some indication of purchasing tendencies. The sales education can be amplified in the appropriate direction.

Casual conversation with clients is fine, but inflammatory subjects should always be avoided. The salesperson should allow no opportunity for disagreement. As soon as there is an indication that the client is ready to discuss business, the salesperson should proceed and thereafter not wander from the subject.

Part of any successful sales performance is the service after the sale. Return calls to ascertain the customer's satisfaction indicate the salesperson's intent to please. Furthermore, these calls exude confidence in the company's performance. Problems that arise are more easily solved at the salesperson's initiative.

Selling to a Couple

Selling to two people differs from selling to an individual, primarily because two personalities are involved. Two different sets of needs and desires may exist, and two sets of objections may be encountered. More possibility of a personality conflict exists with the addition of another person to the transaction.

Normally, one of the two people involved in a transaction will dominate. The salesperson's job is to satisfy that dominant individual. Usually the member of the twosome who shows the most enthusiasm and asks the most pertinent questions is the driving force in the decision. A positive attitude indicates that the salesperson has an ally in convincing the other one to buy.

The other person may voice most of the objections. These objections must be handled with care. Giving poor answers will do nothing to alter the objector's viewpoint but may dampen the second person's enthusiasm.

Deliberation between the two parties to a decision can lead to an argument. When this occurs, the salesperson should carefully avoid involvement on either side. Alienation of either person by the salesperson minimizes the chances for a sale.

Selling to a Committee

Every committee consists of three distinct parts: the leader, the main body, and the anchor. The leader will often, but not always, be the chairperson. This leader makes the committee decide on issues. The anchor serves the opposite function. This individual drags his or her feet on decisions, usually taking a negative role. Many of the objections voiced will probably come from the anchor. The remaining committee members make up the main body, which will flow with the leader or the anchor, whoever makes the most convincing argument. Roles often change from one issue to another.

Identification of the leader and the anchor is the salesperson's first task when selling to a committee. The leader is usually a strong and persuasive person; if the leader demonstrates a positive attitude toward making the purchase, it can do much to help make the sale. By stimulating discussion toward the positive aspects of the sale and by instigating action, the leader helps the sales cause. The objections raised by the anchor offer ample opportunity for the salesperson to eliminate doubts that members of the more silent main body might share.

The main-body members participate minimally in the discussion but are instrumental in the rendering of a final decision. Since private discussion is usually required before a committee makes its decision, the salesperson can only present his or her case as convincingly as possible before leaving. Having done a good job with the leader and anchor, the salesperson should be able to predict the decision.

Showing a landscape plan to a large committee offers unique challenges in visibility. One set of landscape plans shared by a table full of committee members is unsatisfactory. Those seated far away from the plans will be unable to see details. Specially prepared plans that have been enlarged for easy visibility, or separate sets of plans for each committee member, are in order. Most satisfactory, but more difficult to prepare, is a set of slides that project the plans onto a screen. That way, the salesperson can highlight individual details with a pointer, knowing that all committee members are looking in the right place. Some additional graphical preparation for a committee sale is well worth the effort.

Selling to a Businessperson

Businesspeople are also individuals with likes and dislikes. Unlike homeowners, though, businesspeople share in the common goal of profit-making. A businessperson is likely to regard the landscaping of his or her business property in a completely different light from that of his or her own home. Any way that the salesperson can emphasize the increased profit potential to be realized through business landscaping should be used to increase the chances of sales success.

Potentially profit-stimulating landscape devices should be pointed out in an educational fashion. This information should be brief and concise but not to the exclusion of important details. The point is that businesspeople are usually tightly scheduled, and they appreciate recognition of their busy status. Taking an undue amount of time will not promote the sale.

Written cost estimations and terms for payment, delivery, and performance times may be even more important to businesspeople than to the private individual. Businesspeople are accustomed to dealing with written documents, and they like having all terms spelled out.

Selling from Quick Sketches

Although this book is primarily concerned with the design of complete landscapes in formal plans arrangements, practicing landscape designers often find that their clients want something less. Many landscaping problems are solved by quick sketches completed on the site. The speed with which a design is completed should not reflect on its quality, however. Some of the finest landscapes have been designed rapidly on scraps of paper. Experienced designers often find that their best ideas are their first ones, anyway, so spending additional design time might be counterproductive. When a rapid design is completed on the site, quality graphical representation may be sacrificed to a degree, so the sales success becomes more dependent on the verbal skills of the designer/salesperson. However, a positive savings of design and drafting time also results. To most landscaping businesses, time-saving is the greatest saving of all. If design quality can be maintained, that saving is welcomed. Experienced designers usually have little difficulty substituting verbal communication of design intent for graphical representation. With increased design-speed capabilities comes confidence in design abilities—a confidence that manifests itself in better verbal communication.

Quick sketches may be done in many different ways. Some are drawn only in rough plan view on any paper available. Others are drawn in plan view on graph paper, which makes the scaling of the drawing easier. Still others are completed on copy-producing forms so that both client and designer retain copies of the drawing. Individual company policies dictate procedures. Some firms are reluctant to leave copies of landscape drawings with customers unless the products and services are already sold. They fear the client will take the drawings elsewhere for cost estimates, giving competitors an unfair advantage since they encounter no design or sales cost.

If a designer has the ability to draw quick perspective sketches, elevational drawings, or isometric views of the proposed landscaping, sales are greatly facilitated (see Figure 14–2). The added communicative value of these drawings is well worth the time spent. The old adage "one picture is worth a thousand words" applies. Remember, though, that in the client's eye, drafting quality quite often represents the designer's attitude toward a landscaping project. Any sketches or drawings completed quickly must still be of high quality in order to be effective.

Final Notes about Sales

Sales are often made most readily when the designer/salesperson listens rather than talks. Perhaps the image of a smooth-talking, happy-go-lucky, glad-handing salesperson should be replaced by the image of a sincere listener. As mentioned earlier, sales are facilitated by listening to and observing the needs and desires of customers, then providing for those as much as possible. Since the same requirement is made of a good landscape designer, the two tasks are a natural combination.

POINTS TO REMEMBER

- The sale of landscaping is a natural extension of the design process, since designers are the most knowledgeable about their own designs and also have a naturally high degree of interest in their implementation.

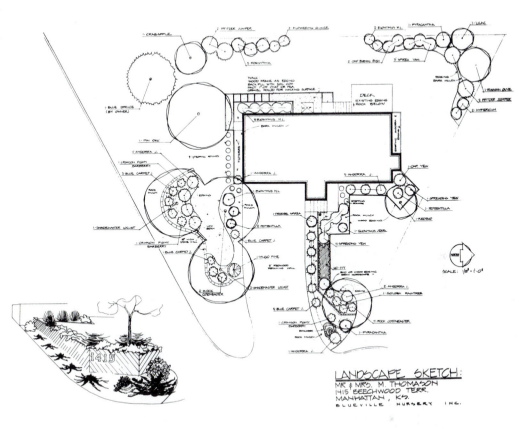

Figure 14–2.   A quick landscape sketch and elevational drawing can often produce large sales. A photograph of a completed portion of this design appears in Figure 5–21, page 99. (Design by Marguerite Koepke)

- Purchases are motivated by the customer's desires or needs for products and services, which may exist individually or in tandem.
- A good salesperson simply educates the customer, emphasizing his or her own needs and desires for products.
- Allowing a client to wait for long periods of time without contact during the design process diminishes sales possibilities.
- The salesperson serves best as an interpreter of the design intentions communicated on landscape plans and specifications.
- Information should be carefully sequenced so a property owner can understand the purpose of all landscape elements.
- Although color, texture, and form are all important physical features to be used during the design process, the sales effort might best emphasize the colors and forms, since texture is more difficult for the novice to understand.

- Questions should be encouraged at all times during a sales presentation. Information given in answer to questions is more likely to be retained.
- Objections should be viewed as opportunities by the salesperson. The answers to objections should always be feasible and positive.
- Anyone who wishes to be a successful salesperson must possess certain important character traits, including honesty, the ability to teach, knowledge of products and services, enthusiasm, articulate speech habits, good grooming habits, and so forth. Many of these traits can be cultivated.
- Prospecting is the act of hunting for potential customers by a business. Advertising by various means and direct contact are the most frequently used ways of prospecting.
- Individual firms may develop either active or passive sales attitudes, depending on whether or not they seek potential clients and sales aggressively.
- Sales strategies vary with the size and composition of the group to which the sale is being made. Individuals, couples, committees, and businesspeople all respond to different variations in sales approaches.
- With larger groups, more attention is necessarily given to the type of graphical representation required for selling from a landscape plan.
- Good design and sales volume can result from quick-sketch landscape planning, as long as high standards of design and graphic representation are maintained and they are supplemented by good verbal communications.
- High-quality perspective sketches, elevational drawings, or isometric representations all help the salesperson to communicate the design intent.
- Sales are often made by listening, instead of talking.

REVIEW QUESTIONS

1. Why is the sale of a landscape by its designer considered to be a natural extension of the designer's job?
2. Why might the sale of a landscape be called a sales education?
3. How do customer objections to making a purchase offer the salesperson an opportunity for success?
4. What are some of the qualities of a good salesperson?
5. What is meant by the term *prospecting*?
6. What are the two general sales attitudes?
7. Why is selling to a couple different from selling to an individual?
8. How can elevational or isometric drawings help sell a landscape?
9. Why is a good salesperson usually a good listener?

PRACTICAL TIP FROM A PRACTICING DESIGNER

I like to bring people to my office when they first see the landscape plans I've drawn for their property. I put the plan on my drawing board, which sits below a wall full of photographs of my completed landscapes. These photos are selected to demonstrate particular landscape features. I also show clients plant photos, to supplement verbal descriptions. Many designers find it effective to use videotapes of their completed work. When meeting in a client's home or office, I carry a portfolio of completed job photos, along with a book of plant photos.

15

COMPUTERS IN
LANDSCAPE DESIGN

In this chapter, the uses of computers in the landscape design process, including computer-aided-design systems and the computer-imaging system, will be discussed.

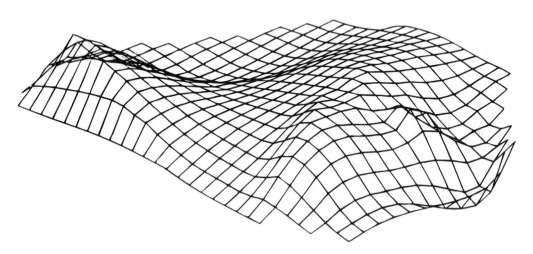

Illustration courtesy of LANDCADD, Inc., 10418 East Tanglewood Road, Franktown, CO 80116.

One of the most beneficial by-products of an ambitious United States space program in the 1960s and 1970s was a tremendous increase in computer technology. Miniaturization, particularly the invention of the microchip, which enables the storage of vast amounts of information in small storage spaces, allowed the development of the microcomputer. This spawned a whole new generation of computers that were affordable for small businesses.

One of the developing technologies most useful by those in the landscape-related industries was that of computer-aided-drafting (CAD) systems. Although new developments occur almost daily, state-of-the-art technology at the time of this writing will be discussed here.

CAD SYSTEMS

Requirements for a CAD system include hardware and software. *Hardware* is a term used to describe the machinery used in CAD, whereas the *software* may be thought of as the programs or instructions required to make that hardware function. The success of a CAD system depends equally on proper selection and use of both hardware and software.

Hardware

Necessary hardware includes input devices, a central processing unit, data storage devices, and outlet devices. A closer look at each is warranted.

Input devices could include a keyboard, a lightpen, a trackball, a joystick, a mouse, or a scanner. Voice-command systems, utilizing a headset microphone and the operator's own voice to issue commands, are also in the developmental stage, although better software is needed to make these systems practicable.

The most commonly used input device is the *keyboard,* which is a standard component of most small computers. Many commands are issued by typing "word command" instructions to the computer. Regardless of other input devices, the keyboard is usually an integral part of a CAD system.

A *lightpen* is a relatively inexpensive input device. It is moved over the monitor, which probably makes it most closely relate to normal drafting procedures. It is used to select figures displayed on the screen or to move crosshairs about on the screen. Operator fatigue is a problem with the lightpen because the pen must be held up to the screen.

A *joystick* is an input device familiar to many from its popular use in video games. Moving the joystick causes a cursor, which is usually crosshairs or an arrow, to move about the monitor. The cursor can point to figures for selection, or identify points on the screen to be marked. For those not accustomed to the joystick, it may seem awkward.

A *trackball* causes a cursor to be moved about as the ball is rolled. Relative to the joystick, more movement is required to make the trackball move the cursor. Some operators might find this makes them move accurately and more comfortably during the trackball's operation.

A *mouse* is a hand-held rolling device. It contains two wheels that contact the table surface. One wheel rotates for movement along a side-to-side plane, while the other wheel moves in an up-and-down plane. The wheels generate electrical voltages that position the cursor on the screen. The mouse does not require a special table or surface for operation, and positions are marked by pressing switches on it.

The use of a *graphics tablet* and *stylus* comprise the method of input that most clearly resembles normal drafting procedures. The tablet is laced with wires along *X* and *Y* planes. When the stylus moves over the tablet, electrical pulses are rapidly applied to the wires in sequence, identifying locations at each wire intersection. Using this type of input device, the operator can trace drawings onto the screen and into the computer's memory, there to be altered by the addition of other design elements.

A *digitizer* is a special type of graphics tablet and stylus that is useful as an input device, but it is also used to measure and calculate areas, lengths, volumes of item counts, and so forth, which makes it important as a cost-estimation tool (see Figure 15–1).

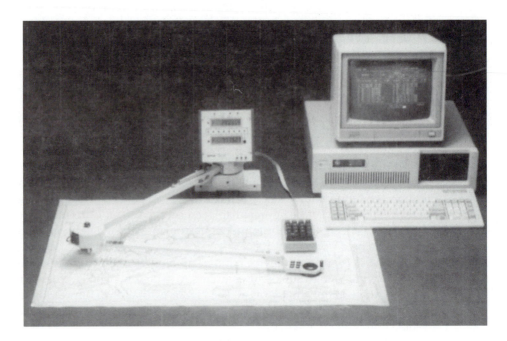

Figure 15–1.   Lasico's Series 1280 digitizer, tied in with a microcomputer by means of a built-in computer interface. (Photo courtesy of Lasico, 2451 Riverside Drive, Los Angeles, CA 90039.)

The *central processing unit* is the computer itself, which takes commands from the input device, then processes those commands, resulting in information being fed to an output device. At minimum, an IBM compatible 80486 processor or its equivalent, is required to operate most CAD systems. A pentium processor operates at greater speed and capability, so it is most satisfactory.

Data storage devices comprise the computer's memory. The memory of a microcomputer may be comprised of both internal and external storage units. The internal memory of microcomputers must usually contain at least 8 megabytes of RAM (random access memory), with a recommended 8 megabytes of added memory to operate a CAD system. External storage units, consisting of magnetic tapes, soft (floppy) disks, or hard disks, can be added to greatly increase the data storage capability of a microcomputer. Many systems now contain 2 gigabyte or larger hard disks. A math coprocessor might also be required.

Output devices consist of monitors, printers, and plotters. While printers can produce drawings of a limited size, they are primarily used for printed text. Plotters, with a much greater size range, produce drafted plans or even three-dimensional renderings. Drawings, charts, or other written material generated by computers is referred to as *hard copy*.

Plotters range greatly in size and, of course, expense. The size of the plotter dictates the flexibility in scale available to the designer through a CAD system. The American National Standard sheet sizes are:

Size A 8 1/2" x 11"
Size B 11" x 17"
Size C 17" x 22"
Size D 22" x 34"
Size E 34" x 44"

International Standard Sizes are:

Size A4 210 mm x 297 mm
Size A3 287 mm x 420 mm
Size A2 420 mm x 594 mm
Size A1 594 mm x 841 mm
Size A0 841 mm x 1189 mm

Plotters may print in only one color or in several, depending on model and price. Most will print on paper, vellum, or plastic film, rendering high-quality graphics that rival the best drafting techniques.

Software

Software refers to all programs that are written to be performed on a computer. These instructions are turned into a code that tells the computer how to input data, operate the system, and output data. In a CAD system, the software enables the computer to output data in the form of *hard copy* drawings. There are several computer languages, but the operator does not have to know any of them. The authors of the software used to program a CAD system have done the programming—operators merely use it.

A computer program that controls the execution of other programs and manages the operation of the physical equipment of the system is called an *operating program.* This type of system provides a language that the computer can understand, and establishes the foundation for such "application programs" as *AutoCAD* or *Drafix,* which are specific for computer-aided drafting. Complex and specific as these programs are, however, other, more specific, application programs exist to allow the user to put even more detail into drawing and to utilize the computer for more functions. *LANDCADD* is an example of a program that goes beyond being specific for CAD, to being specific for landscape and irrigation design. It provides many time-saving routines that customize *AutoCAD* for land planners and an interface that allows users to perform specialized tasks using familiar names. LANDCADD automates complex calculations, customizes the interface for land planners, and provides predrawn landscape symbols.

More specifically, LANDCADD converts units used by landscape designers to units used by the computer (for example, LANDCADD allows users to input property descriptions in bearings and distances, instead of having to convert thefts to lines and angles).

The interface is more intuitive for land planners than a basic CAD interface. For example, to draw a parking lot you would select "Parking," and select stall width and length, instead of using the CAD features "polyline," "line," "offset," and "rotate." In addition, the commands can be selected just by pointing to icons on a tablet menu. To select parking, then, the user can simply point to a drawing of a parking stall on the LANDCADD tablet menu. (Note: There are other ways to select commands; from pull-down menus to screen menus to quick keyboard entry.)

LANDCADD also performs complex calculations. For example, cut and fill calculations are performed by the Site Planning and Landscape Design module, and irrigation pipe sizing and flow rates are calculated by the Irrigation Design module.

A basic CAD program such as *AutoCAD* has a symbols library that can provide tools for drawing lines, arcs, and circles. Because the basic CAD programs generally do not provide symbols libraries, the users must draw each tree or shrub individually. With LANDCADD, this work has already been done for the user. The time it would take for an individual to create the same number of symbols available with the LANDCADD package is overwhelming, because over 500 symbols are provided in plan view, section view, and three dimensions. The symbols range from very simple to very complex. To give an idea of the time saved by using the LANDCADD symbols library, drawing one three-dimensional tree would be a full day's work (or more!) for an experienced CAD user.

LANDCADD was originally developed by practicing professionals for their own use. It was released to the public in 1984. Using *AutoCAD* as a main operating program, LANDCADD expands and customizes *AutoCAD*'s capabilities for land planning and design applications. Various software packages included in the LANDCADD inventory include Site Planning and Landscape Design, Irrigation Design, EZ-Estimate, Plant Specifier, Quadrangle, and Construction Details. These allow the designer to use his or her computer to facilitate an entire project, from site planning through plant selection and cost estimating (see Figures 15–2, 15–3, 15–4, and 15–5).

Although the symbol library of an application program like LANDCADD might be extensive, a designer can add symbols of his or her own making, if desired. By adding symbols, the designer makes the computer-generated hard copy more closely resemble that drawn by his or her own hand. Many application programs have hand-lettering fonts in their symbol library to give that "hand-drawn" look.

COMPUTER IMAGING

Computer imaging, developed for the landscape industry by New Image, Inc., of Canoga Park, California, involves the use of a computer, a video camcorder or a digital camera, a high-resolution color monitor, and a mouse or a graphics tablet with stylus. The designer takes the camcorder or digital camera to the client's site, shoots a few seconds of videotape from each angle he or she wishes to address on the property, then returns to the design studio and hooks the camcorder to the computer by means of a still-picture capture system. The videotape of the client's property will appear on the color monitor. Using the mouse or the stylus, the designer calls up landscape features, such as plant materials usable in the area, placing them on the images of the client's property. These features can be moved around while viewed on the monitor screen and can be reduced or enlarged as needed to fit the scale of the image on the screen. Retaining walls, decks, fences, and other features are all part of the system's extensive data bank, appearing in color when called for by the system operator. Additionally, by videotaping or digitally scanning trees, shrubs, or other design features, the designer can expand the library's databank. Videotapes of successful projects completed by a landscape contractor can be added to the system's library. For example, the tapes of a particular type of brick patio can be stored so the designer can call it up later when designing a patio of the same style.

When adding grass to the image on the screen, the designer calls up the image, placing it like a blanket over areas to be turfed. Since it also covers areas that are not to be grassed, the designer uses the mouse or the stylus as an eraser, removing the grass and trimming it to the proper dimensions. If there are still areas needing grass, the mouse or the stylus can be used like a paint brush, filling those areas.

Figure 15–2. The menu portion of Drafix Plus 1, containing landscape symbols. (Courtesy of Softdesk, Kansas City, MO.) A more complete menu of selections for LANDCADD's site planning and landscape design symbol library. (Courtesy of LANDCADD, Inc., 10418
East Tanglewood Rd., Franktown, CO 80116.)

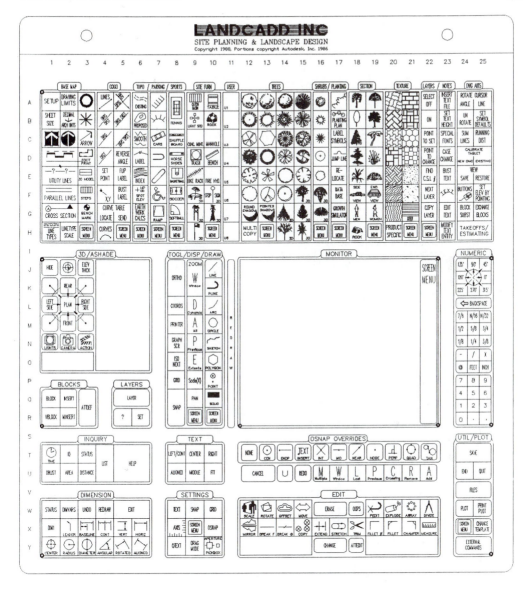

Figure 15–2 (continued)

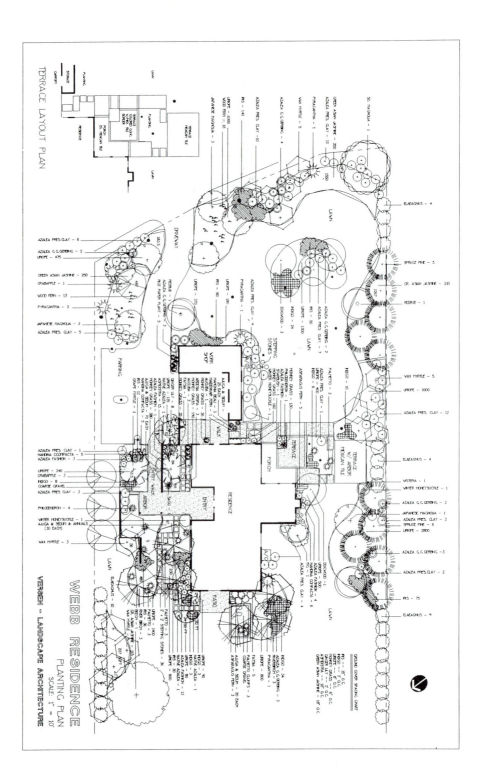

Figure 15-3. A computer-generated residential landscape plan. (Courtesy of Versen-Huh, The Land Design Group, and LANDCADD, Inc., 10418 East Tanglewood Rd., Franktown, CO 80116.)

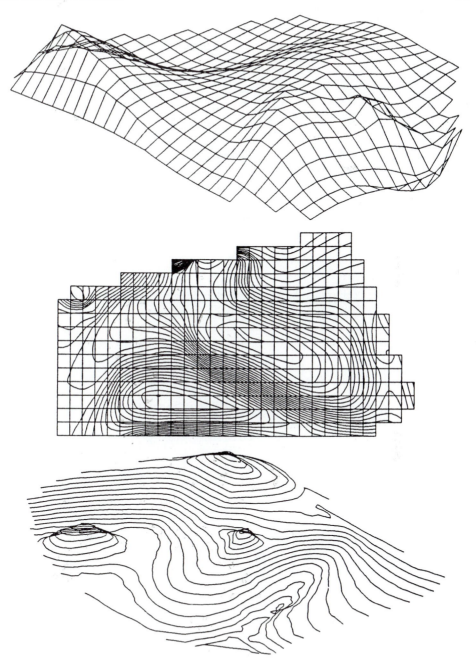

Figure 15–4. A computer-generated topographical map (bottom) can be quickly demonstrated in three dimensions by means of triangular connecting lines or a "fishnet" grid. (Courtesy of LAND-CADD, Inc., 10418 East Tanglewood Rd., Franktown, CO 80116.)

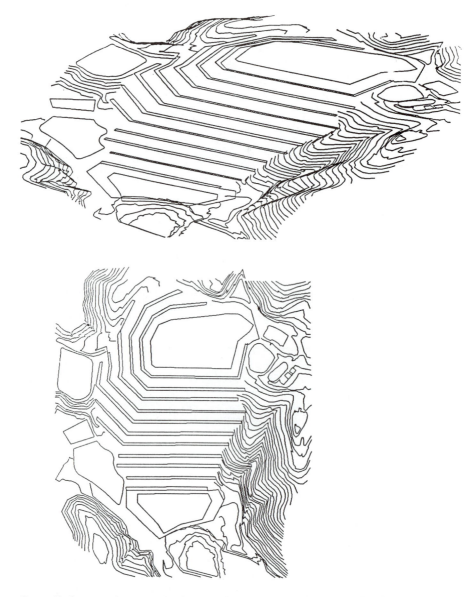

Figure 15–5. Another way a CAD system shows contours. The topographical map (bottom) is shown in three dimensions (top). (Courtesy of LANDCADD, Inc. 10418 East Tanglewood Rd., Franktown, CO 80116.)

To make erasing or painting easier, the area can be magnified up to eight times on the screen, then returned to normal size following the operation. New features allow textures to be placed in a one-point perspective in any direction.

To enlighten clients, the designer can call for plants as they will look when mature, when they are first planted, and at intermediate stages. Blooms, berries, and fall colors can also be shown. Color development is almost infinite, since the system exceeds 32,000 color hues.

To duplicate plants in a mass planting, the operator simply points the stylus at the position where another plant is needed, until the total number needed are pictured on the screen. If perspective is needed to make the picture accurate, the stylus can be used to resize shrubs as they are perceived progressively further from the viewpoint.

When an item is to be placed behind another object—a shrub partially hidden by the corner of a deck, for example—the item is placed over the corner of the deck, then pattern masking enables only the proper portions of the plant to show. (See Figure 15–6.)

Using this system, it is possible to prepare as many landscape designs as desired, giving the client various options. The client can even be given a videocassette to view, using the VCR and television set in his or her own home. Adding a high-resolution color printer to the system enables the printing of the picture seen on the monitor. In addition to giving the client a copy, some contractors might find it useful to send a copy out with the installation crew. This will clarify the designer's intent.

Computer imaging can even be used to suggest building remodeling, if necessary. Changing the color of siding or trim on a house can be done quickly and easily. Moving a window or adding or rerouting a walk can be done right before the customer's eyes.

The addition of a high-resolution, high-speed digital scanner to the system's hardware provides the ability to copy material from books, photographs, or advertising copy, which can then be inserted into the system's data base library. Virtually anything that can be photocopied can be copied into the system by such a scanner.

Effective advertising tapes can be created by the computer imaging system, to be used in television ads or given directly to prospective clients. Videotaping "before" and "after" views of installations a firm has designed and sold can give potential clients a solid reason to desire similar treatment of their own property.

Landscape maintenance applications exist with computer imaging also. A poorly maintained landscape can be videotaped and the operator can use the stylus to "prune" plants by erasing portions of them. Similarly, landscape features that need to be removed can be erased from the picture, showing the client how the property would look without the feature in question.

Perhaps the most important function of the computer imaging system can be summed up by saying that it allows the client to see the images that must occur in a good designer's imagination. With blueprints, even with photographs, that is often a difficult achievement.

Figure 15–6.   A computer image, created on Softdesk® Landscape Assistant by the author. (Image was done on a Softdesk Landscape Assistant imaging system by the author. Printed by a Hewlett-Packard 855 inkjet printer.)

Figure 15–6 (continued)

Figure 15–6 (continued)

POINTS TO REMEMBER

- The abbreviation CAD stands for computer-aided-drafting or computer-aided-design.
- A CAD system requires both hardware and software to operate.
- Necessary hardware includes input devices, a central processing unit, data storage devices, and output devices.
- Input devices include lightpens, joysticks, trackballs, mouses, and graphic tablets with stylus.
- The central processing unit is the computer itself.
- Data storage devices comprise the memory of the computer.
- Magnetic tapes, soft (floppy) disks, and hard disks are all data storage devices.
- Output devices include monitors, printers, and plotters.
- Drawings, charts, or other written material produced by computers is called *hard copy*.
- Software refers to all programs that are written to be performed on a computer.

- A computer program that controls the execution of other programs and manages the operation of the system's hardware is called an *operating system.*
- *Application programs* are specific programs for expanding the computer's abilities in a given area. CAD is an application program.
- Computer imaging combines the use of a microcomputer, a video camcorder, a videocassette recorder (VCR), a color monitor, and a graphics tablet with stylus, to create a system that allows video images of landscape elements to be overlaid on a videotape of a client's house.

REVIEW QUESTIONS

1. What do the initials CAD stand for?
2. What is computer hardware? Give examples.
3. What is computer software? Give examples.
4. How does a lightpen differ from a digitizer?
5. What is a graphics tablet?
6. What is a central processing unit?
7. Differentiate between an *operating program* and an *application program.*
8. What hardware components are necessary for the computer-imaging system?
9. Give an example of how the computer-imaging system can be used to sell maintenance to a landscape customer.

PRACTICAL TIP FROM A PRACTICING DESIGNER

CyberScapes, an exciting new design tool based on a system of "virtual reality" is under development at LANDCADD. By donning a special computer-fed helmet, the designer will be able to design a landscape from within. It will look and feel as though the wearer of the helmet is standing, walking, or sitting in the landscape area as designed. The designer will be able to shift landscape elements about as desired. It will even be possible to "hear" streams and waterfalls!

This system will provide a great sales tool, because the client can also wear the helmet and experience the proposed landscape before the purchase is made.

LANDCADD is also developing its own version of computer imaging. VideoScapes™ utilizes software to replace some of the more expensive hardware of the previously available systems. Users of the VideoScapes™ system will be able to generate realistic renderings of proposed landscaping elements for viewing on their computer monitors, eliminating the need for a videocassette recorder, television monitor, graphics tablet, and lightpen.

Chapter **16**

DESIGNING AUTOMATIC IRRIGATION SYSTEMS

In this chapter, you will learn the basics of automatic irrigation system design, including site analysis and layout, sprinkler head layout, zoning, and piping.

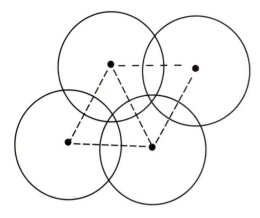

TRIANGULAR SPACING

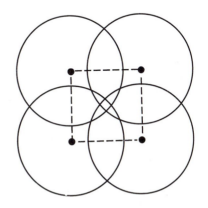

SQUARE SPACING

Among the services many landscape operators offer is irrigation installation. The responsibility for designing and estimating the cost of these systems often falls to a firm's landscape designers. In this chapter, we will discuss the design of automatic irrigation systems. This is not to indicate that everything a person needs to know to become a successful irrigation designer can be written in one chapter of a book. Indeed, there are complete books about the subject. Rather, it is the intent here to create a rudimentary understanding of this complex subject, which, along with experience in the field, can help that person to become a successful irrigation designer.

There are four steps in designing irrigation systems:

1. Providing site analysis, measurements, and layout
2. Planning the sprinkler head layout
3. Zoning the system
4. Piping the system

These steps are normally followed in the order presented above. Following is a discussion of each step.

SITE ANALYSIS AND LAYOUT

Locating Property Corners and Boundaries

To accurately design an irrigation system for a property, it is necessary to know exactly where the property's boundaries are. If property corners are not marked, it might be necessary to have the property surveyed by engineers. However, if at least one corner and one property line can be located, the others can be found with accurate information from a plat, which can be obtained from the property's owner, the building contractor, or the city or county engineering departments.

From the existing property corner, other adjacent property corners may be found. First, a transit or a builder's level (see Chapter 4, "Studying the Land Forms") is set directly over the known property corner, with a plumb bob used to assure the surveyor that the instrument is directly over the corner pin. The instrument is set so that the protractor on the instrument's base reads zero as the telescope sights directly down the known property line. The angle between the known property line and the other property line emanating from the known corner will be shown on the plat. As the telescope on the instrument is swiveled to reach the number of degrees shown on the plat, the new line of sight shown on the instrument's protractor will be the second property line emanating from the known corner. A tape measure can then be stretched along that line, extending the distance shown on the plat, to locate the second corner of the property. The third corner is located by measuring the distance shown on the plat along the known property line from the known corner.

To find the fourth corner, the transit/builder's level is moved to one of the newly found corners, and the procedure is repeated. If the property contains more than four corners, the instrument is moved until all corners and property lines are located.

Measuring to Accurately Locate Structures on the Property

When property lines and corners have been found, structures existing on the property can be measured. To accurately locate these structures, triangulating measurements from the corners of structures to known property corners are taken. For example, from the front corner of a house a line is measured to each of the front property corners. When those measurements are scaled out on paper, the house corner is located where the two measurements coincide (see Figure 16–1). If all corners on the structure are 90° angles, locating two corners by triangulating measurement should accurately define the building's location, but triangulating measurements from other corners can serve as a check.

Any permanent feature on the property is measured. This includes swimming pools, decks, patios, vegetable gardens, storage sheds, retaining walls, and fences. Locating the water meter, whether it is in the lawn or in the basement, is critical. The size of that meter must be determined as well.

Underground utilities must all be pinpointed so they may be noted on the irrigation plan. For their own protection, utility companies are normally eager to provide location services.

Analyzing Other Site-related Factors

Existing trees and shrub beds are located, and individual shrubs, which would block part of a sprinkler pattern, must also be noted.

Changes in terrain should be studied as part of the site analysis. Steep slopes cause problems in locating pipes, and even gradual changes in elevation magnify changes in water pressure.

A thorough site analysis should include researching below as well as above ground. Sampling the soil profile with a probe is wise, wherever underground rock is suspected. Underground rock can prove to be a strong obstacle to placing pipe in the soil.

Finally, the static water pressure should be checked. A pressure gauge, which can be screwed onto a hose bib, gives a reading when the water hydrant is open. This reading, the *static pressure*, is the pressure of the water in the system when the water is not moving. The pressure existing in the system at any point when water is flowing is called *working pressure*.

Laying out the Property on Paper

At the drawing board, all measurements taken on the site are scaled onto paper. Any scale the designer chooses can be used, as long as it results in a manageable drawing. Possible architechtural scales include 1/8", 1/16", or 3/32" = 1'.

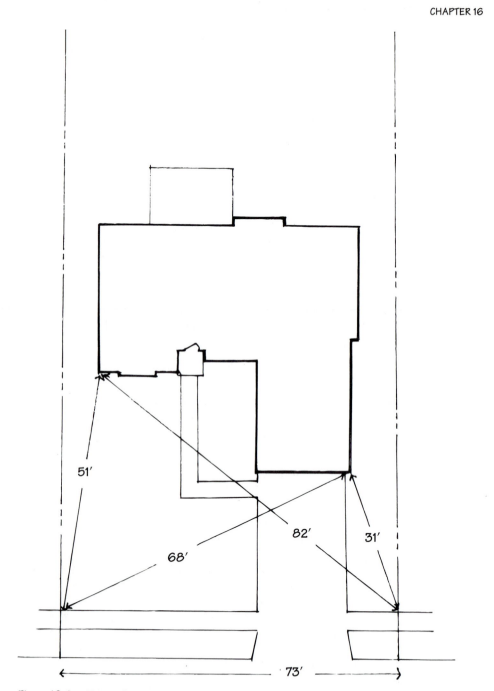

Figure 16–1. Triangulating measurements from each corner of a house allows the accurate location of a house on a lot.

Engineer's scales include 1" = 10, 20, or 50'. Many designers favor scales for which design simplifying head pattern templates are available. When all information gleaned from the site analysis has been transferred to paper, the designer enters the sprinkler head layout phase of irrigation design.

SPRINKLER HEAD LAYOUT

Types of Sprinkler Heads

Two general classes of sprinkler heads exist: spray heads and rotary heads. Spray heads pop up and spray through a fixed nozzle. Neither the head nor the nozzle move during operation. The spray pattern of these heads is determined by the size and shape of the nozzle orifice. Rotary heads rotate while they are spraying, and their spray pattern is determined by the degree of rotation.

Most spray heads have matched-precipitation-rate nozzles, which means that they supply equal amounts of precipitation over an area regardless of the angle of spray coverage. In other words, the smaller the area covered by a matched-precipitation-rate spray nozzle, the smaller is the volume of water passing through it. Many types of rotary heads, on the other hand, emit equal streams of water at all times. Since a half circle rotary head covers its pattern twice during the same time that a full circle head covers its pattern once, the half circle head applies twice as much precipitation to its coverage area. Some rotary heads, usually of the gear-driven type, have interchangeable nozzles, which allows them to become matched-precipitation-rate nozzles.

Selecting Sprinkler Patterns and Nozzle Sizes

System design varies with the type of heads being used. Spray heads may be arranged in either a triangular or a square pattern. Triangular spacing provides for the most even distribution of water, and it is by far the most popular method of irrigation design. Square sprinkler patterns are usually reserved for small areas, where it is most convenient to place a head in each of four corners (see Figure 16–2).

The coverage of spray heads ranges up to 24' diameter. Although the nozzle size selected for an area depends mostly on the size of the area, that area's configuration also plays a part. Many designers opt not to design with the largest diameter nozzles available to them, preferring to maintain a margin of safety should the coverage be inadequate. For example, if a section is designed and installed with 20' diameter nozzles, but one or more heads fail to cover all the area expected, 24' diameter nozzles can be substituted as long as the water volume is sufficient to operate the zone with the larger nozzles.

Fitting Sprinkler Heads to an Area

For a particular area of lawn, then, the designer selects the largest nozzle diameter he or she thinks might work and fits it to the area. This "fitting"

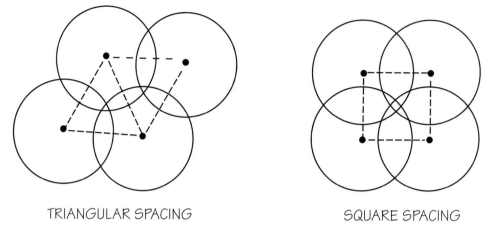

TRIANGULAR SPACING   SQUARE SPACING

Figure 16–2. Triangular head spacing (left) and square head spacing (right) are the two ways to lay out sprinkler heads.

process is greatly facilitated by the use of irrigation templates, when they are available. These templates are sheets of clear mylar, with a sprinkler pattern of a given diameter at a particular scale printed on them (see Figure 16–3). The designer can overlay an area scaled out on paper, checking the fit. Different overlays can be tried, until the pattern is found which most adequately covers the area.

If templates are unavailable, or if none fit properly, the designer measures two sides (if the area is square or rectangular), then divides those distances by the spacings required for various nozzles until one can be identified that comes closest to an even number of heads. When a triangular head arrangement is used, the heads are closer together than the heads in a row would be. In fact, the spacing between rows is 86% of the head spacing within a row. This allows all heads to be equally spaced in triangular arrangement (see Figure 16–4). So, when using nozzles requiring 20′ spacing between heads, row spacing would be 17′ (20′ x .86 = 17.2′), causing all heads to be spaced 20′ apart when arranged as an equilateral triangle.

Often an exact fit cannot be found, so nozzles of one diameter may be used to fill an area. Accordingly, it may be necessary either to use another diameter nozzle to fill out the design or to "squeeze" the pattern to make a fit (see Figure 16–5). Sometimes neither of these options gives satisfactory results, necessitating the use of "filler" heads shown in Figure 16–6. Although the use of these fillers results in less water efficiency because of the overspray, it is necessary at times to assure 100% coverage.

When an area is neither square nor rectangular, more variety in nozzle size might be required, but the principles of design remain the same. When each area of the landscape has been fitted with heads, the irrigation design is ready to be zoned.

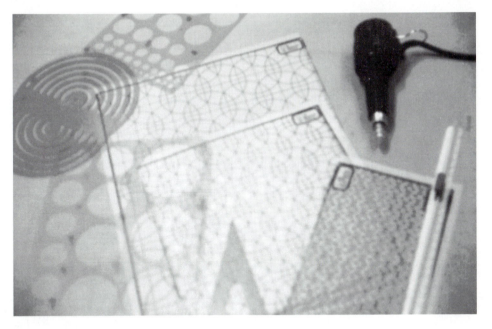

Figure 16–3.   Clear mylar irrigation templates are available in different scales. These templates greatly speed head layout.

ZONING THE SYSTEM

Determining the Total Water Volume Required by a Designed Irrigation System

Zoning begins by determining the volume of water required to service the system. Each manufacturer of sprinkler nozzles publishes charts that tell how much water volume passes through each of its nozzles at minimum required operating pressure. To calculate the water requirements, the designer counts and lists the nozzles designed for each area of the landscape and multiplies the number of each type by the gallonage consumed, arriving at the total gallonage required to service the entire area. To assure a safety margin suitable for all conditions it is a good idea to add a 10% buffer, as in the example that follows.

Backyard Area

12 Full-circle 20′ diameter @ 4.0 gpm	= 48.0 gpm
4 Quarter-circle, 20′ diam. @1.4 gpm	= 5.6 gpm
23 Half-circle, 20′ diam. @ 2.3 gpm	= 52.9 gpm
Sub-total Gallonage	= 106.5 gpm
10% Buffer	= 10.7 gpm
Total Gallonage	= 117.2 gpm

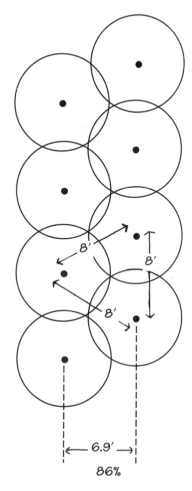

Figure 16–4. When laying out sprinkler heads in a triangular pattern without templates, rows of heads are spaced at 86% of the head spacing desired.

Now, the irrigation designer can determine how many sprinkler zones would be necessary to service the system from the available water supply.

Determining the Volume of Water Available to Operate a Designed Irrigation System

If the water supply is metered, the size of that meter determines the amount of water that can pass through it at a given pressure. Typically, residential water meters supplied to service the house will be 5/8", 3/4", or 1" in size. They often are served by piping that is marginally larger in diameter. For example, a 5/8" meter is often served by 3/4" copper pipe, especially when there is low water

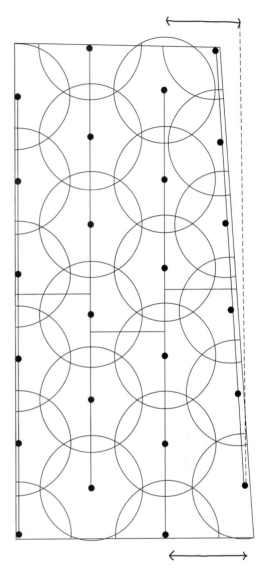

Figure 16–5. When equally spaced head patterns will not fit a given area, it is sometimes necessary to "squeeze" the pattern.

pressure in the area. Typical water meter sizes and their maximum safe flows are listed in Table 16–1. By dividing the total water requirement for each landscape area by the maximum safe flow through each size meter, the designer can determine the minimum number of sprinkler zones required and, thus, the size of the controller that will be required. When many zones will be required for the existing meter, it might prove more economical to have a larger meter installed.

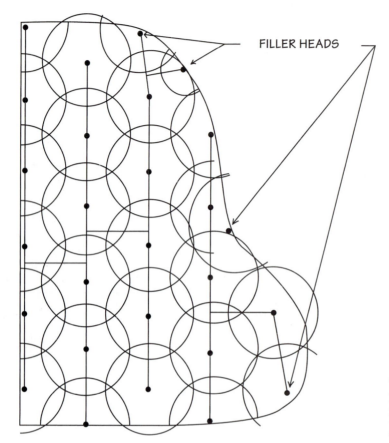

FILLER HEADS

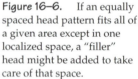

Figure 16–6.   If an equally spaced head pattern fits all of a given area except in one localized space, a "filler" head might be added to take care of that space.

TABLE 16–1

Meter Size inches	Maximum Flow gpm	Safe Capacity Pressure Loss lb./sq. inch	Flow in Type K Copper @ 9 ft./second gpm
5/8	20	15.0	
3/4	30	15.0	12.2
1	50	15.0	21.8
1 1/2	100	20.0	48.3
2	160	20.0	84.6

Using the 117.2 gallons required for the backyard considered earlier, divided by 12.2 gpm above, we find that ten zones would be required to service that area with a 3/4" water meter, while only six zones would be needed with a 1" meter, or three zones with a 1 1 /2" meter. Costs vary by water district, but it would seem that a 1" meter might be most cost-effective in this instance.

When the water source is a pump, the process is the same. Pumps are rated by the number of gallons they will produce in an hour, but also considered is the vertical distance the pump must pull the water. This vertical distance is called *head*. In terms of pressure, 1' of head is equal to .433 lb./sq. inch. A pump might be capable of 50 gallons per minute at 15' of head, for instance, but only 40 gpm at 20' of head.

If a pump will not produce adequate water volume or pressure, and a larger pump is not an option, the problem might, in some cases, be solved by adding pressure tanks. Pressure builds as water is pumped into these tanks. Water is then released at a pressure adequate to operate the system.

System Operating Time

Another consideration to be made about the size of the water supply involves the system's necessary operating time. The larger the number of zones required, the longer the operating time, provided all heads are of the same type. Spray heads require much less operating time than rotaries, because of the greater volume of water passing through them per area of coverage. If a system consists of 12 zones, for example, and each zone must operate for 20 minutes to supply adequate irrigation, the entire cycle will require 4 hours for completion (240 minutes). With a larger water supply, however, the system might be reduced to 7 zones, which would operate for 2 hours and 20 minutes per cycle. The difference might be important. Required operation time becomes more important when rotary heads are used. Rotary systems apply water much more slowly than do spray heads, so a rotary system with many zones can require many hours per cycle. The need to control watering time relates mostly to a desire to confine irrigation to certain times of the day, such as early mornings, when pressure is maximum and wind and evaporation are minimum.

PIPING THE SYSTEM

The next step in designing an irrigation system involves piping. There are two types of piping—lateral piping and mainline piping. Mainline piping extends from the water source to the last zone valve, or back to the source if the main is looped. Lateral piping is the pipe within individual zones that connects all sprinkler heads with the zone valve.

Types of Piping Material

Two kinds of piping material are used in modern irrigation systems. Polyvinylchloride (PVC) pipe is a rigid pipe that is usually sold in 20' lengths, and in a variety of diameters and pressure ratings. Most lengths are manufactured with one end plain and the other end belled, so the lengths may be joined without fittings. Fittings attached to lengths of pipe must be solvent-welded. Polyethylene (PE) pipe is made in long coils, usually 50' or 100' (see Figure 16–7).

Figure 16–7.   The two types of pipe most often used in irrigation systems arc PVC (white) and PE (black).

This makes it quicker to install in long runs than PVC, because 20' lengths of PVC must be solvent-welded together to make up the necessary length. PE is more flexible than PVC, but generally is not as strong. Plastic insert fittings, secured by hose clamps, are used with PE. Where it is necessary to change from PE to PVC, insert fittings, which are threaded on one end, can be connected to threaded PVC fittings with slip fit on the other end to be welded to PVC pipe.

Considerations for Freeze Protection

Auto drains, which are small ball valves, are installed at all low elevations in PVC piping. This causes the pipe to drain automatically whenever the pressure is off. Auto drains are usually not used with PE pipe because of the pipe's flexibility. To completely drain PE pipe, it is necessary to blow water out with an air compressor. However, PE pipe is not as susceptible to freeze damage as PVC, so often gravity drainage out the lowest heads is considered adequate protection for PE pipe. Many sprinkler installers prefer to use PE in lateral piping and PVC for the main line. A manual drain valve is placed just above the main shutoff valve in the main line, to ensure that water trapped between the main shutoff valve and the master valve is released when the irrigation system is winterized.

Volume, Velocity, and Pressure Considerations

The pipe used in an irrigation system is selected based on three criteria— the velocity at which water will travel through the pipe, the water pressure within the line, and the volume of water per minute required to service the system and the pressure loss within the pipe, in sizes adequate to provide that volume.

Type K copper tubing is most often used as the service line from the city water main to the water meter. The maximum safe velocity flow in Type K copper tubing is 9' per second. The maximum flow within an irrigation system should also be 9' per second, to avoid a condition called *water hammer*. Water hammer is a condition that occurs when the pressure in a line is suddenly abated or stopped. This results in a vibration within the piping that causes a pounding noise. If it is severe enough, water hammer can cause damage to pipe and connections, or it can cause material fatigue over a period of short or long duration. To minimize water hammer in a system, piping should be selected in a size that will not allow flow velocities greater than 9' per second.

Pipe should be selected with a pressure rating of at least twice the expected pressure in the line. In a main line, where static pressure is 70 psi, for example, 160 psi pipe would be the minimum satisfactory quality, and 200 psi would yield greater safety, because of pressure surges that occur when valves close. Pipe with less wall strength might stretch or even rupture.

Each type of irrigation nozzle requires a certain minimum pressure for operation, and everything that water must pass through en route to the final nozzle of each zone causes a *pressure loss*. Another way to define pressure loss is to say that it is the difference between static pressure and working pressure. Each diameter and type of pipe experiences its own unique pressure losses. Generally, increasing pipe diameter by one size will reduce pressure loss, given equal water volume. For example, given a main line using 200 psi PVC pipe and a volume of 48 gpm, the pressure loss in a 1 1/4" pipe is 8.10 psi per 100' of pipe. When 1 1/2" pipe is substituted, also at 48 gpm, pressure losses are reduced to 4.15 psi per 100' of pipe. When velocity flow is considered, the 1 1/4" pipe will carry 48.3 gpm at a flow of 9' per second, while the 1 1/2" pipe will carry 49.5 gpm at 7' per second. Considering that flow should be kept under the maximum safe flow through type K copper tubing, (9' per second), thereby minimizing water hammer, and the reduction of pressure loss, 1 1/2" would be a clear choice in this example. Similar choices are made all the way through the piping, whether it is PVC or PE pipe. As piping progresses through each zone, diameter requirements shrink as some of the volume in the main line is used up by sprinkler heads in the zone. Pressure decreases progressively through the zone also, as more and more pressure loss occurs throughout the route.

Generally it is best if the lateral piping originates in the middle of a zone,with approximately the same length of lateral piping extending in two directions from the zone valve. This is not always possible, however. Installation efficiency is gained through longer pipe runs, particularly when a vibratory plow is used to pull pipe into the ground (see Figure 16–8). With longer pipe runs, fewer runs must be made, so less time is spent connecting and disconnecting pipe. From a watering efficiency standpoint, however, long, continuous end-fed sections of pipe with sprinkler heads experience greater pressure loss and

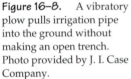

Figure 16–8. A vibratory plow pulls irrigation pipe into the ground without making an open trench. Photo provided by J. I. Case Company.

less uniform pressure from the first nozzle on the line to the last. Figure 16–9 shows three possible arrangements of the piping in an area. Ultimately, the final choice often is a compromise between the most efficient irrigation arrangement and the most efficient installation arrangement. If a zone is side-fed, start with a 5% deduction from the static pressure gauged. Use 10% if it is end-fed, and 15% if it is end-fed into a single row.

To ensure that each zone will operate properly, it is necessary to determine that this pressure loss is not severe enough to cause the sprinkler heads in a zone not to function. The designer must determine which sprinkler zone will be the weakest (usually the zone with the most sprinkler heads or the zone furthest from the water source), then calculate the pressure losses from the water source to release at the last nozzle on that zone. If this weakest zone will function, it can be reasoned that the other zones will also.

The water meter, back flow preventer, manual and electric valves, pipe, and fittings all contribute to pressure losses along the water's route to the final nozzle in each section. The amount of pressure loss to be expected for each item mentioned above can be obtained from their manufacturers or from charts. Each type and size of pipe experiences its own pressure loss for each foot of run.

The static pressure taken by the designer from a hose bib at the site is the same as static pressure in the water supply, except for differences caused by a change in elevation. Remember, though, that it is only static pressure if no water is circulating through the house plumbing when the pressure is gauged. If the site is in a newer housing area, existing static pressure may be greater than could be expected when the area becomes fully populated. To be safe, it is best not to

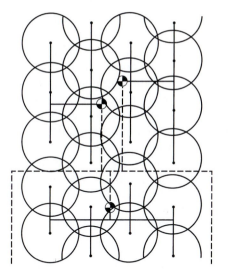

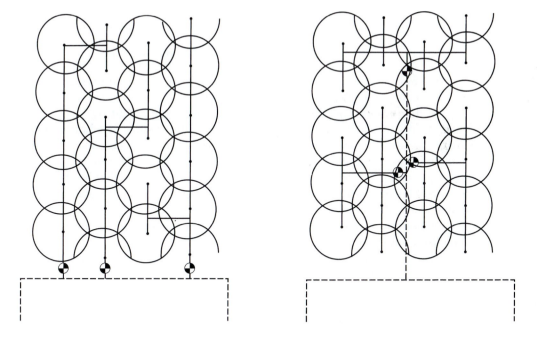

Figure 16–9. Three different piping arrangements of the sprinkler heads in an area.

consider that static pressure as typical. Generally, static pressures between 50 psi and 75 psi might be considered most normal, and as such, might be discounted by 10%, for safety. Pressures in the 100 to 125 psi range, however, might be discounted by as much as 25%. Another way to ensure that the static pressure expected is realistic is to call the engineering department of the city or rural water district. They can usually project a typical pressure for the location.

Expected pressure losses are subtracted from the adjusted static pressure, and if the remainder is greater than the required minimum operating pressure for the type of sprinkler heads being used, the system can be expected to operate. A sample calculation of pressure losses, not to be considered average, follows.

Assume a static pressure of 50 psi, pressure vacuum-breaker, end-fed circuit, pop-up spray heads that require 18.0 psi to operate.

Adjusted static pressure 45 psi (10% safety adj.)

End-fed circuit adj.	-4.5 psi
Loss before meter	-5.5 psi
1 1/2" water meter	-4.6 psi
1 1/2" vacuum-breaker	-4.0 psi
Piping, fittings	-8.2 psi
Total Pressure Loss	-22.8 psi

45.0 psi -22.8 psi = 22.2 psi -18.0 psi = 4.2 psi

So, in this case, after anticipated pressure losses, enough pressure remains to operate the spray heads, with 4.2 psi left over.

System operating pressure can be enhanced somewhat by "looping" the main. Many times, the mainline stretches around three sides of a house in horseshoe shape in order to service all sprinkler zones. If it is possible to continue that mainline to join with itself at its origin, pressure is equalized throughout its length (see Figure 16–10). The value of looping the mainline is such that it often enables the use of the next size smaller pipe. A disadvantage of looping the mainline is that it often necessitates boring under a driveway, and this can be expensive.

A few more notes about pressure loss are in order. Insert fittings, of the type used with pipe, cause greater friction loss than the slip or threaded fittings used with PVC pipe. When water must flow uphill, the friction losses are greater than when it flows across level ground or a downhill slope. The total distance in feet the water must climb is known as the *head*. When a pump is rated, for example, the performance chart will indicate that it produces a certain water pressure at 20′ of head, and a higher pressure at 15′ of head.

Final Design Notes

Most automatic irrigation systems are designed with a master valve. This electric valve is positioned immediately after the main turn-on valve, on the mainline.

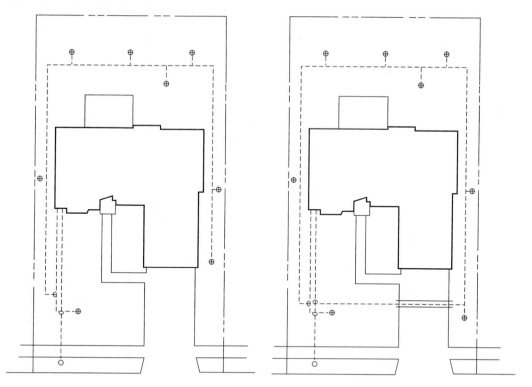

Figure 16–10. "Looping" the mainline by connecting it into a continuous circle front to end reduces friction loss, often allowing the next size smaller diameter main line pipe.

Whenever the system operates, the master valve must open simultaneously with each zone valve. This affords a safety margin, because it prevents the mainline from being pressurized with water when the system is not operating. It also prevents unimpeded water flow through a zone valve, should that zone valve fail to close for any reason.

Zone valves are normally positioned near the mainline, partly to facilitate the burial of electric cable. One wire extends from each valve, including the master valve, to the controller and to a common ground wire, which links all electric valves with the controller.

Location of the controller may or may not be noted on the irrigation plan, but usually the size and type will be specified on the plan, in the accompanying specifications, or in both places. Typically, residential controllers are located in a garage, attached to a retaining wall or fence, or mounted on a pedestal somewhere in the landscape (see Figure 16–11).

If the backflow preventer required is a vacuum-breaker, which must extend upward to a height at least 1' higher than the highest sprinkler head, it is usually located near a house, or somewhere easily concealed from sight (see Figure 16–12).

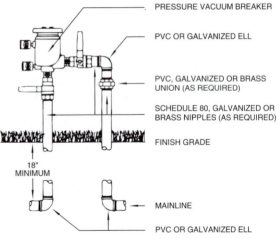

FACE OF WALL

RESIDENTIAL CONTROLLER –
SEE MANUAL FOR WALL MOUNTING
INSTRUCTIONS, ALL WIRING TO BE
INSTALLED AS PER LOCAL CODES

JUNCTION BOX

CONDUIT FOR CONTROL AND
COMMON UF DIRECT BURIAL
WIRES TO REMOTE CONTROL
VALVES – EXTEND CONDUIT 6"
OUT FROM BASE OF WALL

CONDUIT FOR 120 VOLT WIRE
FROM POWER SOURCE

Figure 16–11. A typical computer-type irrigation controller.

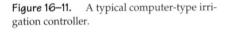

PRESSURE VACUUM BREAKER

PVC OR GALVANIZED ELL

PVC, GALVANIZED OR BRASS
UNION (AS REQUIRED)

SCHEDULE 80, GALVANIZED OR
BRASS NIPPLES (AS REQUIRED)

FINISH GRADE

18"
MINIMUM

MAINLINE

PVC OR GALVANIZED ELL

NOTE:
INSTALL 12" ABOVE HIGHEST
HEAD PER MANUFACTURER'S
RECOMMENDATIONS

INSULATE PER LOCAL CODES

Figure 16–12. A typical pressure-type vacuum-breaker installation.

DESIGNING ROTARY SYSTEMS

Irrigation systems that use rotary heads differ from spray head systems in several ways. Since each of these heads, which may be of the impulse, gear-driven, or ball-driven type, cover much larger diameters than spray heads, their use is usually restricted to larger areas (see Figure 16–13). These heads are more influenced by wind than spray heads are, and they are more susceptible to becoming maladjusted. They also may not be matched-precipitation-rate, meaning that part-circle heads apply more irrigation to the area they cover than do full-circle heads, given the same irrigation time. In order to provide equal irrigation to an area, then, each zone must be made up of heads of the same coverage. In other words, combining half-circle heads with full-circle heads on the same section results in uneven irrigation. It is usually not too difficult to separate half-circle heads from full-circle heads, but is often difficult to separate quarter-circle heads from half-circle heads. In many cases the two are combined, even though some of the corners of the property, covered by the quarter-circle heads, might receive double doses of irrigation. This is done instead of installing extra electric zone valves, extra pipe and/or a larger controller, which might be required to zone very few heads separately.

Figure 16–13.   Types of rotary sprinkler heads; ball-driven (bottom), gear-driven (upper right), and two sizes of impulse rotaries.

Because they are more influenced by wind and maladjustment, rotary systems can create more of a traffic hazard on streets adjacent to areas being irrigated. For that reason, if areas being irrigated are adjacent to busy streets, one or two rows of spray heads are often used as a buffer between the first row of rotaries and the curb.

Rotary sprinkler heads are more exposed to damage from outside elements in two ways. Since they are larger and more complex than spray heads, there is more opportunity for moving parts to wear out or suffer damage. Also, since these heads are used in larger areas, the maintenance equipment used to groom the irrigated area is usually larger and heavier. To avoid damage by tractors or mowers, swing-joint assemblies are often specified. These are assemblages of threaded ells and nipples that flex when pressure is applied to the top of the head (see Figure 16–14). Since the swing-joint assembly flexes, no extra pressure is applied to the piping below the head, and breakage is avoided.

COMPUTER-AIDED-DRAFTING (CAD)

Several CAD systems are now available that have software specifically created for irrigation design applications. These systems not only save time, but they are also very accurate and produce clean, easily interpreted drawings.

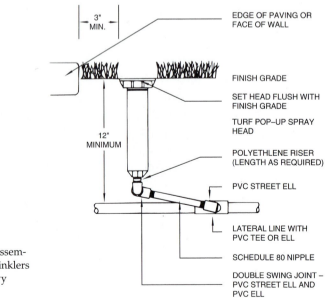

Figure 16–14.   A typical swing-joint assembly, which is used with large rotary sprinklers to prevent damage by tractors and heavy equipment.

CAD systems generally require a computer processor that is at least the equal of a PC compatible 80386 with at least 4 megs RAM, a math coprocessor, a VGA monitor, and either a dot matrix, ink-jet, or laser printer, or a plotter. See Chapter 15 for a more complete discussion of CAD systems.

When interfaced with a digitizer (see Figure 13–7 on page 284) and the appropriate spreadsheet software, CAD systems can greatly reduce takeoff and estimation time. Some of these programs allow the design to be "tested" within the computer, ensuring that it will perform when it is installed. Many of these CAD programs also include symbols libraries that enable the preparation of landscape plans.

A hand-drawn irrigation plan appears in Figure 16–15. A computer-drawn irrigation plan is shown in Figure 16–16.

POINTS TO REMEMBER

- The four steps in irrigation design are site analysis, measurement, and layout; sprinkler head layout; zoning; and piping.
- If one corner pin and one property line can be determined, the other corners and lines can be found using surveying instruments.
- The two general types of sprinkler heads are spray heads and rotary heads.
- The size of nozzles to be used in designing a spray head system depends upon both the size and the shape of the area to be covered.
- The two types of sprinkler head patterns are triangular and square.
- With a triangular head pattern, the spacing between rows will be 86% of the spacing between the heads within a row.
- The zoning process is begun by calculating the volume of water necessary to operate all sprinkler heads in each area of the landscape.
- The two general classes of pipe used in irrigation systems are PVC (polyvinylchloride) and PE (polyethylene) pipe.
- Water hammer, a vibration in the piping that occurs when a valve closes, can cause serious damage to a system.
- Two limitations upon whether a sprinkler system will function are the volume of water available per zone and the pressure losses water encounters en route to and through each zone.
- Rotary sprinkler heads are of three general types: impulse, gear-driven, and ball-driven.
- Swing-joints are used to absorb shock when a sprinkler head is run over by equipment, preventing serious damage to piping below.
- Computer-aided-drafting (CAD) systems help the irrigation designer by rendering usable irrigation designs (with accurate input) at reasonable cost. Some CAD systems are helpful with takeoff and estimation functions, as well.

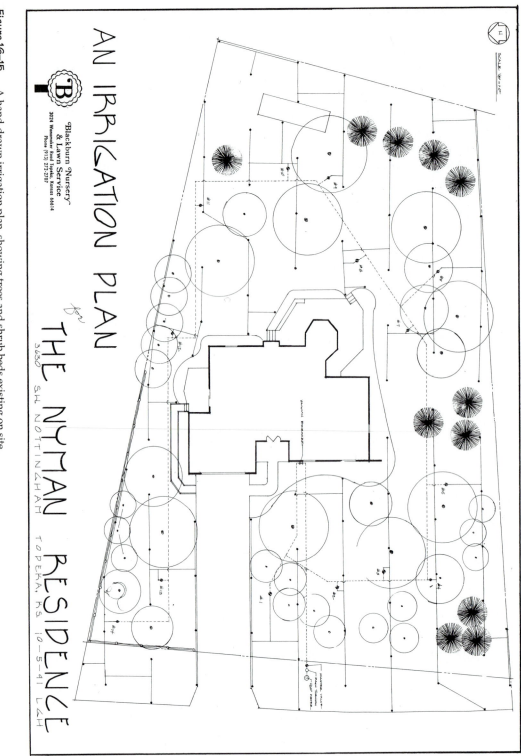

Figure 16–15. A hand-drawn irrigation plan, showing trees and shrub beds existing on site.

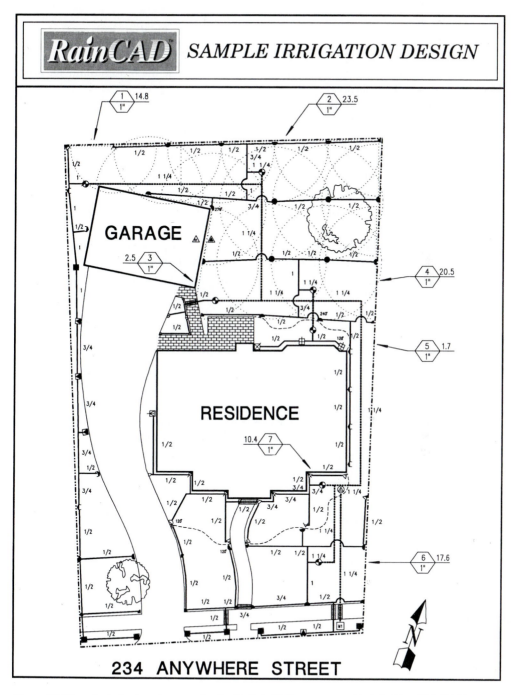

Figure 16–16. An irrigation plan completed with Rain Bird's computer-aided-drafting (RainCAD) program. Courtesy Rain Bird Sprinkler Manufacturing Corp.

REVIEW QUESTIONS

1. Which type of sprinkler head has the fewest moving parts?
2. Why do irrigation designers often not plan to use maximum diameter nozzles unless it is absolutely necessary?
3. Why are rows of sprinkler heads closer together than individual heads within a row when triangular spacing is used?
4. Why is it necessary sometimes to "squeeze" a sprinkler pattern, and what does squeezing mean?
5. Why should the piping in an irrigation system be of a pressure rating that is at least twice the adjusted static pressure?
6. How can a pump be enabled to produce larger water volume for a period of time?
7. Why is it sometimes more feasible to use longer pipe runs in an irrigation system, even though it is not the most efficient watering configuration?
8. What provides the main obstacle to "looping" the main line on many irrigation systems?

PRACTICAL TIP FROM A PRACTICING DESIGNER

Along a sidewalk or drive, where wind usually affects the pattern, I like to overextend the pattern, using a 190° to 210° nozzle instead of the 180° nozzle that usually would be required. Similarly, I might use a 120° nozzle in place of 90°. When the wind is not blowing these nozzles will overspray some of the concrete, but I find that to be less of a problem than dry edges would be.

Much of the necessary drafting on each irrigation plan or landscape plan is redundant. You can save time by using drafting vellum with the title block framework, sheet border, and business name, address, and logo preprinted. Alternatively, you might want to have the business logo, construction details, drawing scales, or directional indicators preprinted onto clear adhesive film, which can be pressed onto the plan wherever needed. When blueprinted at the proper speed, the clear adhesive film does not show up on the blueprint.

Appendix A

PLANT
MATERIALS GUIDELISTS

The following lists of plant names and characteristics are included to aid the designer in the plant-selection processes. However, it must be strongly emphasized that one cannot learn plant characteristics sufficiently from such a list. In order to utilize plant materials wisely in design, one must know the plants themselves intimately in a variety of circumstances. These lists, then, should be used as reminders of knowledge gathered by the designer through plant materials courses, outdoor study of plant materials, and previous experience.

In the first plant list provided, plants are grouped according to their primary functions. Shade trees are listed first, in alphabetical order by botanical names. Following the shade trees are small ornamental trees, deciduous ornamental shrubs, broadleaf evergreen shrubs, narrowleaf evergreen trees, narrowleaf evergreen shrubs, specialty plants, groundcovers, vines, and perennials in that order.

Design characteristics for each plant are given, but it must be understood that these characteristics change somewhat from one set of conditions to another. For example, the height and width attained by each plant varies considerably with location; I have chosen to list what I consider to be their average-to-large ranges. The climatic zone of adaptability is also somewhat general. The intended meaning here is that, under most conditions, the zone given is the northernmost zone in which the plant is hardy. Again, local conditions must be considered.

The plant forms specified correspond to the diagrammatic plant forms represented in Figure 1–2 on page 8. Terms such as *dense* and *open* indicate the density of foliage relative to other species in general. This is another area in which the local growing conditions and cultural treatments can greatly distort normal expectations. Foliage colors are given for summer and fall. Textures are indicated very broadly, but individual impressions are of great importance here since textures are perceived somewhat individually. I would suggest that anyone who wants a thorough grasp of the textural variations among plants should not only study textures visually from varying distances and in various light patterns, but should also become familiar with the "feel" of these textures by closing his or her eyes and touching them.

In the "exposure/soil" column of the first plant list, an attempt is made to indicate each plant's preference for sun or degrees of shade and the types of soil in which the plant will grow well. The term *adapt* appears in the soil-condition portion of this column frequently, meaning that the plant will tolerate various conditions. It does not mean, however, that the plant will grow equally well under all conditions. Local recommendations are important for determining the ideal growing conditions for each plant.

In the "remarks" column, I have tried to give any special information about each plant that might serve as a helpful reminder to the designer. Flower and fruit colors are indicated here, as well as specialized uses to be made of the plant.

The second plant list is alphabetized by common name, so that a plant can be located when the botanical name is unknown. Plants are not listed by group in this list. More information about the design qualities of individual plants is given in this cross-index; the system is explained as a prelude to the list.

An attempt has been made to exclude commercially unavailable plant materials from these lists. However, regional availability varies, so each designer should satisfy himself or herself that a variety is available for purchase before proposing it. Many individual cultivars and varieties are listed, but these are being developed so rapidly that, inevitably, some worthy varieties must be missing from these lists. Such oversights are unintentional and are not meant to indicate that this plant is unworthy. For uniformity, the botanical names used are those specified by *Hortus III*.

The abbreviations used in the botanical plant list and their meanings are given below:

Abbreviation	Meaning	Abbreviation	Meaning
arch	arching	lus	lustrous
ascend	ascending	M	medium
bl	blue	mar	margins
blk	black	mat	mat-like
brd	broad	mound	mounding
brn	brown	nar	narrow
bron	bronze	or	orange
bt	bright	pend	pendulous
C	coarse	pros	prostrate
clp	clump	p-sh	partial shade
col	columnar	pur	purple
com	compact	pyra	pyramidal
con	conical	rd	red
creep	creeping	s (*or* sun)	sun
crim	crimson	scar	scarlet
decid	deciduous	sh	shade
dk	dark	sil	silver
dwf	dwarf	spr	spreading

Abbreviation	Meaning	Abbreviation	Meaning
F	fine	tol	tolerant
fastig	fastigate	trail	trailing
gl	glossy	upr	upright
gr	green	var	variegated
hor	horizontal	weep	weeping
irr	irregular	well-dr	well-drained
layer	layered	wht	white
lt	light	yw	yellow

SHADE TREES

Botanical Name/ Common Name	Zone	Size Ht/Wid	Form	Foliage Summer	Fall	Texture	Exposure Soil	Remarks
Acer platanoides Norway Maple	4	50'/40'	round dense	dk-gr	yw	MC	sun/ adapt	Stately tree of predictable quality.
Acer platanoides 'Cleveland' Cleveland Maple	4	50'/35'	upr-oval	dk-gr	yw	MC	sun/ adapt	More upright and tight.
Acer platanoides 'Columnare' Columnar Maple	4	50'/20'	col	dk-gr	yw	MC	sun/ moist	Columnar Maple. Dense and full.
Acer platanoides 'Crimson King' Crimson King Maple	4	50'/40'	round dense	red-pur	red	M	sun/ moist	Brilliant foliage during growing season.
Acer platanoides 'Drummondii' Variegated Leaved Maple	4	30'/25'	round dense	gr, ivory edges	yw	MC	sun/ moist	
Acer platanoides 'Emerald Queen' Emerald Queen Maple	4	40'/30'	upr-oval	dk-gr	yw	M	sun/ adapt	
Acer platanoides 'Fassen's Black' Fassen's Black Norway Maple	4	60'/50'	round dense	red-gr	red	MC	sun/ well-dr	Good foliage color.
Acer platanoides 'Greenlace' Greenlace Maple	4	50'/40'	upr-round	dk-gr	yw	MC	sun/ well-dr	

SHADE TREES (CONTINUED)

Botanical Name/ Common Name	Zone	Size Ht/Wid	Form	Summer	Foliage Fall	Texture	Exposure Soil	Remarks
Acer platanoides 'Schwedleri' Schwedler Maple	4	50'/40'	upr-oval	red-gr	red	MC	sun/adapt	Slow-growing. Stands city conditions well.
Acer platanoides 'Summer shade' Summer shade Maple	4	60'/50'	upr-oval	dk-gr	yw	MC	sun/adapt	
Acer rubrum Red Maple	3	50'/35'	oval dense	dk-gr	red	M	s-sh/adapt	Red branch tips & buds.
Acer rubrum 'Armstrong' Armstrong Red Maple	3	35'/15'	nar-col	dk-gr	red	M	s-sh/adapt	Columnar Red Maple.
Acer rubrum 'Autumn Flame' Autumn Flame Maple	3	50'/40'	round dense	dk-gr	crim-red	M	sun/adapt	Good fall color.
Acer rubrum 'October Glory' October Glory Maple	3	50'/35'	oval dense	dk-gr	red	M	sun/adapt	Good fall color.
Acer rubrum 'Red Sunset' Red Sunset Maple	3	45'/40'	round oval	dk-gr	red	M	sun/adapt	Good fall color.
Acer saccharinum Silver Maple	3	50'/40'	upr-irr	gr, sil under	yw-brn	M	s-p-sh/adapt	Brittle. Loose form w/o. pruning.
Acer saccharum Sugar Maple	3	80'+/60'	oval dense	m-gr	or-red	M	s-p-sh/well-dr	Strong and slow. A majestic tree with brilliant fall color.
Acer saccharum 'Globosum' Globe Sugar Maple	3	10'+/10'	globe					Dense globe for accent.
Acer saccharum 'Green Mountain' Green Mountain Maple	3	50'/35'	upr-oval	dk-gr	or-red	M	s-p-sh	A little smaller than *saccharum*. Darker foliage.

SHADE TREES (CONTINUED)

Botanical Name/ Common Name	Zone	Size Ht/Wid	Form	Summer	Foliage Fall	Texture	Exposure Soil	Remarks
Acer saccharum 'Newton Sentry' Newton Sentry Maple	3	40'/15'	nar- upr	dk-gr	or-red	M	s-p-sh	Narrow, upright.
Aesculus X carnea Red Horsechestnut	3	50'/40'	round dense	dk-gr	yw-brnC		s-p-sh/ well-dr	Lots of rosy red spring blooms. Cultivars 'Briotii,' 'O'Neill Red.'
Aesculus glabra Ohio Buckeye	4	40'/40'	round	bt-gr	yw	M	s-p-sh/ well-dr	
Aesculus hippocastanum Common Horsechestnut	3	60'/40'	oval	yw-gr	yw-brnC		s-p-sh/ well-dr	Limited com- mercial avail- ability.
Ailanthus altissima Tree of Heaven	4	60'/40'	irr	m-gr	yw	C	s-p-sh/ any soil	Brittle. Fast. Tolerates poor conditions. Last-resort tree.
Alnus glutinosa Black Alder	3	60'/40'	upr- oval irr	gl- dk-gr	yw	M	s-p-sh/ moist	
Alnus rhombifolia White Alder	8	80'/45'	round dense	gl- dk-gr	yw	M	sun/ tol-heat	Slightly pendulant branches.
Betula jacquemontii White-barked Himalayan Birch	5	45'/35'	upr- oval	dk-gr	yw	MF	s-p-sh/ moist well-dr	Very white bark. Resists Birch borer.
Betula maximowicziana Monarch Birch	2	50'/35'	upr oval	bt-gr	yw	MF	s-p-sh/ moist well-dr	Smooth bark turns white early. Vigorous.
Betula nigra River Birch	4	50'/35'	pyra- open	m-gr	yw	MF	s-p-sh/ moist	Bronze, peeling bark. 'Heritage' resists bronze birch borer.

SHADE TREES (CONTINUED)

Botanical Name/ Common Name	Zone	Size Ht/Wid	Form	Summer	Foliage Fall	Texture	Exposure Soil	Remarks
Betula papyrifera Paper Whlte Birch (canoe)	2	60'/40'	pyra-irr	dk-gr	yw	M	s-p-sh/ well-dr	Peeling white bark. Bigger, coarser leaves than *pendula*.
Betula pendula European White Birch	2	50'/30'	upr-oval pend	bt-gr	yw	MF	s-p-sh/ moist	White, peeling bark. Borer problems in many areas.
Betula pendula 'monle' Purple Rain™ Birch	2	45'/35'	upr-oval pend	pur	pur	MF	s	White bark with purple leaves. Pendulous branches.
Betula pendula laciniata Cutleaf Weeping Birch	3	50'/35'	upr-oval pend	bt-gr	yw	MF	s-p-sh/ well-dr moist	Deeply cut leaves. Weeping branches. White bark.
Betula platyphylla japonica Japanese White Birch	2	50'/35'	upr oval	bt-gr	yw	MF	s-p-sh	White bark turns quickly. Firm against the wind.
Betula platyphylla japonica 'Whitespire' Whitespire Birch	2	50'/35'	upr-oval	bt-gr	yw	MF	s-p-sh	Very resistant to bronze birch borer.
Betula populifolia Gray Birch	4	40'/15'	oval irr	bt-gr	yw	MF	s-p-sh/ adapt	Chalky-white, smooth bark.
Carpinus betulus European Hornbeam	5	60'/40'	round	dk-gr	yw	MF	s-p-sh/ adapt	'Columnaris,' 'Fastigiata,' and 'Globosa' cultivars.
Carpinus caroliniana American Hornbeam	2	30'/15'	flat irr	dk-gr	yw-or-red	M	s-p-sh/ acid, moist	Will tolerate dry soils.

SHADE TREES (CONTINUED)

Botanical Name/ Common Name	Zone	Size Ht/Wid	Form	Summer	Foliage Fall	Texture	Exposure Soil	Remarks
Carya illinoinensis Pecan	3	90'/50'	oval	yw-gr	yw	M	sun/ adapt	Protect from wind. Cross-pollination required for nuts.
Carya ovata Shagbark Hickory	3	90'/50'	oval irr	yw-gr	yw	M	sun/ adapt	Coarse, peeling bark. Protect from wind.
Castanea mollissima Chinese Chestnut	4	50'/50'	round	dk-gr	yw-bron	MC	sun/ acid, well-dr	Leaves reddish in early spring.
Catalpa speciosa Western Catalpa (Catawba)	4	60'/40'	oval-open	lt-gr	yw-brn	C	s-p-sh/ adapt	Extra-large leaves. White flower in early summer. Long, messy seed pods. Not very useful in landscape.
Celtis laevigata Sugar Hackberry	5	70'/60'	round	lt-gr	yw-brn	MF	sun/ adapt	
Celtis occidentalis Common Hackberry	4	70'/50'	vase-open	lt-yw gr	yw-brn	M	sun/ adapt	Excellent shade tree. Drought resistant.
Cercidiphyllum japonicum Katsura Tree	4	60'/30'	brd oval	bl-gr	yw-scar	MF	sun/ adapt	Handsome specimen.
Cladrastis lutea American Yellowood	3	50'/40'	round brd	bt-gr	yw	M	sun/ adapt	Tolerant of different pH.
Disopyros virginiana Persimmon	4	50'/35'	oval irr	dk-gr	yw	M	sun/ adapt	Messy, large fruit. Interesting bark and foliage.
Fogus grandifolia American Beech	3	60'/50'	upr oval	bl-gr	yw-or	M	s-p-sh/ acid, moist	

SHADE TREES (CONTINUED)

Botanical Name/ Common Name	Zone	Size Ht/Wid	Form	Summer	Foliage Fall	Texture	Exposure Soil	Remarks
Fagus sylvatica 'Atropurpurea' Copper Beech	5	75'/60'	con- dense	dk-pur	cop- per	MF	sun/ acid, moist	Striking foliage color. Specimen. Usually quite symmetrical.
Fraxinus americana White Ash	3	60'/60'	round to oval	bt-gr	yw to deep maroon	M	sun/ rich, well-dr	'Autumn Ap- plause,' 'Autumn Purple,' 'Cham- paign County,' 'Elk Grove,' and 'Rosehill' cultivars.
Fraxinus holotricha 'Moraine' Moraine Ash	5	35'/25'	nar upr	dk-gr	yw- pur	M	sun/ adapt	
Fraxinus pennsylvanica Green Ash	2	60'/40'	upr irr loose	m-gr	yw	M	sun/ adapt	'Honeyshade,' 'Patmore,' and 'Marshall's Seedless' cultivars.
Fraxinus quadrangulata Blue Ash	3	60'/60'	round broad	bt-yw gr	yw	M	sun/ adapt	Valuable for timber.
Fraxinus velutina Arizona Ash	7	40'/40'	round	bt-gr	yw	M	sun/ adapt	Tolerant of hot sun, winds, and alkali soils.
Ginkgo, biloba Ginkgo	4	60'/40'	pyra irr	lt-gr	yw	M	sun/ adapt	Female fruit smells bad. Plant only male trees. 'Autumn Gold' is best male upright cultivar.
Gleditsia triacanthos inermis Thornless Honeylocust	4	60'/50'	spr open	m-gr	yw	F	sun/ adapt	Mimosa webworm a problem in many locales.
Gleditsia triacanthos 'Green Glory' Green Glory Honeylocust	4	60'/50'	pyra	m-gr	yw	F	sun/ adapt	Some web- worm resis- tance.

SHADE TREES (CONTINUED)

Botanical Name/ Common Name	Zone	Size Ht/Wid	Form	Foliage Summer	Fall	Texture	Exposure Soil	Remarks
Gleditsia triacanthos 'Imperial' Imperial Honeylocust	4	35'/35'	round spr	m-gr	yw	F	sun/ adapt	Smaller than most. Graceful.
Gleditsia triacanthos 'Moraine' Moraine Honeylocust	4	50'/40'	vase	m-gr	yw	F	sun/ adapt	Thornless and seedless.
Gleditsia triacanthos 'Rubylace' Rubylace Honeylocust	4	40'/40'	round	red-edge	bron	F	sun/ adapt	Reddish-tinge to foliage is interesting. Thornless and seedless.
Gleditsia triacanthos 'Shademaster' Shademaster Honeylocust	4	50'/50'	round	m-gr	yw	F	sun/ adapt	Ascending branches. Thornless and seedless.
Gleditsia triacanthos 'Skyline' Skyline Honeylocust	4	50'/40'	pyra	m-gr	yw	F	sun/ adapt	Wide-angled branches. Thornless and seedless.
Gleditsia triacanthos 'Sunburst' Sunburst Honeylocust	4	40'/40'	round	yw on tips	yw	F	sun/ adapt	Colorful accent tree. Commands much atten- tion. Warrants careful use.
Gymocladus dioica Kentucky Coffeetree	4	65'/45'	oval open	dk-gr	yw-gr	M	sun/ adapt	Long coffee- bean pods are messy. Stately, symmetrical tree.
Juglans nigra Black Walnut	4	60'/60'	oval round	dk-gr	yw	M	sun/ moist, rich	Nuts can be messy in land- scape. Roots produce toxic substance to many plants.
Juglans regia Persian Wal- nut	6	60'/60'	oval round	yw-gr	yw	MC	sun/ deep, well-dr	Produces valuable cabi- net wood.

SHADE TREES (CONTINUED)

Botanical Name/ Common Name	Zone	Size Ht/Wid	Form	Summer	Foliage Fall	Texture	Exposure Soil	Remarks
Larix decidua European Larch	2	70'/30'	pyra	dk-gr, yw-edge	yw	MF	sun/ moist, well-dr	
Larix kaempferi Japanese Larch	5	80'/40'	pyra open	gr	yw	F	sun/ moist, well-dr	
Liquidambar styraciflua Sweetgum	5	60'/40'	pyra dense	dk-gr	yw-pur-red	M	sun/ moist	Good, sym-metrical shape Many colors at once in fall. 'Burgundy' & 'Palo Alto' cultivars.
Lirirodendron tulipifera Tuliptree	4	80'/40'	oval	yw-gr	yw	MC	sun/ moist, well-dr	Yellow, "tulip-like" flowers. Smooth bark.
Magnolia grandiflora Southern Magnolia	6	60'/40'	pyra dense	gl dk-gr	ever-green	MC	s-p-sh/ acid, well-dr	Large white flower. Ever-green foliage. Included here because it is used as shade tree. Specimen.
Metasequoia glyptostroboides Dawn Red-wood	5	80'/35'	pyra con	bt-gr	brn	F	sun/ moist, well-dr	Feathery foliage. Ever-green appear-ance.
Morus alba White Mul-berry	4	50'/40'	round open	bt-gr	yw	M	s-p-sh/ adapt	Messy fruit. Tolerates drought.
Morus alba 'Chaparral' Weeping Mulberry	4	12'/15'	weep	gl-dk-gr	yw	M	s-p-sh	Grafted at 6', branches weep. Accent tree.
Morus platanifolid Fruitless Mulberry	4	50'/40'	round open	m-gr	yw	M	s-p-sh/ adapt	Male is fruit-less. Drought-resistant.
Nyssa sylvatica Black Tupelo (Black Gum)	4	45'/30'	pyra open	gl dk-gr	yw or red-scar	MF	s-p-sh/ moist	Horizontal branching. Not tolerant of alkaline soils.

SHADE TREES (CONTINUED)

Botanical Name/ Common Name	Zone	Size Ht/Wid	Form	Summer	Foliage Fall	Texture	Exposure Soil	Remarks
Ostrya virginiana American Hophornbeam	4	40'/25'	pyra to round	m-gr	yw	MF	s-p-sh/ adapt	
Paulownia tomentosa Royal Paulownia	5	40'/40'	round open	rich dk-gr	gr	C	s-p-sh/ adapt	
Phellodendron amurense Amur Corktree	3	40'/40'	round open	bt dk-gr	yw- bron	M	sun/ adapt	Tolerant of air pollution.
Platanus X acerifolia London- planetree	5	100'/60'	pyra to round	dull, yw-gr, large	yw- brn	C	sun/ adapt	Resists anthracnose. Peeling green-white bark. Interesting seed balls. Use carefully be-cause of size.
Platanus X acerifolia 'Bloodgood Strain' Bloodgood London- planetree	5	100'/60'	pyra to round	dull yw-gr, large	yw- brn	C	sun/ adapt	Very resistant to anthrac-nose.
Platanus accidentalis Sycamore	4	100'/60'	pyra to round	dull yw-gr, large	yw-brn	C	sun/ adapt	Fast-growing. Very large. Anthracnose a problem. Use carefully because of size.
Populus alba White Poplar	3	60'/50'	round open	gl gray-gr	or-yw	MC	sun/ adapt	Pollution-tolerant.
Populus alba 'Bolleana' Bolleana Poplar	3	50'/15'	col	dk gray-gr	or-yw	M	sun/ moist	Grow fast and narrow. Brittle. Borer problems. Resists canker.

SHADE TREES (CONTINUED)

Botanical Name/ Common Name	Zone	Size Ht/Wid	Form	Summer	Foliage Fall	Texture	Exposure Soil	Remarks
Populus alba 'Nivea' Silver Poplar	5	60'/60'	irr	dk-gr wht, under	or-yw	M	sun/ moist	Fast & brittle. White under-side of leaves interesting in breeze.
Populus del-toides Cottonless Cottonwood	3	100'/80'	irr spr	dk-gr	yw	M	sun/ moist	Fast & brittle. Musical in breeze. Male does not pro-duce cotton.
Populus nigra 'Italica' Lombardy Poplar	3	60'/10'	nar col	dk-gr	yw	M	sun/ moist	Short life-borers, cankers, & brittle in wind. 'Theves' culti-var lives longest.
Populus tremuloides Quaking Aspen	1	45'/25'	col	lt-gr	yw	M	sun-p-sh moist	Leaves rustle pleasantly in the breeze.
Psuedolarix kaempferi Golden Larch	5	50'/40'	pyra	lt-gr, blue below	yw	M	s-p-sh/ acid, moist	
Quercus acutissima Sawtooth Oak	6	40'/30'	pyra dense	lus dk-gr	yw	M	sun/ adapt	
Quercus alba White Oak	4	70'/70'	round oval	dk-gr	pur-red	MC	sun/ moist, well-dr	Strong & majes-tic. Slow. Holds leaves late. Colorful in fall.
Quercus borealis maxima Northern Red Oak	3	70'/70'	round oval	dk-gr	crim	MC	sun/ adapt	Excellent fall color. Strong & hardy. Can be difficult to transplant.
Quercus cocci-nea Scarlet Oak	4	70'/60'	oval spr dense	gl dk-gr	scar	MC	sun/ adapt	Brilliant red in fall.
Quercus imbricaria Shingle Oak	4	60'/60'	pyra	gl gr	red-brn	M	sun/ adapt	Drought-resis-tant. Interesting long, narrow leaves.

SHADE TREES (CONTINUED)

Botanical Name/ Common Name	Zone	Size Ht/Wid	Form	Summer	Foliage Fall	Texture	Exposure Soil	Remarks
Quercus macrocarpa Bur Oak	2	90'/90'	round spr	dull m-gr	yw-brn	C	sun/ adapt	Extremely fine shade tree, but slow, with lots of character. Very strong.
Quercus muehlenbergii Chinkapin Oak	5	50'/40'	irr	yw-gr	brn	C	sun/ adapt	Picturesque form. White underside on leaves interesting.
Quercus palustris Pin Oak	4	70'/40'	pyra pend	lus dk-gr	scar	M	sun/ moist, well-dr	Holds leaves long in winter. Iron chlorosis a problem. Good specimen tree.
Quercus robur English Oak	5	100'/100'	round broad	dk-gr	brn	C	sun/ fertile, well-dr	Requires large space in sunny location. Holds leaves late into winter.
Quercus robur 'Fastigata' Upright English Oak	5	60'/30'	pyra	dk-gr	brn	C	sun/ well-dr	Narrow upright. Columnar when young.
Quercus shumardii Shumard Oak	5	75'/60'	oval	gl dk-gr	scar	M	sun/ adapt	Very good in an open lawn area. Interesting bark—gray or red-brn.
Quercus virginiana Southern Live Oak	7	60'/60'	pyra low dense	dk-gr	ever- green	M	sun/ moist, well-dr	Glossy foliage.
Robinia pseudoacacia Black Locust	3	50'/35'	round open	dk-bl- gr	yw	MF	sun/ adapt	Thornless varieties best. White flowers Cultivar 'Fastigata' is columnar & thornless.
Robinia pseudoacacia 'globosa' Globe Locust	3	15'/15'	round	dk-bl- gr	yw	MF	sun/ adapt	Head forms a round ball of foliage on a 6' trunk.

SHADE TREES (CONTINUED)

Botanical Name/ Common Name	Zone	Size Ht/Wid	Form	Foliage Summer	Fall	Texture	Exposure Soil	Remarks
Salix alba White Willow	2	90'/90'	round	lt-yw-gr	yw-gr	F	sun/ wet	
Salix alba tristis Golden Weeping Willow	2	50'/50'	round weep	lt-yw-gr	yw-gr	F	sun/ wet	Golden stems add winter color.
Salix X blanda Niobe Weeping Willow	4	50'/50'	round weep	lt-gr	yw-gr	F	sun/ wet	Weeping willow with yellow stems. Messy, but unique.
Salix matsudana 'Tortuosa' Corkscrew Willow	3	40'/40'	flat ovate dense	olive	olive	MF	sun/ wet	Corkscrew stems, lots of character.
Sassafras albidum Common Sassafras	4	50'/35'	round irr	lt-gr	yw to scar-pur	M	s-p-sh/ well-dr	Fragrant yellow blossoms in spring. Good fall color.
Sophora japonica Japanese Pagodatree	4	60'/30'	oval open	bl-gr	bl-gr	MF	sun/ adapt	Drought- & heat-resistant. Greenish bark interesting. Tolerates air pollution. Hard to transplant.
Sorbus aucuparia European Mountainhash	3	35'/25'	broad oval	lt-gr	yw to or	MF	sun/ adapt	Bright red berries in summer, in heavy clusters. Small tree in some locales.
Taxodium distichum Common Baldcypress	4	60'/30'	pyra	m-gr	yw to red-brn	F	sun/ acid, well-dr	Deciduous conifer. Drought-resistant.
Tilia americana American Linden (Basswood)	2	70'/45'	con oval	gr	yw-brn	C	s-p-sh/ moist	Good specimen. 'Fastigata' more pyramidal

SHADE TREES (CONTINUED)

Botanical Name/ Common Name	Zone	Size Ht/Wid	Form	Summer	Foliage Fall	Texture	Exposure Soil	Remarks
Tilia cordata Littleleaf Linden	3	60'/40'	oval	gl dk-gr	yw-gr	M	sun/ adapt	
Tilia cordata 'Greenspire' Greenspire Linden	3	60'/25'	nar oval	m-gr	yw-brn	M	sun/ adapt	Works well in urban sites. Good street tree.
Tilia X euchlora 'Redmond' Redmond Linden	4	60'/30'	pyra to col	gl bt-gr	yw-brn	MC	sun/ adapt	Straight & well-shaped. Red tip on branches in winter.
Ulmus parvifolia Chinese Elm	5	50'/40'	round	m-gr	yw-brn	F	sun/ adapt	True Chinese Elm. Nice little shade tree that should be used more.
Zelkova serrata Japanese Zelkova	5	60'/60'	broad vase	dk-gr	yw-or- red	MF	sun/ moist	Resists drought. Often used in place of American Elm.

SMALL ORNAMENTAL TREES

Botanical Name/ Common Name	Zone	Size Ht/Wid	Form	Summer	Foliage Fall	Texture	Exposure Soil	Remarks
Acer ginnala Amur Maple	2	20'/15'	broad irr	dk-gr	scar	MF	s-p-sh/ adapt	Usually multi-stemmed. Good character
Acer ginnala compacta Dwarf Amur Maple	2	8'/8'	upr-round	dk-gr	scar	MF	s-p-sh	Grows like a big shrub. Ex-cellent fall color.
Acer griseum Paperbark Maple	5	25'/20'	oval open	dk-gr	red-bron	MF	sun/ well-dr	
Acer japonicum Japanese Maple (Fullmoon)	5	20'/20'	round irr	red-gr	pur-red	F	s-p-sh/ well-dr	Red fruit in summer. Strong color accent.

SMALL ORNAMENTAL TREES (CONTINUED)

Botanical Name/ Common Name	Zone	Size Ht/Wid	Form	Foliage Summer	Fall	Texture	Exposure Soil	Remarks
Acer palmatum Dwarf Japanese Maple	6	15'/15'	irr layer	m-gr	scar-pur	F	p-sh/ rich, well-dr	Exotic tree. Slow growth. Cultivars include 'Bloodgood,' 'Burgundy,' 'Dissectum,' 'Oshi-Beni.'
Acer tataricum Tatarian Maple	4	25'/25'	oval irr	m-gr	yw & red	M	s-p-sh/ adapt	Red fruit in August. Good background tree.
Albizia julibrissin Mimosa (Silktree)	6	25'/25'	broad round	yw-gr	yw-brn	F	s-p-sh/ adapt	Lacy foliage. Pink flowers in summer. Seedlings from fallen seed a pest. Protect from wind
Asimina triloba Common Pawpaw	5	20'/20'	round	m-gr	yw	MC	sun/ moist, acid	
Cercis canadensis Eastern Redbud	4	25'/20'	broad round	dk-gr	yw-brn	MC	s-p-sh/ adapt	Prolific pink flowers in early spring. Heart-shaped leaves. Dark, gray, black bark.
Cercis canadensis 'Forest Pansy' Forest Pansy Redbud	4	25'/20'	broad round	dk-pur	dk-pur	MC	s-p-sh/ adapt	Maroon foliage, sometimes fades to green in extreme heat. Pink flowers.
Cercis canadensis 'Oklahoma' Oklahoma Redbud	4	25'/20'	broad round	gl-dk-gr	yw-brn	MC	s-p-sh	Glossy leaves. Rosy-lavender blooms.
Cornus alba Tatarian Dogwood	2	10'/8'	erect arch	yw-gr	red-pur	M	s-p-sh/ adapt	

SMALL ORNAMENTAL TREES (CONTINUED)

Botanical Name/ Common Name	Zone	Size Ht/Wid	Form	Summer	Foliage Fall	Texture	Exposure Soil	Remarks
Cornus florida Flowering Dogwood	4	20'/20'	broad round	dk-red-gr	red-pur	M	p-sh-sh/ well-dr	Many cultivars: 'Cherokee Chief,' 'Cherokee Princess,' 'Cloud Nine,' 'Rubra,' 'Pendula.' Pink, white, and red flowers.
Cornus kousa Kousa Dogwood	4	20'/20'	vase	dk-gr	red-pur	M	sun/acid well-dr	White flowers, red fruit. Later bloom than c. florida.
Cornus mas Cornelian cherry Dogwood	4	20'/15'	oval	dk-gr	red-pur	M	s-p-sh/ adapt	
Cornus racemosa Gray Dogwood	4	15'/15'	round	gray-gr	red-pur	M	s or sh/ adapt	Brushy. Background or screen planting. Shrub-like plant with white flowers in spring.
Cotinus coggygria Common Smoketree (Purple Fringetree)	5	15'/15'	round spr	bl-gr	red-pur	M	sun/ adapt	Pink, "smoky" flowers in June 'Rubrifolia' cultivar has glossy purple foliage.
Crataegus crus-galli Cockspur Hawthorn	4	25'/25'	round	gl-dk-gr	or-scar	MF	sun adapt	White flower in May. Bright red fruit. Long, sharp thorns. Good tree for birds.
Crataegus crus-galli inermis Thornless Cockspur Hawthorn	4	25'/25'	round	gl-dk-gr	or-scar	MF	sun/ adapt	Thornless. White blooms. Red berries.

SMALL ORNAMENTAL TREES (CONTINUED)

Botanical Name/ Common Name	Zone	Size Ht/Wid	Form	Summer	Foliage Fall	Texture	Exposure Soil	Remarks
Crataegus X lavellei Lavelle Hawthorn	4	25'/25'	round	gl-dk-gr	red-bron	M	sun/ adapt	
Crataegus mollis Downy Hawthorn	4	25'/25'	round	gr	yw-brn	MF	sun/ adapt	White flowers in May. Ornamental red fruit. Long sharp thorns.
Crataegus oxycantha 'Pauli' Paul's Scarlet Hawthorn	4	18'/15'	round flat	dk-gr	yw-gr	MF	sun/ heavy soil	Double-red flowers in May. Red showy fruit. Small accent tree with thorns.
Crataegus phaenopyrum Washington Hawthorn	4	30'/20'	oval	dk-gr, red-tinge.	red-bron	MF	sun/ adapt	More upright. Usually multi-stemmed Thorny.
Crataegus viridis 'Winter King' Winter King Hawthorn	4	30'/30'	round dense	gl m-gr	yw-brn	MF	sun	
Elaeagnus angustifolia Russian olive	2	25'/25'	irr spr	sil-gr	yw-brn	MF	sun/ adapt	Attractive foliage, thorny. Fast. Drought-tolerant.
Elaeagnus umbellata Autumn Elaeagnus (Autumn olive)	4	15'/15'	vase	sil-gr	yw-brn	M	sun/ adapt	Shrublike. Good screen planting.
Koelreuteria paniculata Goldenraintree	5	25'/20'	round spr	dk-gr	yw-brn	M	sun/ adapt	Cascades of yellow pani-cled flowers. Bronze seed pods in fall. Good character.
Magnolia X soulangiana Saucer Magnolia	5	25'/25'	round	m-gr	yw-brn	C	sun/ deep, acid, moist	Large, tulip-like blossoms that disinte-grate quickly in wind.

SMALL ORNAMENTAL TREES (CONTINUED)

Botanical Name/ Common Name	Zone	Size Ht/Wid	Form	Summer	Foliage Fall	Texture	Exposure Soil	Remarks
Magnolia virginiana Sweetbay Magnolia	5	15'/15'	upr irr spr	dk-gr	red-bron	M	s-or sh/ moist to wet	
Malus atrosanguinea Carmine Crabapple	4	20'/25'	round	gl dk-gr	yw	M	sun/ adapt	
Malus sargentii Sargent Flower-ing Crabapple	5	10'/10'	flat mound	m-gr	yw	M	sun/ adapt	White flowers in spring. Very dwarf and picturesque.
Malus X zumi calocarpa Zumi Crab-apple	4	25'/18'	round irr	m-gr	yw	MC	sun/ adapt	Flowers open pink, turning white. Bright red fruit.
Malus species (Crabapple vari-eties)	4							
'American Beauty'		25'/12'	fastig					Pink flowers (large), red fruit.
'Bechtel's'		15'/10'	upr-spr					Double-pink. Green fruit.
'Beverly'		20'/20'	round					Pink flowers, red fruit.
'Coralburst'		10'/10'	round					Double pink flowers.
'Dolgo'		35'/30'	round					White flowers. Red fruit.
'Evelyn'		20'/15'	erect					Rose-pink flowers. Yellow fruit.
'Golden Hornet'			upr-oval					White flowers. Yellow fruit.
Malus species 'Gorgeous'		25'/25'	round					White flowers. Red fruit.
'Hopa'		35'/35'	spr					Pink flowers. Red fruit. Large.
'Jay Darling'		30'/30'	round	gr-bron				Purple-red flowers. Purple-red fruit.

SMALL ORNAMENTAL TREES (CONTINUED)

Botanical Name/ Common Name	Zone	Size Ht/Wid	Form	Foliage Summer	Foliage Fall	Texture	Exposure Soil	Remarks
malus species (cont.)								
'Katherine'		20'/25'	open					Pink-white flower. Yellow fruit.
'Marshall Oyama'			nar upr					White flowers. Red and yellow fruit.
'Parkman'		15'/12'	vase					Rose-pink flowers. Red fruit.
'Prince George'		20'/20'	upr spr					Pink flower. No fruit.
'Radiant'		18'/15'	upr	dk-gr red edge				Dark red-pink flower. Red fruit.
'Red Splendor'			upr	pur				Red flowers.
'Roussau'		40'/35'	round					Purple-red flowers. Red fruit.
'Royalty'		18'/15'	round	red-pur				Dark red flowers. Dark red fruit.
'Snowcloud'								White flowers.
'Snowdrift'								White flowers.
'Spring Snow'								White flower. No fruit.
'VanEstletine'		20'/10'	fastig					Dark red flowers. Very upright.
'White Angel'		20'/20'	round					White flowers. Ruby red fruit.
Prunus cerasifera Cherry Plum	4	20'/20'	ascend	dk-gr	red-bron	M	sun/ adapt	Cultivars 'Thunder-cloud' and 'Newport' have dark red-purple foliage. Pink flowers in in May. Red-purple fruit.
Prunus cerasifera 'Krauter Vesuvius' Krauter's Purple Plum	5	18'/15'	dscend	dk-pur	red-bron	M	sun/ adapt	Very dark purple-black leaves. No fruit.

SMALL ORNAMENTAL TREES (CONTINUED)

Botanical Name/ Common Name	Zone	Size Ht/Wid	Form	Summer	Foliage Fall	Texture	Exposure Soil	Remarks
Prunus persica Flowering Peach	4	20′/12′	upr round	yw-gr	yw	M	sun/ adapt	'Cardinal' (double red); 'Pink Charming' (double pink); 'Iceberg' (white); 'Rutgers' (purple leaves).
Prunus serrulata 'Kwanzan' Kwanzan Cherry	5	20′/10′	vase	gl dk-gr	yw to red	M	sun/ adapt	Double pink flowers. Red fruit. New leaves are copper-red.
Prunus subhirtella 'Pendula' Weeping Higan Cherry	5	25′/20′	erect weep	red-gr	bron	F	sun/ adapt	
Prunus tomentosa Manchu Cherry (Nanking)	2	10′/12′	irr	dk-gr	red	M	s-sh/ rich, moist	
Pyrus calleryana 'Aristocrat' Aristocrat Pear	5	40′/25′	pyra	gl dk-gr	bron-scar	M	sun/ adapt	Dense, glossy and symmetrical. White flowers in spring & good fall color. Specimen/ accent.
Pyrus calleryana 'Bradford' Bradford Pear	5	40′/30′	pyra oval	gl dk-gr	bron-scar	M	sun/ adapt	Same as 'Aristocrat.' Tolerates drought and pollution.
Pyrus calleryana 'Capital' Capital Pear	5	35′/8′	upr-fast	gl-dk-gr	red-pur	M	s-p-sh/ adapt	Very narrow upright. Good replacement for Lombardy Poplar.
Pyrus calleryana 'Redspire' Redspire Pear	5	35′/25′	pyra oval	gl-dk-gr	yw-red	M	s-p-sh/ adapt	A little narrower form than Bradford.

SMALL ORNAMENTAL TREES (CONTINUED)

Botanical Name/ Common Name	Zone	Size Ht/Wid	Form	Foliage Summer	Fall	Texture	Exposure Soil	Remarks
Pyrus calleryana 'Whitehouse' Whitehouse Pear	5	35'/20'	upr oval	gl-dk-gr	bron-scar	M	s-p-sh	Upright and narrow, but not as narrow as Capital.

DECIDUOUS ORNAMENTAL SHRUBS

Botanical Name/ Common Name	Zone	Size Ht/Wid	Form	Foliage Summer	Fall	Texture	Exposure Soil	Remarks
Abelia X 'Edward Goucher' Pink Abelia	6	5'/5'	round	gl dk-gr	bron-pur	MF	s-p-sh/ well-dr	Pink flowers in summer.
Abelia X grandiflora Glossy Abelia	5	5'/5'	round	gl dk-gr	bron-pur	MF	s-p-sh/ well dr	White flowers in summer. Semi-ever-green. Grace-ful.
Aesculus parviflora Bottlebrush Buckeye	4	10'/12'	broad round	m-gr		MC	s-p-sh/ rich	"Bottlebrush" flowers are interesting.
Alnus rugosa Speckled Alder	3	10'/15'	upr spr	dull gr	yw	MF	s-p-sh/ moist, wet	
Amelanchier arborea Downy Serviceberry	4	20'/12'	upr oval	gray-gr	yw to red	MF	s or sh/ well-dr	
Amelanchier stolonifera Dwarf Juneberry	5	3'/3'	irr	dk-gr		MC	s or sh/ adapt	White flowers in May. Purplish fruit.
Amorpha fruiti-cosa Indigo bush	4	10'/10'	irr open	lt-gr	yw-gr	M	sun/ dry	Thrives in dry conditions.
Aralia spinosa Devil's Walkingstick	4	12'/12'	oval irr	dk-gr	yw-bron	M	s-p-sh/ adapt	Twisted stems are main fea-ture. Interesting accent.

DECIDUOUS ORNAMENTAL SHRUBS (CONTINUED)

Botanical Name/ Common Name	Zone	Size Ht/Wid	Form	Summer	Foliage Fall	Texture	Exposure Soil	Remarks
Aronia arbutifolia Red Chokeberry	4	5'/4'	upr round	gl dk-gr	crim	M	s-p-sh/ adapt	White flowers in May. Red fruit in fall.
Aronia melanocarpa Black Chokeberry	4	4'/3'	round open	gl dk-gr	crim	MF	s-p-sh/ adapt	
Berberis X gladwynesis 'William Penn'™ William Penn™ Barberry	6	3'/5'	spr	gl dk-gr	gl-gr red	M	sun/ adapt	Evergreen zone 6 & south. Many yellow flowers. Dwarf growth habit.
Berberis koreana Korean Bar- berry	4	5'/4'	oval	m-gr	red	M	s-p-sh/ adapt	Fall berries. Thorns.
Berberis X mentorensis Mentor Barberry	5	7'/6'	upr globe	dk-gr	or	M	s-or-sh/ adapt	Very dense foliage. Sharp thorns.
Berberis thunbergii Japanese Barberry	4	6'/6'	round	dk-gr	red	MF	sun/ adapt	Withstands dry conditions. Thorns.
Berberis thunbergii 'Atropurpurea' Redleaf Barberry	4	5'/4'	round	crim- gr	red	MF	sun/ adapt	Bright red color for good accent. Thorns.
Berberis thunbergii 'Nana' Crimson Pygmy Barberry	4	2'/3'	mound	crim- gr	red	F	sun/ adapt	True dwarf. Excellent small colorful shrub. Thorns flexible, not as sharp as other Berberis.
Berberis thunbergii 'Aurea' Golden Barberry	4	5'/5'	round dense	gold		MF	sun/ adapt	Thorns.
Berberis thunbergii 'Erecta' Truehedge Barberry	4	6'/5'	upr- com	lt-gr	or-red	MF	s-or-sh/ adapt	Good, upright hedge plant. Thorny.

DECIDUOUS ORNAMENTAL SHRUBS (CONTINUED)

Botanical Name/ Common Name	Zone	Size Ht/Wid	Form	Foliage Summer	Fall	Texture	Exposure Soil	Remarks
Berberis thunbergii 'Kobold' Kobold Barberry	4	3'/4'	mound dense	bt-gr		F	sun/ adapt	Very full, dense, and dwarf. Good edging or facer.
Berberis thunbergii 'Rosy Glow' Rosy Glow Barberry	4	3'/4'	round dense	red-wht mottled		MF	sun/ adapt	Mottled foliage over-cast with rosy-red tint.
Buddleia davidii Butterflybush	6	6'/6'	oval round	gr	brn	M	sun/ adapt	Violet, pink, and white flowering vari-eties available. Summer flow-ering. Grows in zone 5, but freezes back to ground each year.
Callicarpa dichotoma Beautyberry	6	4'/4'	irr open	lt-gr		MC	s-p-sh/ adapt	Pink flowers in August. Violet-purple berries in fall & winter.
Calycanthus floridus Common Sweetshrub	4	7'/6'	upr round	yw-gr	yw	MC	s-or-sh/ moist	
Caragana arborescens Pea Shrub	2	18'/15'	erect oval	lt-gr	yw-gr	MF	s-p-sh/ adapt	Pale yellow flowers in late spring. Good screen or hedge, but needs facer.
Caragana pygmea Pygmy Pea Shrub	2	1 1/2'/1 1/2'	round	gr	yw	MF	s-p-sh/ adapt	Pale flowers in May. Good shrub, but difficult to obtain.

DECIDUOUS ORNAMENTAL SHRUBS (CONTINUED)

Botanical Name/ Common Name	Zone	Size Ht/Wid	Form	Summer	Foliage Fall	Texture	Exposure Soil	Remarks
Caryopteris incana Blue Mist Bluebeard (B. M. Spirea)	5	2'/2'	mound	dk-bl-gr	grayish	MF	sun/ adapt	Nice mound of powder-blue flowers from August to frost.
Chaenomeles japonica Japanese Flowering Quince	4	4'/5'	round spr	gl dk-gr	bron	MF	sun/ adapt	Scarlet-orange flowers in March & April. One of the earliest bloomers.
Chaenomeles speciosa Common Flowering Quince	4	6'/8'	round spr	gl dk-gr	bron	M	sun/ adapt	Pink flowers in March & April. Jet Trails' culti-var (white blossoms); 'Texas Scarlet' (red blos-soms).
Clethra alnifolia Sweet Pepperbush	4	6'/6'	round com	dk-gr	yw	M	s-or-sh/ acid, moist	White, fra-grant, summer flowers of interesting form.
Cornus baileyi Bailey's Dogwood	3	6'/5'	round oval	gr	red-bron	C	s-p-sh/ adapt	White summer flowers. Red twigs in winter.
Cornus stolonifera Redosier Dogwood	3	8'/6'	upr open	dull gr	yw-brn	MC	s-or-sh/ adapt	White flowers in summer. Red twigs in winter.
Cornus stoloni-fera 'Flaviramea' Yellowtwig Dogwood	3	8'/6'	upr open	yw-gr	yw-brn	MC	s or sh/ adapt	White flowers in May. Yellow twigs in win-ter.
Cotoneaster acutifolius Peking Cotoneaster	4	8'/8'	round	gl dk-gr	gr-brn	F	sun/ adapt	Pink flowers in May. Good hedge or tall border plant.

DECIDUOUS ORNAMENTAL SHRUBS (CONTINUED)

Botanical Name/ Common Name	Zone	Size Ht/Wid	Form	Summer	Foliage Fall	Texture	Exposure Soil	Remarks
Cotoneaster adpressus praecox Early Cotoneaster	5	3'/4'	pros	gl-dk gr	bron	F	s-p-sh/ adapt	Heavy red berry set. Very resistant to fire blight.
Cotoneaster apiculata Cranberry Cotoneaster	4	3'/4'	mound	gl dk-gr	bron	F	s-p-sh/ adapt	Pink flowers in May. Many red berries in fall. Holds leaves late in fall.
Cotoneaster apiculata 'Nana' Dwarf Cranberry Cotoneaster	5	2'/4'	pros	gl-dk gr	bron	F	s-p-sh/ adapt	Dwarf form of cranberry cotoneaster. Good rock garden plant.
Cotoneaster dammeri 'Lowfast' Lowfast Cotoneaster	6	2'/6'	pros	gl dk-gr	dk-gr bron	F	s-p-sh/ adapt	Pink flowers in May. Many red berries. Evergreen in South. Good groundcover.
Cotoneaster dammeri 'Coral Beauty' Coral Beauty Cotoneaster	5	1'/10'	pros	gl-dk-gr	bron	F	s-p-sh/ adapt	Trailing form. Pink flowers. Heavy berry set.
Cotoneaster divaricatus Spreading Cotoneaster	5	5'/8'	spr arch mound	gl dk-gr	yw- red- pur	F	sun/ adapt	Pink flowers in May. Red berries in fall. Bacterial fire blight a problem in some areas.
Cotoneaster glaucophyllus Gray-leaved Cotoneaster	6	5'/8'	broad spr	gray- gr	gray- gr-brn	F	sun/ adapt	Pink flowers in May. Red berries in fall. Semi-ever-green in South.
Cotoneaster horizontalis Rock Cotoneaster	5	3'/6'	mound arch	gl dk-gr	red- bron	F	sun/ adapt	Pink flowers in May. Prolific red berries in fall. Good ground-cover plant.

DECIDUOUS ORNAMENTAL SHRUBS (CONTINUED)

Botanical Name/ Common Name	Zone	Size Ht/Wid	Form	Summer	Foliage Fall	Texture	Exposure Soil	Remarks
Cotoneaster horizontalis 'Robustus' Round Rock Cotoneaster	5	3'/6'	mound arch	gl dk-gr	red- bron	F	sun/ adapt	White flowers in May. Red berries. Vigorous grower.
Cotoneaster X 'Monter' Shangri-La™ Cotoneaster	5	2'/8'	flat- spr	gl-dk- gr	red- bron	F	sun/ adapt	Large cran- berry-type berries.
Cotoneaster salicifolius 'Rependens' Rependens Cotoneaster	6	3'/6'	mound pend	gl dk-gr	dk-gr	F	sun/ adapt	White flowers in May. Red berries. Evergreen in South. Good ground- cover.
Deutzia garacilis Slender Deutzia	4	3'/4'	spr round	yw-gr	yw- brn	MF	s-p-sh/ adapt	Small white flowers in May. Graceful, delicate looking plant. Good facer.
Deutzia X rosea Pink Slender Deutzia	5	3'/4'	round	yw-gr	yw- brn	MF	s-p-sh/ adapt	Pink flowers in May.
Deutzia X le- moinei Lemoine Deut- zia	4	5'/5'	upr irr	gr	yw- brn	MF	s-p-sh/ adapt	White flowers in May that are larger than *Deutzia gracilis*.
Deutzia scabra Pride of Rochester Deutzia	4	6'/5'	upr oval	gr	yw- brn	M	s-p-sh/ adapt	Double pink- white blooms in June.
Euonymus alata Winged Euonymus (Burningbush)	3	12'/12'	round	m-gr	bt-red	M	s-p-sh/ adapt	Brilliant red in fall. Interesting, corky "wings" on bark.
Euonymus alata 'Compacta' Dwarf Winged Euonymus	3	8'/8'	round	m-gr	bt-red	M	s-p-sh/ adapt	Accent/speci- men. Good summer and fall foliage. Grows slower and smaller.

DECIDUOUS ORNAMENTAL SHRUBS (CONTINUED)

Botanical Name/ Common Name	Zone	Size Ht/Wid	Form	Summer	Foliage Fall	Texture	Exposure Soil	Remarks
Exochorda racemosa Pearlbrush	4	10'/12'	vase	bl-gr	bl-gr	M	s-p-sh/ acid, well-dr	Abundant white flowers in April. Good for mass planting.
Forsythia X intermedia Forsythia varieties	5	10'/8'	arch round	yw-gr	yw-gr	M	sun/ adapt	Bright yellow flowers in March & April 'Beatrix Farrand,' 'Lynwood Gold,' 'Spring Glory,' 'Karl Sax.'
Forsythia suspensa sieboldii Siebold Forsythia	5	8'/10'	arch weep	yw-gr	yw-gr	M	sun/ adapt	Pendulous branches.
Forsythia viridissima Golden Bell Forsythia	5	8'/6'	vase arch	yw-gr	yw-gr	M	sun/ adapt	Yellow flowers in March.
Forsythia viridissima 'Bronxensis' Bronx Forsythia	5	2'/3'	round dwf	dk-gr	yw	M	sun/ adapt	Very dwarf. Yellow flowers in March.
Hibiscus syriacus Rose-of-Sharon (Althaea)	5	10'/8'	vase	dk-gr	dk-gr	M	s-p-sh/	'Anemone' (pink); 'Ardens' (purple); 'Lucy' (red); 'Blue Bird' (blue); 'Jeanne de Arc' (white). August.
Hydrangea arborescens Annabelle Hydrangea	4	3'/4'	round broad	gr	yw	C	p-sh-sh/ moist, well-dr	White summer blossoms up to 8" in diameter.

DECIDUOUS ORNAMENTAL SHRUBS (CONTINUED)

Botanical Name/ Common Name	Zone	Size Ht/Wid	Form	Summer	Foliage Fall	Texture	Exposure Soil	Remarks
Hydrangea arborescens 'Grandiflora' Snow Hill Hydrangea (Hills of Snow)	5	5'/6'	broad round	gr	yw	C	s or sh/ moist	White summer flowers.
Hydrangea macrophylla Japanese Hydrangea	6	6/6	round	yw-gr	yw	C	s-p-sh/ acid, moist	Very large leaves. Blue flowers in acid soil. Pink flowers in alkaline soil.
Hydrangea paniculata 'Grandiflora' Pee Gee Hydrangea	4	12'/12'	broad spr	gr	gr	C	s-p-sh/ moist, well-dr	Pink, huge flowers in August. Red, purple, blue, and white flowering varieties also available.
Hydrangea quercifolia Oakleaf Hydrangea	5	5'/4'	irr spr	gray-gr	red-bron	C	s-p-sh/ rich, moist	Light pink flowers in August. Oaklike leaves.
Hypericum frondosum Golden St. Johnswort	5	4'/4'	upr round	bl-gr	bl-gr	MF	s-p-sh/ adapt	Yellow-orange flowers in summer.
Hypericum kalmianum Kalm St. Johnswort	4	3'/3'	round	bl-gr	bl-gr	MF	s-p-sh/ adapt	'Pot O'Gold' favorite variety. Yellow-orange flowers in summer.
Hypericum patulum 'Sungold' Sungold St. Johnswort	5	3'/3'	round dense	lt-gr	lt-gr	MF	s-p-sh/ adapt	Yellow-orange flowers from June to September.
Ilex verticillata Winterberry Holly	3	6'/5'	up oval	gr	gr	M	s-p-sh/ adapt	Female produces scarlet fruit. Deciduous holly.

DECIDUOUS ORNAMENTAL SHRUBS (CONTINUED)

Botanical Name/ Common Name	Zone	Size Ht/Wid	Form	Summer	Foliage Fall	Texture	Exposure Soil	Remarks
Kerria japonica Kerria	4	5'/6'	upr broad loose	bt-gr	yw-gr	F	p-sh/ adapt	Yellow flowers in spring. Double-flowering varieties available.
Kolkwitzia amabilis Beautybush	4	8'/8'	arch vase open	gray-gr	yw-gr	M	sun/ well-dr	Pink flowers in spring. 'Rosea' and 'Pink Cloud' varieties
Lagerstroemia indica Crape Myrtle	5	12'/5'	upr tree-like	m-gr	red-gr	M	sun/ moist well-dr	Pink-, white-, and red-flowering varieties. Summer flowering. Dies to ground in zone 5.
Ligustrum amurense Amur River North Privet	3	12'/6'	erect oval	m-gr	gr	MF	s or sh/ adapt	Excellent hedging. White flower in May has unpleasant odor.
Ligustrum obtusifolium regalianum Regal Border Privet	3	6'/6'	round	m-gr	russet	M	s-sh/ adapt	White flowers in May. Flat-layered foliage.
Ligustrum X vicari Vicary Privet	4	12'/8'	upr oval	gold	gold	M	sun/ adapt	Bright accent plant/specimen. Winter injury problems.
Ligustrum vulgare 'Lodense' Lodense Privet	4	5'/3'	round com	dk-gr	gr	M	sun/ adapt	White flowers in June.
Loniceri X amoena 'Arnoldiana' Arnold Gotha Honeysuckle	5	9'/6'	arch round	m-gr	m-gr	F	sun/ adapt	

DECIDUOUS ORNAMENTAL SHRUBS (CONTINUED)

Botanical Name/ Common Name	Zone	Size Ht/Wid	Form	Summer	Foliage Fall	Texture	Exposure Soil	Remarks
Lonicera fragrantissima Winter Honeysuckle (Fragrant)	5	10'/10'	round irr	gray-gr	gray-gr	M	s-p-sh/ well-dr	Very fragrant, off-white blooms in May.
Lonicera morrowii Morrow Honeysuckle	4	8'/10'	round dense	bl-gray	bl-gray	M	sun/ adapt	Off-white, fragrant flowers in May.
Lonicera tatarica Tatarian Honeysuckle	3	10'/8'	broad round	bl-gr	bl-gr	M	s-p-sh/ adapt	'Alba' (white blossoms); 'Rosea' (pink); 'Zabeli' (red). April.
Lonicera tatarica 'Claveyi' Clavey's Dwarf Honeysuckle	4	6'/5'	round dense	gray-gr	gray-gr	M	s-sh/ adapt	Compact, tight shrub, good as facer. Off-white blossoms in May.
Magnolia stellata Star Magnolia	4	12'/12'	round	dk-gr	yw-bron	MC	sun/ moist, well-dr	Does best in slightly acid soil. Large white flowers in early spring. 'Rosea' has pink flowers.
Nandina domestica Heavenly Bamboo	6	5'/6'	round loose	dk-gr	red-scar	M	s-p-sh/ well-dr, acid	White flowers in spring. Red berries in fall. Semi-evergreen.
Nandina domestica 'Harbour Dwarf' 'Harbour Dwarf' Nandina	6	2'/3'	mound	lt-gr	or-red	MF	sh-p-sh	Lacy-type foliage. New leaves bronze-red.
Philadelphus coronarius Sweet Mockorange	4	10'/10'	upr round	m-gr	m-gr	C	s-p-sh/ adapt	White flowers in May, very fragrant. Leggy needs facer.

DECIDUOUS ORNAMENTAL SHRUBS (CONTINUED)

Botanical Name/ Common Name	Zone	Size Ht/Wid	Form	Summer	Foliage Fall	Texture	Exposure Soil	Remarks
Philadelphus coronarius aureus Golden Mockorange	4	6'/6'	round dense	bt-yw-gr	bt-yw-gr	M	sun/ adapt	Bright yellow accent plant. Fragrant white flowers in May.
Philadelphus coronarius 'Nana' Dwarf Sweet Mockorange	4	4'/4'	round com	gr	yw-gr	M	s-p-sh/ adapt	Dwarf and compact. White flowers in May.
Philadelphus lemoinei Lemoine Mockorange	5	8'/8'	round dense	m-gr	m-gr	M	s-p-sh/ adapt	'Enchantment' double white flower. 'Innocence' and 'Mont Blanc'—all favorite cultivars.
Philadelphus X lemoinei 'Silver Showers' Silver Showers Mockorange	4	4'/4'	round dense	gr	gr	MF	s-p-sh/ adapt	Profuse white, fragrant blooms in May.
Philadelphus X virginalis 'Minnesota Snowflake' Minnesota Snowflake Mockorange	3	8'/6'	round dense	m-gr	m-gr	M	sun/ adapt	Double-white flowers in June. Dwarf variety avail-able that only reaches 3'.
Philadelphus X virginalis 'Glacier' Glacier Mockorange	3	5'/5'	round dense	m-gr	m-gr	M	s-p-sh/ adapt	Fragrant, double-white flowers in June. Semi-dwarf. Most popu-lar mock-orange.
Philadelphus X virginalis 'Natchez' Natchez Mockorange	3	8'/6'	round dense	m-gr	m-gr	M	s-p-sh/ adapt	Very large white flowers in June.

DECIDUOUS ORNAMENTAL SHRUBS (CONTINUED)

Botanical Name/ Common Name	Zone	Size Ht/Wid	Form	Foliage Summer	Fall	Texture	Exposure Soil	Remarks
Physocarpus monogynus Dwarf Ninebark	2	4'/3'	spr dense	bt-gr	yw	MC	s-sh/ adapt	Good textural accent. White flowers in May.
Physocarpus opulifolius Ninebark	2	8'/10'	round dense	yw-gr	yw	C	s-sh/ adapt	Very coarse texture. White flowers in May.
Physocarpus opulifolius 'Luteus' Goldleaf Ninebark	2	8'/10'	round dense	yw	yw-gr	C	sun/ adapt	Only yellow in full sun. Accent. White flowers in May.
Potentilla fruiticosa Cinquefoil (Potentilla)	2	3'/4'	upr round	m-gr	yw-brn	MF	s-p-sh/ adapt	Tiny yellow blossoms all summer. 'Gold drop,' 'Katherine Dykes,' 'Jack-mannii,' 'Klon-dike,' 'Gold-finger,' 'Tang-erine' cultivars.
Potentilla fruiticosa 'Abbotswood'	3	2'/3'	upr round	m-gr	yw-brn	MF	s-p-sh/ adapt	White flowers.
Prunus besseyi Western Sand Cherry	3	5'/4'	irr pros	m-gr	yw	MF	s-p-sh/ adapt	
Prunus X cistena Purple-Leaf Sand Cherry (Cistena Plum)	2	8'/6'	oval vase	pur	pur	M	sun/ adapt	Accent shrub. Needs facer. White blooms in May, purple fruit in fall.
Prunus glandulosa Flowering Almond	4	4'/4'	arch round	yw-gr	yw	F	sun/ adapt	Double-pink flowers in April & May.
Prunus tomentosa Nanking Cherry	2	10'/12'	upr irr	bron-gr	gr	M	sun/ rich, moist	Pink flowers in April. Good tall screen plant.

DECIDUOUS ORNAMENTAL SHRUBS (CONTINUED)

Botanical Name/ Common Name	Zone	Size Ht/Wid	Form	Foliage Summer	Fall	Texture	Exposure Soil	Remarks
Rhammus frangula 'Columnaris' Tallhedge	2	15'/4'	upr col	gl dk-gr	yw	M	s-p-sh/ adapt	Excellent for tall, narrow hedge.
Rhodotypos scandens Black Jetbead	5	6'/8'	round	bt-gr	yw-gr	M	s-sh/ adapt	White flowers in April. Black berries persist.
Rhus aromatica Fragrant Sumac	3	5'/8'	round spr	red-gr	yw-scar-crim	M	s-sh/ adapt	Colorful in fall.
Rhus typhina Staghorn Sumac	3	20'/20'	irr	m-gr	or-scar	MC	s-sh/ adapt	Picturesque accent. Seldom used.
Ribes alpinum Alpine Current	2	8'/8'	arch erect	bt-gr	yw	MF	s-sh/ adapt	Scarlet berries. Good in shade. Good hedging plant.
Salix discolor Pussy Willow	2	10'/12'	upr vase	gr	yw	MF	sun/ moist	Pink-gray flowers in May. Usually cut for early indoor bloom.
Salix purpurea 'Nana' Dwarf Arctic Blue Willow	2	4'/4'	mound	sil-bl	sil-bl	MF	sun/ moist	Gray flowers in March. Purple twigs in winter.
Sambucus nigra 'Aurea-variegata' Golden Elder	4	8'/8'	round dense	gold	gold	M	sun/ adapt	Yellow-green accent plant. White flowers in June. Edible black fruit.
Spiraea X arguta Garland Spirea	4	6'/3'	round dense	yw-gr	yw	F	s-p-sh/ adapt	
Spiraea X billardii Billard Spirea	4	6'/5'	round	lt-gr	yw	MF	sun/ adapt	Bright pink, conelike flowers in July.
Spiraea X bumalda Bumald Spirea	5	3'/4'	mound	red-gr	red-bron	MF	sun/ adapt	Red-pink flowers during summer. 'Anthony Waterer' and 'Froebelii' are popular culti-vars.

DECIDUOUS ORNAMENTAL SHRUBS (CONTINUED)

Botanical Name/ Common Name	Zone	Size Ht/Wid	Form	Summer	Foliage Fall	Texture	Exposure Soil	Remarks
Spiraea X bumalda 'Goldflame' Goldflame Spirea	5	3'/4'	mound	bron- yw- gr	red- or	MF	sun/ adapt	New foliage bronze first, then gold, then green at maturity. Pink flowers in summer.
Spiraea X bumalda 'Goldmound' Goldmound Spirea	5	2'/3'	mound	yw- gr	br- red	F	sun/ adapt	Golden outer foliage—light green inner foliage. Light pink flowers in summer.
Spiraea X bumalda 'Limemound' Limemound Spirea	3	2'/3'		lt-yw gr	or-red	F	sun/ adapt	Light pink flowers. Yellow-green outer foliage— light green inner foliage.
Spiraea X bumalda 'Little Princess' Little Princess Spirea	4	2'/3'		lt-gr	yw- brn	F	sun/ adapt	Light pink summer flowers. Good border plant.
Spiraea dolchica Dolchica Spirea	4	3'/4'		dk-gr	red	F	s-p-sh/ adapt	Distinctive serrated foliage. Purplish-pink flowers.
Spiraea japonica 'Coccinea' Red Flowering Japanese Spirea	5	3'/3'	round	gr	red- bron	MF	sun/ adapt	Rose-pink flowers in July.
Spiraea japonica 'Shirobana' Shirobana Spirea	4	3'/4'		brt- gr	red	F	s-p-sh	Flowers white, pink, and red blooms simultaneously.
Spiraea nipponica 'Snowmound' Snowmound Spirea	4	4'/4'	round dense	bl-gr	bl-gr	MF	sun/ adapt	Completely covered with white blossoms in May.

DECIDUOUS ORNAMENTAL SHRUBS (CONTINUED)

Botanical Name/ Common Name	Zone	Size Ht/Wid	Form	Summer	Foliage Fall	Texture	Exposure Soil	Remarks
Spiraea prunifolia Bridalwreath Spirea	4	6'/6'	upr loose	bl-gr	or	F	sun/ moist	White flowers in April. 'Plena' culti- var has dou- ble flowers.
Spiraea reevesiana Reeves Double Bridalwreath Spirea	4	3'/4'	upr round	dk- gr	red- pur	F	sun/ adapt	Double-white spring flowers.
Spiraea X vanhouttei Vanhoutte Spirea	4	8'/8'	pend	bl-gr	bl-gr	F	sun/ adapt	Prolific white flowers in April. Shrub stays full to the ground.
Stephandra incisa Cutleaf Stephandra	5	8'/8'	arch round	red-gr	red- pur	F	s-p-sh/ moist, well-dr	Graceful, arch- ing branches Green-white flowers in May.
Symphoricarpos X chenaulti Chenault Coralberry	3	3'/4'	round open	bl-gr	bl-gr	F	s-sh/ well-dr	Pink blossoms in July. Red berries with white under- side. Flowers borne on spikes.
Symphoricarpos vulgaris— orbiculatus Indiancurrent Coralberry	3	4'/5'	upr dense	gray-gr	crim	MF	s-sh/ well-dr	White flowers in June. Red berries in fall.
Symphoricarpos albus Snowberry	3	6'/6'	round dense	bl-gr	bl-gr	M	s-sh/ well-dr	Light pink flowers in June. Does well in shade & poor soil.
Syringa Palibiniana Dwarf Korean Lilac	4	5'/5'	round	dk-gr	yw-br	M	sun/ well-dr	Compact size. Lavender flowers.

DECIDUOUS ORNAMENTAL SHRUBS (CONTINUED)

Botanical Name/ Common Name	Zone	Size Ht/Wid	Form	Foliage Summer	Fall	Texture	Exposure Soil	Remarks
Syringa X persica Persian Lilac	5	8'/8'	upr round	bl-gr	bl-gr	MF	s-p-sh well-dr	Fragrant, purple flowers in May.
Syringa reticulata Japanese Tree Lilac	4	15'+/ 15'+	upr oval	dk-gr	dk-gr	MC	sun/ acid, well-dr	White flowers in May.
Syringa vulgaris Common Lilac	2	10'/10'	round	gray-gr	gray-gr	MC	sun/ well-dr	Purple flowers in May. Large leaves.
Syringa vulgaris 'French Hybrid' Lilacs	3							Many cultivars. Purple, red, white, pink, and blue flowers. Are not really hybrids.
Viburnum acerifolium Mapleleaf Viburnum	3	5'/4'	upr round	bt-gr	yw-red	M	p-sh-sh/ adapt	
Viburnum carlesi Koreanspice Viburnum	4	5'/5'	round dense	dk-gr	red-wine	M	sun/ acid, well-dr	White flowers in April. Blue-black fruit that birds like.
Viburnum dentatum Arrowwood Viburnum	4	10'/12'	upr oval	dk-gr lus	yw-red-pur	MC	s-p-sh/ well-dr	White flowers in May. Crimson fruit, turning blue.
Viburnum lantana Wayfaring Tree	3	12'/12'	round	dk-bl-gr	pur-red	MC	s-p-sh/ adapt	White flowers in May. Red fruit turns black.
Viburnum opulus Cranberrybush	4	12'/12'	round	dk-gr lus	red	MC	s-sh/ adapt	White flowers in May. Clear red berries. Good shrub for many purposes.

DECIDUOUS ORNAMENTAL SHRUBS (CONTINUED)

Botanical Name/ Common Name	Zone	Size Ht/Wid	Form	Summer	Foliage Fall	Texture	Exposure Soil	Remarks
Viburnum opulus 'Nanum' Dwarf Cranberrybush	5	2'/2'	round	dk-gr	red	M	s-sh/ adapt	Good plant for edging and hedging. Very dwarf. No flower or fruit.
Viburnum opulus 'Sterile' Common Snowball	4	10'/12'	round	m-gr	yw-red	MC	sun/ adapt	Large, white, snowball-like flowers in May. Red fruit.
Viburnum plicatum Japanese Snowball	5	10'/10'	round irr	bl-gr	red-gr	MC	sun/ adapt	White flowers in May are better than those on Common Snowball.
Viburnum plicatum 'Tomentosum' Doublefile Viburnum	5	10'/10'	round	bron-gr	red-pur	MC	s-p-sh/ moist	White flowers in May. Red berries. Good specimen or border plant-ing.
Viburnum X pragense Pragense Viburnum	5	8'/8'	round	gl-dk gr	gl-dk gr	MC	s-p-sh/ moist	Semi-ever-green. Erect branches. Red berries become black in winter. Glossy, leath-ery leaves.
Viburnum sargentii 'Onandaga' Onandaga Viburnum	5	4'/5'	round	dk-gr	red-pur	MC	s-p-sh/ moist	New leaves bronze. White flowers & red fruit.
Viburnum trilobum Highbush Cranberry	2	10'/10'	round	dk-gr lus	yw-red pur	M	s-p-sh/ adapt	White flowers in May. Red berries. 'Compactum' cultivar only get 4' to 6' tall.

DECIDUOUS ORNAMENTAL SHRUBS (CONTINUED)

Botanical Name/ Common Name	Zone	Size Ht/Wid	Form	Summer	Foliage Fall	Texture	Exposure Soil	Remarks
Viburnum wrightii Wright Viburnum	5	8'/8'	round	m-gr	crim	C	s-p-sh/ adapt	White flowers in May. Brilliant red fruit.
Weigela florida Old Fashioned Weigela	5	6'/8'	arch round	m-gr	yw-gr	C	sun/ adapt	Rose-pink flowers during summer, beginning in May.
Weigela florida 'Minuet' Minuet Weigela	4	3'/4'	arch round	dk-gr	red-pur	MC	sun/ adapt	Very dwarf form. Dark rosy-pink blooms.
Weigela florida 'Rosea' Pink Weigela	5	6'/8'	arch round	m-gr	yw-gr	C	sun/ adapt	Deep pink flowers in summer attract hummingbirds and bees.
Weigela florida Red Prince Red Prince Weigela	4	3'/3'	round	m-gr	yw-gr	C	sun/ adapt	Red flowers do not fade.
Weigela florida 'Vaniceki' Vanicek Weigela (Newport Red)	5	6'/8'	arch round	m-gr	yw-gr	C	sun/ adapt	Dark red flowers all summer and late into fall.
Weigela florida 'Variegata nana' Variegated Weigela	4	4'/4'	arch round	m-gr wht var	yw-gr	C	sun/ adapt	Variegated foliage, soft green edged in white.
Wisteria sinensis 'Alba' White Wisteria	5	to 30'	tree vine	dk-gr	yw	M	sun/ moist, well-dr	White flowers in spring.
Wisteria sinensis 'Purpurea' Purple Wisteria	5	to 30'	tree vine	dk-gr	yw	M	sun/ moist, well-dr	Purple flowers in spring.
Wisteria floribunda Japanese Wisteria	4	to 30'	tree vine	bt-gr	yw	M	sun/ well-dr	Purple, grape-like clusters of flowers. Spring blossoms.

BROADLEAF EVERGREEN SHRUBS

Botanical Name/ Common Name	Zone	Size Ht/Wid	Form	Summer	Foliage Fall	Texture	Exposure Soil	Remarks
Berberis julianae Wintergreen Barberry	5	6'/5'	upr dense	dk-gr	dk-gr	MF	sun/ adapt	Semi-ever-green in zone 5. Thorny plant particu-larly used for for screening or traffic control.
Buxus microphylla Littleleaf Box	5	3'/3'	round dense	m-gr	yw-gr	MF	s-p-sh/ adapt	Needs protec-tion from dry-ing winds, particularly in winter.
Buxus microphylla koreana Wintergreen Boxwood	5	4'/5'	round dense	dk-gr	m-gr	MF	s-p-sh/ adapt	Hardiest box-wood. Protect from drying winds.
Buxus sempervirens Common Box	5	15'/12'	round dense	lus dk-gr	dk-gr	MF	s-p-sh/ adapt	Size listed can be mislead-ing—depends upon locale. Slow-growing 'Inglis' is popular culti-var.
Buxus sempervirens 'Suffruticosa' Edging Boxwood	5	3'/3'	round dense	dk-gr	dk-gr	F	s-p-sh/ adapt	Very dense and compact. Slow growing Good small hedge.
Daphne cneorum Garland Flower	5	2'/2'	pro-cum-bent	gray-gr	gray-gr	MF	sun/ moist, well-dr.	Rose-pink, fra-grant flowers in spring
Euonymus fortunei 'Emerald Cushion' Emerald Cushion Euonymus	6	3'/4'	upr mound	dk-gr	dk-gr	M	s-p-sh/ adapt	

BROADLEAF EVERGREEN SHRUBS (CONTINUED)

Botanical Name/ Common Name	Zone	Size Ht/Wid	Form	Foliage Summer	Fall	Texture	Exposure Soil	Remarks
Euonymus fortunei 'Emerald Gaiety' Emerald Gaiety Euonymus	5	3'/4'	erect mound	var	var	MF	sun/ adapt	Green leaves with white margins.
Euonymus fortunei 'Emerald 'n Gold' Emerald 'n Gold Euonymus	5	3'/4'	upr mound	var	var	M	sun/ adapt	Green leaves with gold margins.
Euonymus fortunei 'Emerald Pride' Emerald Pride Euonymus	5	3'/4'	erect mound	dk-gr	dk-gr	MF	s-p-sh/ adapt	Very dense and compact.
Euonymus fortunei 'Golden Prince' Golden Prince Euonymus	4	3'/4'	erect mound	gr-yw-mar	gr-yw-mar	M	s-p-sh/ adapt	Older leaves solid green. Hardiest of variegated Euonymus.
Euonymus fortunei 'Kewensis' Kewensis Euonymus	5	2'/3'	creep	dk-gr	dk-gr	F	s-p-sh/ adapt	Tiny, dense foliage. Makes a good groundcover, particularly for small areas.
Euonymus fortunei 'Sarcoxie' Sarcoxie Euonymus	5'	6'/3'	erect	dk-gr gl	dk-gr	MF	s-sh/ adapt	Very upright, and will vine on walls. Makes excellent doorway accent plant.
Euonymus japonica 'Aurea-marginata' Golden Euonymus	6	5'/5'	round com	var	var	M	sun/ adapt	Gold margins. Showy accent.

BROADLEAF EVERGREEN SHRUBS (CONTINUED)

Botanical Name/ Common Name	Zone	Size Ht/Wid	Form	Foliage Summer	Fall	Texture	Exposure Soil	Remarks
Euonymus japonica 'Aurea-marginata' Gold Spot Euonymus	6	5'/5'	round com	var	var	M	sun/ adapt	Same as Golden Euonymus but gold center with green edges.
Euonymus japonica 'Grandfolia' Japanese Euonymus	6	15'/8'	upr	dk-gr gl	dk-gr gl	MC	sun/ adapt	Fast grower. Compact and dense. Shears well.
Euonymus japonica 'Miocrophylla' Dwarf Euonymus	6	1'/1'	erect dense	dk-gr	dk-gr	F	s-p-sh/ adapt	Small leaves. Slow and compact. Makes a good small hedge.
Euonymus japonica 'Silver King' Silver King Euonymus	6	6'/6'	upr	gl gr-wht mar	gl gr-wht mar	M	sun/ adapt	Irregular white variegation on leaf margins.
Euonymus kiautschovica 'Jewel' Jewel Euonymus	5	4'/6'	mound	gr	wine	MF	s-sh/ adapt	Semi-evergreen in zone 5. Good small hedge plant.
Euonymus kiautschovica 'Manhattan' Manhattan Euonymus	5	6'/6'	round	dk-gr gl	dk-gr gl	M	s-p-sh/ adapt	Glossy bright green leaves. May turn tan-brown before falling in late winter.
Euonymus kiautschovica Large Leaf Euonymus	5	8'/8'	round open	m-gr	m-gr	C	s-p-sh/ adapt	Many pink white fruits. Inconspicuous flowers attract flies.
Euonymus kiautschovica Medium Leaf Euonymus	5	5'/4'	round open	m-gr	m-gr	M	s-p-sh/ adapt	Many pink-white fruits. Flowers attract flies. Semi-evergreen in zone 5.

BROADLEAF EVERGREEN SHRUBS (CONTINUED)

Botanical Name/ Common Name	Zone	Size Ht/Wid	Form	Summer	Foliage Fall	Texture	Exposure Soil	Remarks
Euonymus kiautschovica 'Dupont' Dupont Euonymus	5	5'/4'	round com	m-gr	gr-brn	M	s-p-sh/ adapt	More dense and compact than most.
Euonymus paulii Pauli Euonymus	5	6'/6'	round upr	gl dk-gr	dk-gr	M	s-p-sh/ adapt	Holds good foliage color well in winter.
Ilex X attenuata 'Fosteri' Foster Holly	6	20'/15'	pyra	gl dk-gr	gl dk-gr	MC	sh-p-sh/ acid, well-dr	Bright red berries on female if male pollinator is present. Is a tree, but often used as accent shrub
Ilex cornuta 'Burfordii' Burford Holly	6	10'/8'	round dense	gl dk-gr	gl dk-gr	M	s-sh/ acid, moist	Profusion of bright red berries in fall. Excellent foliage color.
Ilex cornuta 'Burfordii Nana' Dwarf Burford Holly	6	6'/5'	round dense	gl dk-gr	gl dk-gr	M	s-sh/ acid, moist	Slower, more dwarf version of Burford. Many red berries.
Ilex cornuta 'Carissa' Carissa Holly	6	4'/4'	round dense	gl dk-gr	gl dk-gr	M	s-sh/ acid, moist	Has a leaf like Dwarf Burford. Many red berries in fall.
Ilex cornuta 'Dazzler'	6	6'/8'	upr com	gl dk-gr	gl dk-gr	M	s-sh/ acid, moist	Large clusters of large red berries
Ilex cornuta 'Delcambre' Needlepoint Holly	6	10'/12'	broad round	gl dk-gr	gl dk-gr	M	s-sh/ acid, moist	Long, narrow, slightly twisted leaves. Blood-red berries. Dense lateral branching.
Ilex cornuta 'Rotunda' Dwarf Chinese Holly	6	4'/4'	mound	gl dk-gr	gl dk-gr	MF	s-sh/ acid, moist	Produces no berries. Good small foliage plant.

BROADLEAF EVERGREEN SHRUBS (CONTINUED)

Botanical Name/ Common Name	Zone	Size Ht/Wid	Form	Summer	Foliage Fall	Texture	Exposure Soil	Remarks
Ilex crenata 'Compacta' Dwarf Japanese Holly	6	3'/4'	oval com	dk-gr	dk-gr	M	s-sh/ acid, moist	Black fruit, not showy. Good, dense foliage.
Ilex crenata 'Hellerii' Heller's Japanese Holly	6	4'/5'	round com	dk-gr	dk-gr	MF	s-sh/ acid, moist	Black fruit. Good substitute for boxwood.
Ilex crenata 'Hetzii' Hetz Japanese Holly	6	5'/6'	round com	dk-bl-gr	dk-bl-gr	F	s-sh/ acid, moist	Black fruit. Extremely compact. Excellent foliage plant.
Ilex X meserveae 'Blue Angel' Blue Angel Holly	4	6'/8'	round dense	gl dk-gr	gl dk-gr	M	sh/ adapt	Crinkled leaves on purple stems. Large red berries.
Ilex X meserveae 'Blue Prince' Blue Prince Holly	4	15'/12'	pyra	gl dk-gr	gl dk-gr	MC	sh/ adapt	Very attractive crinkled foliage.
Ilex X meserveae 'Blue Girl' Blue Girl Holly	4	15'/10'	globe	gl dk-gr	gl dk-gr	MC	sh/ adapt	Probably the hardiest blue holly.
Ilex X meserveae 'Blue Princess' Blue Princess Holly	4	15'/10'	pyra	gl dk-gr	gl dk-gr	C	sh/ adapt	Heavy red fruit production.
Ilex X meserveae 'Blue Stallion' Blue Stallion Holly	5	15'/10'	pyra	gl dk-gr	gl dk-gr	MC	sh/ adapt	Snag-free leaves. Improved form of Blue Prince.
Ilex X meserveae 'China Boy' China Boy Holly	5	8'/8'	round	gl-gr	gl-gr	C	sh-p-sh/ acid-rich	Pollinator.

BROADLEAF EVERGREEN SHRUBS (CONTINUED)

Botanical Name/ Common Name	Zone	Size Ht/Wid	Form	Summer	Foliage Fall	Texture	Exposure Soil	Remarks
Ilex X meserveae 'China Girl' China Girl Holly	5	8'/8'	round	gl-gr	gl-gr	C	sh-p-sh/ acid-rich	*I. Cornuta*-type. Excellent berryset. Very hardy.
Ilex vomitoria Yaupon Holly	5	12'/10'	round dense	dk-gr	dk-gr	M	s-sh/ adapt	Heavily fruit-ed, red. Drought-resis-tant.
Ilex vomitoria 'Nana' Yaupon Holly	5	4'/5'	round dense	gl dk-gr	gl dk-gr	F	s-sh/ adapt	Black berries. Dwarf and compact.
Kalmia latifolia Mountain Laurel	4	10'/10'	round dense	gl dk-gr	bron-gr	M	s-sh/ acid, moist, well-dr	Clusters of pink-white, cup-shaped blossoms in May. Narrow leaves.
Ligustrum japonicum Waxleaf Ligustrum	7	10'/10'	upr round	gl dk-gr	gl dk-gr	MC	s-p-sh/ adapt	White blos-soms in spring. Dark blue berries in fall. Good foliage plant.
Ligustrum lucidum 'Recunifolium' Curly Leaf Ligustrum	7	10'/10'	upr round	dk-gr	dk-gr	C	s-p-sh/ adapt	Curly, crinkled leaves on heavy, gnarled stems.
Mahonia aquafolium Oregon Grape	5	6'/5'	round irr	gl dk-gr	gr-red-bron	M	p-sh-sh/ adapt	Holly-like leaves. Yellow flowers in May. Powder blue berries.
Mahonia aquafolium 'Compacta' Compact Oregon Grape	5	4'/4'	round dense	gl dk-gr	gr-red-bron	M	p-sh-sh/ adapt	Same as Maho-nia aquafolium but much more compact.

BROADLEAF EVERGREEN SHRUBS (CONTINUED)

Botanical Name/ Common Name	Zone	Size Ht/Wid	Form	Summer	Foliage Fall	Texture	Exposure Soil	Remarks
Mahonia bealei Leatherleaf Mahonia	5	4'/5'	upr round	bl-gr	bl-gr	MC	s-p-sh/ well-dr	Leathery leaves Yellow flowers in spring. Blue-black berries.
Nandina domestica Heavenly Bamboo	6	6'/6'	round open	gr	red-gr	M	s-p-sh/ acid, well-dr	Red berries in fall. Slender leaves. Semi-evergreen in zone 5.
Photenia X fraseri Fraser Photenia	6	12'/10'	round	dk-gr	dk-gr	M	s-p-sh/ well-dr	Good hedging plant. New leaves red.
Pyracantha angustifolia 'Yukon Belle' Pyracantha (Firethorn)	4	8'/8'	round	gr	gr-wine	M	sun/ adapt	Hardiest pyracantha. White flowers & orange berries.
Pyracantha angustifolia 'Gnome' Gnome Pyracantha (Firethorn)	5	6'/8'	round	dk-gr	gr-wine	M	sun/ adapt	Compact form. White flowers & orange berries.
Pyracantha coccinea 'Kasan' Kasan Pyracantha (Firethorn)	5	10'/12'	round irr	dk-gr	gr-wine	M	sun/ adapt	White flowers in May. Orange-red berries. More compact than Lalandi.
Pyracantha coccinea 'Lowboy' Lowboy Pyracantha (Firethorn)	6	4'/6'	broad mound	dk-gr	gr-wine	M	sun/ adapt	Very compact. Broader than tall. White flowers & orange berries.
Pyracantha coccinea 'Rutgers' Rutgers Pyracantha	6	3'/6'	broad spr	gl-dk-gr	gl-dk-gr	M	sun/ adapt	Excellent foliage. Very compact. Good red-berries.
Pyracantha X 'Mojave' Mojave Pyracantha	6	6'/8'	round flat	dk-gr	gr-wine	M	sun/ adapt	Large masses of red-orange berries.

BROADLEAF EVERGREEN SHRUBS (CONTINUED)

Botanical Name/ Common Name	Zone	Size Ht/Wid	Form	Summer	Foliage Fall	Texture	Exposure Soil	Remarks
Pyracantha X 'Red Elf' Red Elf Pyracantha	7	4'/6'	mound	dk-gr	gr	MF	sun/ well-dr	Dense foliage. Many bright red berries. Dwarf.
Rhododendron carolinianum Carolina Rhododendron	6	5'/5'	round	dk-gr	pur-gr	M	p-sh/ acid, well-dr	Pale rose-red flower in spring.
Rhododendron catawbiense Catawba Rhododendron	5	15'/6'	round	dk-gr	gr- to yw	MC	p-sh/ acid, well-dr	Lilac-purple or white flowers in late spring.
Rhododendron X kosteranum Mollis Hybrid Azaleas	6	3'/3'	round	dk-gr	dk-gr	M	p-sh/ acid, well-dr	Red, orange, yellow, white varieties available. Protect from winds.
Rhododendron obtusum Kurume Azaleas	6	4'/4'	round	dk-gr	red- gr	M	p-sh/ acid, well-dr	Red, orange, salmon, white varieties available, with both single and double flowers.
Viburnum rhytidophyllum Leatherleaf Viburnum	5	10'/10'	round	dk-gr	gr-pur	C	p-sh/ well-dr	Yellow-white flower in May. Black fruit. Large leaves look like green leather. Protect from wind.

NARROWLEAF EVERGREEN TREES

Botanical Name/ Common Name	Zone	Size Ht/Wid	Form	Summer	Foliage Fall	Texture	Exposure Soil	Remarks
Abies balsamea Balsam Fir	4	60'/20'	pyra	gl dk-gr	dk-gr	M	sun/ well-dr	
Abies concolor White Fir	4	40'/20'	pyra	bl-gr	bl-gr	M	sun/ well-dr	
Abies fraseri Fraser Fir	5	35'/25'	pyra	gl dk-gr	dk-gr	M	s-p-sh/ well-dr	

NARROWLEAF EVERGREEN TREES (CONTINUED)

Botanical Name/ Common Name	Zone	Size Ht/Wid	Form	Foliage Summer	Fall	Texture	Exposure Soil	Remarks
Abies procera Noble Fir	5	60'/30'	pyra	bl-gr	bl-gr	M	s-p-sh/ well-dr	
Abies veitchii Veitch Fir	3	60'/30'	pyra	gl dk-gr	dk-gr	M	s-p-sh/ well-dr	
Cedrus atlantica 'Glauca' Atlas Blue Cedar	6	50'/40'	broad pyra	bl-gr	bl-gr	M	s-p-sh/ well-dr	Bright blue, rustic look. Too large for most land-scape uses.
Cedrus deodara Deodar Cedar (California Christmas Tree)	7	60'/45'	broad pyra	gray-gr	gray-gr	F	sun/ well-dr	Arching, graceful branches. Very broad.
Cedrus libani Cedar of Lebanon	6	50'/50'	broad pyra	bl-gr	bl-gr	M	sun/ well-dr	Biblical inter-est. Hardiest strain.
Chamaecyparis lawsoniana 'Ellwoodii' Ellwood False-cypress	5		nar pyra	sil-bl	sil-bl	M	s-p-sh/ well-dr	Dwarf, slow-growing, grafted variety.
Chamaecyparis lawsoniana 'Stewartii' Stewart Golden Cypress	5	40'/30'	upr pyra	gold tips	gold tips	M	s-p-sh/ well-dr	Best color in full sun.
Chamaecyparis obtusa Hinoki Falsecypress	3	60'/15'	con	dk-gr gl	dk-gr	M	sun/ well-dr	
Chamaecyparis pisifera Sawara Falsecypress	4	60'/15'	pyra loose	dk-gr	dk-gr	M	sun/ well-dr	
Cryptomeria japonica Japanese Cyrptomeria	6	50'/25'	pyra	bt-bl-gr	bl-gr	M	sun/ acid, rich	Foliage similar to Sequoia.
Cryptomeria japonica 'Nana' Dwarf Japanese Cedar	6	Not available	com pyra	dk-gr	dk-gr	M	sun/ acid, rich	Extremely dwarf and compact.

NARROWLEAF EVERGREEN TREES (CONTINUED)

Botanical Name/ Common Name	Zone	Size Ht/Wid	Form	Foliage Summer	Fall	Texture	Exposure Soil	Remarks
Cunninghamia lanceolata Common Chinafir	7	60'/30'	pyra pend	m-gr	bron- gr	MF	p-sh-sh/ acid, moist, well-dr	
Cupressus arizonica Arizona Cypress	6	30'/25'	broad pyra	bl- gray	bl- gray	M	sun/ well-dr	Withstands drought. Windbreaks and screens.
Cupressus sempervirens 'Glauca' Blue Italian Cypress	7	40'/15'	col dense	bl-gr	bl-gr	M	sun/ well-dr	Background or accent tree.
Juniperus chinensis 'Ames' Ames Juniper	4	12'/8'	broad pyra	bl-gr	bl-gr	F	sun/ adapt	Compact and dense. Requires little pruning.
Juniperus chinensis 'Blaauwii' Blaauw's Juniper	4	15'/10'	upr vase	gray- gr	gray- gr	MC	sun/ adapt	Dense and heavily textured.
Juniperus chinensis 'Blue Point' Blue Point Juniper	4	15'/10'	pyra	bl- gray	bl- gray	F	sun/ adapt	Very dense. Good color accent.
Juniperus chinensis 'Denserecta' Spartan Juniper	4	20'/6'	pyra	bt-gr	bt-gr	F	sun/ adapt	Narrow upright with rich color.
Juniperus chinensis 'Keteleeri' Keteleer Juniper	5	20'/12'	broad pyra	dk-gr	dk-gr	M	sun/ adapt	Ascending branches. Fast.
Juniperus chinensis 'Robusta Green' Robusta Green Juniper	5	20'/8'	upr irr	dk-gr	dk-gr	M	sun/ adapt	Informal, irregular, rugged.

NARROWLEAF EVERGREEN TREES (CONTINUED)

Botanical Name/ Common Name	Zone	Size Ht/Wid	Form	Foliage Summer	Fall	Texture	Exposure Soil	Remarks
Juniperus chinensis 'Torulosa' Hollywood Juniper	5	20'/8'	upr irr	rich gr	rich gr	M	sun/ adapt	Rustic, informal, irregular, and rugged.
Juniperus excelsa 'Stricta' Spiney Greek Juniper	4	10'/6'	con	gray-gr	gray-gr	MF	sun/ adapt	Spiney foliage. Irregular edge. Fast grower.
Juniperus scopulorum 'Blue Haven' Blue Haven Juniper	3	20'/12'	pyra	blue	blue	M	sun/ adapt	One of the bluest uprights.
Juniperus scopulorum 'Cologreen' Cologreen Juniper	3	20'/12'	broad pyra	bt-gr	bt-gr	MF	sun/ adapt	Upright branches. Rich green color. Symmetrical.
Juniperus scopulorum 'Medora' Medora Juniper	3	12'/8'	col	bl-gr	bl-gr	F	sun/ adapt	Slow-growing. Columnar form. Easily controlled.
Juniperus scopulorum 'Gray Gleam' Gray Gleam Juniper	3	30'/10'	tall col	sil-bl	sil-bl	F	sun/ adapt	Symmetrical. Accent or specimen. Dense.
Juniperus scopulorum 'Welchii' Welch Juniper	5	30'/15'	nar pyra	sil-gr	sil-gr	MF	sun/ adapt	Dense compact upright.
Juniperus scopulorum 'Wichita Blue' Wichita Blue Juniper	3	15'/8'	pyra	blue	blue	F	sun/ adapt	More compact than 'Blue Haven.'
Juniperus virginiana Eastern Redcedar	5	20'/15'	pyra	gr	gr-wine	MF	sun/ adapt	Many variations in nature. Good windbreak plant.

NARROWLEAF EVERGREEN TREES (CONTINUED)

Botanical Name/ Common Name	Zone	Size Ht/Wid	Form	Foliage Summer	Fall	Texture	Exposure Soil	Remarks
Juniperus virginiana 'Canaertii' Canaert Juniper	4	20'/8'	pyra irr	dk-gr	dk-gr	MF	sun/ adapt	Shears well. Rich dark green color and many blue berries in fall. Horizontal irregular branches.
Juniperus virginiana 'Cupressifolia' Hillspire Juniper	5	30'/15'	broad pyra	dk-gr	dk-gr	F	sun/ adapt	Dense foliage. Good wind-break or screening tree.
Juniperus virginiana 'Manhattan Blue' Manhattan Blue Juniper	5	20'/10'	pyra com	bl-gr	bl-gr	MF	sun/ adapt	Good back-ground screen.
Juniperus virginiana 'Oxford Green' Oxford Green Juniper	5	30'/15'	pyra com	bt-gr	bt-gr	F	sun/ adapt	
Juniperus virginiana 'Sky Rocket' Sky Rocket Juniper	5	20'/6'	nar col	blue	blue	F	sun/ adapt	Very narrow columnar juniper. Excellent blue color for accent or background.
Picea abies White Spruce	2	50'/15'	pyra dense	bl-gr	bl-gr	M	s-p-sh/ adapt	Slow, but sym-metrical.
Picea glauca Norway Spruce	2	50'/25'	pyra dense	lus dk-gr	lus dk-gr	M	s-sh/ moist	
Picea glauca 'Densata' Black Hills Spruce	3	25'/20'	broad pyra	dk bl-gr	dk bl-gr	MF	s-sh/ rich, moist	Good specimen lawn tree.
Picea pungens Colorado Spruce	2	50'/30'	broad pyra	bl-gr	bl-gr	M	sun/ rich, moist	Symmetrical. Slow.

NARROWLEAF EVERGREEN TREES (CONTINUED)

Botanical Name/ Common Name	Zone	Size Ht/Wid	Form	Foliage Summer	Fall	Texture	Exposure Soil	Remarks
Picea pungens 'Glauca' Colorado Blue Spruce	2	50'/30'	broad pyra	blue	bl-gr	M	sun/ rich, moist	One of the best specimen trees available. Brilliant blue. Slow & expensive. "Shiners" include 'Kosters' and other grafted varieties.
Pinus densiflora Japanese Red Pine	4	50'/50'	broad irr	bl-gr	yw-gr	M	sun/ acid, well-dr	Very broad and irregular.
Pinus densiflora 'Umbraculifera' Japanese Umbrella Pine	4	20'	mushroom	gr	gr	M	sun/ well-dr	Canopy drapes like an umbrella.
Pinus elliotti Slash Pine	7	80'/35'	broad pyra	bt-gr	bt-gr	MC	sun/ moist	
Pinus flexilis Limber Pine	2	40'/20'	pyra	bl-gr	bl-gr	M	s-p-sh/ moist, well-dr	Fine needles in clusters of five.
Pinus nigra Austrian Pine	4	50'/30'	pyra	dk-gr	dk-gr	MC	sun/ well-dr	Darkest green colored pine. White buds.
Pinus ponderosa Ponderosa Pine	3	50'/40'	broad pyra irr	yw-gr	yw-gr	C	sun/ well-dr	Twisted, long needles.
Pinus strobus Eastern White Pine	3	70'/30'	pyra	dk-bl-gr	dk-bl-gr	F	s-p-sh/ well-dr	Delicate appearance. Fine needle. Clusters of five needles.
Pinus strobus 'Nana' Dwarf Eastern White Pine	3	12'/15'	pyra	bl-gr	bl-gr	F	Sun/ well-dr	Slow-growing, medium sized, wider than tall.

NARROWLEAF EVERGREEN TREES (CONTINUED)

Botanical Name/ Common Name	Zone	Size Ht/Wid	Form	Foliage Summer	Fall	Texture	Exposure Soil	Remarks
Pinus sylvestris Scotch Pine	2	50'/35'	pyra irr	bl-gr	bl-gr	M	sun/ well-dr	Orange bark. Irregular branching. Picturesque tree. One of the faster growing pines.
Pinus sylvestris 'Fastigata' Columnar Scotch Pine	2	50'/20'	col	bl-gr	bl-gr	M	Sun/ well-dr	Narrow, columnar form.
Pinus sylvestris 'French Blue'	2	50'/35'	pyra irr	bl-gr	bl-gr	M	sun/ well-dr	More blue than other Scotch pines.
Pinus sylvestris 'Nana glauca'	4	10'/10'	pyra	bl-gr	bl-gr	MF	sun/ well-dr	Very dwarf.
Pinus thunbergii Japanese Black Pine	5	50'/25'	pyra irr	dk-gr	dk-gr	M	sun/ well-dr	Fast grower. Tolerant of a wide range of soils.
Pseudotsuga menziesii Douglas Fir	4	60'/20'	pyra	bl-gr	bl-gr	M	sun/ moist	The fir most often used for cut Christmas trees. Sparse when young.
Taxus baccata English Yew	6	40'/20'	spr irr	blk gr	blk gr	M	s-sh/ fertile, well-dr	
Taxus cuspidata 'Capitata' Upright Japanese Yew	4	15'/12'	pyra	blk-gr	blk-gr	M	s-sh/ well-dr	Often sheared for accent "shrub."
Taxus media 'Hicks' Hicks Yew	4	6'/3'	vase	dk-gr	dk-gr	MF	sh-p-sh/ fertile, well-dr	Narrow vase shape makes a good hedge or accent.
Thuja accidentalis 'Nigra' Dark Green Arborvitae	4	15'/8'	pyra	dk-gr	dk-gr	MF	sun/ well-dr	Holds winter color well. All arborvitaes are subject to breakage under heavy snow load.

NARROWLEAF EVERGREEN TREES (CONTINUED)

Botanical Name/ Common Name	Zone	Size Ht/Wid	Form	Foliage Summer	Fall	Texture	Exposure Soil	Remarks
Thuja accidentalis 'Techny' Mission Arborvitae	3	8'/6'	pyra	dk-gr	dk-gr	MF	s-sh/ well-dr	Thick foliage. Hedges or windbreaks.
Thuja orientalis 'Aurea Nana' Berkman's Golden Arborvitae	5	10'/6'	pyra	lt-gr, yw-tip	lt-gr, yw-gr	MF	sun/ well-dr	Bright yellow tips. Good accent or specimen tree. Dense foliage. Form tends to be formal.
Tsuga canadensis Canadian Hemlock	3	70'/30'	pyra	dk-gr gl	dk-gr gl	F	p-sh-sh/ acid, moist, well-dr	Protect from winds.

NARROWLEAF EVERGREEN SHRUBS

Botanical Name/ Common Name	Zone	Size Ht/Wid	Form	Foliage Summer	Fall	Texture	Exposure Soil	Remarks
Juniperus chinensis 'Armstrong' Armstrong Juniper	4	4'/8'	upr spr	yw-gr	yw-gr	MF	sun/ adapt	Makes excellent globes. Semi-dwarf.
Juniperus chinensis 'Armstrong Aurea' Old Gold Juniper	4	4'/8'	upr spr	bt-gr yw-tip	bt-gr yw-tip	MF	sun/ adapt	Same as Armstrong, but with yellow growing tips.
Juniperus chinensis 'Aurea' Gold Coast Juniper	4	4'/8'	hor spr	bt-gr yw-tip	bt-gr yw-tip	F	sun/ adapt	Bright yellow growing tips weep slightly at ends. Retains color well in winter. Compact.

NARROWLEAF EVERGREEN SHRUBS (CONTINUED)

Botanical Name/ Common Name	Zone	Size Ht/Wid	Form	Foliage Summer	Fall	Texture	Exposure Soil	Remarks
Juniperus chinensis 'Blue Vase' Blue Vase Juniper	4	5'/4'	vase	bl-gr	bl-gr	MF	sun/ adapt	
Juniperus chinensis 'Glauca Hetzii' Hetz Juniper	4	15'/18'	upr spr	bl-gr	bl-gr	M	sun/ adapt	Very large blue spreader. Unruly without some pruning.
Juniperus chinensis 'Maneyi' Maneyi Juniper	4	8'/12'	vase	dk bl-gr	dk bl-gr	MC	sun/ adapt	Somewhat coarse. Good for screens or hedges.
Juniperus chinensis 'Mint Julep' Mint Julep Juniper	4	8'/8'	arch spr	dk-gr	dk-gr	MF	sun/ adapt	Arching branches give graceful appearance. Mint smell when branch is broken.
Juniperus chinensis pfitzeriana compacta 'Mordigan' Mordigan Pfitzer Juniper	4	2'/4'	spr- com	gray-gr	gray-gr	F	sun/ adapt	Extremely compact.
Juniperus chinensis 'Pfitzerana' Pfitzer Juniper	4	8'/12'	hor spr	gr	gr	F	sun/ adapt	Big spreader. Not for foundation plantings.
Juniperus chinensis 'Aurea-Pfitzerana' Gold Tip Pfitzer	4	6'/10'	hor spr	bt-gr yw-tip	bt-gr	F	sun/ adapt	Slightly smaller than pfitzer. Bright yellowgrowing tips turn green in winter. Good texture.

NARROWLEAF EVERGREEN SHRUBS (CONTINUED)

Botanical Name/ Common Name	Zone	Size Ht/Wid	Form	Foliage Summer	Fall	Texture	Exposure Soil	Remarks
Juniperus chinensis 'Pfitzerana Kallay' Kallay Pfitzer	4	3'/5'	spr com	lt-gr	lt-gr	F	sun/ adapt	Compact, dense, dwarf pfitzer. Good for foundation planting.
Juniperus chinensis 'Nicks compact' Nicks Compact Pfitzer	4	4'/8'	hor spr	gray-gr	gray-gr	F	sun/ adapt	Very compact and dense. Graceful.
Juniperus chinensis 'San Jose' San Jose Juniper	4	1'/6'	pros	lt-gr	lt-gr	M	sun/ adapt	One of the coarsest textures among the conifers. Good ground-cover.
Juniperus chinensis 'Sarcoxie' Ozark Compact Pfitzer	4	4'/8'	hor spr	gr	gr	F	sun/ adapt	Another compact, dense pfitzer.
Juniperus chinensis 'Sargentii Glauca' Sargent Juniper	4	1 1/2' /10'	creep	gray-gr	gray-gr	F	s-lt-sh/ adapt	Heavily branched. Full foliage.
Juniperus chinensis 'Sargentii Viridis' Green Sargent Juniper	4	2'/10'	creep	bt-gr	bt-gr	F	s-lt-sh/ adapt	Holds good green color well in winter.
Juniperus chinensis 'Sea Green' Sea Green Juniper	4	6'/8'	arch spr	dk-gr	dk-gr	MF	sun/ adapt	Arching branches give graceful appearance Good accent.

NARROWLEAF EVERGREEN SHRUBS (CONTINUED)

Botanical Name/ Common Name	Zone	Size Ht/Wid	Form	Foliage Summer	Fall	Texture	Exposure Soil	Remarks
Juniperus conferta 'Blue Pacific' Blue Pacific Juniper	6	2'/8'	trail	bl-gr	bl-gr	F	sun/ adapt	An improved Shore juniper with good color.
Juniperus horizontalis 'Bar Harbor' Bar Harbor Juniper	4	2'/8'	pros	bl-gray	bl-pur	F	sun/ adapt	A ground-hug-ging variety.
Juniperus horizontalis 'Blue Chip' Blue Chip Juniper	4	1'/8'	pros mound	lt-bl	bl	F	s-lt-sh/ adapt	Very good light blue color. Holds color well in winter.
Juniperus horizontalis 'Blue Horizon' Blue Horizon Juniper	4	1'/6'	pros	bl	bl	F	sun/ adapt	
Juniperus horizontalis 'Hughes' Hughes Juniper	4	2'/6'	creep	bl	bl-gr	F	sun/ adapt	Retains blue well in winter.
Juniperus horizontalis 'Plumosa' Andorra Juniper	4	2'/8'	low spr	bt-gr	plum	F	s-lt-sh/ adapt	Plume-like foliage. Upright dense branches.
Juniperus horizontalis 'Youngstown' Compact Andorra Juniper	4	2'/6'	low spr	bt-gr	plum	F	s-lt-sh/ adapt	Slower, more compact than regular Andorra. Stays fuller in center of plant.
Juniperus horizontalis 'Turquoise' Turquoise Juniper	4	1'/8'	pros	tur-bl	tur-bl	F	s-lt-sh/ adapt	Resists mounding. Stays flat and full.

NARROWLEAF EVERGREEN SHRUBS (CONTINUED)

Botanical Name/ Common Name	Zone	Size Ht/Wid	Form	Summer	Foliage Fall	Texture	Exposure Soil	Remarks
Juniperus horizontalis 'Wiltonii' Blue Ring Juniper	4	8"/8'	mat	sil-bl	sil-bl	F	s-lt-sh/ adapt	Carpet-like. Trailing. Will not withstand any traffic.
Juniperus horizontalis 'Yukon Belle' Yukon Belle Juniper	2	1'/8'	mat	sil-bl	sil-bl	F	sun/ adapt	Adaptable for colder ciimatic zones than other junipers.
Juniperus procumbens Procumbens Juniper	4	2'/8'	pros trail	bl-gr	bl-gr	M	s-lt-sh/ adapt	Spiney foliage. Tough plant.
Juniperus procumbens 'Nana' Dwarf Procumbens Juniper	4	8"/6'	mat	bl-gr	bl-gr	F	s-lt-sh/ adapt	Very dwarf. Good for rock gardens or other areas small in scale.
Juniperus sabina Savin Juniper	3	5'/8'	semi-vase	dk-gr	dk-gr	F	sun/ adapt	Good low spreader, but name varieties of Juniperus *sabina* are superior. Disease problems.
Juniperus sabina 'Arcadia' Arcadia Juniper	3	2'/5'	spr hor	bt-gr	bt-gr	F	sun/ adapt	Lacy foliage. Tiered branches
Juniperus sabina 'Blue Danube' Blue Danube Juniper	3	1 1/2' /5'	pros	bl-gr	bl-gr	F	sun/ adapt	Semi-erect form of J. *sabina*.
Juniperus sabina 'Broadmoor' Broadmoor Juniper	3	2'/6'	mound spr	bt-gr	bt-gr	F	sun/ adapt	Soft, very dense foliage. Makes a grace-ful, slightly mounded plant.

NARROWLEAF EVERGREEN SHRUBS (CONTINUED)

Botanical Name/ Common Name	Zone	Size Ht/Wid	Form	Foliage Summer	Fall	Texture	Exposure Soil	Remarks
Juniperus sabina 'Buffalo' Buffalo Juniper	3	2'/6'	mound trail	dk-gr	dk-gr	F	sun/ adapt	Low, dense. Mounded branches trail over center of plant.
Juniperus sabina 'Moordense Monard' Moordense™ Juniper	3	2'/6'	pros	l-gr	l-gr		sun/ adapt	More prostrate form of Broad-moor.
Juniperus sabina 'Scandia' Scandia Juniper	3	1 1/2' /8'	low spr	dk-gr	dk-gr	F	sun/ adapt	Feathery foliage. Full and dense.
Juniperus sabina 'Tamariscifolia' Tamarix Juniper	3	3'/8'	mound trail	dk-gr	dk-gr	F	sun/ adapt	Outstanding form. Branches seem to weep over mounded center of plant.
Juniperus sabina 'New Blue' New Blue Tamarix Juniper	3	3'/8'	mound trail	bl-gr	bl-gr	F	sun/ adapt	Same as Tamarix with blue foliage.
Juniperus sabina 'Von Ehron' Von Ehron Juniper	3	8'/20'	vase	dk-gr	dk-gr	MF	sun/ adapt	Most valued for shearing into globe shape.
Juniperus scopulorum 'Monam' Blue Creeper Juniper	3	2'/6'	pros	bl-gr	bl	F	sun/ adapt	Mounded form. Bright blue color intensifies in winter.
Juniperus scopulorum 'Table Top Blue' Table Top Blue Juniper	5	4'/6'	semi vase	sil-bl	sil-bl	MF	sun/ adapt	Heavily branched. Flat-top.

NARROWLEAF EVERGREEN SHRUBS (CONTINUED)

Botanical Name/ Common Name	Zone	Size Ht/Wid	Form	Foliage Summer	Fall	Texture	Exposure Soil	Remarks
Juniperus squamata 'Meyeri' Meyeri Juniper	4	6'/6'	upr irr	dk bl-gr	dk bl-gr	MC	sun/ adapt	Heavy branch-es. Irregular form and fairly coarse texture. Accent.
Picea abies 'Nidiformis' Bird's Nest Spruce	4	3'/3'	round	dk-gr	dk-gr	F	s-lt-sh/ well-dr	Very dwarf and compact. Slow growing accent plant. Good for rock gardens.
Picea glauca 'Conica' Dwarf Alberta Spruce	4	4'/4'	con	bt-gr	bt-gr	F	s-lt-sh/ well-dr	Symmetrical, slow, and dense accent plant.
Picea pungens 'Globosa' Dwarf Globe Blue Spruce	2	3'/4'	globe	bt-bl	bt-bl	MF	sun/ well-dr	Densely branched, flat-topped globe.
Pinus mugo 'Compacta' Dwarf Mugo Pine	3	6'/8'	round broad	bt-gr	bt-gr	M	s-lt-sh/ well-dr	Popular accent plant. Slow growing. All growth occurs at one time of year for easy maintenance.
Taxus cuspidata 'Capitata' Upright Japanese Yew	4	15'/12'	pyra	blk-gr	blk-gr	M	s-sh/ well-dr	Also listed as evergreen tree. Often used as accent shrub. Shears well.
Taxus cuspidata 'Densiformis' Densiformis Yew	4	5'/5'	spr	blk-gr	blk-gr	M	sh-p-sh/ well-dr	Dense, compact. Recovers well from winter-burn. Probably the most popular spreading yew.

NARROWLEAF EVERGREEN SHRUBS (CONTINUED)

Botanical Name/ Common Name	Zone	Size Ht/Wid	Form	Summer	Foliage Fall	Texture	Exposure Soil	Remarks
Taxus cuspidata 'Sebian' Sebian Yew	4	4'/8'	spr	blk-gr	blk-gr	M	sh-p-sh/ well-dr	Among the most shades tolerant evergreens, along with other spreading yews.
Taxus cuspidata 'Nana' Dwarf Japanese Yew	4	5'/5'	spr	blk-gr	blk-gr	M	sh-p-sh/ well-dr	Dense and compact.
Taxus X media 'Brownii' Brown's Spreading Yew	4	8'/8'	spr	blk-gr	blk-gr	M	sh-p-sh/ well-dr	Many red berries in fall. Makes a good sheared globe.
Taxus X media 'Hatfieldii' Hatfield Yew	4	8'/8'	pyra	blk-gr	blk-gr	M	sh-p-sh/ well-dr	Accent plant. Good small pyramid.
Taxus X media 'Hicksii' Hicks Yew	4	8'/6'	vase col	blk-gr	blk-gr	M	s-p-sh/ well-dr	Accent or hedge plant.
Taxus X media 'Tauntonii' Taunton Spreading Yew	4	8'/8'	spr	blk-gr	blk-gr	M	sh-p-sh/ well-dr	Resistant to winterburn.
Taxus media 'Wardii' Ward's Spreading Yew	4	4'/6'	spr	blk-gr	blk-gr	M	sh-p-sh/ well-dr	Dense, com- pact spreading yew.

SPECIALTY PLANTS

Botanical Name/ Common Name	Zone	Size Ht/Wid	Form	Summer	Foliage Fall	Texture	Exposure Soil	Remarks
Bambusa species Bamboo	6	to 15'	tall clump	gr	gr- brn	C	sun/ moist	Semi-tropical plant. Several species. Good for accent, background. Good around pools.

SPECIALTY PLANTS (CONTINUED)

Botanical Name/ Common Name	Zone	Size Ht/Wid	Form	Foliage Summer	Fall	Texture	Exposure Soil	Remarks
Bambusa arundaria pygmaea Pygmy Bamboo	4	1'/4'	spr	gr	gr-brn	MC	sun/ moist	Aggressive spreader. Good border effect.
Cortaderia selloana Pampas Grass	5	to 10'	tall clump	gr	gr-brn	MC	sun/ moist	Beautiful white seed plumes in fall, persisting through winter. Strong accent requires careful use.
Erianthus ravenae Hardy Pampas Grass	5	6'/3'	clump	gr	brn-pur	MC	sun/ moist	Blooms brown with orange and purple.
Festuca glauca Blue Fescue	5	to 12"	clump	blue	blue	F	sun/ adapt	Attractive, fine-textured accent.
Liriope muscari Green Liriope	6	to 3'	grass	gr	gr-brn	M	s-p-sh/ moist	Borders, edging, accent.
Liriope muscari 'Variegata' Variegated Liriope	6	to 3'	grass	gr-yw var	var, brn	M	sun/ moist	Borders, edging, accent. Variegated foliage.
Miscanthus sinensis 'Gracillimus' Maidengrass	5	4'/3'	clump	gr	tan	F	sun/ moist	Delicate, silvery-white blooms. Good medium size.
Ophiopogon japonicus Mondo Grass	6	to 1'	grass	gr	gr-brn	F	s-sh/ moist	Fine-leaved grass. Good for edging, borders, or accent. Tolerates shade well.
Pennisetum alopecuvoides 'Hamelin' Dwarf Fountaingrass	5	2'/2'	clump	gr	tan	MF	sun/ moist	Buff-colored, foxtail-type blooms. Very dwarf plant.
Pennisetum setaceum 'Rubrum' Purple Fountaingrass	7	4'/2'	clump	red-brn	tan-brn	MF	sun/ moist	Grown as an annual north of zone 7. Rose-red flower spikes in fall.

SPECIALTY PLANTS (CONTINUED)

Botanical Name/ Common Name	Zone	Size Ht/Wid	Form	Summer	Foliage Fall	Texture	Exposure Soil	Remarks
Phalaris arundinacea variegata Variegated Ribbon Grass	6	to 5'	grass	var	var, brn	M	s-p-sh/ moist	Interesting green-and-white striped foliage. Borders, accent. Can be used as groundcover.
Yucca aloifolia Spanish Dagger Yucca	7	15'	tall clump	gr	gr	C	sun/ dry	Dagger-like leaves. White flower on tall spike in summer.
Yucca filamentosa Adam's Needle Yucca	4	3'	clump	gr	gr	C	sun/ dry	Stiff, upright leaves like blades. Spike of white blooms extends high above plant.
Yucca recurvifolia Pendula Yucca	7	6'	clump	bl-gr	bl-gr	C	sun/ dry	Blue-green, recurving leaves. Branches out with age.

GROUNDCOVERS

Botanical Name/ Common Name	Zone	Size Ht/Wid	Form	Summer	Foliage Fall	Texture	Exposure Soil	Remarks
Aegopodium podagraria 'Variegatum' Variegated Bishops Weed	5	6"/1'	low dense	gr, wht, margin	var	MC	sun/ adapt	Tiny white flower in June. Aromatic fruit.
Ajuga pyramidalis 'Metallica Crispa' Curly Bugle	4	6"/1'	low	pur-bron	pur-bron	MC	s-sh/ adapt	Blue flower spike in June. Excellent, colorful foliage.

GROUNDCOVERS (CONTINUED)

Botanical Name/ Common Name	Zone	Size Ht/Wid	Form	Summer	Foliage Fall	Texture	Exposure Soil	Remarks
Ajuga reptans 'Atropurpurea' Carpet Bugle	4	6"/1'	low	dk-bron	dk-bron	MC	s-p-sh/ adapt	Blue, red, purple, or white blooms in June.
Ajuga reptans 'Rubra' Red Bugle	4	6"/1'	low	dk-pur	dk-pur	MC	s-p-sh/ adapt	Blue, red, purple, or white blooms in June.
Ajuga reptans 'Variegata' Variegated Bugle	4	6"/1'	low	yw & gr var	yw & gr var	MC	s-p-sh/ adapt	Blue, red, purple, or white blooms in June.
Artemisia schmidtiana 'Nana' Silver Mound	4	1'/2'	mound	sil-gr	brn	F	sun/ adapt	Must be tightly grouped to cover the ground. Dies to ground in fall.
Chaenomeles japonica alpina Alpine Flowering Quince	4	1'/3'	dense mound	gr	yw	F	sun/ adapt	Thorny low groundcover.
Coronilla varia Crown Vetch	4	2'/6'	spr dense	gr	tern	M	sun/ adapt	Tough, leguminous groundcover. Improves poor soils.
Cotoneaster adpressus Creeping Cotoneaster	4	1 1/2' /10'	mound	gr	red	MF	sun/ adapt	
Cotoneaster apiculata Cranberry Cotoneaster	5	1 1/2' /6'	mound	red-gr	red-or	F	s-p-sh/ adapt	Pink flowers in spring. Lots of red berries in fall.
Cotoneaster dammeri 'Lowfast' Lowfast Cotoneaster	6	2'/6'	pros	gl dk-gr	dk-gr	F	sun/ adapt	Pink flowers. Red berries. Evergreen.
Cotoneaster horizontalis Rock Cotoneaster	5	2'/6'	arch mound	gl dk-gr	red-or	F	sun/ adapt	Red berries that attract birds. Evergreen in South.

GROUNDCOVERS (CONTINUED)

Botanical Name/ Common Name	Zone	Size Ht/Wid	Form	Summer	Foliage Fall	Texture	Exposure Soil	Remarks
Cotoneaster salicifolius 'Repandens' Repandens Cotoneaster	6	3'/6'	mound pend	gl dk-gr	gl dk-gr	F	sun/ adapt	White flowers in spring. Red berries. Ever-green.
Euonymus fortunei 'Colorata' Purpleleaf Wintercreeper	5	2'/6'	upr irr	dk-gr	plum	M	s-sh/ adapt	Irregular with-out pruning. Will vine into trees. Good fall & winter color.
Euonymus fortunei vegeta Bigleaf Wintercreeper	5	3'/3'	upr irr	dk-gr	plum	MC	s-sh/ adapt	Red berries in fall. Will vine into landscape plants if un-checked.
Hedera helix English Ivy	4	8" tall	trail	dk-gr	dk-gr	M	sh-p-sh/ cool, moist	Vine on walls. Good ground-cover.
Hedera helix 'Bulgaria' Bulgarian Ivy	5	8" tall	trail	dk-gr	dk-gr	M	sh-p-sh/ cool, moist	Vines on walls.
Hypericum linarioides Creeping St. Johnswort	5	6"/5'	pros	gr	brn	F	sun/ well-dr	Yellow flowers during sum-mer.
Iberis sempervirens Candytuft	4	1'/ 1 1/2'	mound dense	dk-gr	dk-gr	F	sun/ adapt	Evergreen. 'Christmas Snow,' 'Snow-flake,' and 'Little Gem' popular culti-vars. White flowers.
Juniperus chinensis 'San Jose' San Jose Juniper	4	1'/6'	pros	lt-gr	lt-gr	M	sun/ adapt	Evergreen. No traffic.
Juniperus chinensis 'Sargentii' Sargent Juniper	4	1 1/2' /10'	creep	gray-gr	gray-gr	F	s-lt-sh/ adapt	Evergreen. No traffic.

GROUNDCOVERS (CONTINUED)

Botanical Name/ Common Name	Zone	Size Ht/Wid	Form	Foliage Summer	Fall	Texture	Exposure Soil	Remarks
Juniperus chinensis 'Sargentii Viridis' Green Sargent Juniper	4	2'/10'	creep	bt-gr	bt-gr	F	s-lt-sh/ adapt	Holds color well in winter. No traffic.
Juniperus conferta 'Blue Pacific' Blue Pacific Juniper	4	2'/8'	trail	bl-gr	bl-gr	F	sun/ adapt	No traffic. Evergreen.
Juniperus horizontalis 'Bar Harbor' Bar Harbor Juniper	4	2'/8'	pros	bl-gr	bl-pur	F	sun/ adapt	Ground-hugging Evergreen. No traffic.
Juniperus horizontalis 'Blue Chip' Blue Chip Juniper	4	1'/8'	pros mound	lt-bl	bl	F	sun/ adapt	No traffic. Evergreen.
Juniperus horizontalis 'Hughes' Hughes Juniper	4	2'/6'	low spr	bl	bt-gr	F	sun/ adapt	Evergreen. Holds color well in winter. No traffic.
Juniperus horizontalis 'Plumosa' Andorra Juniper	4	2'/8'	spr	bt-gr	plum	F	s-lt-sh/ adapt	Good winter color. No traffic.
Juniperus horizontalis 'Youngstown' Compact Andorra Juniper	4	2'/8'	spr	bt-gr	plum	F	s-lt-sh/ adapt	Very dense evergreen. Good winter color. Stays full in centers. No traffic.
Juniperus horizontalis 'Turquoise' Turquoise Juniper	4	1'/8'	pros	tur-bl	tur-bl	F	s-lt-sh/ adapt	Stays full. Does not mound in centers. Evergreen. No traffic.

GROUNDCOVERS (CONTINUED)

Botanical Name/ Common Name	Zone	Size Ht/Wid	Form	Summer	Foliage Fall	Texture	Exposure Soil	Remarks
Juniperus horizontalis 'Wiltoni' Blue Rug Juniper	4	8"/8'	mat	sil-bl	sil-bl	F	s-lt-sh/ adapt	Carpetlike evergreen. Drapes. Particularly susceptible to traffic.
Juniperus horizontalis 'Yukon Belle' Yukon Belle Juniper	2	1'/8'	mat	sil-bl	sil-bl	F	sun/ adapt	Adaptable in colder climates. Evergreen. No traffic.
Juniperus procumbens Procumbens Juniper	4	2'/8'	pros trail	bl-gr	bl-gr	F	s-lt-sh/ adapt	Spiney, tough evergreen. No traffic.
Juniperus procumbens 'Nana' Dwarf Procumbens	4	8"/6'	mat	bl-gr	bl-gr	F	s-lt-sh/ adapt	Very slow. Good for small areas. Evergreen. No traffic.
Juniperus sabina 'Broadmoor' Broadmoor Juniper	3'	2'/6'	mound	bt-gr	bt-gr	F	sun/ adapt	Taller than most junipers. No traffic.
Juniperus sabina 'Buffalo' Buffalo Juniper	3	2'/6'	mound	dk-gr	dk-gr	F	sun/ adapt	Evergreen, no traffic. Branches trail.
Juniperus sabina 'Scandia' Scandia Juniper	3	1 1/2'/6'	spr	dk-gr	dk-gr	F	sun/ adapt	Feathery foliage. Evergreen. No traffic.
Liriope muscari Green Liriope	6	3'/1'	clp	gr	gr-brn	M	s-lt-sh/ moist	Grass-like groundcover.
Liriope muscari 'Variegata' Variegated Liriope	6	3'/1'	clp	gr-wht, var	brn	M	sun/ moist	Variegated leaves. Grass-like groundcover. Purple flowers.

GROUNDCOVERS (CONTINUED)

Botanical Name/ Common Name	Zone	Size Ht/Wid	Form	Summer	Foliage Fall	Texture	Exposure Soil	Remarks
Lonicera heckrotti Goldflame Honeysuckle	4	4'/6'	trail	m-gr	m-gr	M	s-p-sh/ adapt	Coral red or yellow flowers in summer. Tall, tangled groundcover also vines.
Lonicera japonica 'Halliana' Hall's Honeysuckle	4	4'/6'	trail	m-gr	wine	M	s-p-sh/ adapt	White flower in summer. Tall and tangled groundcover. Also vines.
Lonicera japonica 'Purpurea' Purple Leaf Honeysuckle	5	3'/6'	trail	red-gr	pur	M	s-p-sh/ adapt	White flower in summer. Tall and tangled groundcover that also vines.
Mahonia repens Creeping Oregon Grape	5	1'/2'	irr	dk-gr	bron-gr	C	s-sh/ well-dr	Holly-type leaves. Yellow flowers in June. Black berries.
Pachysandra terminalis Japanese Spurge (Pachysandra)	4	6"/2'	low spr	gr	yw-gr	C	s-sh/ adapt	Popular groundcover under trees.
Parthenocissus tricuspidata 'Vetchii' Boston Ivy	4	6" tall	trail	dk-gr	crim	M	sh-p-sh/ cool, moist	Vines on walls.
Paxistima canbyi Ratstripper Paxistima	4	1'/2'	low spr	dk-gr	bron	F	sh-p-sh/ well-dr	Neat evergreen with tiny red flowers.
Potentilla aurea	3	4"/2'	mat	dk-gr	yw	F	sun/ adapt	Golden yellow flowers.
Sedum acre Goldmoss Stonecrop	5	3" tall	low spr	gr	red-gr	F	sun/ adapt	Will grow in thin soil and dry conditions.
Sedum album White Stonecrop	5	8" tall	low spr	gr	gr	MF	sun/ adapt	Mat-forming. White flowers in August.

GROUNDCOVERS (CONTINUED)

Botanical Name/ Common Name	Zone	Size Ht/Wid	Form	Summer	Foliage Fall	Texture	Exposure Soil	Remarks
Sedum spurium Dragon's Blood Sedum	5	6" tall	low spr	red-gr	red-brn	F	s-sh/ adapt	Crimson flowers in June. Tolerates very dry conditions.
Thymus serpyllum Mother-of-Thyme	5	1"/1'	very low	gr	gr	F	sh-p-sh/ adapt	Lowest of groundcovers. Good between stepping stones
Vinca major Bigleaf Periwinkle	4	1' tall	low	dk-gr	dk-gr	M	sh-p-sh/ cool, moist	
Vinca minor Periwinkle trail (Myrtle)	4	6"/2'	low	dk-gr	dk-gr	F	s-sh/ cool, moist	Tiny blue flowers in May and September. One of the most popular groundcovers.
Vinca minor 'Bowlesii' Bowles Periwinkle	4	8"/2'	low trail	dk-gr	dk-gr	MF	s-sh/ cool, moist	Has large blue flowers. Grows a little taller.
Vinca minor 'Alba' White Periwinkle	4	6"/2'	low trail	dk-gr	dk-gr	F	s-sh/ cool, moist	White flowers.

VINES

Botanical Name/ Common Name	Zone	Size Ht/Wid	Form	Summer	Foliage Fall	Texture	Exposure Soil	Remarks
Akebia quinata Akebia	6	to 30'		yw-gr	yw-gr decid	M	sun	Fragrant flowers though not conspicuous. Purple berries. Strong and woody vine.
Arctostaphylos uva-ursi Bearberry	3			yw-gr	bron	M	sun	Evergreen, with white or pink flowers. Red berries.

VINES (CONTINUED)

Botanical Name/ Common Name	Zone	Size Ht/Wid	Form	Summer	Foliage Fall	Texture	Exposure Soil	Remarks
Aristolochia durior Dutchman's Pipe	6	to 30'		gr	gr	C	sun	Large, kidney-shaped leaves. Brown flowers shaped like a pipe.
Campsis radicans Trumpet Creeper	4	30'+		gr	yw-brn	C	sun/ well-dr	Large, orange trumpet-shaped flowers in July-August.
Campis X tagliabuana Madam Galen Creeper	4	30'+		gr	yw-brn	C	sun/ well-dr	Dark orange bloom in July-August.
Celastris orbiculatus Oriental Bittersweet	4	30'+		gr	yw-gr	M	s-p-sh/ adapt	Bright yellow-red fruit. Male and female plants required for fruit produc-tion.
Celastris scandens Bittersweet	5	30'+		gr	yw	M	s-p-sh/ adapt	Bright orange-red fruit. Male and female plants required for fruit produc-tion.
Clematis X jackmannii Jackman Clematis	4	6' to 18'		gr	gr, decid	M	s-p-sh/ alkaline	Many different flower colors available by varieties.
Clematis X lawsoniana 'Henryii' Henry Clematis	5	5' to 8'		gr	gr, decid	M	sun/ rich	White flowers in June. Protect from wind.
Clematis dioscoreifolia 'Robusta' Sweet Autumn Clematis	4	to 30'		gray-gr	gr, decid	M	s-p-sh/ rich	Fragrant white flowers in Sep-tember.

VINES (CONTINUED)

Botanical Name/ Common Name	Zone	Size Ht/Wid	Form	Foliage Summer	Fall	Texture	Exposure Soil	Remarks
Euonymus fortunei Wintercreeper Euonymus	5	to 15'		gr	gr	M	s-sh/ well-dr	Will climb on walls or trellis.
Euonymus fortunei 'Colorata' Purpleleaf Wintercreeper	5	to 15'		gr	pur-wine	M	s-sh/ adapt	Foliage becomes heavy, will pull away from wall after rain or snow.
Euonymus fortunei 'Kewensis' Kewensis Euonymus	5			gr	gr	F	s-sh/ well-dr	Tiny leaves. Slow growing.
Euonymus fortunei radicans Common Wintercreeper	5	to 15'		gr	gr	MC	s-sh/ well-dr	Orange berries.
Euonymus fortunei 'Sarcoxie' Sarcoxie Euonymus	5	to 15'		dk-gr	dk-gr	M	s-sh/ adapt	Upright shrub that vines when placed next to a wall. Makes a good accent for entryway.
Euonymus fortunei vegeta Bigleaf Wintercreeper	5	to 15'		gr	gr	MC	s-sh/ well-dr	Orange berries.
Hedera helix English Ivy	4	to 20'		dk-gr	dk-gr	M	s-p-sh/ cool, moist	Vigorous attachment. Can damage sidings. 'Baltica' and 'Bulgarian' cultivars available.
Lonicera heckrotti Goldflame Honeysuckle	4	to 30'		gr	gr	M	s-sh/ adapt	Coral-red blooms. Orange-red berries. Vines by twinning.

VINES (CONTINUED)

Botanical Name/ Common Name	Zone	Size Ht/Wid	Form	Summer	Foliage Fall	Texture	Exposure Soil	Remarks
Lonicera japonica 'Halliana' Hall's Honeysuckle	4	to 20'		gr	wine	M	s-p-sh/ adapt	Twinning. Needs trellis for support. Creamy-white flowers.
Lonicera japonica 'Purpurea' Purpleleaf Honeysuckle	5	to 20'		red-gr	pur	M	s-p-sh/ adapt	Twinning, with white flowers.
Lonicera sempervirens Scarlet Trumpet Honeysuckle	5	20'+		bl-gr	bl-gr	M	sun/ adapt	Scarlet-yellow flowers. Twinning vine.
Parthenocissus quinquifolia Virginia Creeper	4	to 50'		gr	red, decid	MC	s-sh/ adapt	Aggressive wall climber.
Parthenocissus quinquifolia 'Engelmannii' Engleman Ivy	4	to 50'		gr	red-brn	MC	sh-p-sh/ adapt	Has finer texture than Virginia Creeper.
Parthenocissus tricuspidata 'Vetchii' Boston Ivy	4	60'+		red-gr	red	M	s-sh/ cool moist	Better fall color than standard Boston Ivy.
Polygonum aubertii Silver Fleece Vine	5	25'+		red-gr	red-gr	MF	sun/ adapt	Vigorous twinning vine. White, lacy flowers during summer.
Wisteria sinensis 'Alba' White Wisteria	5	20'+		bt-gr	yw, decid	MC	sun/ adapt	Pendulous clusters of white flowers in June. Twinning.
Wisteria sinensis 'Purpurea' Purple Wisteria	5	20'+		bt-gr	yw, decid	MC	sun/ adapt	Pendulous clusters of purple flowers in June. Twinning.

PERENNIALS

Common Name Botannical Name	Sun/ Shade	Height	Flower Color	Flower Timing	Soil Type	Remarks
Achillea filipendula Cloth of Gold Yarrow	s	30–36"	golden	All summer	drought- resistant	Fern-type foliage. Cut or dried flowers.
Achillea tayetea 'Summer Pastels' Summer Pastels Yarrow	s	24"	Pastel Blend	June–Sept.	drought- resistant	Unique color mix. Cut or dried flowers.
Adiantum Pedatum Maiden Hair Fern	sh	12–24"			well-dr	
Adiantum pedatum 'Miss Sharples' Miss Sharples fern	sh	12–24"				
Allyssum saxatile *'compactum'* Basket of Gold Alyssum	s-p-s	8–12"	yw	Spring		Borders or rock gardens.
Alchea rosea 'Powderpuff Mix' Powderpuff Mix Hollyhock	s	4–5'	wht, pink, pur, red, yw	June/July		Double flowers.
Anemone pulsatilla Pasque Flower	s-p -sh	12"	bl- reddish -pur	Spring	alkaline moist	Mulch for winter.
Aquilegia flabellata 'Ministar' Ministar Columbine	sh-p -sh	6–8"	bl-wht	Spring		Very dwarf.
Aquilegia X hybrida 'McKana Giant Mix' McKana Giant Columbine	sh-p -sh	30"	bl-wht	Spring	most soils	Large blooms; dark blue-green foliage.
Arabis procurrens Rock Cress	s	12"	wht	Spring	sandy	Groundcover-type plant.
Armeria maritima Sea Thrift	s	12"	pink, wht,red	May– June	Tolerates poor soil	Grassy evergreen foliage. Rock gardens.
Artemisia schmidtiana Silvermound	s	12"			well-dr	Silver mound of foliage.
Ascleplas tuberosa Butterfly Milkweed	s	24'	or-red	Summer	drought- tolerant	Attracts butterflies.
Aster alpinus 'Dwarf Mix' Alpine Aster	s-p-s	12"	lav, bl, pink	May–June	well-dr; limey	Good dwarf form.
Aster alpinus 'goliath' Goliath Aster	s-p-s		bl	May–June	Well-dr limey	

PERENNIALS (CONTINUED)

Common Name Botannical Name	Sun/ Shade	Height	Flower Color	Flower Timing	Soil Type	Remarks

Aster novi-belgi
'Professor Kippenburg'
    Professor Kippenburg
    Aster
	s	12–15"	bl	Aug.–Oct.		Dk gr foliage;
						compact form.

Aster novi-belgi 'Alert' Alert Aster	s	8–12"	red	Aug.–Oct.		Dk gr foliage; compact form.
AstilbeX arendsii Astilbe	sh-p -sh	12–24"		early summer		Excellent glossy foliage. Varieties: 'fanal'-red, Deutchland-white, 'Peach Blossom'-pink, 'Granaat '-red, 'Showstar'-pink, red, or white 'Rheinland'-pink.
Athyrium flex-femina Lady fern	sh	24–30"				Great for woodland areas.
Athyrium goeringianium 'Pictum' Japanese Painted Fern	sh	18"			moist	Gray-green fronds with red stems & veins.
Bergenia cordifolia Bergenia	sh-p -sh	18"	rose pink	Apr.–June	adaptable	Glossy green leaves. Good groundcover.
Buddleia davidii Butterflybush	s-p -sh	4–6'	pur, red, wht	July–Sept.	adaptable	Attract butterflies; shrub in south 'Black Knight'-deep pur, 'Royal Red'-red, 'White Profusion'- white.
Buddleia davidii 'Petite Plum' Petite Plum Buddleia	s-p -sh	1–2'	pur	July–Sept	adaptable	Very dwarf.
Buphthaimium salicifolium Oxeye Daisy	s	2'	yw	July–Sept.	adaptable	Good cut flowers.
Campanula calycanthema Cup and Saucer	s-p -sh	3'	wht, rose, violet	early summer		Cup and saucer- shaped flowers.
Campanula carpatica 'Blue Chips' Blue Clips Bellflower	s-p -sh	8"	bl	June–Oct.		Bell-shaped flowers above glossy green foliage.

Campanula persicifolia
'Mix'
    Peach Leaved
    bellflower
	s-sh	30–36"	bl-wht	June–July	adaptable	Cutflower and
						borders.

PERENNIALS (CONTINUED)

Common Name / Botannical Name	Sun/ Shade	Height	Flower Color	Flower Timing	Soil Type	Remarks
Caryopteris X clandonensis Blue Mist Spirea	s-sh	4'	bl	July—frost	adaptable	Shrublike. Dk gr foliage.
Catananche coerulea Cupid's Dart	s	18"	violet-bl	June–Aug.	drought-resistant	Excellent dried flowers.
Centaurea cyanus Bachelor's Button	s-p-s	18–24"	dp violet-bl	June–frost	drought-resistant	Popular old perennial.
Centaurea dealbata Persian Cornflower	s-p-s	18–24"	rosy-lilac wht inside	May–Sept.	drought-resistant	
Centranthus ruber 'cocineus' Red Valerian	s-p-s	2–3'	dp pink	July–Sept.	well-dr; drought-resistant	Fragrant flowers.
Cerastium tomentosum Snow-in-Summer	s-p-s	8"	wht	May–June	well-dr	Silvery-white foliage; good rock garden.
Ceratostigma plumbaginoides Plumbago	s-p-s	8"	dk bl	July–Aug.	adaptable	Good groundcover; soil erosion control.
Chrysanthemum maximum 'Double Exhibition' Shasta Daisy	s	3–4'	wht	Spring, summer	adaptable	Good cut flower.
Chrysanthremum X coccineum Painted Daisy	s	24"	red, rose, wht	Late spring	adaptable	Good cut flower; fernlike foliage.
Chrysanthemum X superbum Daisy	s	8–36"	wht	June–Aug.	adaptable	Dwarf to semi-dwarf; 'Miss Muffet,' 'Snow lady,' 'Thomas Killen' varieties.
Convallaria majalis Lily-of-the-Valley	sh	6–8"	wht	May–June	adaptable	Good groundcover; orange berries.
Coreopsis grandiflora 'Early Sunrise' Early Sunrise Coreopsis	s	24"	golden yw	All summer	adaptable	Good narrow foliage; compact plant.
Coreopsis verticillata Coreopsis	s	12–18"	yw, pink	Summer to fall	adaptable	Excellent total plant; fernlike foliage; 'Moonbeam'-pale yellow, 'Rosea'-pink.
Coronilla varia Crown Vetch	s	15–18"	pink	Summer	dry soils	Good groundcover, especially steep,arid banks. Leguminous-builds soil.

PERENNIALS (CONTINUED)

Common Name Botannical Name	Sun/ Shade	Height	Flower Color	Flower Timing	Soil Type	Remarks
Delosperma cooperi Ice Plant	s	1–2″	rose-pink	June–Sept.	well-dr	Good groundcover; succulent foliage.
Delphinium chinensis 'Butterfly Compacta' Blue Butterfly Delphinium	s	12–15″	med. bl	June–Sept.	adaptable	Good border plant; fernlike foliage.
Delphinium cultorum 'Magic Fountains' Magic Fountains Delphinium	p-s-s	36″	bl, wht	June–Sept.	adaptable	Dense foliage; good cut flower.
Delphinium elatum 'Pacific Giants Mix' Pacific Giants Delphinium	p-s-s	5–7′	bl, wht, pink, lav	June–Sept.	adaptable	Good cut flower.
Dianthus barbatus 'Indian Carpet' Indian Carpet Dianthus	s	6–8″	bright color mix	June–Aug.	adaptable	Good border plant; good for rock garden.
Dianthus caryophyllus 'Grenadin Mixed' Grenadin Mixed Carnation	s	18–20″	pink, red, yw, wht	Early spring	well-dr	Winter protection.
Dianthus deltoides 'Zing Rose' Maiden Pink Zing Rose	s	10–14″	carmine-rose	May–June	adaptable	Vivid blooms; good rock gardens.
Dianthus grandiflorus Pinks	s	12″	rose-pink	Spring–early summer	adaptable	Fragrant; dense green foliage.
Dicentra eximia Fringed Bleeding Heart	sh-p-sh	15″	pink	May–Sept.	fertile	Heart-shaped flower; good for cutting.
Dicentra spectablis Old-Fashioned Bleeding Heart	sh-p-sh	2–3′	pink	May–June	fertile	Heart-shaped flower; mulch in winter.
Dictamnus albus Gas Plant	s	2–3′	wht	Summer	moist	Vapors from flowers and leaves will faintly ignite if lit.
Digitalis purpurea 'Foxy' Foxy Foxglove	s-p-s	2–3′	wht, pink, pur	July–Sept.	adaptable	Good cut flower.
Dryopteris marginalis Eastern Wood Fern	sh	20″			adaptable	Evergreen zones 5–9.

PERENNIALS (CONTINUED)

Common Name Botannical Name	Sun/ Shade	Height	Flower Color	Flower Timing	Soil Type	Remarks
Echinacea purpurea 'Magnus' Magnus Purple Coneflower	s	2–3'	pur-red	July–Sept.	adaptable	Good cut flower; attracts butterflies.
Echinacea purpurea 'White Swan' White Swan Coneflower	s	4'	wht	Aug.–Sept.	adaptable	Fragrant-attracts butterflies.
Erigeron x karvinskianus 'Profusion' Profusion Fleabane	s	8–12"	wht	Spring–fall	tolerates dry soils	Dp gr foliage.
Euphorbia polychroma Cushion Spurge	s	16"	yw	Spring	tolerates poor/dry	Crimson foliage in fall. Good ground cover. Good border.
Gaillardia aurea 'The Sun' Golden Goblin Gaillardia	s	12–14"	yw	Summer	tolerates drought	
Gaillardia x grandiflora 'Dwarf Goblin' Dwarf Goblin Gaillardia	s	14–18"	maroon-red	June–Nov.	adaptable	Good cut flower.
Geranium sanguineum Cranesbill Geranium	s-p-s	6–8"	pink	Spring–summer	adaptable	Long blooming period. Good in border or rock garden.
Gypsophila paniculata Baby's Breath	s	36"	wht	June–July	well-dr; alkaline	Good cut or dried flower.
Gypsophila repens 'Rose' Rose Creeping Baby's Breath	s	6"	rose pink	April–May	well-limed	Mats of trailing stems with bl-gr leaves. Good rock garden plant.
Helenium hoopsii Helen's Flower	s	2–3'	red, yw	July–Aug.	tolerates wet	Good cut flower.
Helianthemum nummularium 'Multiple Mixture' Rock Rose	s	8–10"	pink & wht	June–Aug.	adaptable	Good rock garden. Evergreen foliage.
Heliopsis elianhoides 'Summer Sun' Summer Sun Heliopsis	s	2.5–4'	yw	July–Sept.	tolerates poor & dry	Semi-double flowers.
Hemerocalis spp. Daylily	s-p -sh	20–36"	yw, red pink, or	Mid to late summer	adaptable	Many varieties. Broad range of uses.

PERENNIALS (CONTINUED)

Common Name Botannical Name	Sun/ Shade	Height	Flower Color	Flower Timing	Soil Type	Remarks
Hemerocalis 'Stella de Oro' Stella de Oro Daylily	s	9–12"	yw	Periodically all summer	adaptable	Repeat bloomer and a true dwarf. Very useful in many capacities.
Heuchera americana 'Palace Purple' Palace Purple Coral Bells	sh-p -sh	8–10"	wht	Early– mid-summer	rich, moist, well-dr	Purplish-red foliage all summer.
Heuchera sanguinea 'Bressingham hybrids' Bressingham hybrids Coral Bells	sh-p -sh	24"	pale pink to dp crimson	May–June	adaptable	Good mass planting.
Hibiscus moscheutos Hibiscus	s	18"–4'	wht, pink, red	July–frost	adaptable	Large, showy flowers. Many varieties. 'Blue River II'-white, 'Disco Belle'-red, 'Lord Baltimore'-red, 'Disco Belle'-pink, 'Southern Belle' white, pink & red, 'Sweet Caroline' bright pink.
Hosta spp. Plantainlily	sh	8–40"	wht, lav	Mid–late summer	well-dr, rich	Very useful for shade gardens, borders, perennial gardens. Many varieties, grown mostly for foliage impact.
Houttuynia cordata 'Variegata' Variegated Houttuynia	s-sh	12"			moist-boggy	Variegated foliage, pink, green & yellow; can be invasive.
Hydrangea macrophylla 'Nikko Blue' Nikko Blue Hydrangea	sh	3–4'	bl or pink	Early summer	acid	Blue flowers in acid soil, pink in alkaline. Large flower clusters —good foliage.
Iberis sempervirens Candy tuft	s-p-s	6–10"	wht	April–May	adaptable	Dense flower clusters.
Iris germanica Iris	s-p -sh	2'	Red, pur, pink, wht	Spring	average, well-dr	Very hardy, old-fashioned perennial. Many varieties— some bearded.
Iris siberica Siberian Iris	s	2–4'	wht, lilac,or pur	Summer	moist, slightly acid	Hollow stems. Spearlike.

PERENNIALS (CONTINUED)

Common Name Botannical Name	Sun/ Shade	Height	Flower Color	Flower Timing	Soil Type	Remarks
Kniphofia hybrids 'Royal Castle Mix' Royal Castle Mix red Hot Poker	s-p-s	4'	red, yw	May–June	adaptable	Best in mass planting. Unique flower.
Lagerstroemia indica 'Dwarf' Low Flame Crepemyrtle	s	4'	red	Late summer	adaptable	Very dwarf. Profuse bloom.
Lagerstroemia indica 'Dwarf' Royalty Crepemyrtle	s	4'	pur	Late summer	adaptable	Profuse bloomer and dwarf.
Lathyrus latifolius 'Pearl Mixture' Everlasting Sweet Pea	s	6'	red, wht, pink	Summer– fall	adaptable	Vine-like. Needs support.
Lamium maculatum Spotted Dead Nettle	p-s– p-sh	12–18"	wht, pink, pur-red	Spring– early summer	moist	Excellent groundcover. 'Beacon Silver'and 'White Nancy' are favorite cultivars.
Lavender vera Lavender	s	12–24"	lav- bl	July– Sept.	well-dr	Good for potpourri.
Liatris spicatata 'Blazing Stars Purple' Kansas Gayfeather	s	36"	pur	Late spring– summer	drought- resistant	Unusual spike flowers. Drought- resistant. Good cut and dried flowers.
Liatris spicata 'Blazing Stars White' Blazing Stars White Gayfeather	s	36"	wht	Late spring– summer	drought- resistant	Same as above but white flowers.
Linum flavum 'Compactum' Yellow Flax	s	12–14"	yw	Summer	drought- resistant	Very bright flowers.
Linum perenne 'Sapphire' Blue Flax	s-p-s	12–14"	bl	Mid-May– August	adaptable	Fluorescent quality to flowers.
Liriope muscari 'Big Blue' Big Blue Liriope	sh-p -sh	9"	bl	Mid-summer	adaptable	Grasslike leaves make a good border. Good groundcover.
Liriope muscari 'Variegata' Varigated Liriope	sh-p -sh	6–9"	pur-bl	Mid-summer	adaptable	Variegated foliage— green with silver edge. Excellent border. Good low accent.

PERENNIALS (CONTINUED)

Common Name Botannical Name	Sun/ Shade	Height	Flower Color	Flower Timing	Soil Type	Remarks
Lobelia cardinalis Cardinal flower	p-sh	2–4'	crimson	July– Sept.	adaptable	Green foliage. Good red flowers.

Lupinus
'Russell Hybrids'
    Russell Hybrids
    Lupine
	s-p
	-s
		3–4'	bl, pink,
			red, wht
			yw
				May–July	rich, acid
					soil
						Dk gr foliage. Unusual flower.

Lychnis calcedonica Maltese Cross	s-p-s	18–20"	scarlet	June– August	adaptable	Glossy green foliage.
Lythrum salicaria Purple Loosestrife	s-p-s	2–4'	pink– rosy crimson	Summer– fall	tolerates wet	Good accent or background plant. Long bloom period. Good foliage.
Matteuccia struthiopteris Ostrich Fern	sh-p -sh	to 5'			moist, well -dr	Fronds resemble ostrich feathers.
Monarda didyma Bee Balm	s-p -sh	2–3'	red tints	June–July	adaptable	Attracts hummingbirds & bees. Mint-scented foliage. Varieties include 'Monarda Mix' and 'Cambridge Scarlet.'
Myosotis alpestris Forget-Me-Not	sh-p -s	6–8'	dp bl	April–June	prefers moist	Very small & compact. Good blue color.
Oenothera missouriensis Missouri primrose	s	12"	lemon -yw	Summer	tolerates poor soil	Sweetly scented. Front of border and rock garden.
Oenothera speciosa 'Siskiyou' Siskiyou primrose	s	8–10"	lt pink	Summer	tolerates drought	Flowers close at night.
Osmunda cinnamomea Cinnamon Fern	sh	2–3'			adaptable	Young fronds brown, turning dark green.
Osmunda regalis Royal Fern	sh	2'			likes wet soils	
Paeonia lactiflora hybrids Peony	s	36"	red, wht, pink	Late May– June	adaptable	Excellent dark green foliage.
Papaver orientale Poppy	s	36"	yw, red, or	May–June	adaptable	Good cut flower. Excellent color.
Pardencanda x norresii Candylily	s	12–14"	yw, bl, red, pur, wht, or	July–frost	drought- tolerant	Swordlike foliage.

PERENNIALS (CONTINUED)

Common Name / Botannical Name	Sun/ Shade	Height	Flower Color	Flower Timing	Soil Type	Remarks
Penstemon hirsutus Scarlet Queen Beardtongue	s	12–14″	scarlet	Mid-summer	deep, well-dr soil	Evergreen, rosette foliage.
Penstemon hirsutus 'Husker Red' Husker Red Beardtongue	s	24–36″	wht	June–Aug.	well-dr	Bronze, upright spike foliage. Attracts hummingbirds.
Perovskia atriplicifolia Russian Sage	s	3–5′	violet-bl	Aug.–Sept.	well-dr	Silvery foliage. Aromatic. Good backdrop plant in border.
Phlox paniculata Tall Phlox	s-p -sh	2–3′	bl, pur, wht, pink, red	June–Aug.	adaptable	Strong presence in garden.
Phlox sublata Creeping Phlox	s	4–6″	blue, red, pink, bl, wht	Spring	adaptable	Good groundcover. Needlelike foliage. Good in rock gardens.
Physostegia virginiana Obedient Plant	s-p-s	24″	rose	June–Aug.	adaptable	Dk gr foliage. Good cut flower.Long blooming. Easy to grow.
Platycodon grandiflorus Balloon Flower	s	24–30″	blue, wht	July–Aug.	adaptable	Bell-shaped flowers.
Polystichum acrostichoides Christmas Fern	sh	30″			adaptable	Dark green, leathery fronds. Evergreen.
Potentilla nepalensis 'Miss Willmott' Miss Willmott Potentilla	s	12–18″	carmine-scarlet	June–July	adaptable	Good cut flower. Nice, mounded shape.
Primula x polyantha 'Pacific Giants Mix' Pacific Giants	sh-p -sh	10″	bl, red, pink, yw, wht	April–June	adaptable	Vibrant, fragrant flowers.
Ranunculus repens Creeping Buttercup	s-p -sh	12–24″	yw	Summer	adaptable	Some varieties with wht or red flowers.
Rudbeckia fulgidia 'Goldsturm' Goldsturm Black-Eyed Susan	s	3–4′	golden -yw	Aug.–frost	adaptable	Old favorite.
Rudbeckia hirta 'Indian Summer' Black-Eyed Susan	s	3–4′	golden -yw, black center	Summer–fall	adaptable	

PERENNIALS (CONTINUED)

Common Name Botannical Name	Sun/ Shade	Height	Flower Color	Flower Timing	Soil Type	Remarks
Rudbeckia hirta 'Irish Eyes' Irish Eyes Green-Eyed Susan	s	2.5'	golden -yw, green center	Summer	adaptable	Good cut flower.
Sagina subulata Pearlwort (Irish Moss)	s-p	2"	wht	July	adaptable	Mosslike foliage. Often used in sidewalk cracks.
Salvia x superba Blue Salvia	s	12"	bl	June–Aug.	drought-tolerant	Intense flower color. Good cut flower. 'Rose Queen' is a pink variety.
Santolina chamaecyparissus Lavender Cotton	s	12'	yw	June	well-dr	Buttonlike flower. Silver-grey, aromatic foliage.
Saponaria ocymoides Soapwort	s	8–10"	bt pink	May–June	adaptable	Rock gardens. Edging. Groundcover.
Saxifraga Purple Robe Purple Robe	s-p -sh	8–10"	crimson	Spring	adaptable	Good for rock gardens or edging.
Scabiosa caucasica 'House's hybrid Mix' House's Hybrid Pincushion Flower	s	24–30"	blue	June–Aug.	adaptable	Good cut flower. Plant in groups. Bl fringed & frilled double blooms.
Sedum spectable 'Autumn Joy' Autumn Joy Live -forever	s-p-s	15–24"	pink	Aug.–Sept.	adaptable	Fleshy foliage, low water consumption. Flowers turn to russet. Excellent perennial.
Semperviren tectorum Hen and Chicks	s	6–15"			adaptable	Will grow in anything. Great in boulder pockets.
Stachys byzantina Lamb's Ear	s-p-s	12–18"	rosy -mauve	Summer	adaptable	Dense, wooly, greyish-white foliage. Good edging plant.
Teucrium chamaedrys Germander	s	5–8"	pur	Summer	adaptable	Small, glossy green foliage.
Thalictrum aquilegifolium Meadowrue	s-p-s	40"	rosy -pur	June–July	moist, even, damp	
Verbena canadensis Vervain	s	24"	lilac	Spring–summer	ordinary garden soil	Broad, dense mats of foliage.
Veronica spicata Veronica	s-p -sh	18"	lav-bl, rosy -pink	June–frost	well-dr	'Rose Veronica'-pink. 'Blue Spires Veronica' -lavender-blue.

PERENNIALS (CONTINUED)

Common Name Botannical Name	Sun/ Shade	Height	Flower Color	Flower Timing	Soil Type	Remarks
Viola spicata Viola	s-sh	6–8″	violet, bl, pur, wht, yw	Spring	adaptable	Tend to reseed themselves.

CROSS-INDEX: COMMON NAMES TO BOTANICAL NAMES

In the index following, all plants that were listed by botanical names in the plant list on the previous pages are again listed this time in alphabetical order by their common names. The botanical name follows the common name so that the botanical list can be consulted, and all common names known to the author are listed. For example, the pfitzer juniper is listed as both "pfitzer" and "Juniper, pfitzer." *Vinca minor* is listed under both "periwinkle" and "myrtle," since both names are commonly used.

Additional information about each plant is also given. The preceding list was divided into Shade trees; Small ornamental trees; Deciduous ornamental shrubs; Broadleaf evergreen shrubs; Narrowleaf evergreen trees; Narrowleaf evergreen shrubs; Specialty plants; Groundcovers; Vines; and Perennials. Included after the botanical name for each plant in this list are abbreviations indicating the best uses to be made of it. These abbreviations and their meanings are as follows:

(S) Plant is suitable for use as a specimen plant.

(A) Plant works well as an accent plant within a planting unit.

(M) Plant is suitable for massing in numbers.

(H) Plant is suitable for hedging.

(W) Plant is good for windbreaks.

In some cases, several of these abbreviations may follow one plant name, meaning that the plant has multiple uses, depending on the situation. In other cases, no abbreviation follows the plant name. This simply means that the plant has already been labeled according to its best use in the plant list by botanical names. For instance, many of the vines are only suitable for use as vines or groundcovers. Since those two categories are already given in the list by botanical names, no further use is specified in this list.

Abelia Glossy: *Abelia X grandiflora* (A) (M)

Abelia Pink: *Abelia X 'Edward Goucher'* (A) (M)

Akebia: *Akebia quinata*

Alder, Black: *Alnus glutinosa* (M)

Alder, Speckled: *Alnus rugosa* (M)

Alder, White: *Alnus rhombifolia* (M)

Almond, Flowering: *Prunus, glandulosa* (M)

Althaea: *Hibiscus syriacus* (A) (M)

Amorpha, Indigobush: *Amorpha fruiticosa* (M)

Arborvitae, Berkman's Golden: *Thuja occidentalis* 'Aurea Nana' (S) (A) (H) (W)

Arborvitae, Dark Green: *Thuja occidentalis* 'Nigra' (S) (A) (H) (W)

Arborvitae, Mission: *Thuja occidentalis* 'Techny' (H) (W)

Ash, Arizona: *Fraxinus velutina*

Ash, Autumn Applause: *Fraxinus americana* 'Autumn Applause' (S)

Ash, Blue: *Fraxinus quadrangulata*

Ash, Champagne County: *Fraxinus americana* 'Champaign County' (S)

Ash, Elk Grove: *Fraxinus americana* 'Elk Grove'

Ash, Green: *Fraxinus pennsylvanica*

Ash, Honeyshade: *Fraxinus pennsylvanica* 'Honeyshade'

Ash, Moraine: *Fraxinus holotricha* 'Moraine'

Ash, Marshall's Seedless: *Fraxinus pennsylvanica* 'Marshall's Seedless'

Ash, Patmore: *Fraxinus pennsylvanica* 'Patmore'

Ash, Rosehill: *Fraxinus americana* 'Rosehill' (S)

Ash, White: *Fraxinus americana*

Aspen, Quaking: *Populus tremuloides* (S) (A) (M)

Autumnolive: *Elaeagnus umbellata* (S) (A) (M)

Azalea, Kurume: *Rhododendron obtusum* (A) (M)

Azalea, Mollis hybrids: *Rhododendron X kosteranum* (A) (M)

Baldcypress, Common: *Taxodium distichum* (S)

Bamboo: *Bambusa species* (S) (A)

Bamboo, Pygmy: *Bambusa arundaria* (A) (M)

Bamboo, Heavenly: *Nandina domestica* (A) (M)

Barberry, Crimson Pygmy: *Berberis thunbergii* 'Nana' (S) (A) (M) (H)

Barberry, Golden: *Berberis thunbergii* 'Aurea' (S) (A)

Barberry, Japanese: *Berberis thunbergii* (M) (H)

Barberry, Kobold: *Berberis thunbergii* 'Kobold' (M) (H)

Barberry, Korean: *Berberis koreana* (M)

Barberry, Mentor: *Berberis X mentorensis* (M) (H)

Barberry, Paleleaf: *Berberis candidula* (M) (H)

Barberry, Redleaf: *Berberis thunbergii* 'Atropurpurea' (A) (S) (M) (H)

Barberry, Rosy Glow: *Berberis thunbergii* 'Rosy Glow' (S) (A) (M)

Barberry, Truehedge: *Berberis thunbergii* 'Erecta' (H)

Barberry, William Penn™: *Berberis gladwynensis* 'William Penn' (M) (H)

Barberry, Wintergreen: *Berberis julianae* (M) (H)

Basswood: *Tilia americana* (S)

Bearberry: *Arctostaphylos uva-ursi*

Beautyberry: *Callicarpa dichotoma* (A) (M)

Beautybush: *Kolkwitzia amabilis* (A) (M)

Beech, American: *Fagus grandifolia* (S)

Beech, Copper: *Fagus sylvatica* 'Atropurpurea' (S)

Birch, Canoe: *Betula papyrifera*

Birch, Cutleaf Weeping: *Betula pendula laciniata* (S) (A)

Birch, European White: *Betula pendula* (S) (A)

Birch, Gray: *Betula populifolia* (S) (A)

Birch, Japanese White *Betula platyphylla japonica* (S) (A)

Birch, Monarch: *Betula maximowiczlana* (S) (A)

Birch, Paper White: *Betula papyrifera* (S) (A)

Birch, Purple Rain™: *Betula pendula* 'Monle' (S) (A)

Birch, River: *Betula nigra* (S) (A)

Birch, Whitebarked Himalayan: *Betula jacquemantii* (S) (A)

Birch, Whitespire: *Betula plataphylla japonica* (S) (A)

Bittersweet: *Celastris scandens*

Bittersweet, Oriental: *Celastris orbiculatus*

Bishop's Weed, Variegated: *Aegopodium podagraria* 'Variegatum'

Bluebeard, Blue Mist: *Caryopteris incana* (M)

Box, Common: *Buxus sempervirens* (S) (M) (H)

Box, Littleleaf: *Buxus microphylla* (S) (M) (H)

Boxwood, Edging: *Buxus sempervirens* 'Suffruticosa' (M) (H)

Boxwood, Wintergreen: *Buxus microphylla* 'koreana' (S) (M) (H)

Buckeye, Bottlebrush: *Aesculus parviflora* (A)

Buckeye, Ohio: *Aesculus glabra*

Bugle, Carpet: *Ajuga reptans* 'Atropurpurea'

Bugle, Curly: *Ajuga pyramidalis* 'Metallica Crispa'

Bugle, Red: *Ajuga reptans* 'Rubra'

Bugle, Variegated: *Ajuga reptans* 'Variegata'

Burningbush: *Euonymus alata* (S) (A)

Burningbush, Dwarf: *Euonymus alata* 'Compacta' (S) (A) (M)

Butterflybush: *Buddleia davidii* (A) (M)

Candytuft: *Iberis sempervirens*

Catalpa, Western: *Catalpa speciosa*

Catawba: *Catalpa speciosa*

Cedar, Atlas Blue: *Cedrus atlantica glauca* (S)

Cedar, Deodar: *Cedrus deodara* (S)

Cedar, Dwarf Japanese: *Cryptomeria japonica* 'Nana' (S)

Cedar, Japanese: *Cryptomeria japonica*

Cedar of Lebanon: *Cedrus libani* (S)

Cherry, Kwantzan: *Prunus serrulata* 'Kwanzan' (S) (A)

Cherry, Manchu: *Prunus tomentosa* (M)

Cherry, Nanking: *Prunus tomentosa* (M)

Cherry, Purple Leaf Sand: *Prunus X cistena* (S) (A)

Cherry, Weeping Higan: *Prunus subhirtella* 'Pendula' (S)

Cherry, Western Sand: *Prunus besseyi* (S) (A) (M)

Chestnut, Chinese: *Castanea mollissima*

Chinafir, Common: *Cunninghamia lanceolata*

Chokeberry, Black: *Aronia melanocarpa* (M)

Chokeberry, Red: *Aronia arbutifolia* (M)

Cinquefoil: *Potentilla fruiticosa* (M)

Clematis, Henry: *Clematis X lawsoniana* 'Henryi' (S)

Clematis, Jackman: *Clematis X jackmannii* (S)

Clematis, Sweet Autumn: *Clematis dioscoreifolia* 'Robusta' (S)

Coffeetree, Kentucky: *Gymnocladus dioica*

Coralberry, Chenault: *Symphoricarpos X* 'Chenaultii' (M)

Coralberry, Indiancurrent: *Symphoricarpos vulgaris-orbiculatus* (A) (M)

Corktree, Amur: *Phellodendron amurense*

Cotoneaster, Coral Beauty: *Cotoneaster dommeri* 'Coral Beauty' (A) (M)

Cotoneaster, Cranberry: *Cotoneaster apiculatus* (M)

Cotoneaster, Creeping: *Cotoneaster adpressus* (M)

Cotoneaster, Dwarf Cranberry: *Cotoneaster apiculata* 'Nana' (A) (M)

Cotoneaster, Early: *Cotoneaster adpressus praecox* (M)

Cotoneaster, Gray-leaved: *Cotoneaster glaucophyllus* (M)

Cotoneaster, Lowfast: *Cotoneaster dammeri* 'Lowfast' (M)

Cotoneaster, Pecking: *Cotoneaster acutifolius* (M) (H)

Cotoneaster, Rependens: *Cotoneaster salicifolius* 'Rependens' (M)

Cotoneaster, Rock: *Cotoneaster horizontalis* (M)

Cotoneaster, Round Rock: *Cotoneaster horizontalis* 'Robustus' (M)

Cotoneaster, Shangri-La™: *Cotoneaster X* 'Monter' (M)

Cotoneaster, Spreading: *Cotoneaster divaricatus* (M) (H)

Cottonwood, Cottonless: *Populus deltoides*

Crabapple, Carmine: *Malus atrosanguinea* (S) (A) (M)

Crabapple, Sargent: *Malus sargentii* (S) (A)

Crabapple varieties: *Malus species*

Crabapple, Zumi: *Malus X zumi calocarpa* (S) (A) (M)

Cranberrybush: *Viburnum opulus* (S) (M)

Cranberrybush, Dwarf: *Viburnum opulus* 'Nanum' (M)

Cranberry, Highbush: *Viburnum trilobum* (S) (M) (H)

Crape Myrtle: *Lagerstroemia indica* (S)

Creeper, Madame Galen: *Campsis X tagliabuana*

Creeper, Trumpet: *Campsis radicans*

Creeper, Virginia: *Parthenocissus quinquifoli*

Crown Vetch: *Coronilla varia*

Cryptomeria, Japanese: *Cryptomeria japonica*

Current, Alpine: *Ribes alpinum* (M) (H)

Cypress, Arizona: *Cupressus arizonica* (S) (W)

Cypress, Blue Italian: *Cupressus sempervirens* 'Glauca' (S)

Cypress, Stewart Golden: *Chamaecyparis lawsoniana* 'Stewartii' (S) (W)

Deutzia, Lemoine: *Deutzia X lemoinei* (M)

Deutzia, Pink Slender: *Deutzia X rosea* (M)

Deutzia, Pride of Rochester: *Deutzia scabra* (M)

Deutzia, Slender: *Deutzia gracilis* (M)

Dogwood, Bailey's: *Cornus sericea* (A) (M)

Dogwood, Cherokee Chief: *Cornus florida* 'Cherokee Chief' (S) (A)

Dogwood, Cherokee Princess: *Cronus florida* 'Cherokee Princess' (S) (A)

Dogwood, Cloud Nine: *Cornus florida* 'Cloud Nine' (S) (A)

Dogwood, Corneliancherry: *Cornus mas* (M)

Dogwood, Flowering: *Cornus florida* (S) (A)

Dogwood, Gray: *Cornus racemosa* (M)

Dogwood, Kousa: *Cornus kousa*

Dogwood, Pendula: *Cornus florida* 'Pendula' (S) (A)

Dogwood, Redosier: *Cornus stolonifera* (A) (M)

Dogwood, Tatarian: *Cornus alba*

Dogwood, Yellowtwig: *Cornus stolonifera* 'Flaviramea' (A) (M)

Dutchman's Pipe: *Aristolochia durior*

Elaeagnus, Autumn: *Elaeagnus umbellata* (A) (M)

Eldor, Golden: *Sambucus nigra* 'Aurea-variegata' (A) (M)

Elm, Chinese: *Ulmus parvifolia*

Euonymus, Bigleaf Wintercreeper: *Euonymus fortunei vegeta*

Euonymus, Dupont: *Euonymus kiautschovica* 'Dupont' (M) (H)

Euonymus, Dwarf: *Euontmus japonica* 'Microphylla' (M)

Euonymus, Dwarf Winged: *Euonymus alata* 'Compacta' (S) (A) (M)

Euonymus, Emerald Cushion: *Euonymous fortunei* 'Emerald Cushion' (M)

Euonymus, Emerald Gaiety: *Euonymus fortunei* 'Emeraid Gaiety' (A) (M)

Euonymus, Emerald 'n Gold: *Euonymus fortunei* 'Emerald 'n Gold' (A) (M)

Euonymus, Emerald Pride: *Euonymus fortunei* 'Emerald Pride' (M)

Euonymus, Golden: *Euonymus japonica aurea-marginata* (A)

Euonymus, Golden Prince: *Euonymus fortunei* 'Golden Prince' (A) (M)

Euonymus, Gold Spot: *Euonymus japonica* 'Aurea-marginata' (A)

Euonymus, Japanese: *Euonymus japonica* 'Grandifolia' (M)

Euonymus, Jewel: *Euonymus kiautschovica* 'Jewel' (M) (H)

Euonymus, Kewensis: *Euonymus fortunei* 'Kewensis' (M)

Euonymus, Large-leaf: *Euonymus kiautschovica* (M)

Euonymus, Manhattan: *Euonymus kiautschovica* 'Manhattan' (A) (M) (H)

Euonymus, Medium-leaf: *Euonymus kiautschovica* (M)

Euonymus, Pauli: *Euonymus paulii* (M) (H)

Euonymus, Purpleleaf Wintercreeper: *Euonymus fortunei* 'Colorata'

Euonymus, Sarcoxie: *Euonymus fortunei* 'Sarcoxie' (A) (H)

Euonymus, Silver King: *Euonymus japonica* 'Silver King' (A)

Euonymus, Winged: *Euonymus alata* (S) (A)

Euonymus, Wintercreeper: *Euonymus fortunei radicans*

Falsecypress, Ellwood: *Chamaecyparis lawsoniana* 'Ellwoodii' (S)

Falsecypress, Hinoki: *Chamaecyparis obtusa* (S)

Falsecypress, Sawara: *Chamaecyparis pisifera* (S)

Fescue, Blue: *Festuca glauca* (S) (A)

Fir, Balsam: *Abies balsamea* (S)

Fir, Douglas: *Pseudotsuga menziesii* (S)

Fir, Fraser: *Abies fraseri* (S)

Fir, Noble: *Abies procera* (S)

Fir, Veitch: *Abies veitchii* (S)

Fir, White: *Abies concolor* (S)

Firethorn: *Pyracantha coccinea* (A) (M) (H)

Fleece Vine, Silver: *Polygonum aubertii*

Forsythia, Beatrix Farrand: *Forsythia X intermedia* (M)

Forsythia, Bronx: *Forsythia viridissima* 'Bronzensis' (M)

Forsythia, Golden Bell: *Forsythia viridissima* (M)

Forsythia, Karl Sax: *Forsythia X intermedia* (M)

Forsythia, Lynwood Gold: *Forsythia X intermedia* (M)

Forsythia, Siebold: *Forsythia suspensa* 'Sieboldi' (M)

Forsythia, Spring Glory: *Forsythia X intermedia* (M)
Forsythia, Purple: *Cotinus coggygria* (S)

Garland Flower: *Daphne cneorum* (M)
Ginkgo: *Ginkgo biloba*
Goldenraintree: *Koelreuteria paniculata (S)* (A)
Grass, Dwarf Fountain: *Pennisetum alopeuroides* 'Hamelin' (S) (A) (M)
Grass, Hardy Pampas: *Erianthus ravenae (S)* (A) (M)
Grass, Maiden: *Miscanthus sinensis* 'Gracillimus' (S) (A) (M)
Grass, Pampas: *Cortaderia selloana* (S) (A) (M)
Grass, Purple Fountain: *Pennisetum setaceum* 'Rubrum' (S) (A) (M)
Gum, Black: *Nyssa sylvatica*

Hackberry, Common: *Celtis acidentalis*
Hackberry, Sugar: *Celtis laevigata*
Hawthorn, Cockspur: *Crataegus crus-galli* (S) (A) (M)
Hawthorn, Downy: *Crataegus mollis* (S) (A) (M)
Hawthorn, Lavelle: *Crataegus X lavellei* (S) (A) (M)
Hawthorn, Paul's Scarlet: *Crataegus oxycantha* 'Paulii' (S) (A)
Hawthorn, Thornless Cockspur: *Crataegus crusgalli inemis* (S) (M) (A)
Hawthorn, Washington: *Crataegus phaenopyrum* (S) (A) (M)
Hawthorn, Winter King: *Crataegus viridis* 'Winter King' (S) (A) (M)
Hemlock, Canadian: *Tsuga canadensis* (S) (H)
Hickory, Shagbark: *Carya ovata*
Holly, Blue Angel: *Ilex X meserveae* 'Blue Angel' (A) (M) (H)
Holly, Blue Girl: *Ilex X meserveae* 'Blue Girl' (A) (M)
Holly, Blue Prince: *Ilex X meserveae* 'Blue Prince' (S)
Holly, Blue Princess: *Ilex X meserveae* 'Blue Princess' (S)
Holly, Blue Stallion: *Ilex X meserveae* 'Blue Stallion' (S)
Holly, Burford: *Ilex cornuta* 'Burfordii' (A) (M) (H)
Holly, Carissa: *Ilex cornuta* 'Carissa' (A) (M) (H)
Holly, China Boy: *Ilex X meserveae* 'China Boy' (S)
Holly, China Girl: *Ilex X meserveae* 'China Girl' (S) (M)
Holly, Dazzler: *Ilex cornuta* 'Dazzler' (A) (M) (H)
Holly, Dwarf Burford: *Ilex cornuta* 'Burfordii Nana' (A) (M) (H)
Holly, Dwarf Chinese: *Ilex cornuta* 'Rotunda' (M) (H)
Holly, Dwarf Japanese: *Ilex crenata* 'Compacta' (M) (H)
Holly, Dwarf Yaupon: *Ilex vomitoria* 'Nana' (M) (H)

Holly, Foster: *Ilex X attenutata* 'Fosterii' (S)
Holly, Heller's Japanese: *Ilex crenata* 'Helleri' (M) (H)
Holly, Hetz Japanese: *Ilex crenata* 'Hetzii' (M) (H)
Holly, Needlepoint: *Ilex cornuta* 'Delcambre' (S) (A)
Holly, Winterberry: *Ilex verticillata* (A) (M)
Holly, Yaupon: *Ilex vomitoria* (A) (M)
Hollygrape, Compact Oregon: *Mahonia aquafolium* 'Compacta' (A) (M)
Hollygrape, Oregon: *Mahonia aquafolium* (A) (M)
Honeylocust, Green Glory: *Gleditsia triacanthos* 'Green Glory'
Honeylocust, Imperial: *Gleditsia triacanthos* 'Imperial'
Honeylocust, Moraine: *Gleditsia triacanthos* 'Moraine'
Honeylocust, Rubylace: *Gleditsia triacanthos* 'Rubylace' (S)
Honeylocust, Shademaster: *Gleditsia triacanthos* 'Shademaster'
Honeylocust, Skyline: *Gleditsia triacanthos* 'Skyline'
Honeylocust, Sunburst: *Gleditsia triacanthos* 'Sunburst' (S)
Honeylocust, Thornless: *Gleditsia triacanthos inermis*
Honeysuckle, Arnold Gotha: *Lonicera X amoena* 'Arnoldiana' (M) (H)
Honeysuckle, Clavey's Dwarf: *Lonicera Tatarica* 'Clavey' (M)
Honeysuckle, Fragrant: *Lonicera fragrantissima* (M) (H)
Honeysuckle, Gold Flame: *Lonicera heckrottii*
Honeysuckle, Hall's: *Lonicera japonica* 'Halliana'
Honeysuckle, Morrow: *Lonicera morrowii* (M) (H)
Honeysuckle, Purple Leaf: *Lonicera japonica* 'Purpurea'
Honeysuckle, Tatarian: *Lonicera tatarica* (M) (H)
Honeysuckle, Winter: *Lonicera fragrantissima* (M) (H)
Honeysuckle, Zabeli: *Loncicera tatarica* 'Zabeli' (M) (H)
Hophornbeam, American: *Ostrya virginiana*
Hornbeam, American: *Carpinus caroliniana*
Hornbeam, European: *Carpinus betulus*
Horsechestnut, Common: *Aesculus hippocastanum*
Horsechestnut, Red: *Aesculus X carnea*
Hydrangea, Annabelle: *Hydrangea arborescens* (S) (A)
Hydrangea, Japanese: *Hydrangea macrophylla* (S) (A)
Hydrangea, Oakleaf: *Hydrangea quercifolia* (M)
Hydrangea, Pee Gee (P.G.): *Hydrangea paniculata* 'Grandiflora' (S) (A)
Hydrangea, 'Snow Hill' (A.G.): *Hydrangea arborescens* 'Grandiflora' (S) (A)

Ivy, Boston: *Parthenocissus tricuspidata* 'Veitchii'

Ivy, Bulgarian: *Hedera helix* 'Bulgarian'
Ivy, Engleman: *Parthenocissus quinquifolia* 'Englesmannii'
Ivy, English: *Hedera helix*

Jetbead, Black: *Rhodotypos scandens* (M)
Juneberry, Dwarf: *Amelanchier stolonifera* (M)
Juniper, Ames: *Juniperus chinensis* 'Ames' (S) (A) (W)
Juniper, Andorra: *Juniperus horizontalis* 'Plumosa' (M)
Juniper, Arcadia: *Juniperus sabina* 'Arcadia' (M)
Juniper, Armstrong: *Juniperus chinensis* 'Armstrong' (M)
Juniper, Bar Harbor: *Junipers horizontalis* 'Bar Harbor' (M)
Juniper, Blaauw's: *Juniperus chinensis* 'Blaauw' (S) (W)
Juniper, Broadmoor: *Juniperus sabina* 'Broadmoor' (M)
Juniper, Buffalo: *Juniperus sabina* 'Buffalo' (M)
Juniper, Blue Creeper: *Junipers scopulorum* 'Monam' (M)
Juniper, Blue Danube: *Juniperus sabina* 'Blue Danube' (M)
Juniper, Blue Haven: *Juniperus scopulorurm* 'Blue Haven' (S) (A) (W) (H)
Juniper, Blue Horizon: *Juniperus horizontalis* 'Blue Horizon' (M)
Juniper, Blue Pacific: *Juniperus conferta* 'Blue Pacific' (M)
Juniper, Blue Point: *Juniperus chinensis* 'Blue Point' (S)
Juniper, Blue Rug: *Juniperus horizontalis* 'Wiltonii' (M)
Juniper, Blue Vase: *Juniperus chinensis* 'Blue vase' (A) (M)
Juniper, Canaert: *Juniperus virginiana* 'Canaertii' (S) (A) (H)
Juniper, Cologreen: *Juniperus scopulorum* 'Cologreen' (S) (A) (W)
Juniper, Compact Andorra: *Juniperus horizontalis* 'Youngstown' (M)
Juniper, Gold Coast: *Juniperus chinensis* 'Aurea' (A) (M)
Juniper, Gray Gleam: *Juniperus scopulorum* 'Gray Gleam' (S) (W)
Juniper, Dwarf Procumbens: *Juniperus procumbens* 'Nana' (M)
Juniper, Goldtip Pfitzer: *Juniper chinensis* 'Aureo-Pfitzerana' (S) (A) (M)
Juniper, Green Sargent: *Juniperus chinensis* 'Sargentii Viridis' (M)
Juniper, Hetz: *Juniperus chinensis* 'Glauca Hetzii' (M)
Juniper, Hillspire: *Juniperus virginiana* 'Cupressifolia' (W)
Juniper, Hollywood: *Juniperus chinensis* 'Torulosa' (S) (A)
Juniper, Hughes: *Juniperus horizontalis* 'Hughes' (M)
Juniper, Japgarden: *Juniperus procumbens*
Juniper, Kallay Pfitzer: *Juniperus chinensis* 'Pfitzerana Kallay' (M)
Juniper, Keteleer: *Juniperus chinensis* 'Keteleeri' (W)
Juniper, Maneyi: *Juniperus chinensis* 'Maneyi' (A) (M)

Juniper, Manhattan Blue: *Juniperus virginiana* 'Manhattan Blue' (S) (W)
Juniper, Meyer: *Juniperus squamata* 'Meyeri' (S) (A)
Juniper, Mint Julep: *Juniperus chinensis* 'Mint Julep' (S) (A) (M)
Juniper, Medora: *Juniperus scopulorum* 'Medora' (S) (A)
Juniper, Moordense: *Juniperus sabina* 'Moordense Monard' (M)
Juniper, Mordigan Pfitzer: *Juniperus pfitzeriana compacta* 'Mordigan' (M)
Juniper, New Blue Tamarix: *Juniperus sabina* 'New Blue' (S) (A) (M)
Juniper, Nick's Compact Pfitzer: *Juniperus chinensis* 'Nick's Compact' (M)
Juniper, Old Gold: *Juniperus chinensis* 'Armstrong Aurea' (A) (M)
Juniper, Oxford Green: *Juniperus virgiana* 'Oxford Green' (S) (W)
Juniper, Ozark Compact Pfitzer: *Juniperus chinensis* 'Sarcoxie' (M)
Juniper, Pfitzer: *Juniperus chinensis* 'Pfitzerana' (M) (W)
Juniper, Procumbens: *Junipers procumbens* (M)
Juniper, Robusta Green: *Juniperus chinensis* 'Robusta Green' (S) (A)
Juniper, San Jose: *Juniperus chinensis* 'San Jose' (M)
Juniper, Sargent: *Juniperus chinensis* 'Sargenttii Glauca' (M)
Juniper, Savin: *Juniperus sabina* (M)
Juniper, Scandia: *Juniperus sabina* 'Scandia' (M)
Juniper, Sea Green: *Juniperus chinensis* 'Sea Green' (S) (A) (M)
Juniper, Sky Rocket: *Juniperus virginiana* 'Sky Rocket' (S)
Juniper, Spartan: *Juniperus chinensis* 'Densaerecta' (S) (A)
Juniper, Spiney Greek: *Juniperus excelsia* 'Stricta' (S) (W)
Juniper, Table Top Blue: *Juniperus scopulorum* 'Table Top Blue' (M)
Juniper, Tamarix: *Juniperus sabina* 'Tamariscifolia' (S) (A) (M)
Juniper, 'Turquoise': *Juniperus horizontalis* 'Turquoise' (M)
Juniper, Von Ehron: *Juniperus sabina* 'Von Ehron' (S)
Juniper, Welch: *Juniperus scopulorum* 'Wetchii' (S) (W)
Juniper, Wichita Blue: *Juniperus scopulorum* 'Wichita Blue' (S) (W)
Juniper, Yukon Belle: *Juniperus horizontalis* 'Yukon Belle' (M)

Katsuratree: *Cercidiphyllum japonicum*
Kerria: *Kerria japonica* (M)
Kudzu Vine: *Pueraria lobata*

Larch, European: *Larix decidua*
Larch, Golden: *Pseudolarix kaempferi* (S)
Larch, Japanese: *Larix kaempferi*
Ligustrum, Curly-leaf: *Ligustrum lucidum* 'Recurvifolum' (A) (M)

Ligustrum, Waxleaf: *Ligustrum japonicum* (A) (M) (H)

Lilac, Common: *Syringa vulgaris* (M)

Lilac, Dwarf Korean: *Syringa palibinum* (M) (H)

Lilac, French Hybrids: *Syringa vulgaris* (S) (A) (M)

Lilac, Japanese Tree: *Syringa reticulata* (S)

Lilac, Persian: *Syringa X persica* (S) (M)

Lilac, Rothomagensis: *Syringa X Persica*

Linden, American: *Tilia americana*

Linden, Greenspire: *Tilia cordata* 'Greenspire' (S)

Linden, Littleleaf: *Tilia cordata*

Linden, Redmond: *Tilia X euchlora* 'Redmond' (S)

Liriope, Green: *Liriope muscari* (A) (M)

Liriope, Variegated: *Liriope muscari* 'Variegata' (A) (M)

Locust, Black: *Robina pseudoacacia*

Locust, Globe: *Robinia pseudoacacia* 'globosa' (S) (A)

Londonplanetree: *Platanus X acerifolia*

Londonplanetree, Bloodgood: *Platanus acerifolia* 'Bloodgood strain' (S)

Magnolia, Saucer: *Magnolia X soulangiana* (S)

Magnolia, Southern: *Magnolia grandiflora* (S)

Magnolia, Star: *Magnolia stellata* (S)

Magnolia, Sweet Bay: *Magnolia virginiana* (S) (A)

Mahonia, Leatherleaf: *Mahonia bealei* (M)

Maple, Armstrong Red: *Acer rubrum* 'Armstrong' (S)

Maple, Autumn Flame: *Acer rubrum* 'Autumn Flame' (S)

Maple, Amur: *Acer ginnala* (S) (A) (M)

Maple, Dwarf Amur: *Acer ginnala compacta* (S) (A)

Maple, Bloodgood: *Acer palmatum* 'Bloodsood' (S) (A)

Maple, Burgandy: *Acer palmatum* 'Burgandy' (S) (A)

Maple, Cleveland: *Acer platanoides* 'Cleveland' (S)

Maple, Columnar: *Acer platanoides* 'Columnaire' (S)

Maple, Crimson King: *Acer platanoides* 'Crimson King' (S)

Maple, Dissectum: *Acer palmatlum* 'Dissectum' (S) (A)

Maple, Dwarf Japanese: *Acer palmatum* (S) (A)

Maple, Emerald Queen: *Acer platanoides* 'Emerald Queen' (S)

Maple, Fassen's Black Norway: *Acer platanoides* 'Fassen's Black' (S)

Maple, Fullmoon: *Acer japonicum* (S) (A)

Maple, Globe Sugar: *Acer saccharum* 'Globosum' (S) (A)

Maple, Greenlace: *Acer platanoides* 'Greenlace' (S)

Maple, Green Mountain: *Acer saccharum* 'Green Mountain' (S)

Maple, Japanese: *Acer japonicum* (S) (A)

Maple, Newton Sentry: *Acer saccharum* 'Newton Sentry' (S) (A)

Maple, Norway: *Acer platanoides* (S)

Maple, October Glory: *Acer rubrum* 'October Glory' (S)

Maple, Oshi-Beni: *Acer palmatum* 'Oshi-Beni' (S) (A)

Maple, Paperbark: *Acer griseum* (M)

Maple, Red: *Acer rubrum* (S)

Maple, Red Sunset: *Acer rubrum* 'Red Sunset' (S)

Maple, Schwedler's: *Acer platanoides* 'Schwedleri' (S)

Maple, Silver: *Acer saccharinum*

Maple, Sugar: *Acer saccharinum* (S)

Maple, Summershade: *Acer platanoides* 'Summershade' (S)

Maple, Tatarian: *Acer tataricum* (M)

Maple, Variegated Leaved: *Acer platanoides* 'Drummondii' (S)

Mimosa: *Albizia julibrissin* (S)

Mockorange, Dwarf Sweet: *Philadelphus coronarius* 'Nana' (M)

Mockorange, Glacier: *Philadelphus X virginalis* (M)

Mockorange, Golden: *Philadelphus coronarius aureus* (S) (A) (M)

Mockorange, Lemoine: *Philadelphus lemoinei* (M)

Mockorange, Minnesota Snowflake: *Philadelphus X virginalis* 'Minnesota Snow Flake' (M)

Mockorange, Natchez: *Philadelphus X virginalis* 'Natchez' (M)

Mockorange, Silver Showers: *Philadelphus X lemoinei* 'Silver Showers' (M)

Mockorange, Sweet: *Philadelphus coronarius* (M)

Mondo grass: *Ophiopogon japonicus* (A) (M)

Mountain Laurel: *Kalmia latifolia* (A) (M)

Mother-of-Thyme: *Thymus serpyllum*

Mountainash, European: *Sorbus aucuparia* (S) (A)

Mulberry, White: *Morus alba*

Mulberry, Fruitless: *Morus platinifolia*

Mulberry, Chaparral Weeping: *Morus alba* 'Chaparral' (S) (A)

Myrtle: *Vinca minor*

Myrtle, Crape: *Lagerstroemia indica*

Nandina, Harbour Dwarf: *Nandina domestica* 'Harbour Dwarf' (M)

Ninebark: *Physocarpus opulifolius* (A) (M)

Ninebark, Dwarf: *Physocarpus monogymus* (A) (M)

Ninebark, Goldleaf: *Physocarpus opulifolius* 'Luteus' (A) (M)

Oak, Bur: *Quercus macrocarpa* (S)

Oak, Chinkapin: *Quercus muehlenbergii*

Oak, English: *Quercus robur*

Oak, Northern Red: *Quercus borealis maxima* (S)

Oak, Pin: *Quercus palustris* (S)

Oak, Sawtooth: *Quercus acutissima*

Oak, Scarlet: *Quercus coccinea* (S)

Oak, Shingle: *Quercus imbricaria*

Oak, Shumard: *Quercus shummardii* (S)

Oak, Southern Live: *Quercus virginiana*

Oak, Upright English: *Quercus robrur* 'Fastigata' (S)

Oak, White: *Quercus alba*

Oregon Grape, Creeping: *Mahonia repens* (M)

Pachysandra: *Pachysandra terminalis*

Pagodatree, Japanese: *Sophora japonica*

Pampas grass: *Cortaderia selloana* (S) (A)

Paulownia, Royal: *Paulownia tamentosa*

Pawpaw, Common: *Asimina triloba*

Pea Shrub: *Caragana arborescens* (M)

Pea Shrub, Pygmy: *Caragana pygmea* (M)

Peach, Cardinal Flowering: *Prunus persica* 'Cardinal' (S) (A)

Peach, Flowering: *Prunus persica* (S) (A)

Peach, Iceberg Flowering: *Prunus persica* 'Iceberg' (S) (A)

Peach, Pink Charming Flowering: *Prunus persica* 'Pink Charming' (S) (A)

Peach, Rutgers Flowering: *Prunus persica* 'Rutgers' (S) (A)

Pear, Aristocrat: *Pyrus calleryana* 'Aristocrat' (S) (A)

Pear, Bradford: *Pyrus calleryana* 'Bradford' (S) (A)

Pear, Capital: *Pyrus calleryana* 'Capital' (S) (A) (M) (W)

Pear, Redspire: *Pyrus calleryana* 'Redspire' (S) (A) (M) (W)

Pear, Whitehouse: *Pyrus calleryana* 'Whitehouse' (S) (A) (M) (W)

Pearlush: *Exochorda racemosa* (M)

Pecan: *Carya illinoinensis*

Periwinkle: *Vinca minor*

Periwinkle, Bigleaf: *Vinca major*
Periwinkle, Bowles: *Vinca minor* 'Bowlesii'
Periwinkle, White: *Vinca minor* 'Alba'
Persimmon: *Diospyros virginiana*
Pepperbush, Sweet: *Clethra alnifolia* (A) (M)
Pfitzer: *Juniperus chinensis* 'Pfitzerana' (M) (W)
Pfitzer, Nick's Compact: *Juniperus chinensis* 'Nick's Compact' (M)
Pfitzer, Kallay: *Juniperus chinensis* 'Kallay' (M)
Pfitzer, Ozark Compact: *Juniperus chinensis* 'Sarcoxie' (M)
Photenia, Fraser: *Photenia X fraseri* (M) (H)
Pine, Austrian: *Pinus nigra* (S) (M) (W)
Pine, Columnar Scotch: *Pinus sylvestvis* 'Fastigata' (S)
Pine, Dwarf, Mugo: *Pinus mugo* 'Compacta' (S) (A)
Pine, Dwarf Bluescotch: *Pinus sylvestvis* 'Nana glauca' (S)
Pine, Dwarf Eastern White: *Pinus strobus* 'Nana' (S) (A)
Pine, French Blue: *Pinus sylvestris* 'French Blue' (S)
Pine, Eastern White: *Pinus strobus* (S) (M) (W)
Pine, Japanese Black: *Pinus thunbergii* (M) (W)
Pine, Japanese Red: *Pinus densiflora* (M) (W)
Pine, Japanese Umbrella *Pinus densiflora* 'Umbraculifera' (S)
Pine, Limber: *Pinus flexilis* (M)
Pine, Ponderosa: *Pinus ponderosa* (M) (W)
Pine, Scotch: *Pinus sylvestris* (S) (M)
Pine, Slash: *Pinus elliottii* (M) (W)
Poplar, Bolleana: *Populus alba* 'Bolleana' (S)
Polar, Lombardy: *Populus nigra* 'Italica' (S)
Poplar, Silver: *Populus alba* 'Nivea'
Poplar, Theves: *Populus nigra* 'Theves' (S)
Poplar, White: *Populus alba*
Potentilla: *Potentilla fruticosa* (M)
Potentilla, Abbotswood: *Potentilla fruticosa* 'Abbotswood' (M)
Privet, Amur River North: *Ligustrum amurense* (M) (H)
Privet, Lodense: *Ligustrum vulgare* 'Lodense' (M) (H)
Privet, Regal Border: *Ligustrum obtusifolium regalianum* (M) (H)
Privet, Vicary: *Ligustrum X vicari* (S) (A)
Plum, Cherry: *Prunus cerasifera*
Plum, Krauter's Purple: *Prunus cerasifera* 'Krauter Vesuvius' (S) (A) (M)
Plum, Newport Purple: *Prunus cerasifera* 'Newport' (S) (A)

Plum, Thundercloud: *Prunus cerasifera* 'Thundercloud' (S) (A)
Pyracantha, Gnome: *Pyracanthza angustifolia* 'Gnome' (M) (H)
Pyracantha, Kasan: *Pyracantha coccinea* 'Kasan' (A) (M) (H)
Pyracantha, Lalandi: *Pyracantha coccinea* 'Lalandei' (A) (M) (H)
Pyracantha, Lowboy: *Pyracantha coccinea* 'Lowboy' (A) (M) (H)
Pyracantha, Mojave: *Pyracantha X* 'Mojave' (M) (H)
Pyracantha, Red Elf: *Pyracantha X* 'Red Elf' (A) (M)
Pyracantha, Rutgers: *Pyracantha coccinea* 'Rutgers' (A) (M) (H)
Pyracantha, Wyatti: *Pyracantha coccinea* 'Wyatti' (M) (H)
Pyracantha, Yukon Belle: *Pyracantha angustifolia* 'Yukon Belle' (M) (H)

Quince, Alpine Flowering: *Chaenomeles japonica alpina* (M)
Quince, Common Flowering: *Chaenomeles speciasa* (A) (M)
Quince, Japanese Flowering: *Chaenomeles japonica* (A) (M)

Ratstripper, Paxistima: *Paxistima canby*
Redbud, Eastern: *Cercis canadensis* (S) (A) (M)
Redbud, Forest Pansy: *Cercis canadensis* 'Forest Pansy' (S) (A) (M)
Redbud, Oklahoma: *Cercis canadensis* 'Oklahoma' (S) (A) (M)
Redcedar, Eastern: *Juniperus virginiana* (W)
Redwood, Dawn: *Metasequoia glyptostroboides* (S)
Ribbon grass, Variegated: *Phalaris arundinace variegata* (A) (M)
Rhododendron, Catawba: *Rhododendron catawbiense* (A) (M)
Rhododendron, Carolina: *Rhododendron carolinianum* (A) (M)
Rose-of-Sharon: *Hibiscus syriacus* (A) (M)
Russianolive: *Elaeagnus angustifolia* (S) (M)

Sedum, Dragon's Blood: *Sedum spurium*
Serviceberry, Downy: *Amelanchier arborea* (M)
Sassafras, Common: *Sassafras albidum*
Silktree: *Albizia julibrissin* (S)
Silver Mound: *Artemesia schrmidtiana* 'Nana' (S) (A) (M)
Smoketree, Common: *Cotinus coggygria* (S)
Snowball, Common: *Virburnum opulus* 'Sterile' (S) (M)
Snowball, Japanese: *Viburnum plicatum* (S) (M)
Snowberry: *Symphoricarpos albus* (M)
St. Johnswort, Creeping: *Hypericum linarioides* (M)

St. Johnswort, Golden: *Hypericum frondosum* (S) (M)

St. Johnswort, Kalm: *Hypericum kalmianum* (S) (M)

St. Johnswort, Sungold: *Hypericum patulum* 'Sungold' (S) (M)

Spirea, Anthony Waterer: *Spiraea X bumalda* 'Anthony Waterer' (M)

Spirea, Blue Mist: *Caryopteris incana* (M)

Spirea, Billard: *Spiraea X billardii* (M)

Spirea, Bridalwreath: *Spiraea prunifolia* (A) (M)

Spirea, Bumald: *Spiraea X bumalda* (M)

Spirea, Dolchia: *Spiraea dolchia* (M) (H)

Spirea, Double Bridalwreath: *Spiraea reevsiana* (M) (H)

Spirea, Froebel: *Spiraea X bumalda* 'Froebelii' (M)

Spirea, Garland: *Spiraea X arguta* (M)

Spirea, Goldmound: *Spiraea bumalda* 'Goldmound' (S) (A) (M) (H)

Spirea, Limemound: *Spiraea X bumalda* 'Limemound' (S) (A) (M) (H)

Spirea, Little Princess: *Spiraea X bumalda* 'Little Princess' (M)

Spirea, Red Flowering: *Spiraea japonica* 'Coccinea' (M)

Spirea, Shirobana: *Spiraea japonica* 'Shirobana' (M) (H)

Spirea, Snowmound: *Spiraea nipponica* 'Snowmound' (M)

Spirea, Vanhoutte: *Spiraea X vanhouttei* (A) (M) (H)

Spruce, Bird's Nest: *Picea abies* 'Nidiformis' (S)

Spruce, Black Hills: *Picea glauca* 'Densata' (S)

Spruce, Colorado: *Picea pungens* (S)

Spruce, Colorado Blue: *Picea pungens* 'Glauca' (S)

Spruce, Dwarf Alberta: *Picea glauca* 'Conica' (S) (A)

Spruce, Dwarf Globe Blue: *Picea pungens* 'Globosa' (S) (A)

Spruce, Norway: *Picea glauca* (S)

Spruce, White: *Picea abies* (S)

Spurge, Japanese: *Pachysandra terminalis* (M)

Stephandra, Cutleaf: *Stephandra incisa*

Stonecrop, Goldmoss: *Sedum acre*

Stonecrop, White: *Sedum album*

Sumac, Fragrant: *Rhus aromatica* (M)

Sumac, Staghorn: *Rhus typhina* (A)

Sweetshrub, Common: *Calycanthus floridus* (M)

Sweetgum: *Liquidambar styraciflua* (S)

Sycamore: *Platanus occidentalis*

Tallhedge: *Rhamnus frangula* 'Columnaris' (M) (H)

Tamarisk, Pink Cascade: *Tamarix hispida* 'Pink Cascade' (M)
Tree of Heaven: *Ailanthus altissima*
Tulip tree: *Liriodendron tulipifera* (S)
Tupelo: *Nyssa sylvatica*

Viburnum, Arrowwood: *Viburnum dentatum* (M)
Viburnum, Doublefile: *Viburnum plicatum* 'Tomentosum' (S) (M)
Viburnum, Koreanspice: *Viburnum carlesi* (M)

Appendix B

MEASUREMENTS AND WEIGHTS

To use the conversion-multipliers table on the following page, select the unit from which conversion is to be made, on either the right-hand or left-hand side of the table, and match that with the unit being converted into, on the opposite side of the table. For example, if inches are to be converted into feet, the first line of the table will be used, because it gives inches on the left-hand side and feet on the right-hand side. Then use the multiplier that has the arrow pointing from inches to feet. Using this multiplier (.08333333) times the number of inches you want to convert gives a product that is the equivalent in *feet*. To convert feet into their equivalent in inches, the same line of the table would be used, but the multiplier with the arrow pointing the other way (12.0) would be used since the conversion is now to be reversed. A given number of feet multiplied by the multiplier (12.0) gives a product that is the equivalent in inches. For example:

$$12'' \times .08333333 = 0.9999996 \text{ ft.}$$
$$1'' \times 12.0 = 12''$$

METRIC CONVERSION DATA

LINEAR MEASUREMENTS

U.S. Standard	Metric
1 foot = 12 inches	10 millimeters = 1 centimeter
1 yard = 3 feet	10 centimeters = 1 decimeter

Linear Measurements (continued)

U.S. Standard	Metric
1 rod = 16 1/2 feet	10 decimeters = 1 meter
320 rods = 1 statute mile	10 meters = 1 dekameter
5, 280 feet = 1 statute mile	10 dekameters = 1 hectometer
	10 hectometers = 1 kilometer

Equivalents (rounded off)

U.S. Standard to Metric	Metric to U.S. Standard
1 inch = 2.54 centimeters	1 centimeter = .4 inch
1 inch = 25.4 millimeters	1 millimeter = .04 inch
1 foot = 0.3 meter	1 meter = 3.3 feet
1 yard = 0.9 meter	1 meter = 1.1 yard
1 statute mile = 1.6 kilometer	1 kilometer = 0.6 statute mile

Conversion Multipliers

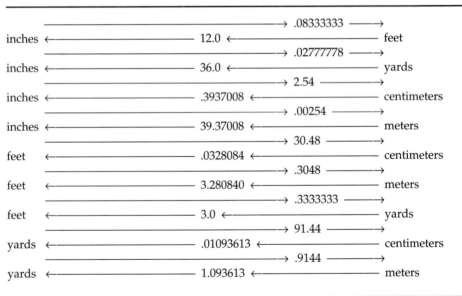

	→ .08333333 →	
inches ←	12.0 ←	feet
	→ .02777778 →	
inches ←	36.0 ←	yards
	→ 2.54 →	
inches ←	.3937008 ←	centimeters
	→ .00254 →	
inches ←	39.37008 ←	meters
	→ 30.48 →	
feet ←	.0328084 ←	centimeters
	→ .3048 →	
feet ←	3.280840 ←	meters
	→ .3333333 →	
feet ←	3.0 ←	yards
	→ 91.44 →	
yards ←	.01093613 ←	centimeters
	→ .9144 →	
yards ←	1.093613 ←	meters

Square-area Measurements

U.S. Standard	Metric
1 square foot = 144 square inches	10 square millimeters = 1 square centimeter
1 square yard = 9 square feet	10 square centimeters = 1 square decimeter
1 square yard = 1, 296 square inches	10 square decimeters = 1 square meter
1 acre = 43, 560 square feet	10 square meters = 1 square dekameter
1 acre = 160 square rods	10 square dekameters = 1 square hectometer
1 square mile = 640 acres	10 square hectometers = 1 square kilometer

Equivalents (rounded off)

U.S. Standard to Metric	Metric to U.S. Standard
1 square inch = 6.5 square centimeters	1 square centimeter = .16 square inch
1 square foot = .009 square meter	1 square meter = 11.0 square feet
1 square yard = .8 square meter	1 square meter = 1.2 square yard

Conversion Multipliers

square inches	←——— 144.0 ←——— →.00694444 →———	square feet
square inches	←——— 1296.0 ←——— →.00771605 →———	square yards
square inches	←——— 1550003 ←——— →6.4516 →———	square centimeters
square inches	←——— 1550.003 ←——— →.00064516 →———	square meters
square feet	←——— 9.0 ←——— →.1111111 →———	square yards
square feet	←——— 10.76391 ←——— →.09290304 →———	square meters
square feet	←——— 43560.0 ←——— →.000022957 →———	acres
square yards	←——— 1.19599 ←——— →.83612736 →———	square meters
square yards	←——— 4840.0 ←——— →.0002066116 →———	acres

WEIGHT MEASUREMENTS*

U.S. Standard	Metric
1 ounce = 437.5 grains	10 milligrams = 1 centigram
1 pound = 16 ounces	10 centigrams = 1 decigram
1 short ton = 2000 pounds	10 decigrams = 1 gram
	100 grams = 1 kilogram

EQUIVALENTS (ROUNDED OFF)

U.S. Standard to Metric	Metric to U.S. Standard
1 grain = 64.8 milligrams	1 milligram = .015 grain
1 ounce = 28.0 grams	1 gram = .035 ounce
1 pound = 0.45 kilogram	1 kilogram = 2.2 pounds
1 short ton = 9.071 kilograms	1 metric ton = 1.102 ton (short)

CONVERSION MULTIPLIERS

	→ .00228571 →	
grains ←	437.5 ←	ounces
	→ .00017361 →	
grams ←	7000.0 ←	pounds
	→ 64.79891 →	
grains ←	.01543236 ←	milligrams
	→ .06479891 →	
grams ←	15.43236 ←	grams
	→ .0625 →	
ounces ←	16.0 ←	pounds
	→ 28.349523125 →	
ounces ←	03527396 ←	grams
	→ .028349523125 →	
ounces ←	35.27396 ←	kilograms
	→ .0005 →	
pounds ←	2000.0 ←	short tons
	→ 453.59237 →	
pounds ←	.00220462 ←	grams
	→ .45359237 →	
pounds ←	2.204623 ←	kilograms
	→ .00045359237 →	
pounds ←	2204.623 ←	metric tons
	→ 907.18474 →	
short tons ←	.00110231 ←	kilograms
	→ .90718474 →	
short tons ←	1.1023113 ←	metric tons

*All U.S. weights are avoirdupois.

LIQUID-VOLUME MEASUREMENTS

U.S. Standard	Metric
1 fluid ounce = 2 tablespoons	10 milliliters = 1 centiliter
1 liquid cup = 8 fluid ounces	
1 liquid pint = 2 liquid cups	10 centiliters = 1 deciliter
1 liquid quart = 2 liquid pints	10 deciliters = 1 liter
1 liquid gallon = 4 liquid quarts	1000 liters = 1 kiloliter

EQUIVALENTS (ROUNDED OFF)

U.S. Standard to Metric	Metric to U.S. Standard
1 fluid tablespoon = 30.0 milliliters	1 milliliter = .02 teaspoon
1 fluid ounce = 2.95735 milliliters	1 milliliter = .07 tablespoon
1 cup = 2.4 deciliters	1 milliliter = .03 ounce
1 liquid pint = 4.73176 deciliters	1 liter = 4.2 cups
1 liquid quart = 9.46353 deciliters	1 liter = 2.1 pints
1 liquid gallon = 3.78541 liters	1 liter = 1.1 quarts
1 liquid gallon = .004 cubic meter	1 cubic meter = 264.0 gallons

CONVERSION MULTIPLIERS

	→ .0625 →	
ounces ←	16.0 ←	pints
	→ .03125 →	
ounces ←	32.0 ←	quarts
	→ .0078125 →	
ounces ←	128.0 ←	gallons
	→ 29.57353 →	
ounces ←	.03381402 ←	milliliters
	→ .02957353 →	
ounces ←	33.81402 ←	liters
	→ .5 →	
pints ←	2.0 ←	quarts
	→ .0125 →	
pints ←	8.0 ←	gallons
	→ 473.176473 →	
pints ←	.0021134 ←	milliliters
	→ .047317647 →	
pints ←	2.113376 ←	liters
	→ .025 →	
quarts ←	4.0 ←	gallons
	→ 946.352946 →	
quarts ←	.00010567 ←	milliliters
	→ .946352946 →	
quarts ←	1.056688 ←	liters
	→ 3785.411784 →	

Liquid-Volume measurements
Conversion Multipliers (continued)

gallons ⟵———————————— .000264172 ⟵——————— milliliters
———————————————→ 3.785411784 ——→
gallons ⟵———————————— .264172 ⟵——————————— liters

Dry-capacity Measurements

U.S. Standard	Metric
1 quart = 2 pints	10 cubic millimeters = 1 cubic centimeter
1 peck = 8 quarts	10 decimeters = 1 cubic decimeter
1 bushel = 4 pecks	1 cubic decimeter = 1 liter
1 bushel = 32 quarts	10 cubic decimeters = 1 cubic meter

Equivalents (rounded off)

U.S. Standard to Metric	Metric to U.S. Standard
1 pint = .05 cubic centimeter	1 liter = 2.1 pints
1 quart = .01 cubic decimeter	1 liter = 1.1 quarts
1 peck = .009 cubic meter	1 cubic meter = 113.0 pecks
1 bushel = .04 cubic meter	1 cubic meter = 28 0 bushels
1 bushel = 35.239 liters	

Conversion Multipliers

————————————————→ .05 ——————→
dry pints ⟵———————————— 2.0 ⟵——————————— quarts
————————————————→ .0625 ——————→
dry pints ⟵———————————— 16.0 ⟵——————————— pecks
————————————————→ .015625 ——————→
dry pints ⟵———————————— 64.0 ⟵——————————— bushels
————————————————→ .55061047 ——————→
dry pints ⟵———————————— 1.816166 ⟵————————— liters
————————————————→ .0125 ——————→
dry quarts ⟵———————————— 8.0 ⟵——————————— pecks
————————————————→ .03125 ——————→
dry quarts ⟵———————————— 32.0 ⟵——————————— bushels
————————————————→ 1.101221 ——————→
dry quarts ⟵———————————— 90808298 ⟵————————— liters
————————————————→ 0.25 ——————→
pecks ⟵———————————— 4.0 ⟵——————————— bushels

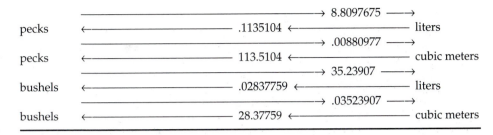

pecks			$\xrightarrow{\hspace{3cm}}$ 8.8097675 $\longrightarrow$	
pecks	$\longleftarrow$	.1135104 $\longleftarrow$		liters
pecks			$\xrightarrow{\hspace{3cm}}$ .00880977 $\longrightarrow$	
pecks	$\longleftarrow$	113.5104 $\longleftarrow$		cubic meters
bushels			$\xrightarrow{\hspace{3cm}}$ 35.23907 $\longrightarrow$	
bushels	$\longleftarrow$	.02837759 $\longleftarrow$		liters
bushels			$\xrightarrow{\hspace{3cm}}$ .03523907 $\longrightarrow$	
bushels	$\longleftarrow$	28.37759 $\longleftarrow$		cubic meters

CUBIC-VOLUME MEASUREMENTS

U S. Standard	Metric
1 cubic foot = 1728 cubic inches	10 cubic millimeters = 1 cubic centimeter
1 cubic yard = 27 cubic feet	10 centimeters = 1 cubic decimeter
1 cubic yard = 46, 656 cubic inches	10 cubic decimeters = 1 cubic meter

EQUIVALENTS (ROUNDED OFF)

U.S. Standard to Metric	Metric to U.S. Standard
1 cubic inch = 16.387 cubic centimeters	1 cubic centimeter = .0610237 cubic inch
1 cubic foot = 28.3168 cubic decimeters	1 cubic decimeter = .0353147 cubic foot
1 cubic yard = .764555 cubic meter	1 cubic meter = 1.30795 cubic yards

CONVERSION MULTIPLIERS

cubic inches			$\xrightarrow{\hspace{3cm}}$ .0005787 $\longrightarrow$	
cubic inches	$\longleftarrow$	1728.0 $\longleftarrow$		cubic feet
cubic inches			$\xrightarrow{\hspace{3cm}}$ .00002143 $\longrightarrow$	
cubic inches	$\longleftarrow$	46656.0 $\longleftarrow$		cubic yards
cubic inches			$\xrightarrow{\hspace{3cm}}$ .000016387 $\longrightarrow$	
cubic inches	$\longleftarrow$	61023.74 $\longleftarrow$		cubic meters
cubic feet			$\xrightarrow{\hspace{3cm}}$ .03703704 $\longrightarrow$	
cubic feet	$\longleftarrow$	27.0 $\longleftarrow$		cubic yards
cubic feet			$\xrightarrow{\hspace{3cm}}$ .02831685 $\longrightarrow$	
cubic feet	$\longleftarrow$	35.31467 $\longleftarrow$		cubic meters
cubic yards			$\xrightarrow{\hspace{3cm}}$ .764554858 $\longrightarrow$	
cubic yards	$\longleftarrow$	1.3079506 $\longleftarrow$		cubic meters

CUBIC VOLUME TABLE

The table in this appendix can serve as a quick reference for calculating volumes of materials from known dimensions. Along the top of the table are lengths from 2 linear feet to 20 linear feet. Along the left side of the table are lengths from 2 linear feet to 30 linear feet. When the dimensions of an area are known and they fit within the boundaries of the chart, it is only necessary to follow the lines to the square where the two axes meet; that square gives the number of cubic feet of material required to cover the specified area to a 1-inch depth. For example, suppose an area that is 30 feet by 20 feet is to be covered by a 1-inch depth of mulch. By locating the junction of the 20-foot column that runs from the top to the bottom of the table and the 30-foot column that runs from left to right, we can easily determine that 50.0 cubic feet of the mulch will be required. To convert that amount into cubic yards, simply divide the number of cubic feet by 27.

If 2 inches of mulch are required, multiply the number of cubic feet by 2. Multiply by 3 if 3 inches of mulch are required, and so forth.

The chart can also be utilized if the dimensions of a given area are multiples of the lengths given in the chart. For example, if an area is 60 feet by 40 feet these dimensions extend beyond the boundaries of the table, but they are multiples of 30 feet by 20 feet. Since *each* dimension is multiplied by 2, the number of cubic feet of material shown on the table should be multiplied by 4 to arrive at the correct total number of cubic feet (2 × 2 = 4). Since we found the total cubic footage for an area of 30 feet by 20 feet to be 50.0 cubic feet, then the cubic footage of material for an area of 60 feet by 40 feet would be 50.0 cubic feet times 4—or 200 cubic feet—to cover the area 1 inch deep. Similarly, if the area dimensions were found to be 90 feet by 60 feet, then each dimension would be a multiple of three, so the cubic footage given by the table for a 1-inch covering for a 30-foot by 20-foot area would be multiplied by nine (3 × 3 = 9). If a thicker covering of material was also desired, then the product of the multiplication above would in its turn be multiplied by the number of 1-inch thicknesses in the depth desired.

When only one dimension is a multiple and the other dimension is found on the chart, the cubic footage given is multiplied only by the multiple of the one altered dimension. For instance, in the previous example, suppose that only the 30-foot dimension had been doubled to 60 feet, while the other dimension remained at 20 feet, a dimension found on the chart. In this instance, the 50.0 cubic feet given as a 1-inch covering for a 30-foot by 20-foot area would be multiplied only by two, since only one dimension had doubled while the other remained as it was on the table (2 × 1 = 2). An area of 60 feet by 20 feet would then require 100 cubic feet of material (50.0 cubic feet × 2 = 100.0) for a 1-inch deep mulch.

No provision has been made in this table for waste or shrinkage of any type. To convert dimensions into their metric equivalents, see the conversion data given in the first part of this appendix.

Cubic Footage Table: For Spaces 1 inch Deep
(All Figures in Squares are Cubic Feet)

	2'	3'	4'	5'	6'	7'	8'	9'	10'	11'	12'	13'	14'	15'	16'	17'	18'	19'	20'
2'	.33	.5	.67	.83	1.0	1.2	1.3	1.5	1.7	1.8	2.0	2.2	2.3	2.5	2.7	2.8	3.0	3.2	3.3
3'	.5	.75	1.0	1.2	1.5	1.7	2.0	2.2	2.5	2.7	3.0	3.2	3.5	3.7	4.0	4.2	4.5	4.7	5.0
4'	.67	1.0	1.3	1.7	2.0	2.3	2.7	3.0	3.3	3.7	4.0	4.3	4.7	5.0	5.3	5.7	6.0	6.3	6.7
5'	.83	1.2	1.7	2.1	2.5	2.9	3.3	3.7	4.2	4.5	5.0	5.4	5.8	6.2	6.7	7.1	7.5	7.9	8.3
6'	1.0	1.5	2.0	2.5	3.0	3.5	4.0	4.5	5.0	5.5	6.0	6.5	7.0	7.5	8.0	8.5	9.0	9.5	10
7'	1.2	1.7	2.3	2.9	3.5	4.1	4.7	5.2	5.8	6.4	7.0	7.6	8.2	8.7	9.3	9.9	10.5	11	11.7
8'	1.3	2.0	2.7	3.3	4.0	4.7	5.3	6.0	6.7	7.3	8.0	8.7	9.3	10	10.7	11.3	12	12.7	13.3
9'	1.5	2.2	3.0	3.7	4.5	5.2	6.0	6.7	7.5	8.2	9.0	9.7	10.5	11.2	12.0	12.7	13.5	14.2	15.0
10'	1.7	2.5	3.3	4.2	5.0	5.8	6.7	7.5	8.3	9.2	10.0	10.8	11.7	12.5	13.3	14.2	15	15.8	16.7
11'	1.9	2.7	3.7	4.6	5.5	6.4	7.3	8.2	9.2	10.1	11.0	11.9	12.8	13.7	14.7	15.6	16.5	17.4	18.3
12'	2.0	3.0	40	5.0	6.0	7.0	8.0	9.0	10.0	11.0	12.0	13.0	14.0	15.0	16.0	17.0	18.0	19	20.0
13'	2.2	3.2	4.3	5.4	6.5	7.6	8.7	9.7	10.8	11.9	13.0	14.0	15.2	16.2	17.3	18.4	19.5	20.6	21.7
14'	2.3	3.5	4.7	5.8	7.0	8.2	9.3	10.5	11.7	12.8	14.0	15.2	16.3	17.5	18.7	19.8	21	22.2	23.3
15'	2.5	3.7	5.0	6.2	7.5	8.7	10.0	11.2	12.5	13.7	15.0	16.2	17.5	18.7	20.0	21.2	22.5	23.7	25.0
16'	2.7	4.0	5.3	6.7	8.0	9.3	10.7	12	13.3	14.7	16.0	17.3	18.7	20.0	21.3	22.7	24	25.3	26.7
17'	2.8	4.2	5.7	7.1	8.5	9.9	11.3	12.7	14.2	15.6	17.0	18.4	19.8	21.2	22.7	24.1	25.5	26.9	28.3
18'	3.0	4.5	6.0	7.5	9.0	10.5	12	13.5	15.0	16.5	18.0	19.5	21	22.5	24.0	25.5	27	28.5	30.0
19'	3.2	4.7	6.3	7.9	9.5	11.0	12.7	14.2	15.8	17.4	19.0	20.6	22.2	23.7	25.3	26.9	28.5	30.1	31.7
20'	3.3	5.0	6.7	8.3	10	11.7	13.3	15	16.7	18.3	20.0	21.7	23.3	25.0	26.7	28.3	30	31.7	33.3
21'	3.5	5.2	7.0	8.7	10.5	12.2	14	15.7	17.5	19.2	21.0	22.7	24.5	26.2	28	29.7	31.5	33.2	35.0
22'	3.7	5.5	7.3	9.2	11	12.8	14.7	16.5	18.3	20.2	22	23.8	25.7	27.5	29.3	31.2	33	34.8	36.7
23'	3.8	5.7	7.7	9.6	11.5	13.4	15.3	17.2	19.2	21.1	23	24.9	26.8	28.7	30.7	32.6	34.5	36.4	38.3
24'	4.0	6.0	8.0	10	12	14	16	18	20	22	24	26	28	30	32	34	36	38	40.0
25'	4.2	6.2	8.3	10.4	12.5	14.6	16.7	18.7	20.8	22.9	25	27.1	29.2	31.2	33.3	35.4	37.5	39.6	41.7
26'	4.3	6.5	8.7	10.8	13	15.2	17.3	19.5	21.7	23.8	26	28.2	30.3	32.5	34.7	36.8	39	41.2	43.3
27'	4.5	6.7	9.0	11.2	13.5	15.7	18	20.2	22.4	24.7	27	29.2	31.5	33.7	36	38.2	40.5	42.7	45.0
28'	4.7	7.0	9.3	11.7	14	16.3	18.7	21	23.3	25.7	28	30.3	32.7	35	37.3	39.7	42	44.3	46.7
29'	4.8	7.2	9.7	12	14.5	16.9	19.3	21.7	24.2	26.6	29.0	31.4	33.8	36.2	38.7	41.1	43.5	45.9	48.3
30'	5.0	7.5	10	12.5	15	17.5	20	22.5	25	27.5	30	32.5	35	37.5	40	42.5	45	47	50

BIBLIOGRAPHY AND SUGGESTED REFERENCES

AJAY, BETTY, *Betty Ajay's Guide to Home Landscape*. New York: McGraw-Hill, 1970.

ASSOCIATED LANDSCAPE CONTRACTORS OF AMERICA. *A Guide to Specifications for Interior Landscaping*. Associated Landscape Contractors of America, Inc., 1979 edition.

ASSOCIATED LANDSCAPE CONTRACTORS OF AMERICA—AND THE AMERICAN SOCIETY OF LANDSCAPE ARCHITECTS. *Landscape Contracting—Guide Specifications—Planting*. Associated Landscape Contractors of America, Inc., 1973.

THE STAFF OF THE L. H. BAILEY HORTORIUM, Cornell University. *Hortus Third: A Concise Dictionary of Plants Cultivated in the United States and Canada*. New York: Macmillan, 1976.

BEARD, JAMES B. *Turfgrass Science and Culture*. Englewood Cliffs, N.J.: Prentice-Hall, Inc., 1973.

BROOKES, JOHN. *Room Outside*. New York: The Viking Press, 1969.

CHING, FRANK. *Architectural Graphics*. New York: Van Nostrand Reinhold Co., 1975.

COUNTRYSIDE BOOKS. *Home Landscaping*. Barrington, Ill.: The A. B. Morse Co., Countryside Books, 1974.

DEMING, RICHARD. *Metric Power: Why and How We Are Going Metric*. New York: Thomas Nelson, Inc., 1974.

DIRR, MICHAEL A. *A Manual of Woody Plants*. Champaign, Ill.: Stipes Publishing Co.

ECKBO, GARRETT. *Home Landscape: The Art of Home Landscaping*, rev. ed. New York: McGraw-Hill, 1978.

450

FAIRBROTHER, NAN. *The Nature of Landscape Design.* New York: Alfred A. Knopf, 1974.

GIVENS, HAROLD C. *Landscape It Yourself.* New York: Harcourt Brace Jovanovich, 1977.

HARLOW, WILLIAM M. *Trees of the Eastern and Central United States and Canada.* New York: Dover Publications, Inc., 1957.

HERUBIN, CHARLES. *Principles of Surveying.* Reston, Va.: Reston Publishing Co., 1978.

INGELS, JACK. *Landscaping: Principles and Practices.* Albany, N.Y.: Delmar Publishers, 1978.

KENNEDY, E. LEE. *CAD: Drawing, Design, Data Management.* Whitney Library of Design, 1986.

LEES, CARLTON B. *New Budget Landscaping.* New York: Holt, Rinehart, and Winston, 1979.

MICHEL, TIMOTHY W. *Homeowner's Guide to Landscape Design.* The Countryman Press, 1978.

MITCHELL, WILLIAM J. *Computer-aided Architectural Design.* New York: Van Nostrand Reinhold Co., 1977.

MUSSER, H. BURTON. *Turf Management.* New York: McGraw-Hill, 1962.

NATIONAL ASSOCIATION OF HOMEBUILDERS. *Cost Effective Site Planning.* Washington, D.C.: National Association of Homebuilders, 1976.

NATIONAL LANDSCAPE ASSOCIATION. *Landscape Designer's and Estimator's Guide.* Washington, D.C.: National Landscape Association, 1971.

NELSON, WILLIAM R. *Landscaping Your Home,* rev. ed. Cooperative Extension Service, University of Illinois, 1977.

———. *Planting Design: A Manual of Theory and Practice.* Champaign, Ill.: Stipes Publishing Co., 1979.

NICKEY, J. M. *The Stoneworker's Bible.* Blue Summit, Pa.: Tab Books, 1979.

OLDALE, ADRIENNE, AND PETER OLDALE. *Garden Construction in Pictures.* New York: Drake Publishers, Inc., 1974.

PIERCEALL, GREGORY M. *Residential Landscapes: Graphics, Planning, and Design.* Reston Publishing Company, Inc., 1984.

ROBINETTE, GARY O. Editor for the American Society of Landscape Architects Foundation. *Landscape Planning for Energy Conservation.* Environmental Design Press, 1977.

———. *Off the Board, Into the Ground.* Dubuque, Ia.: William C. Brown Book Co., 1968.

———. *Plants/People/and Environmental Quality.* Washington, D.C.: Department of the Interior, National Park Service.

SCHIMIZZI, NED V. *Mastering the Metric System.* The New American Library, Mentor Books, 1975.

SCHULER, STANLEY. *Outdoor Lighting for Your Home.* Princeton, N.J.: D. Van Nostrand Co., 1962.

SUNSET BOOKS. *Ideas for Entryways and Front Gardens.* Menlo Park, Ca: Lane Book Co., Sunset Books, 1961.

TURGEON, A. J. *Turfgrass Management.* Reston, Va.: Reston Publishing Co., 1980.

UNITED NATIONS, DEPARTMENT OF ECONOMIC AND SOCIAL AFFAIRS. *World Weights and Measures: A Handbook for Statisticians.* New York: United Nations Publishing Service.

UNTERMANN, RICHARD K. *Grade Easy.* Landscape Architecture Foundation, 1973.

———. *Principles and Practices of Grading, Drainage, and Road Alignment: An Ecological Approach.* Reston, Va.: Reston Publishing Co., 1978.

VAN DER HOEVEN, GUSTAAF A. *Residential Landscape Design.* Manhattan, Ks.: Cooperative Extension Service, Kansas State University, 1977.

Wang, Thomas C. *Plan and Section Drawing.* New York: Van Nostrand Reinhold Co., 1979.

WATKINS, JAMES A. *Turf Irrigation Manual.* Dallas, Tx.: Telsco Industries, 1978.

WEBER, NELVA M. *How to Plan Your Own Home Landscape.* New York: The Bobbs-Merrill Co., 1976.

WYMAN, DONALD. *Shrubs and Vines for American Gardens,* rev. ed. New York: Macmillan, 1969.

———. *Trees for American Gardens,* rev. ed. New York: Macmillan, 1965.

ZION, ROBERT L. *Trees for Architecture and the Landscape.* New York: Reinhold Book Corporation, 1968.

INDEX